Age Shock

How Finance Is Failing Us

Age Shock
How Finance Is Failing Us

◆

ROBIN BLACKBURN

VERSO

London • New York

To the memory of Rudolf Meidner (1914–2005)

First published by Verso 2006
This paperback edition first published 2011
Robin Blackburn © 2011

1 3 5 7 9 10 8 6 4 2

Verso
UK: 6 Meard Street, London W1F 0EG
US: 20 Jay Street, Suite 1010, Brooklyn, NY 11201
www.versobooks.com

Verso is the imprint of New Left Books

ISBN-13: 978-1-84467-765-8

British Library Cataloguing in Publication Data
A catalogue record for this book is available from the British Library

Library of Congress Cataloging-in-Publication Data
A catalog record for this book is available from the Library of Congress

Typeset in Bembo by Hewer Text UK Ltd, Edinburgh
Printed in the US by Maple Vail

Contents

List of Tables

Acknowledgements

I would like to thank Perry Anderson, Larry Beeferman and Matthieu
Leimgruber for reading the MSS and making many helpful suggestions. I
have also greatly benefited from the advice of Yally Avrampour, Ted
Benton, Christopher Blackburn, Per Berglund, Diane Elson, Nancy
Fraser, Jay Ginn, Miriam Glucksmann, Lydia Morris, Lucinda Platt, John
Scott, Lance Taylor and Erik Olin Wright. Of course, none of the
foregoing are responsible for my mistakes or conclusions.

R B, Wivenhoe, July 2006

Preface to the Paperback Edition

When writing this book I had the powerful sensation that the Western economies were hurtling towards disaster, and that, in consequence, many pensions would shrink or disappear. The bias in favour of tax-subsidized, commercially supplied individual pension accounts itself encouraged speculative bubbles, since those running the funds had perverse incentives: money managers received hefty fees as share prices soared, but were not correspondingly penalized when these shares tanked. With the exception of some public-sector pension funds, the majority of institutional investors saw their role as focusing on shareholder value in the short term. Declining the role of responsible stakeholder, they churned their portfolios, earning fees with every transaction. The 'accountability deficits' that I identify in this book contributed to the opacity of the financial system, while 'financialization' swelled the size of the unregulated 'shadow banks'.

Pension systems are very demanding: they aim to deliver large sums over long periods. With an ageing population these demands become even greater and, as I will show, require arrangements that will reliably deliver 'great chunks of GDP' in rising amounts over many decades. Demographic projections, which have not changed significantly in the last few years, still show the over-65s doubling in absolute numbers over the next three decades in both the United States and Europe. However, the economic and political landscape has been subject to seismic changes, and underlines the need for new ways to promote well-being, activity and real security at older ages. If economic growth stalls or goes into reverse, it becomes far more difficult to meet pension promises or fund decent elder care. In *Age Shock*, I argue that pension finance should be diversified, with a strong public, 'pay-as-you-go' old age pension supplying a guaranteed basic cincome, but with a universal second pension supplied by socially managed pension funds. For a time at least, occupational and personal pension schemes will also have a role to play. However, these occupational schemes have many problems, as this book explains, so they should be phased out and their members persuaded to move to the publicly vetted and socially managed second-pension arrangements.

It is difficult to imagine that pensions could long continue to be satisfactory if an economy were in deep trouble. An economy tossed hither and thither by uncertainty, or locked in a stationary state or cycle of underperformance, would inevitably struggle with its pension commitments. And there is the further point that already-existing pension institutions contribute to the dysfunctional wider pattern. For all these reasons, the fate of pensions is bound up with the health of the overall economy. In *Age Shock*, I urge that the powerful thrust in recent years towards commodification, privatization and 'financialization' was inevitably going to undermine pension provision. The advent of crisis in 2007–8 confirmed this view, and there was widespread public anger at the behaviour of dominant financial institutions. While bankers and fund managers have pocketed large sums, the value of savings has suffered and prospective yields are very disappointing. But in the medium term it is quite possible, even likely, that the trends which produced the crisis will gain added momentum.

In this new preface to *Age Shock*, I give an account of the multiplying woes of the post-crisis world, focusing on their impact on pensions. I also build on the proposals for radical reform made in Chapter 6. If extremes of poverty and inequality have helped to generate and perpetuate the crisis, as I believe to be the case, then better pay and conditions for the low paid, and better social protection for all, in the developing as well as developed worlds, would help stimulate and sustain recovery.[1] The crisis has been so persistent because households and banks are both reducing debt ('de-leveraging') while governments are slashing expenditure. 'Defined benefit' pension funds have been part of the problem because as the markets droop, their sponsors (the employers) are required to contribute more to the fund, something that diminishes the resources they have available for investment. DB pension schemes are 'pro-cyclical', that is they aggravate boom-bust cycles. In both the US and the UK occupational pension funds are large – the value of their funds is equivalent to the size of annual GDP – which means that the pro-cyclical effects are significant. So, I will be urging, a critical part of the answer must be to revive demand and remove the pro-cyclical bias.

Global Imbalances and the Great Crash

The Great Credit Crunch of 2007–10 was brought about by persistent global imbalances which had encouraged low interest rates, ready-loans, overborrowing on the part of households and banks, and a succession of asset bubbles. The huge imbalances racked up during the boom years of the global economy (1992–2007) were the product of an ever-widening US deficit and the ever-growing Chinese surplus. Chinese workers or farmers were not paid enough to become good customers for overseas products, while in the US the low-paid and poor ('subprime') borrowers were taking on debt – especially housing debt – that they soon found impossible to service.

The extraordinary extent of inequality, poverty and low pay narrowed markets, but in the richer countries the resulting shortfall in demand could be held off for a time by finding new ways to increase consumer debt, via easier mortgages, credit card facilities and automobile loans. The over-borrowing and asset bubbles which resulted were aggravated by financial deregulation, and by the greed and subterfuge of the banks. The heedless pursuit of short-term profit led to the largest destruction of value in world history. Huge public deficits had to be incurred to prevent collapse. Now these are to be paid for by slashing public spending and shrinking social protection for many decades to come. The welfare state is to be dismantled at a time when higher unemployment and an ageing population make this a certain recipe for destitution and widening misery. The cutbacks weaken recovery and can only result in a further boost to the privatization and commodification of pensions, health and education.

For the last two decades neo-liberals have been insisting that disaster would ensue if we did not have a bonfire of social entitlements. Public pensions were declared to be a nightmare in the making. Now, the disaster has happened – but because of the vices of financialization, not the burden of welfare. The disease had quite different origins and causes from those that were forecast by the doom-mongers, but the medicine needed for this incapacitating ailment is – so they claim – just the same as before.

Grotesquely, a crisis caused by the banks has to be solved at the expense of pensioners, students, teachers, care workers and the unemployed. The banks are still widely thought to be culpable, but governments do not dare to defy the money markets and rating agencies. Fear of the bond traders is excessive, but not irrational: countries that forfeit the confidence of the markets immediately find borrowing more expensive. But the clincher is that if confidence continues to plummet, then bankruptcy looms. As citizens of Argentina discovered in 2002, wholesale default paralyzes economic activity, makes everyday life an obstacle course, and wipes out savings. Attempts to use barter to resuscitate the economy prove extremely cumbersome and ineffective. A currency that is reasonably stable – but not overvalued – is a prerequisite for recovery and growth, as Argentina was to show in the subsequent Kirchner years. An alternative is needed to the grim choice of either defaulting or capitulating to the truncated perspectives of the bond traders and ratings agencies. A viable currency needs a proper tax base – something the EU and eurozone has always lacked. The ECB cannot contribute much to bank bailouts nor can the eurozone issue bonds, since its own fiscal powers are so modest; the fiscal power remains with the member states.

Credit is a wonderful thing, but it must be used to nourish the real economy – producing 'goods' and avoiding 'bads'. Successive speculative bubbles in third-world debt (1980s), dot.com shares (1999–2001), and property and mortgages (2000–2007) did nothing to boost the real economy. Recognizing and writing off losses is an essential part of the recovery process – a deliberate and selective process is to be preferred, with Ecuador's audit of its outstanding debt in 2007 being a useful model. Finally, the real costs of GDP growth – such as the price paid for deforestation or river pollution – must also be used to deflate the advances of commodified output.

In 1998 New Left Review devoted an entire issue to a remarkable study by Robert Brenner, 'The Economics of Global Turbulence'.[2] Brenner's central argument was that the Western economies were confronting a major contraction caused by a steep decline in profitability. There was to be much argument over the precise causes and extent of this underlying crisis. Western governments did their utmost to sustain an illusion of unending growth. Loose credit conditions encouraged households, enterprises and local government institutions to take on large amounts of debt. While entrepreneurs found capital easy to raise, consumer markets were distorted by income inequality. Booming demand for luxury items in the US, Europe, China and the Middle East did not translate into solid advances. The dot.com boom came and went, and the US authorities responded to the attacks of 11 September 2001 by stimulating the economy further. The unlikely idea gained ground that low-income US citizens could become the basis for a lucrative new mountain of specially packaged mortgage debt. At the same time, the large US corporations had dispersed – outsourced – their industrial base and felt no need to invest in capacity in the United States itself. China's rise was adding hugely to productive capacity but much less to global final consumer demand. The rise of the Asian producers could have been good news for *everyone* if those producers had been just a little better paid and if investment had been channelled into new divisions of labour, and producer networks, by trade rules that penalized competition based on poor labour standards or dangerous or wasteful processes of production.[3]

In 1950, financial concerns accounted for just 4 per cent of total corporate profits; by 2006, they accounted for 40 per cent of such profits. Long before the latter date, the workings of the real economy had been dwarfed by derivatives trading in secondary markets. (A derivative is, in essence, a bet that the price of a bond or share, or bundle of such securities, will go up or down on a primary market.) Whereas an old-fashioned fund would content itself with being 'long only' – that is buying, holding and selling shares and bonds – a new species of 'hedge fund' used a portion of its assets to take short positions, that is, to bet that the price of an asset would decline, by borrowing that share and then selling it in the expectation that it would be able to buy it back at a lower price. Traditionally, pension funds were bound by rules that prevented them from speculating in short positions; in recent decades, however, this constraint has often been abandoned. Where markets are very unstable, and downside risks obvious, it seems only prudent to offset 'long' positions by taking out some 'short' positions as an insurance, with, say, 70 to 80 per cent of assets 'long' and the remainder 'short'. Most pension funds will hire a manager to arrange this for them.

Between 2000 and 2008, the percentage of pension funds using hedge funds rose from 2.4 per cent to 26.7 per cent. The hedge funds engaged by the US pension funds made an average annual return of 1.9 per cent during that time, ahead of Canadian pension funds whose average annual return for investments in hedge funds was only 0.9 per cent.[4] Whatever the putative advantages of the long/short hedging style, it has to bear the costs of higher fees and frequent trading. Fees are charged on the 2-and-20 formula – 2 per cent of the principal and 20 per cent of the gain – with, it is hardly necessary to add, no share in the losses. A study of 11,000 hedge funds shows a return of 5.6 per cent in the years 1980–2008, compared with 6.6 per cent for US Treasuries.[5] In order to eke out such modest returns, most pension fund managers were also happy to lend shares they held to hedge funds to enable them to sell short. In normal times the risks were minimal, but such operations could abnormally build up to great waves of speculation. In the housing boom of the years 1993–

2006, bundles of mortgages known as 'collateralized debt obligations' (CDOs) were 'securitized', the process whereby bets on changes in the value of these underlying assets became a saleable 'credit derivative'. The market in CDOs furnished the banks with an artificial and temporary stimulant as they 'originated' (i.e. constructed) credit derivatives and then 'distributed' – or sold – them to institutional investors, notably pension funds. The mortgages being bundled in this way included large numbers taken out by 'subprime' borrowers – that is, the poor and low paid. The financial engineers believed that the consequent risk of default could be massaged away by cutting the bundles into tranches or slices, and by buying insurance. Firstly, the CDOs were tranched, with the lowest tranche being the first 5 per cent of mortgages to default. Because it carried the highest risk this slice was known as the 'equity'. The 'mezzanine' tranche was the next 25 per cent to turn sour, which left as much as 70 per cent of 'senior' debt – the tranche left after the lowest-'equity' slice and the mezzanine slice had all defaulted. The 'equity' slice was prized because it offered the highest return, and the senior tranches because of the supposedly very remote chance that they would default. The CDOs were also typically supplied with insurance in the shape of 'credit default swaps' (CDSs), which would kick in, should one of the counterparties to the deal go bust. Ingenious though all this was, it failed to anticipate the domino effect of interlinked and serial collapse. The statistics used to calculate the likelihood of default were based on two decades of reasonable growth. The devices themselves, moreover, could also assist concealment and deception. For example, it was possible to take out CDS insurance even when not holding the asset being insured, and then to short that asset – a newfangled version of the well-known scam of insuring a derelict building and then setting fire to it, but in this case without even owning the building in the first place. And of course, these highly complex financial instruments posed great difficulties to the tax authorities and lent themselves to a variety of duplicitous accounting treatments across a multitude of jurisdictions around the world, including sixty dedicated tax havens.[6]

During the 'boom' years, trading in the CDOs became hectic, with financial institutions treating them as a licence to print money. But some hedge funds and other investors began to smell a rat. Some public sector pension funds suspected that they were being played for mugs by the 'originate and distribute' model and began to shun CDOs and other credit derivatives. However, the ratings agencies continued blithely to award triple-A ratings to the CDOs – unsurprisingly, given that fees from this work had come to supply half their total revenues.[7] The 'toxic' assets created by the credit derivative bubble were often stored away off-balance-sheet in the special investment vehicles (SIVs) or 'conduits' of the shadow banking system and valued at 'model', not market, prices.

Hot money and financial engineering also chased higher returns through investment in the bonds of struggling public authorities in the US and in the eurozone. The investment banks helpfully explained to the Greek government how it could disguise the extent of its indebtedness using derivatives, since the Eurostat reporting rules did not cover them. In 2001, Goldman Sachs earned $200 million from supplying products that helped the Greek government to understate its debt. Greek bonds looked a better prospect than they really were, and other banks – as well as pension funds – could not resist the temptation.[8]

Losses Trigger Massive Intervention

Reality could not forever be evaded. Defaults rose alarmingly in 2007, though it was not until the Lehman Brothers collapse in September 2008 that the full scale of the disaster became apparent. In a single week, global retirement funds dropped by 20 per cent. Sweeping measures of nationalization were required to avert a meltdown of Wall Street and the world economy. The US Treasury took over some of the world's largest banks and corporations and imposed a straitjacket on them all.[9]

In light of the actions taken in September 2008, the measures that I proposed in the concluding chapter to *Age Shock* suddenly seemed quite modest. In that month, the CEOs of the thirteen largest US banks were summoned to Washington by Hank Paulson, then Secretary of the Treasury. Assembling them in the Treasury's Cash Room, he informed them that they all faced bankruptcy and gave them an hour to decide whether or not to sign a prepared letter. This was an invitation from the banks to the federal authorities to shore up their crumbling balance sheets by injecting new capital from the just-established, $700 billion Troubled Asset Relief Program (TARP) – in return for which the federal authorities would acquire equity stakes in their concerns. Within the hour, after consulting with their boards, all thirteen CEOs signed Paulson's letter. Not only were Wall Street's mightiest begging for help, but Paulson was also answering – or seeming to answer – the question posed by any crisis, especially in the epoch of financialization, namely, 'Who's in charge?'

The Federal authorities acquired a majority holding in Citibank, the world's largest bank, for example – and all the banks undertook to abide by certain rules. In order to qualify for TARP funds, Goldman Sachs changed its legal status to a holding company, thereby gaining access to the 'discount window' and thereby falling into line with the other banks. Before long these measures were followed by a state takeover of AIG, the world's largest insurance company, and of Fannie May and Freddie Mac, the two largest mortgage brokers. (The fact that Hank Paulson was himself a former co-chairman of Goldman Sachs no doubt helped to persuade the banks that these drastic measures were in their best interests.) British finance was as deeply mired in debt as Wall Street – indeed the City of London and its global network of 'offshore financial centres' was vital to the shadow banking arrangements. The British government had been forced to rescue first Northern Rock, then Lloyds TSB group and the Royal Bank of Scotland. Barclays and HSBC did their utmost to avoid becoming entangled in rescue operations, but were nevertheless obliged to accept help from the TARP.

Only the imminent prospect of the collapse of the US financial system – a 'near–death experience', as some called it – allowed for such an extraordinary use of the public purse. Though three of the large US investment banks had gone (Bear Stearns and Merrill Lynch taken over, Lehman Brothers forced into receivership), in the months and years to come it was remarkable to see how the Wall Street survivors and victors reasserted their power. At no point did the Treasury use its power as owner and creditor to impose lending policies on the financial companies that it had saved. In the first place, the banks sought to 'de-leverage' – to contract their balance sheets by calling in loans and being very sparing about making new ones. As the banks persisted in their reluctance to furnish credit to small and medium-sized businesses, the Treasury and the Fed were unhappy but gave no marching orders. The banks were still sheltering huge, unacknowledged losses. Keenly aware of one another's problems, they shunned inter-bank lending. All had invested in a range of very dubious assets – first and foremost subprime mortgage and other credit derivatives, but also vulnerable public bonds (especially state bonds and bonds issued by weaker members of the eurozone). The derivatives were valued at 'model', not market, prices.

The banks held their CDOs in off–balance-sheet special investment vehicles (SIVs), hiding their exposure to debtor defaults, and the resulting shadow banking system had grown to overtake the visible banking system in size. As mortgage holders and bondholders were hit by defaults, the flaws in the credit derivatives market became apparent and the insurance offered by credit default swaps (CDSs) turned out to be illusory. AIG had to be taken over by the Federal authorities a few days after the Lehman collapse because it had made a speciality of taking on insurance for credit derivatives. Insuring triple-A securities seemed like easy money if you neglected to reckon with contagion, synchrony and so-called 'black swan' events.

Rediscovering the State

The US and UK mega-banks had been saved because without the credit lines they extended to their customers the entire economy was threatened by asphyxiation. But the banks, their very existence at stake, declined to expand their loan books, precipitating a generalized 'credit crunch'. The financial authorities stabilized the situation by printing money on a vast scale. The US and UK governments alike cut taxes and increased public spending programmes in massive 'stimulus packages'. Private sector deficits were kept manageable only by transferring them to the public sector – where they soon prompted demands for sweeping austerity and cuts in public pensions. In order to render the bailout more palatable, Britain's new Chancellor of the Exchequer, George Osborne, raised the levy on all UK financial transactions to 0.075 per cent, to yield £2.5 billion annually, triggering similar ultra-modest financial transaction taxes (FTTs) in other European jurisdictions.[10] While Osborne's tax was set far too low to address the crisis, it still proved a point – the very *possibility* of such a levy had earlier been pronounced unthinkable, since it would provoke capital flight.

In the aftermath of the emergency measures there was a widespread call for the reform of the institutions that had permitted it. The 'shadow banking system' was to be brought into the light of day and 'over-the-counter' transactions (OTC) were to be replaced by a public clearing system for all derivative trades. Entrusting the construction of derivatives to a public body would be a straightforward way of achieving transparency, with fees from this activity becoming a useful source of public revenue. Those seeking a credit default swap (CDS) would be required to prove that they held the asset they were insuring; meanwhile, exchange-traded funds (ETFs) and hedge funds could be penalized for 'naked shorts' (i.e. selling shares they did not own). Some accounts of the 'subprime' bubble demonized the very principle of derivatives rather than focusing clearly on how they were used to bamboozle and deceive. Of course many credit derivatives were indeed deliberately over-complex, ratings grades were often consciously manipulated and hollow insurance against default was offered. But in the wake of the crisis many credit derivatives recovered their value, enabling TARP loans to be almost fully repaid and endowing Lehman's creditors with some unsuspected assets. As the Chicago Board has long shown, complex derivatives can work provided that there are stringent rules relating to disclosure, capitalization, collateral and trading standards. The Commodity Futures Trading Commission has demanded better capitalization from banks and hedge funds that wish to trade derivatives.[11] Mutual ownership of trading platforms (i.e. collective ownership by market participants) has often been used to engender the necessary trust – although public ownership would be even better. Anthony Hilton, business editor of London's *Evening Standard*, had a further suggestion: 'Let's nationalize the ratings business', he proposed, pointing out that new aircraft or drugs could not be marketed without a publicly issued licence.[12] Of course any agency that rates securities, including government bonds, would have to be independent of government and have a funding mechanism that was careful not to offer perverse incentives. In the epoch of globalization there should clearly be a number of global ratings agencies and regulators.

The ability of Goldman Sachs to create profit from speculations against its own customers came to sum up the destructive essence of the boom in financialization. The 'vampire squid' was active as buyer or seller in a third of total transactions on the US markets in the years leading up to the crisis. Goldman was frequently found betting huge sums of other people's money on both sides of many 'merger and acquisitions' events. While clients took risks, Goldman could trade on its own proprietary account. Did it ever use customer information to place safe bets? As they say on the Street, 'Goldman are not missionaries'. As Goldman saw the mountain of credit derivatives grow, senior executives invited John Paulson, a very bearish hedge fund manager, to devise credit derivatives that were designed to fail – and which it then sold to customers without any warning. In the aftermath of the crisis and with mounting public anger against bankers, the Securities and Exchange Commission (SEC) charged

Goldman with fraud. Admitting nothing, Goldman later paid $550 million to have the charge dropped.[13]

As noted above, Goldman made a tidy sum from advising the Greek government how to hide debt – but knowing the true situation, the firm also placed a large bet of its own against Greek bonds.[14] Goldman Sachs received $12.9 billion under the terms of the September 2008 bailout – and claimed that it was not a net beneficiary of the rescue of AIG since its $17 billion exposure to the insurer was fully hedged and collateralized to other institutions. That is, aware that AIG might not be able to pay out on the €62 billion of CDOs that it insured, Goldman had also insured against the collapse of one of its insurers (AIG)– all of which simply proves how extensive the house of cards had become.[15]

So large were the losses and so evident the abuses that something had to be done to appease public anger. Eventually complex and extensive legislation was agreed on both sides of the Atlantic. There were new rules, more paperwork and seemingly endless consultations. The Dodd–Frank Wall Street Reform Act was passed in July 2010. The banks solemnly promised to increase collateral. The British authorities proposed to 'ring fence' retail banking operations, awarding them guarantees denied to investment banking. But – strange to relate – both Wall Street and the City of London emerged essentially unscathed, 'too big to fail', complete with outrageous bonuses, slender capitalization, obscure accounting rules, off-balance-sheet items and special purpose entities. The large investment banks still combined a range of activities that put them at an advantage: brokering share issues, arranging M&A, dabbling in consumer finance, running commercial banks and engaging in proprietary trading. Supposedly there were 'Chinese walls' between these various functions. Nevertheless, regulators detected suspicious flurries of trading activity in the days leading up to between a fifth and a third of major corporate events. Such a pattern suggested widespread insider trading. The 1999 repeal of the US Glass–Steagall Act had allowed old-fashioned ideas of 'conflict of interest' to be rebranded as 'synergies'. Even in the aftermath of the crisis, a return to Glass–Steagall-style provisions to separate Main Street from Wall Street failed to attract the support of legislators.

At root, the opposition to reform was driven by the banks' determination to retain a source of badly needed profit in a world where fees from traditional investment banking (IPOs, rights issues and M&A) offered slimmer pickings, and where gains from proprietary trading, OTC derivative transactions and the legerdemain of financialization had become crucial to profits and growth. There was an overwhelming case for increased transparency and more adequate capital cushions, but governments saw no alternative but to safeguard the health of their own financial institutions. A new president in the US and a new coalition government in the UK could have inaugurated completely new policies, but this was not to be. Altogether, *plus ca change, plus ç'est la même chose* best describes the remarkable resilience of the basic practices of the financial sector in the years 2008–11. Despite all the write-offs and bailouts, overall debt levels – national debt, non-financial-corporate debt, banking debt and household debt – remained high, at three to five times GDP.[16]

In January 2008 the French financial expert Jean-Charles Rochet published a book entitled *Why Are There So Many Banking Crises?*[17] In it, Rochet calculated that there had been 46 banking crises since the Bretton Woods system had been allowed to collapse in 1971. In the three years after this book's publication, the world's major financial centres were hit by an even more severe sequence of crises – the most serious since the thirties – and Rochet's total must have climbed by at least a dozen. Between the onset of trouble in 2008 and June 2011 the IMF responded to 22 appeals for crisis lending, but while its resources were generously – though not always effectively – used to ease the predicaments of heavily indebted EU states, large poor states like Ukraine and Pakistan received little help. The very tentative recovery of 2010 ran out of steam and a return to 'stagflation' loomed. There were 14 million unemployed in the US, 15 million in the eurozone and 2.5 million in the UK. Further millions are threatened with foreclosure, many tens of millions face shrunken savings and the prospect of poverty in old age. Small and medium-sized businesses still struggle to find credit.

However, measured against the catastrophic consequences of the 1929 Crash, the measures taken in 2008 were a success. The banks were indeed rescued and restored to profitability. Most of the TARP loans were repaid. The auto companies used 'Chapter 11 bankruptcy' protection to transfer their pension obligations to the Pension Benefit Guaranty Corporation (PBGC). Thus a body set up to insure company schemes from default was being used as an instrument of industrial policy (more on the PBGC in Chapter 3). The rescued auto corporations – under public ownership – became viable businesses once again. In the case of General Motors, the unions played an important role in devising a new strategy – one that included an electric car, the 'Volt'. By early 2011 gross output in the US, France and Germany had returned to the levels of mid-2007.

Yet the success of the bailout and stimulus had a limited focus, and little of the help filtered through to those threatened with foreclosure – the ones whose problems were, after all, at the root of the subprime crisis. Neil Barofsky, the government-appointed 'inspector general' of the TARP program, observed on his last day in office, at the end of March 2011, that claims for the progamme's effectiveness failed to reckon with its very uneven performance:

> . The bank bailout, more formally called the Troubled Asset Relief Program, failed to meet some of its most important goals. From the perspective of the largest financial institutions, the glowing assent is warranted: billions of dollars of tax-payer money allowed institutions that were on the brink of collapse not only to survive but even to flourish. These banks now enjoy record profits and the seemingly permanent competitive advantage that accompanies being deemed 'too big to fail' . . . The legislation that created TARP, the Emergency Stabilization Act, had far broader goals, including protecting home values and preserving home ownership.

Congress had been very reluctant to endorse the TARP – it was rejected when first voted on – and only passed when it was accompanied by warm words about the restraints that would apply to banks and the help that would be extended to families facing eviction. As Barofsky went on to observe:

> [The US] Treasury, however, provided money to the banks with no effective policy or effort to compel the extension of credit. There were no strings attached; no requirement or even incentive to increase lending to home buyers, and against our strong recommen-dation, not even a request that banks report how they used TARP funds . . . The Affordable Home Modification Program was an-nounced [in February 2009] with the promise to help up to four million families with mortgage modifications. That program has been a colossal failure, with far fewer permanent modifications (540,000) than modifications that have failed or been cancelled (over 800,000) . . . As the program flounders, foreclosures continue to mount, with 8 million to 13 million foreclosures forecast over the program's life-time.[18]

If a large slice of TARP funds had gone to debt forgiveness for the low paid, it might have stimulated consumption in an economy threatened by stagnation as well as lightening the load of bad debt.

The method of coordinating an economy by means of a stock exchange is self-evidently plagued by instability and systemic risk. Finance of any sort must expect uncertain outcomes, but the 'free market' exacerbates what is an inevitable problem and allows banks to blackmail the political authorities. Mega-banks are known to be dangerous, yet Western governments continue to indulge them and shelter them from losses. The financial industry lobbies still permeate government, fund the dominant political factions and sustain key 'think tanks'. There is a restless search for methods of tackling the rising costs of an ageing society, methods that socialize losses and privatize profit. Extensions of health care and elder care are designed to offer guaranteed business to commercial suppliers and insurers, despite the latter's poor cost ratios. This approach compromises what might otherwise be positive extensions of welfare entitlement, such as the new health care regime agreed between President Obama and Congress in 2010. In this case participants are required to become customers of private insurers, with no 'public option' and via the construction of 'exchanges' in every state, offering the programme's enemies the opportunity to sabotage its implementation. Moreover, there is no 'single payer' mechanism with the market power to bring down pharma prices.

China's dynamic and semi-collectivist economy, however, has helped it to contain the crisis. China's most important banks are publicly owned and were required to back huge programmes of investment in infrastructure, environmental protection and productive capacity. The Chinese authorities undertook a large and effective stimulus package. China has also used public assets to fund social provision by endowing public welfare bodies with the proceeds of privatization. Echoing the contradictory forces at work in Chinese society, the privatization of public assets has been accompanied by stipulations that entrust a proportion of them to pension provision. The Chinese authorities also proclaim the need to rebalance the economy towards consumption, although implementation remains problematic. China has suffered from a property bubble, as some local governments sell off public land or devote resources to speculative development. But government control of the banking system and the use of taxes on the increase in land values offer some chance of containing the bubble. In Chongqing and some other important regions, the public authorities refused to sell off land, instead letting it out on short-term leases, a tactic which enables them to capture more of the gains from urban development.[19]

In 2009, the G20 extended the US bailout and stimulus package into a vast programme for rehabilitating global finance. The central bankers agreed on programmes of 'quantitative easing' – printing money – on a huge scale. There was a rehabilitation of economic thinkers like Schumpeter, Keynes and Minsky, who challenged the notion of self-regulating finance. Western governments pumped up consumer demand but failed to tackle inequality or to promote new waves of investment. The financial authorities in Brazil and China complained that 'quantitative easing' in the US and Europe was exporting inflation and fostering new asset bubbles in real estate in the emerging economies.

The US Federal Reserve revealed in December 2010 that it had extended no less than $3.5 trillion to US banks, money which these institutions used to escape from their own expensive debts or which they invested, at little or no risk, in public bonds or high-quality consumer debt. To get that $3.3 trillion into perspective, we might note that it is more than four times as large as the TARP, which was just the visible tip of the bank bailout effort.[20] The soft money lent to the banks allowed them to borrow at bargain basement rates – 1 per cent or less – and then to place it in government bonds paying 4 or 5 per cent – or consumer credit paying 12 or 18 per cent. It is not surprising that the big banks became hugely profitable once again and that bankers' bonuses ballooned. (The Fed's disclosure of the scale of the help extended to the banks was one of the few tangible results of the cautious reforms embodied in the Dodd–Frank Act; the scale of 'quantitative easing' was linked to sagging annuity rates, directly reducing the income which a pension pot produces.)

The financial sector was being kept afloat – but with very uneven results. Some hedge funds outperformed but the sector as a whole failed to deliver the absolute returns it had promised. Some large investors came to prefer exchange-traded funds (ETFs), and their funds under management rival those of the shrunken hedge funds. At the close of 2008 global retirement funds had been down 40 per cent, regaining some value over the next six months only to see most of this seep away again over the following two years. If fund-management costs and inflation are included, the generality of 'defined contribution' (DC) funds available to the small saver were struggling simply to achieve zero returns to cap a 'lost decade'.

The US Employee Benefit Research Institute (EBRI) headlined its 2011 Retirement Confidence Survey, 'Confidence Drops to Record Lows, Reflecting the "New Normal"'. This survey reports that 64 per cent of those aged 45–54 have less than $50,000 of savings, excluding the house they live in and membership of the fast-disappearing defined benefit (DB) schemes. In EBRI's 2007 survey, 55 per cent had reported this level of savings or less (savings of $50,000 would buy an annuity of just $300 a month). Of the same cohort, 44 per cent had less than $10,000 (and were most unlikely to have DB membership or wealthy residences). Thus it is Social Security entitlement – averaging $1,100 a month – which will save nearly half the US population who face destitution in retirement. Of those in work, only 13 per cent of all employees were 'very confident' that they would have enough to retire on, with 36 per cent being 'somewhat confident'.[21] Unfortunately, the latter category is likely to include a considerable proportion of the many who underestimate what they will need for retirement. Employees do expect to have to work longer – though whether there will be jobs for them is another matter. The richest tenth of all pension-savers garner half of all tax relief and consequently do well from their pension investments. Most of these, however, will still be invested in so-called 'mutual funds' paying management fees, which greatly limits accumulation in their savings pot. (Although technically 'mutual' – that is, owned by their members – these funds are usually operated by commercial fund managers, who charge an annual fee of 1 to 2 per cent of the sum in the scheme.) Notoriously, the real gains of the boom years accrued to the top 1 per cent, or even top 0.1 per cent of households (on which more in Chapter 4).

The weak and worsening data on US savings and retirement prospects showed the hollowness of Washington's 'success' in tackling the crisis. Moreover, the impetus to international cooperation was not maintained and the huge global imbalances that led to the crisis persisted. The balance sheets of many financial institutions still harboured unrecognised losses.

While Wall Street and the City of London regained some stability in 2009–10, European banks and the holders of bonds issued by weaker European states were soon hit, with large-scale rescues being required in Iceland, Greece, Ireland and Portugal, sometimes with double doses and uncertain results. By 2011 Spain and Italy were next in line. While there was much criticism of those who had over-borrowed, there was little criticism of reckless lenders. Once again, banks had lent unwisely but expected to escape any of the negative consequences. And as I note in Chapter 6 of this book, the euro proved vulnerable because it was not supported by a significant fiscal authority. The bailouts required elaborate negotiations between the various national financial authorities, each of which had special interests to defend, especially where their own banks risked suffering a default or 'haircut'. The rescues imposed drastic austerity programmes on recipient governments, destroying pension entitlements and driving down living standards while requiring the banks to be paid in full. The announcement of a European Stability Mechanism, backed by pledges from national governments totalling over €440 billion, failed to calm fears, because cumbersome to implement and of inadequate size. Suggestions that 'leverage' could be used to enlarge the fund did not help.[22]

From any point of view, European financial institutions had been found wanting. Many of the eurozone's financial titans – notably Deutsche Bank and Société Générale – had participated in the credit derivatives orgy. But the crisis could still have a positive outcome were it to lead to recognition that a new financial regime was required across the eurozone – namely, a financial system geared to public utility and guaranteed by the fiscal authorities. Any real hope of sustaining the euro would require the levying of Europe-wide taxes and the creation of an EU finance ministry. The president of the European Central Bank happily proposed the latter, while neglecting to add that it would need to be subordinate to democratic control.[23] In some ways the original model of the US Federal Reserve system, set up a century ago, contains features from which the eurozone leaders could learn: it has a central bank supported by a powerful Treasury and thirteen regional branches. Unfortunately, the latter do not have either the power or the community representation that was originally envisaged.[24] But even so, elected officials and bodies played a larger part than they do in euroland. Is it utopian to imagine that Europeans could radically improve on the achievements of US progressives in 1913?

The experience of the crisis has given rise to calls for a new international financial architecture based on a recognition that financial markets are not self-correcting and should not be exposed to speculative frenzy. The Chinese authorities urged the creation of a new international reserve currency and, as noted above, the Brazilian authorities criticized the inflationary impact of massive US 'quantitative easing', which threatens the role of the emergent economies as the new engines of the world economy. In the United States, the Dodd–Frank Act introduced a raft of measures offering 'consumer protection' to investors in financial products – but this act was almost immediately hobbled by simultaneous cutbacks in the budgets of the regulatory bodies, and nobbled by loopholes allowing for the continued use of off-balance-sheet vehicles. The *New York Times* dubbed this 'repeal by another name'.[25] The British authorities also sought to introduce measures under the rubric of 'restoring confidence' in financial institutions – but without clearly ensuring that those institutions deserved that confidence. As John Kay pointedly observed: 'The new economy bubble, the sale of complex asset-backed securities, the scale of Greek debt; these problems arose not because consumers did not have enough confidence in the products but because they had too much.'[26]

In the US it is typically the case that any major reorientation requires successive waves of legislation, to correct and radicalize the initial legislative act. In this way, ending slavery required three successive amendments to the Constitution (and even then was incomplete). The 1913 Federal Reserve legislation needed the state of New York's 1921 Martin Act and the 1934 Glass–Steagall Act (as well as other measures) before US financial regulation achieved a certain degree of adequacy. The 1935 Social Security Act was patchy and inadequate, needing major amendments in 1940 and 1950 before today's programme was consolidated. Clearly the Dodd–Frank Act (and Obama's health care bill) will be neutralized without radical improvement and enforcement.[27]

The Eurozone Crisis

The eurozone crisis of 2010–11 has underlined the fact that the bill for the crisis of bubble economics has still not been paid. When the IMF and European Central Bank organized bailouts for 'Greece', 'Ireland' and 'Portugal', they were in fact protecting the large German, British, French and US banks that had lent to those countries. Martin Wolf, the *Financial Times* columnist and a former IMF official, observed in November 2010 that it 'was not the public but the private sector that went haywire in Ireland and in Spain'.[28] Another analyst pointed out that government spending on social protection in Ireland had dropped from 20 per cent of GDP in 1993 to 14 per cent in 2000.[29]

Prior to the financial crisis Ireland's net public debt was only 12 per cent of GDP, compared with 80 per cent for Greece and 50 per cent for Germany. The root of the crisis, according to Wolf, was property speculation in an ultra-'flexible' and deregulated economy, with very low interest rates.[30] With the cost of borrowing so low, private financial entities found property speculations irresistible.

Facilitated by its 1998 Land Act, which scrapped zoning restrictions and environmental norms, and by huge investment in transport infrastructure, Spain enjoyed a huge property boom in the decade that followed. By the end of this period property prices had tripled, fuelling annual economic growth of 5–6 per cent. By 2008, 7 million Spanish households owned two homes, and nearly as many Germans, French and British owned a second home in Spain. While the Spanish state had certainly helped to make this possible, public services and social protection were innocent of the blowout. Yet when property speculations began to turn sour, and to compromise the *cajas* and banks, the Socialist government, pressured and advised by the European Central Bank and IMF, introduced sweeping austerity measures. Unemployment, concentrated particularly among younger and older workers, rose to 20 per cent. In March 2010 an agreement was reached with the unions to cut pensions and raise the retirement age, something which provoked the 'indignado' movement and a wave of demonstrations, strikes and occupations.[31]

The plethora of default swaps in the bond markets made it harder to tackle the return of the Greek debt problem in 2011. It gave many banks a reason to oppose any participation in rescheduling or 'restructuring' the Greek government's debts. Why accept a loss if default triggers compensation? The German Chancellor, Angela Merkel, urged the banks to accept a 50 per cent 'haircut' – writing down the value of their bonds by a half – but the banks procrastinated in the hope of a default event which would allow them to invoke their CDS insurance.[32]

In July 2011, as the crisis ground on, this same constraint prompted some eurozone officials to propose that a new Greek bailout be financed by a levy on the banks. Such a tax, unlike a 'haircut', would not count as a 'credit event' or default. One report commented: 'The plan, which advocates believe could raise 30 billion euros over three years ($42 billion) could help to satisfy German and Dutch demands that private holders of Greek bonds contribute to a new 115 billion euro bailout.'[33] (The 'private holders' referred to being, of course, the banks.) However, resistance from the banks was on this occasion sufficient to block the proposal, despite the seriousness of the situation. The banks accepted a modest €17 billion write-down of their bond-holdings, which they regarded as preferable to a 0.025 per cent levy on their assets throughout the eurozone – since any bank levy, however modest, is seen as the thin end of a very undesirable wedge. By this time, however, angry citizens were prepared to urge their governments' repudiation of what were increasingly seen as 'illegitimate' or 'odious' debts.[34]

The persistence of the crisis stemmed from the continued weakness of demand. The stimulus programmes were too weak and too little focused on investment. The economic weather was being created as households and banks ran down their debts, governments cut spending and the sponsors of DB schemes were obliged to fix the deficits in their pension funds. Unless a path to recovery can be found it will be extraordinarily difficult to meet the costs of an ageing society. So far most of the attempts to stimulate national economies have taken the form of bank bailouts and tax cuts for the rich but the impact on overall demand has been very disappointing. An alternative approach would be to foster the growth of demand by direct measures to boost the income of the low paid and to reduce the debts of the poor by a moratorium. Richard Duncan argues for a minimum wage in the Asian export sector.[35] If the Chinese currency was to rise in value this would also help to raise demand from China. There is certainly a strong case for debt-forgiveness on loans which are simply beyond the means of micro-lenders or of 'subprime' borrowers. If the poor were released from the burden of debt it would begin to rebuild demand from below. The global elderly – two-thirds of them women – are often destitute. In the Afterword I outline a proposal for a global pension. Building the purchasing power of the poorest has the advantage, as I explain there, that they are likely to spend on local and national produce.

Global Coordination

The uncertainty surrounding the euro and resentment at US 'quantitative easing' gave a new relevance to the proposal from the governments of China and Brazil that a new international reserve currency was needed – and that the IMF needed reform in order to remove its domination by the US and EU. An initial package of measures was drawn up in *The Stiglitz Report*, prepared by Joseph Stiglitz and the UN Commission of Financial Experts.[36]

It is not my purpose here to discuss proposals of this sort, other than to agree that global coordination will be needed to tackle issues on the scale of global poverty, ageing and threats to a habitable planet. The anarchy and uncertainty of global exchanges and capital flows must be addressed and regulated in ways that empower and inform the citizens and communities across the world. With this in mind, in *Age Shock* I look at how best to meet the rising costs of the ageing society on a country-by-country basis, but with a view to concerted measures on a regional and global scale. Measures favourable to inclusive pensions and elder-care provision can be taken on a national, regional and global level, combining to build an alternative to the reign of financialization – by which I mean a regime in which banking and finance are both pervasive and sovereign.

At one moment, the crisis itself seemed to threaten the banks' attempts to pose as sovereigns of the financial realm. However, to adapt an aphorism, if a small bank is overstretched then it has a problem, but if a mega-bank is over-extended then the government has a problem. The 'reforms' recommended by the G20 implied considerable regulation, but proved irksome rather than effective. In the end governments felt obliged to bow to the needs of the finance houses. In nearly every case bondholders and shareholders have avoided paying for their own mistakes – instead, taxpayers have had to stump up. Mervyn King, the governor of the Bank of England, became restive at the veto powers wielded by the often feckless or miscreant mega-banks. In a speech in Edinburgh on 21 October 2010, King stressed the virtues of 'narrow banking' – that is, lending to households and companies – and proposed to limit government guarantees to 'utility banks'.[37] If financial engineering brought real benefits then it could fend for itself without government backing.

The repeated distempers of the money markets since 1971 have allowed some to become fabulously rich, but the broader interests of capitalists favour the construction of a more stable and predictable global system of trade and capital.[38] Governments, whether democratic or not, need to court public opinion. Popular movements, and progressive parties and governments will have opportunities to press for their goals in elaborating new national, regional and global institutions and practices.

Public Utility Finance

National governments still have the possibility of developing their own response to the current malaise, but only if they summon up a spirit of collective solidarity and public entrepreneurship. Singapore has shown that even a small state can come to grips with global patterns on its own terms. Social infrastructure, sustainable economics and the cross-border scope for new productive networks furnish many fields for such endeavour. The pressures of capital accumulation should be neither underestimated nor accepted, but rather curbed, controlled and directed. Centrally, this requires the building of public utility banks and finance systems, reaching out from national centres and devolving resources to every locality, on the one hand, and cooperating with regional and global partners on the other.[39] Strategic public ownership is a necessary but not sufficient condition, since public authorities can be tempted into their own speculative excesses (sadly the IMF and World Bank have encouraged this by their privatization euphoria, on which more below).

Management of the crisis, as we have seen, led to public ownership stakes in key financial houses, but the real scale of public help via 'quantitative easing' has not been acknowledged and in several areas losses – on both private securities and pubic bonds – remain concealed. In August 2011, US house prices were still 15 per cent below their August 2008 level, a fact which, it was reported, 'continues to create a drag on the "toxic" mortgage-backed securities that started the problem'.[40] By this time the euro debt problem was even more severe, but with banks in Northern Europe (and North America) often holding the junk.

If financial institutions were required to forgive all household and personal debt below a target level – say $50,000 – this would stimulate the economy; it could, moreover, be accomplished in ways that would both socialize and strengthen the financial sector. The wiping out of the debts of the less well-off would eliminate many non-performing assets; it would also force many financial concerns to seek public help. As Neil Barofsky, the previously cited TARP 'inspector general', explained, a bailout 'from below' – reducing the burdens on the poor and low paid – would have been more effective, and more conducive to public utility, than the banker-friendly bailouts 'from above'.

A public utility finance system would have at its core publicly owned and publicly accountable banks, regulatory agencies and social funds. The latter would inform and empower individual citizens, and regional or local networks. The neo-liberal model, by contrast, hands over public assets and social programmes to private corporations and promotes a pervasive commodification of health, education, pensions and access to the natural environment. Indeed, commodification goes so deep today that it seeks to convert every citizen into a two-legged calculating machine, making their own lives into a financial cost and profit centre. Students are encouraged to take on debt, householders to take out mortgages, consumers to buy on credit and citizens to use commercial entities to insure their own life-course risks rather than sharing and spreading them according to a scheme of intergenerational solidarity and justice.

The wider global cost of financial crises and distortions has been many trillions of dollars in lost output, tens of millions thrown out of employment and many more millions, whether employed or not, losing pension entitlements. And notwithstanding the success of China and Brazil, there has been increasing global inequality, a yawning – and ever-widening – gap between rich and poor, visible in both the rich countries and in the newly emerging markets themselves. In March 2011, the *Economist* reported that 'the benefits of recovery seem to have been distributed almost entirely to the owners of capital rather than workers'.[41] The report went on to note that this was part of both an international and a long-term trend: 'labour's share has been in decline across the OECD since 1980. The gap has been particularly marked in America: productivity rose by 83 per cent between 1973 and 2007, but male, median, real wages rose by just 5 per cent.'[42] Real wages have risen in China, India and Brazil – but labour organization and agitation will be needed to secure and spread such gains which are very unevenly distributed. Levels of inequality have been rising sharply in China, India and Russia; in Brazil levels of inequality have dropped in recent years but remain high. We also see that the crisis has brought no benefit to the poorest areas and has stricken the microfinance movement, even in countries like Bangladesh, where it appeared strongest.[43]

While private finance precipitated the crisis, public finance was needed to stave off disaster and contribute to recovery. The Chinese banking system is still largely publicly owned and controlled, as noted above. China's banks were instructed to maintain or even increase the flow of credit at the risk that they themselves might become weighed down by underperforming loans. Continued growth in the Chinese economy allowed these bets to pay off, and the boost to Chinese demand stimulated the country's imports. German industry was ready to meet the needs of Chinese customers. However, China's growing inequality constrains its trading pattern, with German exporters finding stronger demand for luxury cars than for machine tools or medical equipment. By

2011 there were signs of slackening demand in China, and of government reluctance to undertake a new stimulus package.

German manufacturers retained a competitive edge, in part because they were supported by a public, not-for-profit research network, the Fraunhofer-Gesellschaft, founded in 1947. Today this institution has a research staff of 18,000 and an annual budget of 1.65 billion.[44] This network is vital to German manufacturing prowess.

Although Germany was hit by the crisis, it recovered quite quickly thanks to booming exports to Asia. A system of rebates for younger and older workers reduced both labour costs and the size of the tax wedge on employee incomes (noted as a problem in Chapter 6, below). Firms were also encouraged to retain workers by a special payroll subsidy. Unemployment dropped from 9 per cent in 2006 to 5 per cent in 2011, and growth recovered to a steady 5 per cent on an annual basis. The institutions of 'co-determination' (*Mitbestimmung*) allowed managers and working collectives to make quite good use of the complex new fiscal provisions, albeit that redundancy compensation became much less generous. An *Economist* report was obliged to consider the possibility that 'the crisis seemed to discredit the "Anglo-Saxon model" of growth based on financial wizardry and property bubbles – and vindicate the German one, in which workers cooperate with bosses, managers invest for the long-term and manufacturing holds pride of place over services'.[45] While unions cooperated in containing wage costs, the wages of IG Metal members rose by 13 per cent during the period 2005–2009.

Social ownership and local finance should be encouraged, but stringent safeguards are needed to insulate such funds from commercial and speculative pressures. Thus the network of social funds that I propose in Chapter 7 would be required to hold securities for the long term, and to account for all acquisitions and disbursements to independent auditors. Community banks and building societies have shown that they can give good service if prevented from taking on extraneous 'leverage', but that they soon run into trouble if 'liberated' (that is, deregulated or privatized) and permitted to act like commercial banks. Thus German manufacturing corporations have long benefited from the country's largely publicly owned *Landesbanken*. However, during the last decade or so several of these banks were tempted to speculate with complex mortgage derivatives and ran up huge losses as a result. This phenomenon is yet another example of the perils of deregulating and semi-privatizing public finance networks – other cases in point being the US Savings and Loan banks,

Fannie Mae, many British privatized former mutuals (for example, TSB) and the Spanish *cajas*. Each of these institutions worked well for decades as public-owned and well-regulated institutions; all got into difficulties once deregulated, privatized or demutualized.

A number of states – Norway, Australia, Qatar, China – nurtured sovereign funds or 'future funds' which acted as a buffer during the crisis. Such funds might be invested in ways that promote productive capacity, social housing or environmental protection. Projects like these build long-term assets that can be drawn upon in case of events both un-predictable (natural disaster) and predictable (an ageing population). In some countries public provident and pension funds also play this role. The managers of such funds invest in development or social infrastruc-ture, but are increasingly aware that these should foster environmental sustainability. In the US and EU, though, free-market principles and private lobbies have discouraged sustained public investment pro-grammes. The EU has both a development bank and a 'structural fund' – but both of these have been allowed to lie fallow, with €347 billion in unclaimed funding at the close of 2010.[46]

Twenty-first-century advocates of public enterprise and social plan-ning need to reshape them in ways that avoid their historic pitfalls. Recent years have seen striking successes for publicly sponsored eco-nomic development, but with some serious accompanying problems. Thus, IT manufacturing in Taiwan's science parks and agricultural production in Brazil's *cerrado* backlands have been heralded as great successes; in each case, these countries have become the world's leading suppliers in several of the lines of production chosen for development by the public agencies concerned two or three decades ago. In the Brazilian case, a crucial role was played by EMBRAPA, the Brazilian Agricultural Research Corporation, and its success in rehabilitating the soil of the *cerrado*, previously an inhospitable scrubland.[47] Public subsidies were used strategically to set up viable entities rather than to cover ongoing operational deficits. Yet the very success of the publicly sponsored programmes in Brazil and Taiwan has created unacceptable environ-mental problems. Though worrying, these problems should not be unmanageable if the public authorities and the productive new entities were answerable to local communities for their impacts. Unfortunately, the success of these programmes also makes them juicy targets for privatization, with business interests stepping in to take charge.

Public sector pension funds have also had success in building social housing in many countries – notably Singapore – but attention should always be paid to furnishing housing in ways that are democratically responsive to the wishes of the communities concerned and in ways that promote civic inclusion. China has had huge successes in building an industrial economy, but the extent of local protests shows that it has often done this at great social cost.

Publicly organized pension provision and health care have proven that they can deliver more efficient, reliable and equitable results than commercial suppliers. When private finance fails, public finance invariably has to step into the breach. From the 1990s onwards, the prospect of greater public spending on elder care and the cults of privatization and financialization led to keen interest in elder care as a source of lucrative contracts and dubious financial engineering. Elected officials on the lookout for savings were attracted by financial models that allowed them to reduce care budgets. Financialization contributed the idea that private consortia would take on elder care in return for a stream of future fees and the possibility of taking over publicly owned facilities and reorganizing them according to the 'opco/propco' model. The functions of caring for the elderly and of owning and overseeing care homes would be separated out into care-providing 'operating companies' and real estate-owning 'property companies', with the latter being able to deploy real estate assets in advantageous ways. However, this procedure left the care-supplying company with rent obligations that might quickly eat up its profits. Another problem was that the income stream from the public authority would be subject to crisis-induced austerity cuts. In July 2011 Southern Cross, Britain's largest private care home chain, responsible for 700 care homes, declared bankruptcy. As their 30,000 elderly inmates contemplated ejection, newspapers revealed that the top executives who sponsored this particular piece of financial engineering had shared out £35 million in bonuses. But the financial services company Blackstone and its associates, who devised the opco/propco 'solution', did far better: by the time Blackstone exited this investment, it had made a profit of £1.1 billion on an original investment of £564 million.[48] (It might be noted that in the late 1990s and early 2000s some of the British Labour Party's most generous financial supporters had made their fortunes by running large chains of care homes, a business that depended on public contracts. By 2011 Jeremy Heywood, the financial engineer who had devised the Southern Cross deal, held a senior post in the office of the British prime minister.) The Southern Cross deal was, as a *Financial Times* report explained, just part of the wave of financial 'innovation' that made huge sums by speculating on elder care without taking account of its human cost.[49] Bankruptcy is a normal and necessary discipline for the 'animal spirits' of capitalists – which is why important public services should be publicly owned and run. Pension delivery should likewise be restricted to bodies that will still be in existence in four decades' time. A strong government should recognize the need for an autonomous and well-funded network of pension and elder care agencies, with provision for regular audit, to ensure that they are doing the job assigned to them.

The response to the crisis was overwhelmingly confined to manipulation of interest rates and the money supply. It should have embraced control of the banks and tangible projects of public utility. In the wake of the crisis the British government failed to prevent the closure of a Vestas factory making wind turbine blades in the Isle of Wight, a Pfizer laboratory in Kent, research facilities in Cambridge and a rail plant in Derby – with each closure throwing specialist engineering and research teams on the scrap heap, reducing tax revenue and swelling unemployment costs. In the US the stimulus programme saved some large enterprises, as noted above, but there was little attempt to mount new large-scale projects. In the 1930s Presidents Hoover and Roosevelt had established the Reconstruction Finance Corporation (RFC), which undertook to build badly needed infrastructure and factories. With signature achievements even in the pre-war period, the RFC also worked well in the war years; the Tennessee Valley Authority (TVA), meanwhile, undertook a world-renowned programme of dam-building, electricity generating and irrigation. With the outbreak of war the RFC was given the huge sum of $4 billion (at 1942 prices) to spend building factories for Boeing and Lockheed so that they could produce desperately needed aircraft and lorries.[50] When historians look back at the period 2007–12, however, there will be no remotely comparable monuments to public enterprise.

In early 2009, Paul Krugman in the *New York Times* urged that the US stimulus was seriously inadequate and that resuming real growth required nationalization of the banks. He has been proved right. However, the stymied recovery still demands a new set of institutions going beyond those so far advocated by Krugman and the Keynesians. This should include setting up a public utility finance system, levying taxes on capital and building local networks of democratically controlled social funds. The measures that I canvas below, in Chapter 7, would help to generate the necessary resources. Also helpful is Gerald Holtham's argument that a 'national investment bank' could raise growth and reduce deficits by constructing public facilities that would earn future revenues, such as social housing or toll roads.[51] Holtham suggests that one of the already nationalized banks could be adapted to this function and, if guaranteed by the government, could borrow money cheaply. One could add to this a further proposal: that approved pension funds could be given special access to such investments, with a guaranteed return. For the government to pledge a certain level of future senior income costs it little or nothing, since these pensioners would qualify for state support anyway.

The aim of any new development programme should be to stimulate investment-led growth, foster sustainability, encourage the formation of human capital, and yield a growth in productivity. Without attempting to suppress market relations, such a package would seek to re-embed the market, and to de-commodify major areas of social life, giving everyone free access to decent health care and education, and endowing everyone with a share and say in the control of economic resources.[52] Building better pensions – or even salvaging those that already exist – will require measures which can ensure sustainable growth. Contributions to pension provision can be adjusted to have a countercyclical impact. In my calculation of the growth of the universal pension fund (in Chapter 7), I assume a 5 per cent rate of return. In 2006, and against the background of the promises made by the advocates of pension privatization, this was a comparatively modest rate. The privatizers usually employ a 7 per cent, or even 9 per cent, rate of return – levels which always looked optimistic. In the last deeply troubled decade such rates are clearly unrealistic, and even 5 per cent is demanding. But across several decades, and with concerted, government-backed measures of investment, it would be achievable.

In suggesting measures of regulation and control there is a real danger that one misses the systemic impetus of capitalist accumulation. In this age of financialization this is stronger than ever and is seen in the recklessness with which the great banks pursued the expansion of their balance sheets. From the standpoint of the CEO and board this is often experienced as an external pressure to justify their holdings by sweating them. The shareholders expect them to hunt for profit in even the most unlikely of assets. In June 2007, the Citibank CEO famously explained with reference to easy borrowing and the CDO craze that 'as long as the music is playing you have to get up and dance'.

By the summer of 2011 a new climacteric had been reached, but its advent already bore out the doctrine of Heraclitus that you don't step into the same river twice. The monetary mechanisms that had been at least half-successful in 2009 were no longer available. Dropping interest rates to zero boosts demand, but even negative rates will not overcome the shyness of badly burnt investors. The willingness to engage in stimulus packages had evaporated. In 2007–8 the G20 governments were willing to take concerted measures; in 2010–11 the best that Washington and Brussels aspired to was – as the phrase of the moment had it – 'kicking the can down the road'. The Washington deadlock over the country's debt ceiling and the prevarication of the eurozone leaders told a similar story. Standard and Poor reduced the credit rating of US public debt and China's eagerness for cooperation had subsided. Because the various crises centre on public debt the elements of a solution will have to include the levying of new taxes and the collection of old ones. There should be an audit of public debt, leading to selective debt repudiation, with odious debt wiped out entirely. The debt of poorer and low-income households should be decisively lightened. On the other hand, entitlements to future health care and pension provision should be honoured. The press often harp on very unusual cases, so there is a case for placing a cap or tax on individual pension payouts above, say, 150 per cent of average earnings. There should also be a decent second pension for all employees and citizens. China and Germany will have to play a bigger part in devising solutions to the crisis and cannot reasonably object if their own collectivist approach is emulated. Finally, the need for more secure and wider social protection has been underlined by international experience, as explained in the next section.

'Resource Leverage' and Pension Privatization

The whole experience of the crisis threw into question the supposed success of the IMF and World Bank in urging countries to abandon public pension systems and opt for mandatory private provision. Throughout the 1990s and up to the eve of the crisis these institutions had aggressively promoted commercialization of pension provision, as Mitchell Orenstein has shown in his *Privatizing Pensions*.[53] Between 1994 and 2008, thirty countries in Latin America and Eastern Europe were pressured to abandon their public pension systems and to replace them with personal pension funds managed by commercial finance houses. The international agencies resorted to shameless bullying, and to what Orenstein calls 'resource leverage'. As he explains, countries in the midst of a difficult transition to democracy were denied all financial assistance unless they agreed to pension privatization. In addition, funds were made available by the World Bank to carry through campaigns of public persuasion, while key individuals were offered inducements and attractive employment if they went along with the process.

The success of the World Bank's campaign for pension privatization proved a comprehensive disaster for the countries concerned. The rocky state of stock markets has meant that the promised accumulation targets have been missed by a mile. But even in periods where stock markets grew, commercial funds suffered from exaggerated cost ratios. This underlines a central argument of *Age Shock*, namely, that universal public schemes do not have the expense of marketing and customization that plague private provision. In an attempt to solve this problem, countries were often persuaded to make participation compulsory, but the cost disease problem has remained. This is because either there is no effective competition – in which case the suppliers exploit their monopoly position – or there is competition ('choice') and an expensive marketing war between rival suppliers.[54]

In a re-examination of the 'reformed' regimes undertaken in early 2011, Orenstein notes the following pitfalls:

> Typically, women and lower income earners are the big losers from pension privatization, since they may have significant non-contributory periods, broken employment histories and/or lower levels of savings. High-income earners are usually big winners, since the contributions made to their individual accounts are based on higher earnings through-out relatively uninterrupted work lives   The even bigger winners, however, are financial services companies, who earn enormous administrative fees running pension funds.[55]

Orenstein believes that the pension privatization cause stalled for a while, as a consequence of the crisis – and also because of the impact of forbidding transition costs (that is, the simultaneous cost of paying past pension entitlements while requiring current workers to contribute to their own pension pots). The financial crisis sometimes left governments shortchanging both pensioners and employees, with the former receiving devalued pensions while the later were left dismayed by the insecurity of their savings.

In 2008, newly established pension funds in Poland lost 17 per cent of their value, in Bulgaria 26 per cent, in Slovakia 12 per cent, and in Estonia 32 per cent in one fund, 24 per cent in another and 8 per cent in another.[56] This shock prompted a realization that the privatization strategy was flawed and reform was needed, with caps on management fees, more diversified portfolios and limits on various investment categories (such as investment abroad). Measures were also taken to restore a basic state pension.

In the wake of the crisis, the EU and eurozone authorities became intensely concerned at debt levels, setting rigorous standards for potential new members of the eurozone. These criteria turned the spotlight on the debt countries had taken on as a consequence of the transition to privatization. On the one hand, the burden of state debt had jumped – but on the other, the assets in new private schemes could not be used to offset it. The new member states of the EU protested, but the Eurostat authorities and ECB – having presided over the eurozone debacle and earlier fostered pension privatization – suddenly became the belated guardians of financial rectitude.

Several countries that had adopted private pensions subsequently revised their retirement systems to give greater importance to the 'public pillar' of state pensions. The Chilean government of the 1980s had blazed the trail for a type of privatization. In 2006 Michelle Bachelet, the country's new Socialist president, declared that the Chilean pension regime was badly flawed, with 'low coverage . . . very little competition and high commission charges . . . [while it] discriminates against women'.[57] New legislation created a 'solidarity pension' that would furnish coverage and a living pension to women and the low paid. The commercial practices of the AFPs (pension funds) were curbed, with the aim of avoiding risk and reducing costly marketing, and encouraging the emergence of schemes run by professional rather than corporate organizations.

The pension privatization programme aimed to foster local stock exchanges, but these often proved to be exposed to dramatic swings in value. The Hungarian and Argentine governments felt strong enough to take control of their accumulated funds. Unfortunately the backlash against 'reform' in these countries was often pursued in an ad hoc manner, in crisis conditions, and without sufficient guarantees to ensure the future independence of the pension supplier as a public authority. If only a body with the resources of the World Bank had been available to help with the task of 'de-privatization' (nationalization), its course would have been steadier and more beneficial.

Orenstein notes a certain revival of the privatizing trend as the crisis persists and austerity measures weaken public provision. This new approach replaces 'mandatory' private pension pots with 'automatic enrolment' in a private scheme, but with an opt-out clause. As I explain in *Age Shock*, in 2006 the Labour government in Britain legislated for such a scheme, whereby employees would contribute 5 per cent of salary into a National Employee Savings Trust (NEST) but could withdraw from the scheme whenever they wished. The subsequent coalition government agreed to continue the scheme. It comes into force in 2012, at a time when the living standards of those on low or medium incomes are being tightly squeezed – many may decide to opt out. The extent of bipartisanship (or tripartisanship, as three parties are involved) so far as British pension policy is concerned is impressive. The coalition also asked John Hutton, the former Labour pensions minister, to draw up a report on how to scale back public sector pensions, a report which it subsequently adopted.

While these various measures of 'soft' and 'implicit' privatization were as much as the financial services lobby could reasonably expect in the aftermath of the crisis, politicians were still aware of continuing public unhappiness which they sought to allay by stressing that the level of the basic state pension, and 'pension credit', would be linked to earnings rather than prices. The likelihood of shortfalls and gaps in coverage remains great.

In the US, the sharpness of party and factional cleavage seems to rule out a bipartisan approach to Social Security or other aspects of ageing costs. But though they will be reluctant to admit it, enough Democrats believe in 'saving' Social Security by cutting benefits to make a deal a possibility. If there is a further major lurch in the financial crisis it is even possible that some politicians will bite the hand that feeds them, and agitate for tougher controls on the banks.

In his campaign to become the Democratic presidential candidate, Barack Obama intimated at an early stage that he thought that Social Security needed reform. But as he faced a stronger challenge from Hillary Clinton, who opposed weakening the programme, Obama dropped this theme. Once elected, he appointed a commission to propose ways to reduce the public deficit, some of whose members suggested that Social Security benefits should be cut by raising the retirement age, weakening indexation and other measures. Nevertheless, given the programme's iconic status, and the difficulty of predicting when – or if – a shortfall will be encountered, it was still surprising when Obama offered a 'grand bargain' to the Republican Congressional leaders in July 2011, whereby they would agree to lift the ceiling on official US debt in return for $4 trillion of savings, with the programme of government spending cuts, to include Social Security.[58] While the Republicans refused this tempting concession, benefit cuts to Social Security were no longer off-limits so far as the White House was concerned. The deal eventually reached in August 2011 committed Congress to cutting the federal budget by $917 billion over ten years, entrusting the task of specifying these cuts – and establishing the base line against which the cuts will be made – to a super-committee. Social Security old-age pensions and Medicare, the health programme for the older citizens – will be candidates for butchery.

In *Age Shock*, I identify the typical problems besetting the commercial provision of financial services – excessive fees, on the one hand, and information asymmetry between suppliers and savers, on the other. The high charges stem from the costs of marketing and customization. British governments of several political complexions have passed laws which claim to rein in exorbitant charges and reduce complexity. Yet in a report issued in August 2011, the Workplace Retirement Income Commission found that 'defined contribution' pensions were a bad buy because of excessive fees and obfuscatory terms and conditions.[59] The finance houses have much more information than their customers and use this to secure advantages over them. The vices of commercial money management for customers are not redeemed by effective or enlightened investment policies.

The great investment banks fly far above the level at which small and medium-sized businesses exist, and have no rational criteria to inform their credit decisions – witness their folly in accepting so much exposure to subprime mortgages. Today a similar problem arises with respect to their reluctance to make any productive investments. In contrast, a public utility finance system, buttressed and sustaining networks of social funds, could reconnect finance to its social context and democratize its workings. The traditional socialist model of 'nationalized' and planned economy has had its successes – and in some areas may still have its uses. It

makes sense for railways, electric power, water and other natural mono-
polies to be publicly owned and run.[60] But the command economy
model has had its day. So long as markets are monitored and regulated
they can play a useful, even valuable, role.[61] The social ownership of
pension funds – and their management alongside the pursuit of socially
responsible criteria – can add an extra dimension to this. National and
international regulators will find it difficult to have the information they
need to oversee a myriad of economic actors. Socially owned institutional
investors would add another type of 'regulation from below' to enhance
'regulation from above'.

My argument in *Age Shock* could be caricatured as claiming that the
only way to meet the mounting costs of the ageing society is to take a leap
into socialism. However, the public utility finance system and the
networks of social funds aim to tame and direct capital but not eliminate
it. There would still be competitive final product markets and competition between capitals. The large banks would be socialized and the
remainder required to be far more transparent. For a while, at least, there
would be publicly owned stock exchanges. Improved regulation would
be supplemented by a multitude of well-informed, and broadly owned,
transactors – the network of social funds. The transnational corporations
would be subject to quite new pressures. Eventually, more thorough-
going measures of socialization might be seen as desirable, but for a
considerable time the objective would have to be enhancing the role of
public authorities at all levels in a world where privatization and
financialization have run amok – often by hijacking the state.

Earlier I referred to the Ecuadorean government's audit of the
country's national debt in 2007, preliminary to a rescheduling, or even
a repudiation, of some of its components. If other countries undertook
such an investigation they might well discover undue pressure, the
suborning of public officials and the corruption of legislators. They
might also uncover debts contracted under such onerous terms that even
repaying them several times over did not discharge them.[62] Those who
invested in very high-yielding public bonds were implicitly accepting risk
and should not complain at receiving a 'haircut'. Recognition and default
is the straightforward way to deal with losses. If combined with a vigorous
investment-oriented growth strategy, losses will be replaced by gains. If
such an approach is not adopted then inflation and stagnation are the
likely consequence, with inflation reducing losses but stagnation creating
new deficits.

I have placed the crisis in the context of global imbalances and great inequality. Some commentators believe that there are processes in motion that will lower Western living standards by about a quarter over the next decade or two:

> The imbalances in world trade and growth over the last decade have been hidden from the average voter by the ability of the West to borrow. This has allowed consumers and governments in Europe and America to maintain their living standards and neither recognise or adjust to the fact that the economic tide has turned against us. It's like being unemployed. For a while you can pretend that nothing is happening, while you run up an overdraft or max out on credit cards. But eventually it's payback time. It could hurt a lot. The Centre for Economic and Business Research published a paper today which suggests that our living standards could fall by as much as 25 per cent over the next quarter century as we adjust to the pressure from much cheaper Asian labour, but also to far greater pressure from them for their share of scarce oil and other raw materials.[63]

This line of thought has a certain appeal – and the point about rising raw material costs is a good one – but is as mistaken as faith in the 'law of comparative advantage'. Will Milberg, Anwar Shaikh and Diane Elson and her co-authors have shown that the imbalances that persisted over the recent decades reflect 'absolute' advantage and related technology and skill gaps.[64] Milberg's version of the absolute advantage approach focuses on the deficient aggregate demand, while Skaikh explains how the acquisition of competitive advantage is determinant and not some mythical 'perfect competition'. Feminist authors explain how gender gaps help enterprises in export zones to further their competitive advantage. China's growth was based on low wages for skilled work (the poorly paid young women whose 'nimble fingers' and disciplined conduct generated the wealth of the special export zones constituted an absolute advantage). But the Chinese authorities did not wish to be caught in a low-wage, low-skill trap, so they further boosted the country's development using advanced technology, first imported and then home-grown. China's extraordinary productivity gains – and the awesome trade-surplus mountain achieved in this way – required co-operation between global corporations, international finance, the local state, regional compradors, local producers and the national state. There might seem to be more than enough surplus to go round but capitalist accumulation – with, as Shaikh points out, its inherent struggle for competitive advantage – is likely to produce both conflict between rival alliances of capital and a class struggle between producer networks and gangs of appropriators. The emergence of the previously cited 'Chongqing model' of state capitalism and welfare should perhaps be seen as an expression of the forces at work here. In the age of social media and the internet, debates and struggles address rival development paths, one based on good working conditions, education, decent levels of care, gender equality and high skills, the other based on low wages, long hours and minimal skills. The former has the long-term benefit of creating a wider and more balanced market.

The root of global problems should be sought in the fact that the pools of global demand are shallow and polluted. Milberg's concern for deficient aggregate demand proved prescient. There is too little demand overall because of poverty – that of 'subprime' North American mortgage holders and that of Chinese workers. The demand that does exist is biased – by inequality – towards luxury goods and wasteful modes of consumption. The growth in emergent economies narrows some global inequalities and supplies cheaper industrial goods to the richer nations, acting counter to the tendency to erode Western living standards. But the full Ricardian case for 'comparative advantage' no longer holds because of the often stronger force of absolute advantage: a double-dip recession would hurt emerging economies too. What is needed is the boost to demand that would result from investment in infrastructure and green technologies, on the one hand, and the funding of decent pensions, health care, education and welfare systems on the other. The proposal for new, universal secondary pensions set out in the main body of this book helps to achieve this vision. So far as governments and enterprises are concerned, the objective should be to pursue the 'high road' of competitive advantage, based on improving existing levels of education, skills and care, and shunning the 'low road' which bases competitive advantage on sweated labour, gender gaps and the dumping of social costs.[65]

This approach seeks to humanize the global chain of commodity transactions using international agreements, national legislation, multi-actor codes of conduct, labour rights and collective bargaining, community representation, transparency rules and ethics commitments from corporate and financial agents. The production and sale of commodities presumes the reproduction of the work force, and waged labour is combined with unpaid care work. Support for unpaid care workers dovetails with ensuring decent working conditions. Finally, economic arrangements should be such as to ensure something close to full employment.

Ageing Costs in the Developed World: New Projections

In *Age Shock*, I argue that future ageing costs will be challenging but not overwhelming. I insist that existing provision needs to be supplemented by finding an extra 4 per cent of GDP to cover mid-century ageing costs in most countries. I urge that new resources must be found to meet them. Some countries will find this easier than others because of more advantageous demographics. Immigration can help – but only within limits, as immigrants either return to their native lands or will themselves join the ageing population. Raising the age of retirement can also help – but only if the jobs are there. If we take account of extra time spent in education and training, working lives may not be much extended.

In the US and the EU the number of over-65s is set to double between 2010 and 2050. The US has a higher birth rate and has had more immigration, but such favourable factors will only translate into decent pensions and health care if social provision is defended and extended. I have used estimated proportions of GDP to measure what is needed because this avoids both complacency and alarmism. Projections of expenditure based on existing entitlements for pensions, and for the health and care of the older cohorts of the population, show the impact of the ageing society. Even while per capita expenditure is static – or declines – the proportion of GDP accounted for by ageing costs will rise steeply. If standards of living and of care are not to suffer, tax rates in the US and the UK, particularly the former, will have to rise.

The proposals outlined below, in Chapter 7, are designed to meet these ageing costs and to address the broader issue of ensuring that the living standards of the elderly do not fall far behind the rest of the population. The projections made by the European Commission in 2006 – cited in the first chapter of *Age Shock* – have been further elaborated in the EU's 2009 *Ageing Report* and a 2010 'green paper'. State pensions – comparing 2006 with 2007 – have been further cut in response to the crisis, to 48 per cent of the average wage in France (a cut of 25 points); in Germany, to 42 per cent (a cut of 17 points); and in Italy, to 47 per cent (a cut of 31 points).[66] For Sweden, the same report projects public and private pensions to be equivalent to 46 per cent of average wages in 2060 (a cut of 27 points). But even with these cuts, Europe still needs to find extra funds to plug the gaps in its social care and pension budgets. Looking at the spending envisaged by current legislation, George Magnus estimates that 'in the European Union pensions, health care and long-term care will rise by 4.3 per cent of GDP by 2050'.[67]

In facing up to the costs of an ageing society, it will be helpful if new sources of finance can be found so that existing taxes do not have to carry the whole burden. The alternatives laid out in chapters 6 and 7 of this book retain their validity, as does the need to tax capital rather than labour incomes. But direct contributions from employees also have a role. In an important book, Teresa Ghilarducci urges that in the US the Social Security old-age pension should be supplemented by a universal, mandatory pension for all employees. This would strengthen prospective retirement incomes in a period when so many have found their pension prospects eroded or destroyed. She suggests a solution to the problem of the low paid, who would find it difficult to pay extra from their already straightened budgets: a 'refundable tax credit' worth $600 each year to cushion the blow.[68] Thomas Geoghegan has another way to compensate workers and savers hit by the crisis or by subsequent cuts. He proposes raising US Social Security entitlements and paying for this by raising the income cap above which no further contributions are payable, and perhaps by raising the standard contribution by 1 per cent.[69]

In 2011, US federal taxes account for less than 15 per cent of GDP; Social Security and local taxes take this to around 28 per cent. Britain's tax take is likely to be just below 40 per cent of GDP – still 5 to 10 per cent less than for Germany, France and Sweden. The often-heard argument that high taxes weaken economic performance is contradicted by the fact that these higher-tax countries have stronger economies than the US. Since more needs to be raised from taxes, it should come from tackling the massive tax avoidance by the corporations and the wealthy. Today's tax havens only flourish thanks to the culpable leniency of government in the US, the UK and other OECD countries.[70] One of the great advantages of the Meidner-style share levy is that, as I note in Chapter 7 below, it taxes increases in shareholder value wherever those shares are held. Such a levy would allow national authorities to take measures that undercut 'tax arbitrage' and the use of tax havens. The rate of the levy should be calculated using a number of variables – profits, turnover, valuation – to avoid manipulation of any one number. While states still have real scope for levying taxes on businesses active in their jurisdictions, wider global and regional efforts also need to be made – and as the *Financial Times* columnist John Kay observes, there is much scope for such coordination.[71] In the UK, an extra potential tax on finance could be renegotiation of the €40 billion debt represented by the private finance initiatives of the 1990s and early 2000s. An investigation of PFI charges undertaken by the *Financial Times* identified €20 billion of 'extra costs' of PFIs over the decade 2000–2009 – compared with 'conventional procurement' – to raise just €53 billion. Lawyers and consultants shared €2.8 billion in fees.[72]

The projections I make of ageing costs, and potential revenues to meet them, are couched in terms of future GDP. This is now a standard methodology, though there are some continuing difficulties in projecting income to pension funds. In July 2011 the UK Office of Budget Responsibility offered new estimates of the likely rise in ageing costs and revenues as the over-65s increase from 17 per cent in 2015 to 26 per cent in 2060.

UK Ageing Costs and Revenues as a Per Cent of GDP 2016 and 2050

	2015/16	2060/61
Health	7.4	9.8
State Pension	5.5	7.9
Social Care	1.2	2.0
Public Service Pensions	2.0	1.4

Source: Office of Budget Responsibility, July 2011, pp. 8–9

Made on the basis of existing legislation, these projections only concern the state pensions and public service pensions. They present a serious rather than a crushing challenge. (In view of attacks on public sector pensions, it is interesting to see that the projection for public service pension drops significantly.) The net extra expenditure that is likely to be caused by an ageing population will total 5 per cent of GDP by 2050. To meet these rising costs, the revenue side of the ledger had only a modest countervailing item with projected income from inheritance taxes rising from 1.2 per cent to 1.7 per cent of GDP. The OBR recommended that the best way to meet future ageing costs was to find new taxes or

expenditure cuts of 1.5 per cent of GDP, equivalent to $22 billion in
2015–16. Taking early action would prevent the build-up of deficits and
render public ageing costs easier to meet.

In both the US and the UK, public-sector pension schemes have been
targeted for 'reforms' that will reduce their value. On the whole these are
good schemes and should be vigorously defended. We should respond to
the prospect of an ageing society by expanding pension coverage, not
reducing it. Many public sector schemes are pre-funded; it makes no
sense to convert them to a wholly pay-as-you-go system of finance. In
fact, the pre-funded approach has the merit of reducing the danger that
pension costs and public service budgets will be in competition with one
another. As I have stressed many times, the public sector schemes,
however financed, have good cost ratios and are efficient at turning
contributions into pension incomes. In the British case, official projections of the future cost of public sector employee pensions shows that
they will decline from 2.0 per cent of GDP in 2011 to 1.4 per cent in
2060.

However, it will be easier to retain public support for such schemes if
decent coverage is offered to all employees (and to the unemployed),
with the central or local state making contributions – or offering tax
credits – in order to ensure that all are covered. At the present time it is
the top tenth of earners who benefit most from generous tax relief,
receiving half of it. Government tax relief on private pension contributions has amounted to over $120 billion annually in the US and £18
billion in the UK: here is an overwhelming case for ensuring that the less
well-off are also covered. Abolishing or reducing tax relief at the upper
end of the scale would be one way of doing this – but in Chapter 7,
below, I offer other ideas as well.

The US authorities have still made no assessment of the likely future
share of GDP that will be needed to address ageing costs, or of potential
or actual revenue sources. All too often scary projections are made, using
arbitrary discount rates over long periods, to arrive at a forbidding
mountain of notional debt. A more useful approach is to assess the
proportion of future GDP that will be required by the existence of the
growing proportion of elderly in the population. Magnus cites an exercise
of this sort that projects an increase in Social Security pensions costs
between 2005 and 2050 as 1.9 per cent of GDP, of health care costs as 3.4
per cent of GDP, and of long-term care costs as 2.4 per cent of GDP, a
combined total of 7 per cent.[73] The health care projection is limited to

ageing costs, and the Medicare programme is likely to be somewhat better at controlling costs than other sectors of the health care system, but there is still a problem of paying too much for insurance and pharmaceutical products, something which can only be tackled by further legislation.

In July 2010 the EU Commission produced a green paper, 'Towards Adequate, Sustainable and Safe European Pension Systems', which observed: 'The financial and economic crisis has seriously aggravated the underlying ageing challenge . . . it has acted as a wake up call for all pensions.' The paper estimated that 'the scale of fiscal deterioration during the crisis is equivalent to off-setting 20 years of fiscal consolidation', and also noted that 'increasing reliance on private pensions has fiscal costs' as tax relief reduces public revenues.[74]

This green paper was designed to kick-start a discussion alongside a conference in Brussels in November 2010, at which some participants focused on human need as well as the future fiscal burden. The implicit aim of social policy should be to attend to the needs of the elderly and at least to ensure that the per capita share of GDP received by the elderly does not decline. Such an approach would mean turning the focus away from reducing pension burdens to a minimum, and instead seeking to ensure that pensions are not just adequate but decent, involving no loss of dignity and citizenship.

Global Justice and Ageing

This book focuses mainly on the pension problems of the richer states; it does not address global inequalities. In this new edition of *Age Shock*, I remedy the omission in an afterword which makes the case for a global pension – a modest but real way of redressing the great inequality of life-chances faced by those in the different zones of the world economy. The aim would be to supply an old-age pension of the same amount – $1 a day – to every person over 65 in the advanced countries, or over 60 in the developing world. (I also suggest an educational grant of just $1 a day to every 15- to 18-year-old.) This global pension could be administered by a global network of a thousand funds, covering a population of 6–7 million each and with payment going straight to the beneficiary with the minimum of intermediation. It would be of particular benefit to women as years of unpaid labour leave them poor. The idea of universal, non-contributory pensions is attracting more and more support in the developing countries. One of the most popular proposals of the winning candidate in the 2011 Peruvian presidential elections was for a universal, non-contributory pension starting at age 65. But this proposal is for a new national scheme to be paid from national taxation. The afterword outlines the urgent case for a globally redistributive scheme.[75] In it, I seek to establish the orders of magnitude of such a scheme, and to suggest how it could be implemented. This introduction has made the case for a variety of ways of stimulating demand (minimum wages in emerging economies and debt forgiveness) and the global pension would play its part in promoting this goal.

The various proposals and suggestions I have advanced depend upon an assessment of the seriousness of the crisis and have an undeniably bold and radical character. There are very likely particular claims that will require revision. China and Germany proved themselves stronger in the period 2010 and 2011 but they showed little sign of promoting the long-term measures that will be needed. I am encouraged to believe that the analysis and measures I propose are nevertheless well informed, realistic and right by the publication of *The Way Forward*, authored by Daniel Alpert, Robert Hockett and Nouriel Roubini, and published by the New America Foundation in October 2011. These distinguished authors insist on the gravity of the crisis, estimating that the overhang of household and financial debt will take 5 to 7 years to wind down, during which time great damage will be done. They identify the roots of the asset bubbles as long-term excess global capacity and huge trade imbalances (developments whose ominous character was stressed by Robert Brenner and Andrew Glyn in works referred to above). Like Richard Duncan, they see poverty and inequality (within and between countries) both provoking the crisis and preventing recovery. They propose a three-part plan comprising the following. (1) A $1.2 trillion five-year plan of US infrastructural investment to enable that country to take advantage of a 'historically unique opportunity' to put 'idle capital and labor to work' at an 'extremely low cost'. The size of the effort would be critical since further feeble 'stimulus packages', tax cuts and 'quantitative easing' at a time of excess capacity are 'pushing on a string' while austerity could actually increase overall deficits. (2) Debt overhang reduction, offering relief to debtors and requiring financial institutions to accept write-downs against non-performing assets. (3) 'Global rebalancing' that would see wage increases and welfare improvements in developing states and, most particularly, better social security provision for old age in China to reduce excessive saving and encourage consumption, with the pledging of state assets to such a programme. The 'global rebalancing' rubric also covers a proposal for the setting up of a World Recovery Fund, to be financed by surplus countries but with constitutional changes to give them a position in the World Bank and IMF.

There are aspects of the plan that I would question. For example, I believe that the best way to boost wages in China would be to improve labour rights, not revalue the Chinese currency. Likewise the pamphlet does not address the need for state-sponsored re-capitalization of the large banks. Its approach is avowedly US-centred. But overall the analysis and proposals outlined in *The Way Ahead* are salutary, and tend toward the 'high road' solution. That having been said they are certainly not anti-capitalist. This makes them more realistic, politically, in the short run but perhaps less realistic, economically, in the long run.

August 2011

Notes

1 I have more on this below, but see Richard Duncan, *The Dollar Crisis: Causes, Consequences, Cures,* Singapore 2003.
2 Robert Brenner, 'The Economics of Global Turbulence': A Special Report on the World Economy, 1950–98', *New Left Review,* nos 228–229, May–June 1998, subsequently published in book form with an afterword (London 2006).
3 The case for new trade rules if poverty, joblessness, child labour, discrimination or ecological malpractice are to be avoided has been powerfully made – from contrasting perspectives – by feminist economists and by Jean-Luc Gréau, formerly chief economist of MEDEF, the French employers federation. See Irene van Staveren, Diane Elson, Caren Brown and Nilüfer Çagatay, *The Feminist Economics of Trade,* London 2007; and Jean-Luc Gréau, *Le Capitalisme, malade de sa finance,* Paris 1998. These authors show that 'absolute', rather than 'comparative' advantage and 'technology gaps' and 'skill gaps' rather than 'perfect competition', better explain the persistence of huge trade imbalances. I return to these arguments below.
4 Dan McCrum, 'Studies Question Hedge Fund Returns', *Financial Times,* 31 July 2011.
5 Op. cit.
6 For the extraordinary scope of financial operations in the tax havens, see the very informative study by Nicholas Shaxson, *Treasure Islands: Tax Havens and the Men Who Stole the World,* London 2011.

7   I gave an account of the origins of the crisis in 'The Credit Crunch', *New Left Review*, ser. 2, no. 50, March–April 2008. See also Peter Gowan, 'Crisis in the Heartland', *New Left Review*, ser. 2, no. 55, January–February 2009. What I term 'financialization' is close to Gowan's 'New Wall Street System'; and I have more on financialization in 'Finance and the Fourth Dimension', *New Left Review*, ser. 2, no. 39, May–June 2006.

8   Beat Balzli, 'How Goldman Sachs Helped Greece to Mask its True Debt', *Der Speigel*, 2 August 2010.

9   John Authers, *The Fearful Rise of Markets: Global Bubbles, Synchronized Meltdowns, and How to Prevent Them in the Future*, London 2011.

10 Matt Steinglass, 'Dutch Banks Oppose Plans for €300m Annual Tax', *Financial Times*, 4 July 2011.

11 Ben Protess, 'To Curb Derivatives Risk, Agency Outlines New Capital Rules for Trading', *New York Times*, 28 April 2011.

12 Anthony Hilton, 'Let's Nationalize the Rating Business', *Evening Standard*, 3 June 2010.

13 Jessica Pressler, 'Goldman Settles SEC Fraud Charges for John Paulson's Pocket Change', *New York Magazine*, 15 July 2010.

14 Elisa Martinuzzi and Maria Petrakis, 'EU Seeks Greek Swaps Disclosure After Ministry Probe', *Bloomberg*, 15 February 2010; John Carney, 'Goldman Sachs Shorted Greek Debt After It Arranged Those Shady Swaps', *Business Insider*, 15 February 2010.

15 See, for example, Richard Teitelbaum, 'Secret AIG Document Shows Goldman Sachs Minted Most Toxic CDOs', *Bloomberg*, 23 February 2010.

16 For the dynamic of 'historical cycles' of debt see Elmar Altvater, *The Future of the Market: An Essay on the Regulation of Money and Nature After the Collapse of 'Actually Existing Socialism'*, London 1993, pp. 87–177.

17 Jean-Charles Rochet, *Why Are There So Many Banking Crises? The Politics and Policy of Bank Regulation*, Princeton 2008.

18 Neil M. Barofsky, 'Where the Bank Bailout Went Wrong', *New York Times*, 29 March 2011.

19 'Rising Power, Anxious State: A Special Report on China', *Economist Online* (economist.com), 23 June 2011. See also Philip C. Huang, 'Chonqing: Equitable Development Driven by the "Third Hand"', *Modern China*, forthcoming.

20 Gillian Tett, 'The Lessons in a $3.300 Billion Surprise from the Fed', *Financial Times*, 2 December 2010.

21 Employee Benefit Research Institute, 'The 2011 Retirement Confidence Survey', EBRI Issue Brief No. 355 (ebri.org), March 2011; and for the 2007 figures see George Magnus, *The Age of Aging: How Demographics are Changing the Global Economy and Our World*, London 2008, p. 87.

22 David Oakley, 'Default Tops European Rescue Fund Agenda', *Financial Times*, 22 March 2011; Wolfgang Münchau, 'The Latest Eurozone Fix Is a Con Trick', *Financial Times*, 3 October 2011.

23 Quentin Peel, 'Trichet Calls for a Common EU Finance Ministry', *Financial Times*, 3 June 2011.

24 James Livingston, *Origins of the Federal Reserve System: Money, Class, and Corporate Capitalism, 1890–1913*, Ithaca, NY 1989.

25 Editorial, 'Who Will Rescue Financial Reform?', *New York Times*, 27 March 2011. See here also Tom Braithwaite and Aline van Duyn, 'Regulatory Reform: A Disappearing Act?', *Financial Times*, 20 July 2011.

26 John Kay, 'A Flawed Approach to Better Consumer Protection', *Financial Times*, 29 June 2011.

27 Eliot Spitzer, who – as seen in Chapter 4 – showed the necessary rigour as a regulator of Wall Street, was first triumphantly elected to the governorship of New York state and then, after scarcely a year, felt obliged to resign after it was found that he had used the services of a prostitute.

28 Martin Wolf, 'Ireland Upends the German Perspective on the Eurozone', *Financial Times*, 24 November 2010.

29 Daniel Finn, 'Ireland on the Turn? Political and Economic Consequences of the Crash', *New Left Review*, ser. 2, no. 67, January–February 2011, pp. 5–40, p. 12.

30 Martin Wolf, 'Ireland Upends the German Perspective on the Eurozone'.

31 Isidro Lœpez and Emmanuel Rodríguez, 'The Spanish Meltdown', *New Left Review*, no. 69, May–June 2011, pp. 5–29.

32 Ralph Atkins et al., 'Eurozone Governments Told Not to Rely on Banks Over Greek Bailout', *Financial Times*, 8 July 2011.

33 Peter Spiegel, Quentin Peel and James Wilson, 'Move to Tax Banks Seen as Key in Greece Plan', *Financial Times*, 20 July 2011.

34 See the powerful arguments of François Chesnais, *Les Dettes illégitimes: Quand les banques font main basse sur les politiques publiques*, Paris 2011.

35 Duncan, *The Dollar Crisis*. The minimum wage level in the export sector should be set in country-specific terms, for example as no less than 120 per cent of average per capita income. This would allow poorer countries some edge but target very low wages in what should be a leading sector.

36 Joseph E. Stiglitz, *The Stiglitz Report: Reforming the International Monetary and Financial Systems in the Wake of the Global Crisis*, New York 2010.

37 *The Times*, 21 October 2010.

38 This is the argument of Stiglitz et al. in *The Stiglitz Report*, and of Jean-Luc Gréau in *Le Capitalisme: Malade de sa finance*, Paris 1998.

39 For the concept of the 'public utility finance system' see Gowan, 'Crisis in the Heartland', *New Left Review*, no. 55, January–February 2009, pp. 22–6; and Chenais, *Les Dettes illégitimes*, pp. 17–24, 131–6.

40 John Authers, 'Leadership Needed to Stave Off Fresh Meltdown', *Financial Times*, 5 August 2011.

41 Buttonwood, 'Marx, Mervyn or Mario? What is Behind the Decline in Living Standards?', *Economist*, 24 March 2011.

42 Ibid.

43 Amy Kazmin, 'Cradle of Microfinance Rocked', *Financial Times*, 10 December 2010.

44 'German Business: A Machine Running Smoothly', *Economist*, 3 February 2011.
45 Brooke Unger, 'Europe's Engine', *Economist*, 13 March 2010. The tribute is a little qualified but certainly not withdrawn as the report surveys the impressive strengths – and some weaknesses – of the German model. German unification imposed burdens, but it also weakened the power of organized labour. See Perry Anderson, *The New Old World*, London 2009, pp. 241–77.
46 Stanley Pignall, 'Poor Take-up Reflects the Flaw in Structural Funds', *Financial Times*, 30 December 2010.
47 See 'Brazilian Agriculture: The Miracle of the Cerrado', *Economist*, 26 August 2010. The vicissitudes of public ownership in Latin America are explored by Thomas de Madeiros, 'Asset-Stripping the State', *New Left Review*, ser. 2, no. 55, January–February 2009, pp. 109–32.
48 Richard Wachman, 'Southern Cross's Incurably Flawed Business Model Let Down the Vulnerable', *Observer*, 16 July 2011.
49 Sarah O'Connor, 'Human Cost Forgotten in Race to Invest', *Financial Times*, 30 May 2011; Simon Mundy and Sarah O'Connor, 'Southern Cross Chiefs Netted €35m', *Financial Times*, 3 June 2011.
50 James Stuart Olson, *Saving Capitalism: The Reconstruction Finance Corporation and the New Deal, 1933–1946*, Princeton 1988.
51 Gerald Holtham, 'A National Investment Bank Can Raise Our Growth', *Financial Times*, 21 October 2010. Robert Skidelsky and Felix Martin urge that the British government should sell off its stakes in the banks it has bailed out and use the proceeds to establish a national investment bank. See Skidelsky and Martin, 'Osborne's Austerity Gamble is Fast Being Found Out', *Financial Times*, 1 August 2011.
52 I have more on this in Robin Blackburn, 'Economic Democracy: Meaningful, Desirable, Feasible?', *Daedalus*, vol. 136, no. 2, Summer 2007, pp. 36–45.
53 Mitchell A. Orenstein, *Privatizing Pensions: The Transnational Campaign for Social Security Reform*, Princeton 2008. See also Camila Arza, 'The Limits of Pension Privatization: Lessons from the Argentine Experience', *World Development*, vol. 36, no. 12, 2008.
54 I have more on this in Robin Blackburn, 'The Global Drive to Commodify Pensions', in Bryan S. Turner, ed., *The Routledge International Handbook of Globalization Studies*, New York 2010, pp. 367–92.
55 Mitchell Orenstein, 'Pension Privatization in Crisis: Death or Rebirth of a Global Policy Trend?', *International Social Security Review*, vol. 64, no. 3, 2011, pp. 65-80. See also Nicholas Barr and Peter Diamond, *Reforming Pensions: Principles and Policy Changes* 2008, pp. 207–11.
56 Dariusz Stanko, 'Pension Fund Returns: The Case of Central and Eastern Europe', *Investments and Payouts in Funded Pension Systems*, Santiago de Chile 2009, pp. 26–45.
57 Quoted in Orenstein, 'Pension Privatization in Crisis'.
58 Jackie Calmes, 'Obama Grasping Centrist Banner in Debt Impasse', *New*

York Times, 11 July 2011; Clive Cook, 'Obama's Failed Debt Ceiling Gamble', *Financial Times*, 10 July 2011.

59 Nicholas Timmins, 'Ministers Urged to Cap Pension Charges', *Financial Times*, 1 August 2011. The full report is available on the website of the National Association of Pension Funds which commissioned the report.

60 Prabhat Patnaik, *Re-envisioning Socialism*, New Delhi 2011.

61 As classically argued by Karl Polanyi, *The Great Transformation*, London 1944.

62 Some initial proposals are explored by Chesnais, *Les Dettes illégitimes*, pp. 95–141. Such a scenario might become feasible in a crisis situation, but care would need to be taken in the sequencing of debt rescheduling and nationalization of financial enterprises.

63 Anthony Hilton, 'Markets Have Lost Faith in the Politicians', *Evening Standard*, 5 August 2011.

64 Will Milberg, 'Is Absolute Advantage Passé? Towards a Post-Keynesian/Marxian Theory of International Trade', in Michael Glick, ed., *Competition, Technology and Money: Classical and Post-Keynesian Perspectives*, Cheltenham 1994; Anwar Sheikh, 'Globalization and the Myth of Free Trade', in Anwar Sheikh, ed., *Globalization and the Myths of Free Trade: History, Theory and Empirical Evidence*, London 2007; Diane Elson, Caren Grown and Nilüfer Çagatay, 'Mainstream, Heterodox and Feminist Trade Theory', in Irene van Staveren et al., eds, *The Feminist Economics of Trade*, London 2007, pp. 33–52.

65 See Diane Elson et al., 'Mainstream, Heterodox and Feminist Trade Theory'.

66 European Commission, *Green Paper on Adequate, Sustainable and Safe Pension Systems*, Brussels, July 2010, p. 27.

67 Magnus, *The Age of Aging*, p. 129.

68 Teresa Ghilarducci, *When I'm Sixty-Four: The Plot Against Pensions and the Plan to Save Them*, Princeton 2008, pp. 26–98.

69 Thomas Geoghegan, 'Get Radical: Raise Social Security', *New York Times*, 19 June 2011.

70 See Shaxson, *Treasure Islands*.

71 John Kay, 'There Is No Alternative to Agreeing How We Tax Companies', *Financial Times*, 31 May 2011.

72 Nicholas Timmins and Chris Giles, 'Private Finance Costs Taxpayer £20bn', *Financial Times*, 7 August 2011.

73 Magnus, *The Age of Aging*, p. 129; calculations based on Boris Cornède, 'The Political Economy of Delaying Fiscal Consolidation', *OECD Economics Department Working Paper*, no. 548, 2007.

74 European Commission, 'Green Paper: Towards Adequate, Sustainable and Safe European Pension Systems', Brussels, 7 July 2010, pp. 6–7.

75 First published as Robin Blackburn, 'A Global Pension Plan', *New Left Review*, ser. 2, no. 47, September–October 2007, pp. 71–92.

Introduction: The Need for a New Collectivism

The Woody Allen character sums it up well: 'Why should I worry about posterity? What has posterity ever done for me?' Of course no one puts it this baldly, but a consumer-oriented, commercial civilization lives for the moment and hopes for the best. Climate change? Dead oceans? Toxic waste? The arms trade? Nuclear arsenals? A world of slums? Epidemics? It's really bad but what can we do? *Après nous le déluge.*

The prospect of growing old-age poverty or even of a 'war of the generations' is not as apocalyptic as some of the foregoing. There is nothing intrinsically disastrous in rising longevity and falling birth rates, the forces making for an ageing society. Yet these developments, and the specific costs and strains associated with them, certainly raise the issue of what we owe posterity – and what we owe our forebears. They pose a global challenge and one which is most intense in the already developed world, and in the fast-growing developing countries, since they exhibit the ageing effect in its most marked form. Moreover the shape of the future 'risk' is already clear, in broad outline almost a certainty. This should make meeting it, and turning it into a positive, all the easier. All the advanced countries have discovered through trial and error that collective provision is needed to maintain health and income in retirement. On the other hand, the inherited systems of pension provision are already feeling the strain and need to be better resourced. If the economically more fortunate parts of the world prove incapable of surmounting this quite intimate challenge in an equitable and responsible way it is difficult to imagine them contending successfully with dangers that are greater but, for the moment, more remote and less predictable. The strengthening of collective insurance and social provision, which should be part of the response to the ageing society, is likely to improve our capacity to meet other dangers. This is a book about how best to meet the 'ageing' challenge, but I see this as part of an attempt to address wider, and in many ways more ominous, problems.

Today's 'world without a tomorrow' has taut chains of supply and 'just in time' production with stocks held to a minimum, and little or no surplus capacity. Elemental forces of nature are still a great danger but their impact is multiplied by the cumulative, unintended results of human action. Welcome to the 'risk society', as some of the theorists of globalization would have it.[1] In the early modern period risk stemmed principally from nature and the elements, or from human waywardness and wickedness. It could be managed by using collective risk-pooling and instilling the fear of God into malefactors. But in high modernity and post-modernity, large-scale disasters often stem from seemingly innocent mundane human arrangements, as the decisions of billions of consumers, tens of thousands of corporations and more than a hundred rivalrous states have enormous unintended consequences. This is a world of fortified enclosures and vulnerable marginal communities, of market failure and government failure, of 'financial engineering' and new dimensions of commodification.[2] Fresh air, clean water and personal security are less and less available as public goods, but must instead be individually purchased. It is a world of private prisons as well as private schools and a world where, as we will see in the first chapter, even the different stages of the life course require the purchase of an appropriate financial product. As socio-economic processes become more interdependent, so risk is compounded, with the electric power outage aggravating the effects of the freak weather event, or the danger of a new virus failing to register with pharmaceutical companies because they focus on the existing complaints of the well-off, not the ailments of the poor. The rich and the comfortable middle class will have a better chance of surviving the earthquake or heatwave, but they should be aware their world is also very insecure and dangerous.

The new complex pattern of risk requires a new way of connecting the individual to the collective, new criteria of social responsibility and new norms of regulation and ownership. The misguided prophets of the 'market state' and the 'third way', turning critique into endorsement, instead contend that risk is good and that individuals should learn to confront it on their own. It must be accepted or even welcomed. There is an alternative to the hubris of battling against the current – that of going with the flow 'reflexively' and learning to love boundless commodification and financialization. In *The Third Way* Anthony Giddens argued that individuals and institutions must be weaned from the teat of public finance and learn how to be 'responsible risk-takers', who rise to the challenge, develop entrepreneurial skills, raise needed resources and reject the old forms of dependence, of which the old-age pension was a prime example.[3] While Ulrick Beck pointed to the dangers of the 'risk society', Giddens seemed to find them exhilarating. But if we switch from the language of sociology to that of economics there is good reason to argue that the problem of the ageing society is more akin to that of a 'common shock' than to that of an individually insurable 'risk'.

Nicholas Barr points out that the welfare state arose in the first place to cope with occurrences that had defeated market solutions and commercial insurance methods. As we will see in the second chapter, the first systems of social insurance adapted insurance principles that had been pioneered by finance houses. But it soon became clear that national insurance was able not only to extend coverage to those who had not been able to afford it but also to insure types of risk – or shock – that were beyond the scope of private insurance. For example, commercial insurers have not offered insurance against the risk of losing one's job, partly because joblessness is not random but rather, during downturns, will afflict many at the same time and will be sectorally concentrated. House insurance will cover accidental fire or subsidence but not a wartime bombing raid. While it is possible to buy health insurance for the working adult it is much more difficult for the retired to get health coverage because so many of the elderly will get sick. Some insurers offer limited indexation, but rampant inflation is a common shock and is difficult to insure against. Barr writes: 'Insurance requires a predictable number of winners and losers . . . This condition holds for individual risk such as age at death or the likelihood that one's car will be stolen. With a common shock in contrast, if one person suffers a loss so does everyone else.'[4] Taken as a whole the phenomenon of the ageing society, with its defining demographic constraints and escalating costs, is better seen as a common shock, not a risk. It requires a new development of welfare principles, not their repudiation. In a situation where there may well be many in need and few without a problem we require more collective insurance and larger collective reserves.

Phillip Bobbit, author of the *Shield of Achilles*, also celebrates the new order of things. He is happy that the new market state – a sort of butterfly which is emerging from the chrysalis of market-friendly 'Anglo-Saxon' economics – is defined by the fact that it no longer guarantees the welfare of its citizens. This marks it off, he explains, from the old nation state: 'The nation state undertook to be responsible for economic planning for the society, income distribution, and democratic accountability, and it promised to underwrite (in varying degrees) employment, health care, education and old-age security.'[5] But in contemporary conditions this turns out to be increasingly expensive and generates deficits: 'There is no reason why a state cannot grow out of its deficit, but to do so, however, it will have to increasingly abandon the objective of the government's maintaining the ever-improving welfare of its citizens . . . this is precisely what the Bush administration in the United States and the Blair government in Great Britain were in the midst of doing at the beginning of the twenty-first century.'[6]

In the future the market state will, it is claimed, confine itself to spreading opportunities. Bobbitt's perception that Britain's Labour prime minister had evacuated the terrain of social democracy has also been noted by many others. Brian Barry points out that this apposition between welfare and opportunity was already to be found in the report of the British Labour Party's Commission on Social Justice of 1994, a document that anticipated many key themes of Tony Blair's 'New Labour' philosophy. The report endorsed a notion of social justice that promised to improve 'opportunities and life chances'. Barry comments: 'But social justice is normally understood to be a question of *equal* opportunities. Significantly, however the word does not appear . . . [T]he omission is important because . . . if the notion of equality of opportunity is taken seriously it generates implications . . . To say that you are in favour of *some* opportunities is not to say much . . .'.[7]

And one might add that discrimination is needed because some opportunities are unwelcome. Take, for example, the celebration of 'choice' in contemporary neo-liberal jargon. The privatization of public services has led to a proliferation of choices, or opportunities to exit one arrangement and enter another. The consumer will typically lack the information needed to choose the best supplier and may find acquiring that knowledge difficult and burdensome. The parents of a school-age child might well find that 'voice' – their ability to influence a board of governors or local education authority – is preferable to 'choice' and 'exit', because this requires the wrench of a change of schools and because it might segregate children in undesirable ways. The proliferation of choice can also mean a superstore crammed with product but the closing of speciality shops in a wide area. Telephone subscribers in Britain used to be able to dial a well-known directory number; their lives have scarcely been enriched now that they have a hundred numbers to choose from.

Choice is most likely to be empty or vexatious in the field of financial products. The purchaser usually lacks the information needed to make a good choice, and is required to commit to payments over lengthy periods, when their circumstances and the world could greatly change. Opportunities and choice should be grounded in a social existence that has basic security, well thought-out default options, intelligibility and scope for modifying the overall design.

Public programmes can often be improved but instead the market state replaces them with a confused and costly tangle of commercial facilities, credit networks and financial products. Nowhere is this clearer than in the field of pension provision. As I will show in chapters 3 to 5, private pension provision is both expensive and unreliable. Public provision, discussed in chapters 2 and 6, has proved far more efficient. But the promises of the traditional welfare state, while alleviating many of the worst market failures, were sometimes limited or distorted by patriarchal and ethno-racial assumptions, or corrupted by clientelism. The welfare state might represent lofty ideals but was administered by a mundane and sometimes self-serving bureaucracy. These problems sometimes weaken pension provision and elder care but, as fairer principles have commanded public support, have proved to be far from insuperable. While remaining aware of the potential pitfalls we should realize that the regression promised by the 'market state' would itself discriminate against the weak while still leaving many of the strong vulnerable – a 'common shock' does not only afflict the worst off. The problem with today's public pension arrangements is not so much a paternalist mode of delivery but inadequate resources and the threat of privatization.

Historically the strength of public credit – the national debt – was a vital part of the secret of 'Anglo-Saxon' (in this context, Anglo-Dutch and Anglo-American) capitalism. The size of the national debt was a sign of the confidence of investors. It reflected their estimate of the strength of future state revenues and of the attentiveness of the state and central bank to the interests of investors. While individuals sought to avoid being net debtors, the idea of paying off the national debt had little urgency. A strong national debt was almost as much a hallmark of Anglo-Saxon economics as a strong stock market.

But over recent decades, in an increasingly globalized world, states which hoped to retain some freedom of manoeuvre, and the ability to integrate into the world economy on advantageous terms, came up with new variants of public finance based on earning large trade surpluses and avoiding indebtedness to foreign lenders. They also believed that popular savings should be accumulated under the guidance of strategic public agencies. The latter should engage in large-scale investments and command substantial assets rather than paper balances. Part of the secret of Japan's postwar economic miracle was the use of the huge sums regularly deposited by savers with the public post office and other parts of the state retirement system to finance vital infrastructure investment.[8] The Singapore Provident Fund played a similar role, using social security contributions to construct popular housing, to build roads and harbours, and to finance research and development.[9]

The 'Anglo-Saxon' economies paid down national debt in the late 1990s but since 2002 both the United States and the United Kingdom have reverted to deficit financing, in the US case on a vast scale. The citizens of these countries have also lost their aversion to personal indebtedness. Indeed the buoyancy of modern consumer capitalism rests on ever-growing mountains of private debt. In both the US and the UK, consumer debt runs at around 120–130 per cent of annual disposable income.

So long as credit allows for investments that boost future output or capacity it can be justified, but once it overshoots that mark it reduces future possibilities. Large public and private debts set up a claim on future output. If the enlargement of credit does not enlarge productive capacity, or does so in illusory and destructive ways, then future generations are left poorer and more burdened. Unfortunately current ways of measuring gross national product do not properly reveal the true cost of what simply registers as economic 'growth'.[10]

There is another way and that is to rein in the horsemen, instal a sense of moderation at the heart of the financial system, and build up a cushion of reserves, to be drawn upon when needed. The generals in old-fashioned wars knew that no military plan survives the first encounter with the enemy. They therefore husbanded a strategic reserve with which to parry an unexpected offensive or to exploit an opening. The notion of the reserve is as ancient as the state itself. The priests or the kings had authority to put aside grain during the fat years so that the people would not starve in the lean years. Capitalism and bourgeois revolution introduced a new and different calculus. A non-state elite arose which did not hand over its surplus to wasteful and extravagant public authorities but rather was able to invest it as it thought best, taking a bet on new methods, new products and new tastes. Competition weeded out the unsuccessful and rewarded those who had made shrewd or lucky bets. Capitalists paid wages to workers who needed employment if they were to feed and clothe their families. The visibility of labour costs encouraged a systematic search for labour-saving methods and machinery. Capitalism appeared, at this stage, to have an almost unlimited ability to boost labour productivity and to raise the overall social surplus. Those earning fees, salaries, dividends, rents and wages created a large market. The capitalist might appear the master but needed to serve market demand, and hence cater to consumers' limitless wants, wants which were progressively refined and expanded by the entrepreneur.[11]

The capitalist system is, in its own narrow way, very future-oriented. The capital value set on an enterprise is nothing other than its anticipated future profits – the discounted present value of the return it is thought it will yield. Yet the representation of that potential return as a single, numeric entity flattens and simplifies that future. Capitalist ownership has always earmarked a future stream of revenue to the capitalist. In doing so it allowed the future to be colonized by, and mortgaged to, wealthy individuals and corporations. At various times industrial and national monopoly or regulation sought to render the process more predictable, and better at capturing the anticipated surplus. Today the world's leading financial institutions combine privileged information with computing power, derivatives and mathematical formulae – 'quantitative finance' – to achieve the same end. Of course these institutions, taken individually, are far from being infallible seers. The future always retains an irreducible element of uncertainty. But one or another financial cluster will gain the prize by getting the outcome more right than anyone else. This is today's 'great game'.

Eventually capital can only deliver on expectations by crowding out the expenditures – and absorbing the reserves – which society needs to reproduce and protect itself. In the last couple of decades financialization has greatly boosted the ability of a few wealthy individuals, finance houses and corporations to make these claims on the future. The fiscal system used to allow for a countervailing public claim on future revenue but taxation has steadily lost ground to financialization, and public interests have lost ground to private ones.

Notwithstanding widespread obeisance to the 'free market', modern states have not yet lost contact with the historic function of the public power. They make large-scale provision for physical infrastructure, for education, health, unemployment and, last but not least, pensions. The problem is not that such needs are entirely neglected, but rather that there is a systematic bias to leave too much of the surplus in private hands and to underestimate a rising need for public investments and for safety reserves. Public expenditures require tax revenues or publicly organized contributory systems. There are good reasons for believing that in future increased outlays will be needed for these public purposes, and that existing fiscal arrangements are simply not adequate to the manifold tasks that face them. Private insurers struggle with the consequences of extreme weather, increased longevity and rising medical costs while their customers struggle even more with escalating prices.

The new horizon of public provision has to take the measure of a series of looming demands on the public purse. These include both awesome global challenges – the huge outlays required to achieve an ecological balance favourable to humanity, and the transformations required to overcome global poverty – and apparently more limited and local issues, such as the pension and medical costs of the ageing society, and the educational costs of the knowledge-based economy. These apparently separate challenges will require both resources and social innovation, which is why they may not be as separate as they seem. They will require a new sense of the collective and of the relationship between present and future. The need for more resources for research, for prevention, for restoration, for education, for health, for social infrastructure, for clean technology, for insuring that the global trading of goods does not multiply the exchange of bads, and, last but not least, for social justice. I have already suggested that a society that tolerates the growth of poverty of the old at home will prove mean-spirited and short-sighted in its response to global needs. Likewise financial institutions which indulge greedy CEOs, and cheat employees of their pensions, are not likely to be engines of philanthropy overseas.

Because many social services – especially education and medicine – are people-intensive they find it difficult to match the labour-productivity gains of the manufacturing industry. If wages and salaries in these sectors are not to fall behind they will need rising budgets. The introduction of new technologies makes medical provision more effective, but it means rising costs. The gain represented by a healthier population will not show up in the account books of hospitals or clinics but will rather accrue to all those sectors of the economy which can now count on the input of a person whose healthy working life has been extended. At the level of society as a whole it is not difficult to see the gain of a more healthy population, or of disease prevention. But that gain will not be registered by a given medical practice, or even by the government's health care budget.

I have mentioned some of the public dangers which will require greater collectivism, but there are positive as well as prudential reasons for boosting public provision. It is not just ageing that means that a larger section of the population will be outside formal waged employment. As societies become richer, some will prefer to take more free time, with the latter taking various forms – longer retirement, more study, gap years, career breaks, maternity or paternity leave, part-time employment, a longer holiday, a shorter working week and, an important category, work freely undertaken. The capitalist imperative driving people into paid work to meet obligatory outgoings, or enticing them to work harder and longer as the route to higher consumption, is partially counteracted by the desire for more education, more flexibility and creativeness in work itself, and more free time, or, as the slightly queasy phrase has it, 'quality time'.

Extra free time, or time out of the paid labour force, will have to be subsidized if it is not to lead to penury and starvation. This is true even if it can be shown that the research student or the retired voluntary community care-worker is contributing to the well-being of others as well as themselves. Both the student and the retiree need income entitlements and historically they have often received them in the world's most dynamic societies. One way of pursuing this argument would be to look at the aggregate of all social expenditures and entitlements and explore whether there is pressure for them to rise and, if so, how they might be met in future. I have already cited the frequently labour-intensive character of education and health, urging that this will generate a tendency for costs to rise. Alternatively one might analyze the continuing impetus towards private affluence and public squalor, and how it might be redressed. However, I prefer here to concentrate on just one area, since this is more manageable and since the area in question – that of delivering decent pensions – is a non-optional, big-ticket item. We may or may not see the need for a step change in R&D, or an extra week's holiday for all who want it. Some say they are not convinced by the case for global warming, and many more are puzzled by what can be done about it. But the swelling ranks of seniors, and their sons, daughters and grandchildren, will make sure we don't forget them. So there will be pressure in every part of the world to ensure a minimum flow of resources to the elderly.

The Grey Wave

This book will mainly focus on just one set of challenges – the ageing society – and try to show the far-reaching changes that would be the best way to address these challenges. The raw data of demography do not dictate any particular social outcome as some suppose. A society with a strong and buoyant economy, with some reserves and with efficient pension and medical provision for all, will not be daunted by the costs of an ageing society. But the costs must be met and they will not be modest.

A combination of increased longevity, the postwar baby boom and the subsequent heavy drop in fertility rates means that the proportion of the population over sixty-five will rise to 20 per cent or more in all advanced countries over the next thirty years. The US has a younger population than most other advanced countries, but it will not escape the ageing phenomenon. The onset of ageing in the United States will be slower than in Europe because of a somewhat higher birth-rate, a somewhat higher immigration rate, and the failure of its costly medical system to deliver for many sections of the population – lower life expectancy among the Black, Hispanic and poor reduces the ageing effect. Yet, according to Census Bureau projections, between 2004 and 2034 the number of US citizens who are aged sixty-five and over is expected to double from 35 million to 71 million, and to reach 87 million by 2050 – their proportion of the total population is projected to rise from 12.4 per cent in 2000 to 19.6 per cent in 2030, and to reach 20.7 per cent in 2050. Looking at those who are over sixty-five as a percentage of all those who are over 20, the percentage rises from 17.3 per cent in 2000, to 26.5 per cent in 2030 and is forecast to reach 28 per cent in 2050. This ratio – seeing those of 65 and over as part of the adult population, rather than computing a ratio of 'working age' to 'pensioners' or 'seniors' – has the advantage that it broadly corresponds to households as economic units.

Many of the 'young old' will still hope to be economically active but we should also register that the number of the less strenuous 'old old' – those who are 85 and over – is set to increase sharply, from 4.3 million in the United States in 2000 to 9.6 million in 2030, reaching 20.9 million in 2050. Women are expected to remain more long-lived than men but their proportion of the 'old old' is expected to decline from 70 per cent in 2000 to 63 per cent by 2050.[12]

Peter Peterson points out that in 1940 college-age youths (those aged between 18 and 21 years old) outnumbered 'the elderly' (those sixty-five and over) by 9.6 to 9 million; by 2040 the US Census Bureau has forecast that there will be 20.3 million college-age youths but 77 million 'elderly'.[13] Peterson is surely right to insist that such large-scale demographic shifts will have major consequences and should be anticipated. But we should not make the assumption that terms like 'elderly' and 'college age' will have the same meaning in 2040 as they had in 1940. In 1940 the over-60s were indeed elderly, and nearly all of the small number who actually went to college were between the ages of 18 and 21. But already today there are many very active sixty-year-olds who don't quite qualify as elderly and who may, indeed, be attending college.

The course of life is undergoing far-reaching changes and this should be taken fully into account in reckoning the likely cost of what is not only an undeniably ageing society but also one where people need continuing learning, and remain fit at older ages. In the first chapter I will be assessing the likely costs of ageing, under the assumption that we should be happy to bear them rather than perpetuate the segregation of the generations, and the warehousing of the aged that was characteristic of too much elder care in the richer countries in the twentieth century. If an active ageing policy is pursued then many may return to college in their fifties or sixties, prior to taking up some new role. But their earnings may dip or they may be engaged in voluntary or civic employment performed for little or no remuneration. However, I will continue to use the demographic of those who are sixty-five or over as a convenient proxy for those who will no longer be in regular, full-time salaried or waged employment. While early retirement no longer looks so attractive, employment is insecure and finding new work if you are over fifty-five, let alone over sixty or sixty-five, is difficult. To assume that the average retiring age might rise to sixty-five is optimistic, since currently it is about three years lower.

The ageing of the population is more advanced in Britain where those aged sixty-five and over were already 15 per cent of the total in 2003 and are expected to rise to 24 per cent by 2032.[14] They comprised 28 per cent of all those of 20 and over in 2003 and are expected to reach 40 per cent by 2033 and as much as 47 per cent by 2050. Europe is very much a greying continent. The over-65s are expected to be well over a quarter of the total population and 40 per cent of the adult population by 2030 in the other major Western European states. If those who are sixty-five and over comprise between 28 and 47 per cent of the adult population then they will require a significant slice of national income – less than households with children, to be sure, but still something in the range

15 to 23 per cent of GDP, if those who are sixty-five and over are not to fall way behind the rest of the population. Those who are currently over sixty-five have an income which is between 70 or 75 per cent of average income in most advanced countries, including the United States and Britain, while overall consumption comprises about 70 per cent of US GDP.

The ageing of the population is a feature of developing as well as developed countries. The UN Population Division – whose mid-range 1998 projection used somewhat different categories and ratios to those cited above – told us that the over-60s, who comprised 30.7 persons per 100 adults of working age (15–59) in 1998 in the developed countries, will comprise 62.3 persons per 100 adults of working age in those countries in 2050. In Latin America the proportion rises from thirteen over-60s per 100 working age adults in 1998 to 39 over-60s per 100 working age adults in 2050. The great success story of the last quarter century has been the dynamic growth of the Chinese economy, but this was accompanied by a reduction in the birth rate which will lead to a rapid ageing of the population in coming decades. In Asia, including China and India, the anticipated proportion of those over 60 rises from 14.1 per 100 adults of working age in 1998 to 40.8 by 2050.[15]

The term ageing society should be taken literally. The median age of the world's population – the half-way point in the distribution, with equal numbers above and below this age – was 23.6 years in 1950; it rose to 26.4 in 2000 and is expected to reach 36.8 by 2050 in the UN's 2002 medium projection. The ageing effect is proceeding most rapidly in Europe where 29.2 was the median age in 1950, rising to 35.4 in 2000 and where it is expected to reach 47.7 by 2050. In North America the median age was 28.8 in 1950, reached 35.4 in 2000 and is expected to be 40.2 by 2050. In what the UN calls the 'less developed regions', the median age was 21.3 in 1950, rose to 24.1 in 2000 and is expected to reach 35.7 by 2050.[16]

The over-80s are the most rapidly expanding age cohort globally – they numbered 69 million worldwide in 2000 and are expected to rise to 377 million by 2050. The projections forecast that there will be 29 million Americans over 80 years old by 2050, with 98 million in China, 47 million in India and 13 million in Brazil.[17] In the most advanced countries the proportion of those in their eighties who are reasonably fit is rising – about 80 per cent are now in this category in the United States. On the other hand – and notwithstanding an extensive feel-good literature – being fit at eighty is not the same as being fit at forty. Those over eighty may have wide experience, and good judgment, but their reaction times and energy levels will be less than they were when they were forty or fifty or sixty – the turning point, and rate of change, differing from individual to individual. They will also, a development considered in the first chapter, place greater demands on the health services.

The 'medium range' population estimates I have cited have greater precision than many socio-economic forecasts because they extrapolate the consequences of well-entrenched demographic changes, notably the steady increase in life expectancy and the almost equally steady decrease in birth-rates. Better sanitation and modern medicine has been raising expectation of life for more than two centuries, and the rate of increase has itself risen gently for half a century. Since 1950 life expectancy has increased by ten years, and it continues to increase by two years every decade. In the 1970s and 1980s many actuaries assumed that life expectancy would continue to rise but that there would be a declining rate of growth. But so far no such decline has showed up, leading to renewed debate on whether or not there is a 'natural' human life span.

In most advanced countries the birth-rate has dropped well below the replacement rate, which is an average of roughly 2.1 children per woman. In Europe the birth-rate has dropped to between 1.2 and 1.8 children per woman, with 30 per cent of women having no children and many limiting themselves to one. The next chapter will look at what explains this pattern, and whether it might change. But the overall trend is well-established throughout the developed and developing world. Because the decline became steep three or four decades ago, its consequences will be with us for a long time. While both increased longevity and a lowered birth-rate contribute to the ageing of populations, if the latter drops more heavily than the former rises, the population shrinks.

The Japanese birth-rate has dropped to an average of only 1.3 children for each woman in her child-bearing years. For the first time Japan's population actually dropped in 2005, by a few thousand, and between 2005 and 2030 it is set to fall from 127 million to 100 million.[18] By mid-century fifty states will have populations lower than they were in 2000, and the total world population could well be declining by the last decades of the century. In so far as this development eases the pressure of population on resources, and reduces the emission of greenhouse gases and other pollutants, it could well be very positive. Nevertheless the likely costs of an ageing society will still have to be met and these will be high.

Overall Pension Needs

In this book I attempt what I see as an integrated or 'holistic' approach to pension costs and, though to a lesser extent, ageing costs more generally. I examine whether increasingly fractured public and private systems are capable of supplying the proportion of GDP needed to ensure that pensioner incomes do not lag increasingly far behind the growth of average incomes. This requires us to estimate the likely contribution of private schemes, and not to concentrate exclusively on public schemes and plans, important as they are.

If the over-65s are to comprise between a fifth and a quarter of the population, then they are going to need a big chunk of GDP. While some of their outgoings may be comparatively low, others may be high. Overall those over pension age currently receive an income that is 70 to 75 per cent of average income. This is income from all sources – the state pension, private pensions, earnings and other savings. To maintain the relative income of those past retirement age it is generally necessary for these sources to supply between 15 and 22 per cent of GDP, depending on the dimensions of ageing in that society. In nearly all advanced countries today there is a likelihood, with current programmes, of an income shortfall amounting to between 3 and 6 per cent of GDP showing up between 2030 and 2050. Of course the size of the pension funding gap differs from country to country, varying according to the size of its over-65 population, the effectiveness of existing plans and programmes, and the strength of its economy. While the eventual pension may be paid in a single stream, most pension regimes have a dualistic structure, comprising a basic, subsistence pension and a variable, secondary element which captures both the individual's effort and the overall advance of national and global prosperity.

There was a time when official reports and public discussion in Britain and the United States focused mainly on the publicly provided old-age pension, seeking to establish what would be needed to avoid old-age penury, and how that could be afforded. Separately, and less prominently, some attention was paid to private schemes and private savings. For a little while now this fragmented approach has been seen to be inadequate. It was a merit of the first report of the UK's Pensions Commission, published in 2004, that it sought to establish a target level for overall retirement income by 2050, specified in terms of the share of GDP that it would require. The Trustees of Social Security in the United States consider a great mass of evidence and regularly forecast the programme's incomes and outgoings over a seventy-five-year horizon. But they do not attempt any target figure for retirement incomes in terms of GDP. In order to reach a target figure, the UK Pensions Commission had to work out the implications of rising numbers of those in retirement for the public schemes. It also sought to forecast future pension provision from all other sources, including occupational schemes and individual savings. Since private pension provision enjoys a huge public subsidy in the UK, and since a responsible government should anyway seek to anticipate very significant future needs, the attempt to address both public and private resources was very welcome. The same considerations would apply in the United States.

In the United States it is conservatives and neo-liberals who most loudly proclaim their alarm at the looming costs of the ageing society. Peter Peterson was Reagan's Commerce Secretary though he is now one of those conservatives who is disappointed by George W. Bush's failure to rein in public spending. He has documented the scale of the ageing problem in two informative books: *Gray Dawn* (1997) and *Running on Empty* (2004). Similar alarm, but from a more neo-liberal standpoint, is expressed by Laurence Kotlikoff and John Burns in their study, *The Coming Generational Storm* (2004). While such analysts recognize – and even exaggerate – the pensions and ageing crisis, straight liberals are inclined to downplay it. Thus Paul Krugman criticizes those who 'perceive the issue of an ageing society not as it is – a medium-sized issue that can be dealt with through ordinary changes in taxing and spending – but as an immense problem that requires changing everything.'[19]

The US Social Security problem, by itself, is indeed only medium-sized and may even turn out to be manageable with small adjustments.[20] But if the need for secondary pensions and medical care is taken into account then 'the issue of an ageing society' is certainly large, if not 'immense' – how else to describe 15 to 20 per cent of GDP? – and may well require changing a great deal. Specifically it requires more than 'ordinary changes in taxes and spending'. And it could also be that this intimate problem of coping with the ageing problem will be the spur for changing many things, and Krugman himself often accepts that there is much that needs changing – from galloping inequality to a failing health care system.

The United States could, of course, fail to address the ageing problem, and try to muddle through, but only at the cost of great poverty and distress. The US debate on the prospects for Social Security and Medicare is conducted very publicly, and at a high level, but it is a serious defect that these programmes are usually taken in isolation, with little or no scrutiny of private sector pension prospects.[21] Until very recently British pensions suffered from the enactment of major changes with no real public debate – for example, when Margaret Thatcher decisively weakened the indexation of the basic state pension in 1980 – but at least the failings of the private sector have been so spectacular – from Maxwell's looting spree and the gigantic 'mis-selling' scandal in the early 1990s, to the subsequent ruin of Equitable Life and the fiasco of Tony Blair's attempt to revive British pension prospects by means of a 'partnership' with the financial services industry[22] – that the government's own Pensions Commission has baldly described them as 'not fit for purpose'.[23]

Debate about, and research into, public and private pension provision has often been pursued by different writers, in bodies of work with little overlap or contact. The public and private approach to pension provision usually involves divergent financing methods with pay-as-you-go dominating public provision and pre-funding dominating the private sector. Such contrasts make it difficult to bring both within a common reckoning. Even though I try to do so in this book, most chapters still have a focus either on the public or on the private sector. Yet the important question remains as to whether they add up to a satisfactory solution, or undermine one another.

The modesty or meanness of public provision in so many fields is accompanied by a fantasy of universal salvation through general private provision. The details are rather complicated, and beyond most people's comprehension (they are scrutinized in Chapter 3 so far as pensions are concerned), but the utopian promise is there for all to see. The finance houses offer their expensive services as custodians of people's savings with the promise that a prosperous future awaits the aged – they will be able to maintain if not enhance their standard of living. As Norberto Bobbio points out: 'there is still a rhetorical presentation of old age, but not one that nobly defends the final age of man against the derision or contempt of the first. No, it is found mainly on television and consists of a disguised and highly effective attempt to ingratiate potential new consumers. In these advertisements, the elderly rather than the old, to use the more neutral term, appear sprightly, smiling and happy because they can finally enjoy some fortifying tonic or exceptionally attractive holiday. Thus they too have become highly courted members of the consumer society, depositaries of new demands and welcome participants in the enlargement of the market. In a society where everything can be bought and sold, even old age can become a commodity like any other.'[24] And in the next chapter we will see that while the well-endowed 'young old' are wooed by the tour operators and purveyors of cosmetics, there are still the needy and frail 'old old' whose dependence is commodified by privatized nursing homes and suppliers of geriatric equipment.

The relentless pressure to commodify and commercialize eats away at social trust and eases the problems of the present by shifting them into the future. In the immediately following chapters its growing penetration of all aspects of life, very much including work and production, will be shown to throw a cold shadow of insecurity over retirement hopes as well. The identity and integrity of institutions and companies is threatened by the thought that they are just arbitrary assemblages, like a hand of cards, some to be played for high stakes, others to be thrown away. All too often, employee retirement and health benefits are crucial stakes in this game. In confronting a difficult environment sacrifices may have to be made, but before working collectives are dispersed a value should be placed on collective morale and local commitment. Sometimes it makes sense to harbour reserves and not demand an average rate of return from every asset. Power and transport systems need surplus capacity to meet emergencies, or they may fail when most needed. The turn of the century brought mounting evidence that the market fundamentalism of the financial engineers was a perilous creed. The debacle of rail privatization in the UK, the fiasco of energy deregulation in California, the power outages in Auckland, New York, London and Italy, the financial collapse in Argentina, the failure to anticipate predictable storm-floods in New Orleans, the collapse of new buildings in Eastern Europe, and – of special concern in connection with retirement provision – a succession of scandals at core business institutions, were all signs of vulnerabilities brought on by a perilous experiment in skimping on infrastructure and reserves.[25] Privatization and deregulation have rendered the social fabric vulnerable to short-term commercial calculation. Market institutions do not work properly unless embedded in a strong non-commercial framework. This is just as true of the provisions that must be made for the new life course as it is for basic social infrastructure. And it is part of achieving that balance between the demands of the present and the future which will be a theme of this book.

Questioning the Anglo-Saxon Model

In the 1980s and 1990s a rich literature developed which sought to analyse what were seen to be 'varieties of capitalism' or divergent 'regimes of accumulation' and regulation.[26] These often reflected − among other considerations − the differences in pension financing and provision. French observers took to contrasting 'Anglo-Saxon' arrangements based on stock exchange capitalism, such as prevailed in English-speaking countries, with the organized capitalism − and solidaristic and collective model of social protection − which still prevailed in continental European and Scandinavian states, or the equally distinctive East Asian way of 'governing the market' and mobilizing social security contributions.

By the middle of the first decade of the twenty-first century there can still be no doubt about the claim that there are different types of capitalism − China and India are far from being replicas of any European or North American model. But within the main OECD states the 'Anglo-Saxon', market-based way of organizing economies and social provision has gained much ground. In 2005 the Koizumi government in Japan announced its intention of privatizing the Post Office, a lynchpin of the national savings system. While Post Office savings had helped to finance crucial investments in social infrastructure in the postwar period, by the 1980s there was evidence of a steady decline in macro-social returns and a danger that the precious land not already built on, or reserved for corporate golf courses, was being concreted over with redundant highways, bridges and airfields. Public expenditure on these projects was fuelling a corrupt patronage system that became a target of popular suspicion and anger. The Koizumi government succeeded in presenting the 2005 election as a referendum on this system and emerged the victor as a result, though by a smaller margin than had been expected.[27]

The headlong European retreat from public insurance of the risks of the ageing society is registered in a thorough report submitted by the European Commission and its Economic Policy Committee in February

2006. Looking ahead to 2030 and 2050 the report predicts a declining 'benefit ratio', that is, decline in the ratio of per capita pension benefits to gross output. Indeed, in GDP terms public pension income per aged citizen is expected to drop year by year until by 2050 it will be only a little over half its level in 2004. In absolute terms, public spending on old-age pensions, elder care and health is set to grow very modestly at a time when the absolute and relative numbers of the aged are set to rise steeply. In the 'old' Europe of the fifteen pre-enlargement states, pension spending as a proportion of GDP is now set to rise from 10.8 per cent of GDP in 2004, to 12.3 per cent in 2030 and to 12.9 per cent in 2050. Over this time the numbers of those over sixty-five will grow from 65.2 million in 2004 to 114.2 million by 2050. Since the overall population is projected to decline slightly over the period 2004 to 2050 the elderly will nearly double as a proportion of the total population but the average public pension received by each older person will, in GDP terms, drop by more than 40 per cent.[28] And to finance this scaled-down provision contribution rates will have to be sharply increased.

The US Social Security old-age pension programme in 2050 will only be claiming around half the proportion of GDP due to be paid as pensions in these European states by that date, where the over-65s are expected to be 28 per cent of the population compared with around 20 per cent in the United States. So there is still a greater European emphasis on public provision if the extra contributions can be found, but it is being eroded both by a more rapidly ageing population and by successive waves of neo-liberal reform. The influence of the 'new' Europe on the overall mix is likely to accelerate the shedding of entitlements and the move to 'Anglo-Saxon' style commercial provision.

The Commission's EU-wide projections, covering twenty-five countries and some 450 million people, show overall public pension expenditure growing even more slowly than in 'Old Europe' despite a rapidly increasing aged population.[29] In fact, in many of the new member states the lurch from public to private pensions has been even more precipitate. The collapse of Communism was accompanied by high inflation which further weakened public systems that were not very generous to begin with. Remaining entitlements were then slashed with no attempt to improve them by the tried and tested pay-as-you-go method of finance. The 'reform' process was avowedly designed to leave the field to commercial suppliers. Several of these 'reforms' were undertaken in the mid-1990s, and it will be a long time before they begin to deliver pensions.

Initial indications show a worrying pattern of high charges, poor returns and weak coverage. As yet, it is too soon to judge; pension systems have to prove themselves over several decades. However, commercial pension systems are as old as, if not older than, public systems. The 'Anglo-Saxon' model of publicly subsidized commercial pension provision already has a long track-record in the United States and Britain, which I will be examining in chapters 2, 3, 4 and 5. It has long delivered satisfactory results for some, especially those paying the top rates of tax. But for the majority of employees, let alone citizens, the record is in many ways an ominous one, as I hope to show in this book, especially in Chapter 3.

The past experience of such commercial approaches to pension provision has to be scrutinized to see whether their failings are structural and inescapable, or whether they can be removed or minimized by ongoing reform. It will also be necessary to ask why the privatizers prevailed in so much of Europe. While there was certainly a well-financed and persistent financial services lobby, it encountered stiff opposition in the core states of the European Union, especially Italy, France and Germany. No other public issue has been the occasion of such large-scale manifestations of public unhappiness – demonstrations of millions of citizens, general strikes by many more millions of workers, and stinging electoral rebuffs to the politicians most identified with 'pension reform'. When I published *Banking on Death* in 2002 I feared that this great groundswell of resistance would eventually subside if better ways of financing 'social Europe' were not elaborated, campaigned for and introduced. As it was this opposition was ground down and out-flanked. It was also undermined by the malfunctioning of the European economy, with its high rates of unemployment. The reasons for this are probed in Chapter 6, where it is argued that the European economies retain great strengths, but that they have steadily ceded ground to the 'Anglo-Saxon' model, privatizing public assets, commercializing pension provision and furthering the reign of 'shareholder value'.

Some claim that Anglo–American neo-liberalism has won out because it has all the answers and because the steamroller of globalization – or 'Anglobalization' as Niall Ferguson calls it – is bound to crush all alternatives. Such is the claim of the *New York Times* star contributor, Thomas Friedman.[30] I will be devoting space in this book to pension woes in the United States and Britain in order to show quite how flawed the supposed market model actually is. Pension provision is in deep crisis in both countries, and both are plagued by new insecurities and inequalities. Commercial and corporate pension provision has spawned a dysfunctional 'grey capitalism' based on institutional investors, and fuelled by a stream of privatized pension and insurance contributions. This is not a model which the rest of the world should seek to emulate.

Despite the advice they receive from many politicians and pundits, voters in the US and UK have remained supportive of their existing public pension systems. The citizens of these countries have never been left entirely to the mercy of commercial pension provision, as now threatens to be the case, because of World Bank advice, in large parts of South America, Eastern Europe, China and India. While I am concerned about the failure of private pensions in the United States and Britain, the prospects facing the retired and elderly in these lands threatens to be very much worse. I concentrate in this book on the pensions' record of the Anglo-Saxon states, with sidelights on what is happening in Europe, because these cases are well documented, because they show the relative success of US Social Security, albeit that it deserves to be better funded, and because they show the weakness and vulnerability of private pensions even in prosperous and supposedly law-abiding states.

In this book pensions are placed in the context of other trends in the ageing and learning society, and of the financialized norms and practices of what I call 'grey capitalism'. I do this because the prospects for pension delivery are very much bound up with this wider context. In the early postwar period, the so-called 'Golden Age' of 1945–72, the spread of occupational 'defined benefit' pensions seemed to be perfectly compatible with relatively stable employment, good benefits and rising prosperity. But subsequently pension funds fed the advance of financialization and privatization, becoming in many countries the principal owners of formerly public assets and enterprises. The ageing of the population, the salience of pension funds and the rise of fiancialization are intrinsically quite separate and discrete developments, yet over the last two decades they have become ever more closely intertwined. Techniques of financialization – such as a contract to buy or sell a ton of wheat, or so many thousand pork bellies, in six months time – have a long history, from seventeenth-century Amsterdam to nineteenth-and early-twentieth-century London and Chicago. But they acquired qualitatively new scope in the 1970s and 1980s because of the breakdown of stable exchange rates and monetary conditions.[31] Many companies and banks then used swaps and derivatives mainly to reduce uncertainty, locking in a known and viable current rate rather than be exposed to an unknown future rate, even if the latter might be more favourable. However, we will see that techniques which hedge uncertainty can also be used to mislead tax inspectors, shareholders and the representatives of pension plan beneficiaries.

Chapters 3, 4 and 5 attempt to explain the connection between the way pension funds are organized and the advance of financialization. Pension fund managers should seek the greatest clarity in the arrangements they make for their policy holders yet they seem to thrive on obfuscation and concealment. They should be utterly obsessed with investments that will ensure a more productive economy in coming decades. Why, so often, does this seem to be the last objective they have in mind? The characteristic institutions of Anglo-Saxon capitalism now suffer from a crisis of governance which allows a tiny social layer – chief executives and financial intermediaries – to extract exorbitant 'compensation', as they call it. It has never been much good at husbanding reserves, investing in social infrastructure or anticipating the requirements of future collective provision. But it is now prey to insider-looting on a grand scale. The hallmark of grey capital is absence of accountability.

While pension fund cash-flows have many charactieristics that suit the financial services industry, the relationship is highly asymmetrical and can lead to worrying cash-ebb. The aristocrats of financialization are those with huge computing power, and access to privileged information. This category also includes the CEOs of large corporations, as we will see. Financialization hates idle pools of money, or assets that are not serving as collateral. No sooner has the pension contribution been logged in than it is used to expand credit networks. These days this often means buying a credit derivative or 'collateralized debt obligation' packaged by an investment bank. By this and other means corporate borrowing and personal debt are ramped up, with a consequent reduction in macro-social reserves. A rise in asset prices can also, via a so-called 'wealth effect', stimulate consumption, but if divorced from real productivity gains, this will prove unsustainable.

Financial instability is aggravated by the fact that, as people spend longer in retirement, the returns on their savings become more important than their size. If the retiring employee has on average only four years to live then a pension pot of $100,000 will quite easily deliver a pension of somewhat over $25,000 each year, simply by running down capital, with returns on top of this being a bonus. But if the retiring person has the average prospect of living a further twenty years then the running down of their pension pot will only allow for $5,000 a year of capital draw down and the rate of return becomes a vital consideration. Life insurers refine such crude calculations when they sell an annuity for a capital sum. Finance houses find it easier to persuade companies and consumers to take on debt when the interest rates are low, as they were in the early 1990s and since 2000, but these have dire effects for long-run provision of annuities and are awkward for borrowers if interest rates rise.

In *Banking on Death* (2002), I sought to supply a largely hisorical account of the evolution of pension arrangements, with particular attention to the outcome of major social struggles over retirement provision in the 1980s and 1990s. This was designed as a history of the present, with an attempt to identify some of the roots and operating principles of 'grey capitalism'. In the present book the historical dimensions are only briefly sketched and the focus is on the structural flaws of a pension regime which is moving from under-performance to outright failure. In *Banking on Death* I offered a broad-brush account of the pension crisis and how to meet it. Here I explore in more detail how big the projected pension shortfall is likely to be, how it might be filled by new revenue sources and what reforms to financial institutions would promote, over the long run, greater stability, equity, efficiency and responsibility.

Today's murky 'grey capitalism' is good neither for business nor social insurance. It breeds irresponsibility and insecurity. It encourages governments and employers to try to escape past promises in their effort to stay in business yet it will be incapable of delivering on its own claims. The failings of commercial and particularized schemes of provision will make it impossible to maintain pensioners' relative incomes, and threaten a return of large-scale poverty among the elderly. I show in Chapter 3 that commercial and individualized provision is inherently costly, cumbersome and risky and will therefore compound pension inadequacy. Such private schemes, with all their problems, are better than nothing, yet in countries where they have been longest in operation – notably the US and UK – they cover only half of the population and give good coverage to only some of these.

The situation can be retrieved only by bold egalitarian and collectivist solutions. Both public and private pension systems are already failing in various ways even before the onset of the demographic shock of the baby-boomers' retirement – which will not really start until around 2010. New fiscal instruments and new models of provision could better enable the challenge of pension provision to be met and could also help to foster a more responsible model of accumulation in the wider society. There could be, I will argue, a link or affinity between assuring our future as individuals and assuring a better future for all.

If we try to prepare responsibly for an uncertain but surely testing future we need to embrace a new type of longitudinal thinking, one which leaves space for the measures we will or may need to take. In its own way capitalism is intensively concerned about the future, as investors seek to colonize it. The capitalist seeks to reap the rewards of patience, to cover immediate costs economically, to anticipate a surge in demand and then, by meeting it, to claim the residual or surplus. Indeed, the price of capital is determined by expectation of future profit. Pensions fit in awkwardly here since they too exert a claim to a future revenue stream, just as capital itself does. The true capitalist is not feckless, like the Woody Allen character, but instead insists on what posterity will owe to him or her. And in the era of 'financialization' the ways of colonizing the future and commodifying the present have become incredibly sophisticated, as we will see.

Notes

1 Ulrich Beck, *The Risk Society*, Oxford 1989.
2 The insidious quality of commodifying tendencies is powerfully conveyed in Naomi Klein, *No Logo*, London and New York 2000, and their frequent disguise as liberation and self-realization is explored in Luc Boltanski and Eve Chiapello, *The New Spirit of Capitalism*, London and New York 2005, especially pp. 167–216, 245–418. See also Randy Martin's trenchant survey, *The Financialization of Daily Life*, Philadelphia PA, 2002.
3 Tony Giddens, *The Third Way*, Oxford 1998, pp. 119–20.
4 Nicholas Barr, *The Welfare State as Piggy Bank*, Oxford 2002, p. 19.
5 Philip Bobbitt, *The Shield of Achilles*, London 2002, p. 240.
6 Ibid., p. 222.
7 Brian Barry, *Why Social Justice Matters?*, Oxford 2006, p. 7.
8 Bernard Ecclestone, *State and Society in Postwar Japan*, Oxford 1989, p. 97.
9 Michael Hill and Lian Kwen, *The Politics of Nation-Building in Singapore*, London 1995.
10 The growth registered in US and UK national statistics since the 1970s

should, in any comprehensive social calculus, be reduced by the cost of the waste and destruction of finite natural resources that stemmed from economic activity. A harrowing example from a very poor country is represented in Hubert Souper's film *Darwin's Nightmare* (2004). It recounts how the European Union and International Monetary Fund were happy to sponsor the 'Nile perch' fishing industry in Lake Victoria, Tanzania. A processing industry developed which purchased all the perch the fishermen could find, employing a thousand workers filleting, freezing and packaging the fish, with the product being flown to Europe aboard huge Russian planes. Even if these planes had not been carrying a return cargo of arms the results of this 'successful' project were hugely destructive. The Nile perch, a predator not previously present in the lake, has largely wiped out some two hundred species of fish, ruining the local fishery industry. The effect on villages that were anyway plunged in poverty and HIV/AIDS has been disastrous. The 'gains' from processing are far more than outweighed by the losses to a million villagers living around the lake.

11 I sought to explore this dynamic in *The Making of New World Slavery: From the Baroque to the Modern*, London 1997, Chapters VIII and XII. But see also Slavoj Žižek, 'The Parallax View', *New Left Review*, no. 25, February 2004 pp. 121–34.

12 US Census Bureau website, Interim Projections, March 2004.

13 Peter Peterson, *Running on Empty*, New York 2004, pp. 6–79.

14 UK Government Actuary's Department, London, December 2003.

15 United Nations, Population Division, *World Population Prospects, The 1998 Revision*, New York 2000, pp. 150–74.

16 UN Population Division, *World Population Prospects: The 2002 Revision*, vol. 2, New York 2003, p.16.

17 Ibid., p. 17.

18 'Greying Japan', *Economist*, 6 January 2006.

19 Paul Krugman, 'America's Senior Moment', *New York Review of Books*, 10 March 2005.

20 As is argued in a most informative and cogent study by Dean Baker and Mark Weisbrot, *Social Security: The Phony Crisis*, Chicago 2000.

21 In Chapter 3 I will be drawing on the work of those who have investigated this aspect, such as Edward N. Wolff, *Retirement Insecurity: the Income Shortfall Awaiting the Soon-to-Retire*, Economic Policy Institute 2002.

22 Tony Blair looked forward to private pensions supplying 60 per cent of future retirement incomes by 2050, a goal that the Pension Commission report of 2004 recognized as hopelessly unrealistic. For the initial 'partnership' strategy see the prime minister's preface to Secretary of State for Social Security, *A New Contract for Welfare: Partnership in Pensions*, Cm 417, London, December 1998, p. 103.

23 Pension Commission, *A New Pension Settlement for the Twenty-First Century, The Second Report of the Pension Commission*, London 2005, p. 115.

24 Norberto Bobbio, *Old Age*, Oxford 1990.

25 It is capitalist pressures on social infrastructure that were implicated in most of
    these cases, as I argued in Chapters 2 and 7 of *Banking on Death*, rather than
    the mathematical techniques of financialization as such. The high natural gas
    prices of winter 2005–6 in the United States furnished an example of private,
    de-regulated suppliers failing either to invest in adequate capacity or to hedge
    gas prices, steps which could have been combined to avoid the price spikes.
    See Rebecca Smith and Russell Gold, 'Years of Short-Term Strategy Create
    a Crunch in Natural Gas', *Wall Street Journal*, 17 October 2005.
26 For a survey by a leading exponent of the 'regulation school' see Robert
    Boyer, 'How and Why Capitalisms Differ', *Economy and Society*, vol. 34, no.
    4, November 2005, pp. 509–35.
27 Gavan McCormack, 'Koizumi's Coup', *New Left Review*, no. 35, September–
    October 2005, pp. 3–18.
28 Economic Policy Committee and the European Commission, Directorate
    General for Economic and Financial Affairs, *The Impact of Ageing on
    Government Expenditure: Projections for the EU25 Member States on Pensions,
    Health Care, Long Term Care, Education and Unemployment Transfers (2004–
    2050)*, Brussels, February 2006, p. 71.
29 Ibid.
30 Thomas Friedman, *The Lexus and the Olive Tree*, New York 2000 and *The
    World is Flat*, New York 2005. Niall Ferguson has his own take on the
    argument in *Colossus: The Rise and Fall of the American Empire*, New York
    2004, which I address in 'Imperial Margarine', *New Left Review*, no. 35,
    September–October, 2005, pp. 124–36.
31 For ways in which the impasses of the 1970s led to financialization see Robert
    Brenner, *The Economics of Global Turbulence*, London 2006, pp. 276–8.

1

The New Life-Course: Its Shape and Costs

Today we are moving towards unprecedented family forms and a new life-course. Parents find themselves economically responsible for adult children and, increasingly, they will find that they have fewer siblings with whom to share care of the elderly. In Europe as in North America, young couples start a family by acquiring a pet instead of having a child. The majority of people now have more parents than children. In most advanced countries women have fewer children than are needed to reproduce the population. This, as was observed in the Introduction, is as powerful a factor behind the ageing of populations as is increased longevity. The ageing and learning society is expensive and so, as public authorities and employers seek to contribute less and less to such costs, families struggle to cope. The multitudinous and extended families of the nineteenth and early twentieth century had greater resources and flexibility. Grandparents were younger, and better able to help with childcare, while there were far fewer of the really old. The modern family is quite small and vulnerable, with many one-parent and one-child families, and with two-parent households where both partners now go out to work. Domestic intimacy and family ties are still fundamental to the development of identity, character and social capacity, but families struggle with expensive and lengthening periods of dependency in youth and old age.

Instead of making timely provision for the future costs of the ageing and learning society there is, rather, a foreshortening of perspectives, with the claims of both past and future sacrificed to a greedy present. Public pensions have been attacked nearly everywhere, successfully in much of Europe, without success, so far, in the United States. This is part of a wider social pattern in which time is flattened by 'financialization', with its techniques for denominating every future liability in terms of discounted present values. Individuals and generations are expected to look out for themselves and not to rely on social insurance or to count on spreading risk between generations. Instead they are invited to enter an unequal partnership with finance houses and commercial suppliers. These privatizing trends have provoked widespread resistance because they target established and well-understood programmes. But it is still far from clear whether these will continue to receive the extra resources they need in societies where both the family form and the life course are undergoing a far-reaching transformation, and where privatizing trends are backed by influential lobbies. The predictable costs of new social patterns, with their widening horizons, should be anticipated in good time.

Consider the new life course. The periods spent outside work – the years of schooling and of retirement and old age – have become extended. Working life itself is interrupted by spells of sickness, un-employment, retraining, maternity leave, or, less commonly, paternity leave. The young often stay at college until they are in their mid- or late twenties. The years spent in retirement have been extended by growing life expectancy – and 'early retirement', whether voluntary or not, has often added to the years outside the labour force. The student will take a gap year and intersperse learning with paid work or travel. The employed will go back to college for a refresher course or extra qualification. Someone retiring at the age of fifty-five or sixty well hope to have decades of busy life ahead of them. The trend to early retirement is being resisted. Indeed the word 'retirement' is itself becoming a misnomer. Many look forward to it as an opportunity either to get on with their real work, or as an opportunity to devote themselves to something new, perhaps something less demanding but more engaging, something they are really interested in. This species of retirement would be best thought of as an extension of *free time*.

The need for enhanced spending on education has a utilitarian component. Some spend on education for clearly vocational reasons, whereas some see it as an investment in the hope of a future middle-class status. But rising levels of culture and skill, and a more generous framework of civic formation, benefit others apart from the immediate recipient and are therefore worthy of public support. And even such external justifications of expenditure on education would not work unless those on the receiving end identify with the educational process. Much education is centred on personal self-development, or on finding a meaningful niche in the wider reproduction of culture and social life. In the changeable context of the knowledge-based economy even highly vocational studies need to incorporate general aptitudes, a global per-spective, awareness of a diversity of traditions and openness to learning.

The challenge of financing these new social patterns is considerable. We live in societies where what is called 'human capital' looms ever larger. This terminology reminds us that many varieties of human self-development later turn out to have economic advantages – advantages for the whole society, not just the individual concerned. Such terms have their uses. But it would be upside-down thinking to believe, as some calculations might imply, that the use of free time is implicitly justified only because it later turns out to be economically beneficial. The same goes for 'social capital' and the acquisition of cooperative, networking and entrepreneurial capacities harnessed to personal development rather than to financial gain.

The more that complex possibilities open up, the longer it takes to become fully adult. A newspaper reports: 'Once you were an adult at 18 but now, say researchers, that should read at least thirty . . . Research in Britain and America found that less than a third of thirty-year-olds pass three tests of adulthood – having completed their schooling, left home and become financially independent. If a fourth test – marriage and parenthood – is added, the figure falls further. The results illustrate the rate of change in western societies. There are also implications for later generations – around a quarter of the cost of raising children is now incurred after they are 17 years old.'[1] The high rates of youth unemployment in continental Europe have had the same effect there, and one by no means confined to the middle class. In Italy, a pioneer of new demographic trends, the phenomenon of 'mammismo', the young adult's dependence of their parents, has become a familiar stereotype. Young men don't just show up to dinner at Hotel Parent (with a bag of washing), but they live there and also need cash. On a visit to Naples in 2002 I read a report in the local newspaper of a thirty-three- year old who was suing his parents for continued maintenance because they had stopped his allowance – he won his case.

Social research shows that there is something beyond anecdotal evidence to support this stereotype, with adult children often living at their parents' home in Europe's Mediterranean countries. But this research also suggests the reverse pattern – namely that parents receive support, or are even rescued from poverty, by co-residence with their adult children. In Northern Europe young adults are much keener on living on their own, and often experience poverty as a result. While it is common knowledge that young children, the very old and the unemployed are all disproportionately likely to live in poor households, poverty is also widespread among young adults, even where they are able to find a job.[2]

Yet those who are deemed old enough to vote or to die in foreign wars should not be kept in an infantilizing dependence on parental support, but rather given the resources to acquire the long-term skills and autonomy they will need in the knowledge-based society. Obviously such help should be universally available, perhaps, as Bruce Ackerman has suggested, in the form of a lump sum available to all from the age of eighteen. While Ackerman urges that no restriction should be set on the use of this grant, Unger proposes that it should only be used to acquire education, or a house, or to establish a business.[3]

The new life-course is the result of a variety of developments involving, no doubt, the greater time needed to acquire a diverse set of skills, but also economic constraints and the search for self-fulfilment. Greater longevity and smaller families interact with the demands of unceasing waves of innovation. The succession of generations is no longer rapid enough to carry forward the torch, so the re-learning process has to be intra-generational as well as inter-generational. Thanks to medical science and a healthier environment we not only live longer but, on average, remain fitter and more active as well. UN demographic figures still assume that those aged 15 and under, and those who are sixty and over, will be economically dependent while those between sixteen and fifty-nine will be employed. But in the developed world, and some developing countries, people are now beginning to spend nearly a third of their life learning and they may spend almost another third outside regular, full-time employment. We should allow for even more inter-mingling of life stages and late learning, but must resource them better, since neither extended education nor active ageing are cheap. And while it is vital to nourish the autonomy of the young adult and the older person this should by no means be confused with the compulsions of commodification.

The Debt Generation

Already a century ago Thorsten Veblen warned that 'business principles' were infiltrating every aspect of life. Veblen did not deny the formidable efficiency of these principles but he did think that they were corroding education, literary production, politics and welfare.[4] The huge effort to defeat the fascist powers in the Second World War engendered a striking advance in economic equality and a surge in free public provision. 'Business principles' were held in abeyance as education and health were extended, and great scientific and construction projects undertaken, at public expense. This fed into the remarkable postwar boom. But over the last three or four decades 'business principles' have staged a strong comeback and are scarcely less important now than they were in the Gilded Age, with its robber barons, self-help manuals for a pinched middle class, and poor, huddled, migrant labourers.

Higher education, with its elaborate hierarchies, is more than ever an engine of privilege. US tuition fees at the top private universities reached an average of around $20,000 a year in 2005 and had risen by nearly a third since 2000. If books, room and board are added the total cost reached $29,000 a year at private colleges. Fees at public universities are lower, averageing just over $12,000 a year in 2005, but subsistence costs add to these and they are rising too.[5] The overall cost of going to college for four years – which can easily reach six figures – is daunting to the poorer student, notwithstanding loans and 'needs-blind' admissions. Access to the best schools shows a strong link to parental social class. By 1993 children from the richest 25 per cent of families were ten times more likely to go to university than children from the poorest 25 per cent of families. In 1979 the multiple – at four times more likely – had been much less while today we may be sure it has grown.[6] The education available at elite private institutions, with their generous endowments, is better insulated from the crasser pressures of 'business principles' than the colleges that cater to the mass of students. With diminished public support, the great public universities and historic 'land grant' colleges are now often reduced to bidding for sponsorship by tailoring their research and courses to the needs of business.

In Britain the fees that universities could charge nearly tripled to £3,000 a year in 2004, and up to £9,000 in 2010, with further student loans available to help meet the cost. Parents of students from poorer backgrounds could submit to a means test to claim some rebate but total costs – including subsistence – remain intimidating. Early indications showed a drop in application rates. In January 2006 it was reported by the Student Loans Company that already 4,000 recent graduates had filed for bankruptcy, with 3,486 still insolvent. Average indebtedness at graduation was expected to rise to about £33,700 by 2012.[7] According to one estimate, the cost of raising and educating a middle class child in the United States over twenty-two years was no less than $1.45 million.[8] College education can spell debt for parents as well as children.

Government-sponsored loans in the US are taken up by 60 per cent of students. Most also need to take term-time jobs to help get them through college. The proponents of the financial revolution hope that those indebted to pay for their own study will learn the calculus and compulsions of a financialized world. This may work at the lucrative end of highly vocational fields of study like law or medicine, but it has problematic results for many students. On the one hand it leads to what researchers call 'debt blindness', as students with access to loans are caught up in the peer pressure to buy another round of drinks in the bar. On the other hand many branches of higher education lack a readily identifiable investment grade, as too many credentials chase too few premium jobs.[9] There is the further problem that debt-burdened graduates are encouraged to chase good pay rather than pursue satisfying careers.

A study by the UK's Financial Services Authority (FSA) published in March 2006 found 'worrying levels of financial literacy and capacity centered around 18- to 40-year olds'.[10] They were more likely to be in debt than other age groups and around one quarter of this age group had fallen into financial difficulty over the previous five years. Rising house prices and declining employer provision of savings facilities led the FSA's chief executive to conclude: 'The under-40s face a considerably more demanding environment than their parents did, and can ill afford to make mistakes or ignore the need to take action'.[11] But this parade of official concern was belied by the proposed remedy. The agency was to launch an educational campaign costing $10 million to reach ten million in the affected age group. It transpired that this modest sum would suffice, since those charged with the educational mission were to be none other than representatives of the various finance houses and so-called 'Independent Financial Advisors', who make their income from commissions paid by the providers they represent (in chapter 3 we will see that the high level of charges is a major problem with all commercial suppliers, but it is one which is aggravated in the UK by the fees, including the 'continuation fees' charged by IFAs. The government did not think to entrust the task of raising financial literacy to the network of Citizen's Advice Bureaus, which is supported by a rather meager government grant and accepts no such fees and commissions).

The finance houses which supply three quarters of US student loans have found it very profitable because 98 per cent of the value of the outstanding loan has been guaranteed by government and they have been allowed to charge annual interest at the ample level of 9.5 per cent. About 40 per cent of US students do not apply for loans but are thereby dependent on their parents. Pell grants are supposedly available to those from poor backgrounds. But these are worth only $4,050 a year, leaving around $8,000 a year of fees, and perhaps $5,000–$8,000 a year of subsistence, to raise through loans and part-time work. A study quoted by *The Economist* showed that such costs deterred 44 per cent of qualified high school graduates from attending a four-year institution. Many of those who do complete a four-year course, with perhaps a post-graduate degree as well, will often owe $60,000–$90,000 and their parents may have borrowed too. The effect is to pressure graduates to pursue high-paying careers and to shun low-paid public professional work. These pressures are likely to intensify as the US Congress votes to cut the level of public subsidy to higher education.[12]

To be deeply in debt by the age of twenty-three used to be an achievement reserved to the *jeunesse dorée*. Today the indebted youngster is more likely to have reached this condition by hard study rather than by playing cards and consorting with fast women. College fees and student loans have taken the place of gambling dens and haunts of the demi-monde. In December 2005 the *Wall Street Journal* reported: 'Over the past five years, total annual borrowing through student loans has soared 89 per cent, easily outpacing the 41 per cent rise in public college costs and the 28 per cent increase at private schools. Indeed among kids graduating last year from not-for-profit four-year colleges, 73 per cent had taken out loans, typically borrowing $19,400.'[13] The report quoted a College Board analyst as observing: ' "The problem is they have all kinds of other debts." . . . Kids are . . . leaving college with a fistful of credit card debt." '[14] Students often feel pressured by government, parents and university authorities to take out a loan, since this is convenient to all these parties, and do not feel fully responsible for the debt they have incurred. In December 2005 student loans in default totaled $33 billion, of which $5.7 billion had been outstanding for more than ten years. But eventually the debt catches up with the debtor as they lose tax rebates, forfeit federal entitlements or suffer from the effects of a poor credit rating. On the day of the previously cited report, the US Supreme Court ruled that it was perfectly constitutional for those with unpaid student debt to be deprived of Social Security payments, including disability entitlements.[15]

The logic of financialization is that each citizen will have to learn how to hedge life risks and spread income over their life cycle, through the sophisticated techniques of contemporary financial engineering. Each

individual is to convert him or herself into a two-legged cost centre and
profit centre, with loans and insurance used to shift costs to where they
can most advantageously be borne. In the 1950s Milton Friedmann was
one of the first to frame a 'life cycle' hypothesis according to which
individuals saved during their working lives in order to be able to meet
the costs of old age. In so far as the model aimed to be descriptive rather
than prescriptive it needs to be taken seriously, and might describe the
observable pattern for a proportion of the population. But actual
behaviour does not conform to the model now, if ever it did. Savings
rates in the 'Anglo-Saxon' countries have dropped into the low single
digits. Many of the low- and medium-paid spend much of their working
lives in debt, while even higher earners find so many invitations to spend
that they put little away. There are also many signs that those who have
managed to accumulate try to conserve a margin of wealth in their
retirement years, rather than running down their capital as the hypothesis
supposes.

Since the 1980s the 'life-cycle hypothesis', with its individualizing
logic, has been extended to separately-conceived age cohorts, each taken
in isolation.[16] According to the influential partisans of 'generational
accounting' each age cohort must look to pool risk on its own. This
approach takes no account of the debt which each generation owes to its
predecessor or of the value of the devices that have been developed for
inter-generational risk-pooling. It assigns an arbitrary present value to
future pension and medical liabilities across huge periods of time and then
gauges whether existing sources of revenue are adequate to them.
Theoretical objections to this model will be considered in chapter 5.
But whatever their validity, exercises in 'generational accounting' now
play an important part in framing policy options in the United States,
having informed projections made by the Social Security trustees and by
the Congressional Budget Office.[17]

The globalized world is gripped by a spirit of parsimony in public
pension provision, and by a belief that commodification and financialization can be made to fill the growing gaps that this will leave. Rich
societies begrudge extra social expenditures although governments also
know that if they skimp on them they run serious political risks. In a false
compromise they turn to commodifying techniques which break down
each life phase, or segment of the public sphere, in order to match it with
a financial product. The techniques for packaging each life stage seek to
make it stand, as it were, by itself. The young spend much longer in the

educational system, but are expected to finance this themselves by taking out larger loans. The middle-aged, knowing that the state pension is modest if not miserable, are goaded to make a stream of payments to financial concerns which will (supposedly) finance their retirement. The 'old old' are invited to sell their homes to pay for care, though selling their homes may be bad for them. Alternatively, those approaching retirement are urged to consider 'equity release', selling all or part of their dwelling to a mortgage company but continuing to live in it. A British consumer group finds this to be an inefficient and high-risk strategy; 'If one were to borrow £80,000 through a lump sum roll-up scheme on a £350,000 property, that might end up costing an owner £256,750 after twenty years.'[18]

Old Age Poverty and the 'Risk Shift'

Between 1972 and 2002 US hourly earnings rose very modestly, but household income grew by more than a third because of the advent of the two-income family. The large-scale entry of women into the labour force between the early 1970s and the early twenty-first century has not reduced household risk by much, if at all, and has not been accompanied by higher savings for eventual retirement. Elizabeth Warren and Amelia Warren Tyagi were alerted to this problem by rising US bankruptcy rates and explain it by showing that the two-income family of today has, after taking account of necessary outgoings for mortgages, child care, health insurance, and transport, a lower proportion of discretionary spending to fixed costs than the single- earner household of the early 1970s.[19] Indeed the 1970s family had a safety net. If the husband lost his job, the wife could go out to work. By the opening years of the new century 'mom as safety net' was replaced by re-mortgageing the house or cashing in the 401(k) pension savings. Families that had nearly paid off their mortgages did indeed have greater leeway and could congratulate themselves on rising house prices. But the latter are a greater obstacle to first-time buyers and to those moving from stagnant or declining areas to the more dynamic regions where jobs are to be found.

The combination of marriage break-up with a mild recession – about three million US workers lost their jobs in 2000–3 – help to explain both high levels of bankruptcy and a rising sense of insecurity. Jacob Hacker reports that a Panel Study of Income Dynamics, which has tracked a sample of US families since the late 1960s, shows that they are 'increasingly insecure'. He explains: 'The volatility of family incomes – how much family finances, adjusted for inflation, and society-wide income gains, fluctuate from year to year – is up sharply . . . Indeed the rise in volatility has outpaced the much-discussed increase in income inequality. Not surprisingly, therefore, the probability that American families will experience a sharp drop in their income has grown dramatically. And this increase in economic instability has occurred despite the dramatic movement of women into the work force . . . My own research leads me to believe that the rise [of economic insecurity] reflects a much larger trend, which I call the "Great Risk Shift". In the past generation, in a wide range of areas – from health care and retirement planning to the job market and the balancing of work and family – the responsibility for economic risk has shifted from the government and corporations to workers and their families.'[20]

The new insecurity not only threatens less income in retirement but also tends to weaken informal support networks. While the best form of pension is a reliable stream of cash, with the bare minimum of form-filling and no complicated conditions, it will help if this is embedded within a meaningful set of social relationships. The public pension which is cashed at the local post office can help to meet this criterion if several older men and women are involved and they come to know the post office staff. Some traditional occupational pension schemes still offer a way in which former co-workers can keep in touch with one another and the world of work, ranging from regular get-togethers to occasional reunions. The closure of such schemes (discussed in the next chapter) is not just an economic loss but also a blow to a 'little platoon' which linked the workplace to recreational facilities and the wider society. Too much discussion on pension provision fails to ask whether there are non-financial advantages to existing forms of public and collective provision that would not be replicated by some big, anonymous scheme linking each ageing individual with a national system of pension accounts, let alone a commercial fund manager.

Old age poverty, as we have noted, is higher in the US and UK, is strongly gendered and, as we see in Table 1.1, especially afflicts women living on their own.

Table 1.1: *Old-Age Poverty Rates:*
Some Cross-National Comparisons c. 2000

Income	Less than 40% of Median	Less than 50% of Median
All those 65+		
United States	15.0	24.7
United Kingdom	10.2	20.9
Germany	3.9	10.1
Canada	1.7	7.8
Sweden	2.1	7.7
Italy	5.6	13.7
65+ Women Living Alone		
United States	29.6	45.5
United Kingdom	25.3	40.7
Germany	7.1	19.6
Canada	1.2	17.7
Sweden	3.6	16.5
Italy	11.0	28.7

Source: Timothy Smeeding and Susanna Sandstrom, 'Poverty and Income Maintenance in Old Age', *Feminist Economics*, vol. 11, no. 3, November 2005, pp. 163–86, p. 167.

Perusing Table 1.1, it is difficult to understand why the states which are relatively more successful at tackling poverty among older people are energetically seeking to copy the states which are least successful in this task. In the US and UK the proportion of the elderly who are poor is at least double the rate in most other advanced countries and encompasses 40–45 per cent of women living alone (who themselves comprise 29 per cent of the total of those sixty-five and over). The fact that women live longer than men, and that they are often younger than their husbands, means that a high proportion of older women live alone, whether divorced or widowed – in the UK the average married woman can expect to live as a widow for nine years.[21] In 2002 the median income of women pensioners in the UK was only £92 a week.[22] At under £5,000 a year, this was less than the annual cost of the livery of a pony in a stables in England's Home Counties. Marriage break-up – with about a half of divorcees not remarrying – also raises the number of single men, many of whom will find it difficult to maintain workplace networks in retirement and who have less contact with kin than older, single women.[23] The forlorn widower played by Jack Nicholson in the 2003 film *About Schmidt*, illustrated this problem in a North American setting. Of course, all is not gloom and doom. The dating scene amongst single 70- and 80-year-olds, who sometimes see themselves as 'senior teens', can be quite lively. But for things to go with a swing resources and networks greatly help.

Poverty in old age is now more likely to rise than fall as existing formulas of pension provision are stretched. For some this will not be a new experience. The high incidence of poverty among the old in three 'Anglo-Saxon' states – the United States, Britain and Australia – in the 1990s was matched by the similarly high incidence of poverty amongst the young.[24] The prosperity of the top fifth of pensioners and the relative adequacy of the next fifth contrasts with the much less visible deprivation of those without property and 'qualifying years'.[25]

When storms lashed Florida in 2004, and Hurricane Katrina devastated New Orleans and the Gulf Coast in 2005, the vulnerability of the poor and elderly became starkly apparent. Those without a car, or the means for a hotel stay, were left to rough it in the Astrodome. Old-age poverty is highest among women, who comprise close to 60 per cent of the elderly, and two thirds of the very old, because of their greater longevity. Public and private retirement systems both reward continuous and high earnings, and they both penalize women whose home cares left them with weak earnings records. Married women could claim a spousal right to a (reduced) pension – but whatever extra contributions they made during their spells in work would not count towards a higher pension. Moreover the contribution-based pattern is shared by all commercial and most state systems of pension provision. The few exceptions (e.g. New Zealand) have been based on flat-rate citizens' pensions rather than explicitly on recognition of the role of care providers and home makers.

Old-age poverty is aggravated by growing social divisions, by segregation of the elderly and by a mass culture which promotes civic passivity. Over thirty years ago, Simone de Beauvoir, in her great work *Old Age* (1970), drew attention to the vulnerability of so many of the aged. The death of some 15,000 or more older persons in France in the heat wave of August 2003 was a sad illustration of one of her central arguments, namely that it is social isolation, rather than poverty or frailty alone, that puts the older person at mortal risk. The deaths prompted a sense of national shame to which the government felt it had to respond by setting aside a day of solidarity in May each year. It proposed that employees should work rather than take the traditional May holiday, with their earnings to be set aside in a special fund for the aged. The first 'day of solidarity' in 2005 was not widely observed – it wasn't clear to many exactly how, and who, their unpaid work would help and the decree of an unpopular government lacked legitimacy.

The cynical narrator of Michel Houellebecq's novel *The Possibility of an Island* recollects: 'The now ugly, deteriorated bodies of the elderly were, however, already the object of unanimous disgust, and it was undoubtedly the heat wave of 2003, particularly deadly in France, which provoked the first consciousness of the phenomenon. "The Death March of the Elderly" was the headline in *Libération* on the day after the first figures became known . . . In the weeks that followed that same newspaper published a series of atrocious reports . . . "Scenes unworthy of a modern country", wrote the journalist without realizing that they were in fact proof that France was becoming a modern country, that only an authentically modern country was capable of treating old people as rubbish, and that such contempt for one's ancestors would have been inconceivable in Africa.'[26] The flooding of New Orleans and other Gulf Coast towns in 2005 provoked similar scenes and similar reactions while in the UK newspaper reports of elderly hospital patients abandoned for hours in corridors or overcrowded wards became a press staple.

Just as 'business principles' increasingly permeate education and medicine, so too do they shape long-term care for the elderly. In the mid-twentieth century it was often regarded as the duty of public authorities to supply residential care homes for the dependent elderly, and not a few such authorities themselves built and ran the homes that were needed. The staff in such homes had to meet minimum professional standards and themselves enjoyed job security and quite good benefits when they retired. The public authorities also regulated the provision of care services by not-for-profit charitable organizations. But from the 1970s cost-cutting exercises coupled with 'business principles' led to 'privatization' and a regulatory 'light touch'. The qualifications needed to work in the 'industry' declined and along with this trend so did wages and benefits, making care workers amongst the worst compensated of employees. While elder care was increasingly organized as a business it remained one profoundly shaped by public subsidies and contracts. Private insurers are reluctant to cover the need for long-term care; in the US they cover only 10 per cent of such costs leaving the rest to be picked up by Medicaid – a means-tested public programmeme – and out of pocket payments by the elderly. The average annual cost of residence in a nursing home is at least $60,000, and the nursing home industry's annual turnover is in the region of $100 billion.[27]

At the top end the well-off, perhaps helped by a premium care plan, have access to high-quality medical attention and relative ease, often part-subsidized by tax relief. But large numbers of the dependent elderly are in more modest care homes run by a string of commercial suppliers who persuade public authorities that they can house them more cheaply than was done in public and not-for-profit facilities. In the UK outfits such as Barchester Healthcare, ANS group, Craegmoor, Runwood Homes, Life Style Care and Southern Cross Healthcare, several of them part of transatlantic groups, became large-scale businesses, furnishing thousands of beds and receiving contracts worth tens or hundreds of millions each year. The companies that supplied such services live on public contracts, and the business leaders who thrived most were usually those who cultivated contacts with local and national political leaders. While the latter might be routine in the United States, the British public was disturbed to learn that the owner of Westminster Health Care, with homes offering 5,700 beds, had received large public-care contracts and also been a major donor to the Labour Party. The man in question, Chai Patel, was appointed to the Cabinet's own Task Force for Older People, where he was able to dilute attempts to curb abuse in privatized care homes – for example the practice of multi-occupancy of tiny rooms. However media concern only became acute when it transpired that Patel, whose business was making £45 million profit a year, had secretly loaned the Labour party £1.5 million in the run-up to the 2005 election, and that he had subsequently been nominated for a peerage by Downing Street. The peculiar structure of the long-term health-care industry can foster tension as well as collusion between suppliers and public authorities. Budget constraints lead both central and local authorities to cut back on long-term care expenditure. Once private suppliers have established a dominant position in a given locality – usually by offering economies – they can, after an interval, threaten to close the facility on the grounds that the fees are too low. The resulting tug-of-war is usually better for profits than for those who live or work in the care homes. [28]

The costs of institutional care have also led public authorities to offer care services to dependent elderly who stay at home. In this way the efforts of spouses and other relatives or friends can be assisted and supplemented at lower costs than might be entailed by full residential care. But unfortunately glib phrases about 'care in the community' can sometimes conceal neglect, isolation and a failure properly to fund support services.

A recent study of heatwave deaths which carried off 800 older people in Chicago in the summer of 1995 stressed isolation as a cause of death.[29] Those who perish in such events usually do not include the most frail, since they are in care or under observation, but rather those who are living on their own but not in touch with anyone who could sound the alarm. On one day towards the end of the Chicago heat wave a local historian heard on the morning news that sixty-eight cadavers, forty-one of whom had died of heat-related causes, were to be given a mass burial in the municipal facility. She decided to attend the interment and persuaded a friend to accompany her. She found that there were no mourners or family present, simply the cemetery workers, a local pastor who tried always to attend such events, and, most unusually, over a dozen press and TV reporters. Each cadaver was encased in a plywood box, costing, she discovered, $100 rather than the $1,000 needed for a cheap coffin. The boxes were placed in a single ditch which was then covered with earth-moving equipment. 'Meaghan and I were the only civilians there. So the media converged on us wanting quotes because we were the only people to interview. It was almost as if we became symbols of the mourners, the family that was not there.'[30] The pastor explained that, on his own initiative, he had some time back decided to attend such mass burials and that between 1980 and 1995 he had offered his prayers as some 4,000 unidentified bodies were buried.

Simone de Beauvoir believed that impoverishment and isolation in later life had a cultural as well as an economic dimension. While unsparing in her chronicle of the decline of physical powers in the ageing person, she evoked the power of culture to manage, and at least partially to outwit, this ultimately inevitable process. She quotes Baudelaire's observation, prompted by Goya's extraordinary late work, drawing attention to a 'strange law' which sometimes allowed that 'lives and intelligences should run in opposite directions, that what they lose on the one hand they should gain on the other. And that they should thus go on . . . gathering fresh strength, new spirit and ever greater daring right up until the very edge of the grave.' De Beauvoir's passionate indictment of the utilitarianism of Western culture argued that the empty and passive quality of so much work, education and entertainment, and correspond-ingly the lack of control over their lives which so many feel, left a large number, at retirement, beached on the shallows of life and either segregated in communities of seniors, or secluded in an urban tenement. De Beauvoir concluded: 'Once we have understood what the state of the aged really is we cannot satisfy ourselves with calling for a more generous "old age policy", higher pensions, decent housing and organised leisure. It is the whole system that is at issue and our claim cannot be otherwise than radical – change life itself.'[31] Not for the first time, De Beauvoir's sensibility was attuned to a shift in the tectonic plates of the social order.

The Third Age

Ageing is not just about demography and economics, important as they both are. We are, as Margaret Morganroth Gullette put it in the title of a recent book, *Aged by Culture*.[32] From birth we enter a succession of life stages each accompanied by culturally-framed definitions and expectations. Almost the first thing a child learns to say after mamma and dada is to lisp its age. And as they grow every child will be repeatedly quizzed as to how old they are. Five-year-olds know that they shouldn't behave like two-year-olds and ten-year-olds know that they shouldn't behave like five-year-olds. And so it goes on with each phase of life. If cultural maturing takes longer and longer it is accompanied, Gullette believes, by a contrary process, which she calls the 'decline' thesis. In a society increasingly defined by a cult of youth, there is a magical turning point – nearer to thirty than forty – after which life starts to go downhill. At first this ageing is quite slow and there are ways to disguise it, or compensate for it, but then it relentlessly picks up speed – before we know it we are on the scrap heap. The ageing experience is gendered, and women are beset by the pressures of 'ageing' earlier and more intensely than is the case for most men. But before long a wider culture intensely concerned with youth also puts pressure on the balding, middle-aged male. Richard Sennett's interviews with middle-aged, middle-class workers confirms that they often find that their skills and perspective are now deemed useless. The young are not only quicker and more open but also easier to order around.[33]

In past societies very few lived to be sixty or seventy years old, but now it is youth which has rarity value in the more developed societies. Elaborate grooming, cosmetic surgery and the cult of the body allow those with the necessary inclination, time and resources to fend off ageing and perpetuate a simulacrum of youth. But denying time risks failing to grasp the compensatory perspective of middle life, somewhat brutally asserted by Elizabeth Jennings in her poem 'Accepted':

> You are no longer young,
> Nor are you very old,
> There are homes where those belong.
> You know you do not fit
> When you observe the cold
> Stares of those who sit
>
> In bath-chairs or the park
> (A stick, then, at their side)
> Or find yourself in the dark
> And see the lovers who,
> In love and in their stride,
> Don't even notice you
>
> This is a time to begin
> Your life. It could be new.
> The sheer not fitting in
> With the old who envy you
> And the young who want to win
> Not knowing false from true,
>
> Means you have liberty
> Denied to their extremes.
> At least now you can be
> What the old can't recall
> And the young long for in dreams,
> Yet still include them all.
>
> (Elizabeth Jennings,
> *Collected Poems*, p. 106)

A writer who made large claims for late middle age in the 1980s and 1990s was Peter Laslett, the historical demographer. In his book *A Fresh Map of Life* (1986) he argued that increases in life expectancy had created the possibility and reality of what he called – adopting a term current in France – 'the Third Age'. The first age, a period of learning and dependence, was stretching into early adulthood. The second age, that of entering the workforce, pursuing a career and bringing up children, was followed by a 'third age', according to Laslett, the potential culmination of the narrative of personal development. This third age, which could last twenty years or more, allowed for new interests and a new freedom, to be followed by a shorter 'fourth age' of decline, decrepitude and death. Laslett's belief in the potential of the third age led him to help found what he termed 'the university of the third age'.[34] As a historian Laslett was aware of the profound novelty of a society in which the over sixties were set to become a quarter of the total population. (Disrupting the tripartite division of life stages, one might also compare the 'third age' with the concurrent emergence in the mid-twentieth century of another novel life stage, that of 'teenagers' and 'youth culture').

Laslett evoked past attitudes by citing the controversial London physician who lectured in 1906 on 'the comparative uselessness of people over forty' and of the need for 'peaceful departure by chloroform at 61.'[35] Today ageism is less blatant but more serious. In reaction to it Laslett was drawn somewhat to overstate the distinctness and destiny of his third-agers, portraying them as the real leaders of society, using their experience and numbers to establish a mildly gerontocratic utopia. But Laslett was not wrong to stress either the significance of the new demographic pattern, or its likely costs and benefits. He wanted each person to 'live their lives in the presence of their future selves' and to enter the third age with a reasonable endowment. He added: 'The use of taxation funds to provide the requisite top-ups in order to ensure that everyone at the end of the second age has the necessary capital sum is a straightforward example of successors at large undertaking the support of their prede-cessors at large. And they are doing so, our theory would add, because they can rely on successors doing the same for them.'[36]

While the third age would entail larger outlays on medicine and income support, its members would help both to identify new possibi-lities and needs, and to ease the burdens of their 'successors at large' caught in the constraints of work and of bringing up a young family. Understood in this way the third age could be seen, as I have suggested, as an installment of *free time*, time not dominated by the need to earn a crust but allowing for a different link between the personal and the collective. The potential social contribution of the third-agers could help to introduce more free time into the lives of those in the second age. This approach rejects generational segregation and individualization while also aiming at economic self-reliance for the third-agers, since only this protects self-respect and ensures that they will not become a burden on their children just when the latter are themselves wrestling with the costs of bringing up their own offspring. Laslett distinguished between the 'third' and 'fourth' ages while leaving the exact boundary rather vague. We have seen that the over-eighties are the most rapidly growing cohort of the population. Those who remain reasonably fit and active are still enjoying a 'third age' in Laslett's term, but those who are infirm will have slipped over into the fourth age. The third- and fourth- agers have significant interests in common. They are more likely to need medical attention and care, and they both need to sustain non-employment income. Notwithstanding the increase in longevity, those who reach the age of sixty or sixty-five already have much experience of illness, death and disability, afflicting not only their parents but a surprising number of people of their own age group who never make it to sixty-five years, or who do so with seriously impaired health.

The annual health costs of those over sixty-five are roughly three times as great as the average per capita costs for the whole population, and four times as great as those of the under-65s. In 1997 the US was already spending $12,000 a year on the over-65s, compared with average per capita health costs for the population as a whole of $3,945. Recent years have seen a rapid escalation of costs but this ratio remains the same. Canada has costs better under control: in 1997 health spending on older people was $6,764 a year compared with $2,095 for the average per capita health spend. The UK at this time was spending each year only $1,847 per capita but $3,614 on older people, a still considerable, if somewhat narrower, gap.[37] The continental European states were closer to the 3 to 1 ratio, so the need to anticipate more spending on an ageing population remains the same. Overall figures for life expectancy and fitness for these countries are very similar, though the UK health system badly needed an injection of funds if it was to improve a number of indicators of poor health outcomes. On the other hand, the higher level of US spending largely reflected cost factors and brought no equivalent improvement in average health – though no doubt outcomes reflected quality of coverage. So prevailing patterns do not have to be accepted fatalistically. The UK raised its health spending overall in 2001–6 while there is growing awareness that US health costs are out of control.

Improvements in the social opportunities, diet and exercise regime of the older person can reduce their medical outlays, but have a price tag of their own. Much of the cost of medical attention for the old is concentrated in the last six months of life. Since we only die once this cost could be addressed separately from other medical costs of ageing. And whether costly or not there is good reason for increasing the chances that each of us will have a good death. In past epochs people were anxious to leave this life on good terms with their maker. Today, another idea of a good death would define it not as a technological challenge to keep the heart going for as long as possible, but instead would involve yielding up life without too much pain, on good terms with one's family and friends, and with a sense that our life has added up to something. Some of the savings reaped by less elaborate medical procedures in the last months would, however, be offset by greater expenditure on agreeable surroundings and decent care.[38]

The buoyant economic conditions of most of the 1980s and 1990s allowed those in the Anglo-Saxon countries with good occupational or personal coverage to retire on substantial pensions. But there were still large differences between three broadly defined income groups, with about 40 per cent lacking any supplementary coverage, a similar number with reasonable or good coverage, and the rest strung out in between. This polarization has at least helped to illustrate the thesis that material endowment greatly assists making the best of the 'third age', just as the plight of the elderly poor suggests that deprivation may be more difficult to bear in old age than at other life stages. Over the last decade US gyms have come to cater for the active elderly who can afford fees that start at $100 a month. The over-55s are the most rapidly expanding group among gym members. In some cases health insurers have been prepared to subsidize membership for those covered by their programmes, not just as a goodwill gesture but in the hope of keeping down medical claims. Enrolment in 'Silversneakers', a US gym membership programme for seniors sponsored by health insurers, grew from 25,000 to 500,000 members between 1996 and 2005. Senior sessions not only allow for less spandex and raucous music but also encourage camaraderie.[39] Local authorities and public sector employers – indeed all employers – would do well to follow this example if they don't already have such facilities.

I have portrayed commercialization and commodification as forces which aggravate the problem but I should make it clear that the proper financing of the 'third' and 'fourth' ages require cash outlays which will allow for the purchase of goods and services. Entitlements should not be calibrated simply to past cash contributions. Those of retirement age should have sufficient independent resources not to constitute a burden on their children, or, as the cant phrase has it, 'the community'. 'Regressive de-commodification' – which urges families to shoulder the cost of elder care – should be avoided; instead we should look to construct a 'progressive de-commodification', which allows the aged the dignity of financial independence.[40]

If women, in particular, are to have adequate retirement income this will have to stem from some mixture of new taxation, employers' contributions and their own savings, with incentives directed at the less well-off – unlike today's tax relief, which offers the best breaks to the rich. From the beneficiaries' standpoint pension finance is not best organized by commercial bodies because of the latter's costly charges and because they are liable to conflicts of interest, as we will see. Non-commercial criteria should help to shape entitlements, requiring further 'de-commodification' of retirement provision.

Crisis, What Crisis?

There is undoubtedly a strain of hyperbole and alarmism in much that is written about the ageing society. The possibility that the ratio of workers to pensioners will drop from 3 to 1 in 2000, to 2 to 1 by 2050, is presented as a threat to civilization as we know it, with little or no account taken of such off-setting factors as immigration, later retirement, higher employment rates or productivity growth. The effect – if not intention – of such panic-mongering is to undermine belief in the future of public retirement programmes and to render private alternatives thereby more attractive. Very understandably, the defenders of public programmes point to countervailing considerations which will enable public programmes to be sustained. They also rightly warn that privatization will aggravate, not improve the situation. But it is important that such a defence of public-pension programmes does not lead to complacency about, or denial of, the real costs of ageing, or to a belief that there is already in place some providential mechanism that will translate favourable conditions into decent pensions and health care. Sadly, there is a great deal of evidence – to be cited in the chapters that follow – which shows that existing public and private pension arrangements can be bad for employment. Pension adequacy will be easier to achieve in a buoyant economy, but it will also require mechanisms that are effective in pension delivery and which do not themselves compromise sustainable and equitable employment and growth.

There are a variety of possible offsets to the likely costs of the ageing society, and their potential should be carefully assessed. The declining ratio of workers to pensioners can be offset by later retirement and more immigration. The simultaneous raising of employment and productivity could boost public revenues in ways which make adequate pensions and health care more affordable. These points all have some substance so long as it is recognized that the help they can bring is limited, conditional and in need of further elaboration. More favourable ratios and increased public revenue would still need to be turned into effective pension outcomes.

Improved health at older ages makes work more attractive to those in their sixties and seventies. Such considerations mean that compulsory retirement ages should be abandoned or raised. In professions where specific physical or mental aptitudes are essential, age bars could be replaced by tests of competence. In general, employees should be allowed to postpone retirement if they wish, and employers' prejudices against older employees should be challenged. While there is scope for raising the age of exit from employment, it is limited, and dependent on the availability of employment opportunities. Supposing success in furnishing such opportunities, extra time at work in later life will very likely simply offset later entry to the workforce and increasing numbers of career breaks occasioned by parenthood and retraining. The overall length of working life will not grow by much, if at all. 'Active ageing' policies could encourage those who have retired from their main lifetime occupation to find more fulfilling or flexible work, perhaps on a voluntary basis, but it is unlikely to allow them to maintain anything like peak earnings. Education and training to ensure a productive 'third age' will require new social investments, as Laslett was well aware.

While lifting barriers to the employment of older workers is desirable, depriving people of pension entitlements in order to force them back into work is a quite different matter. Where it involves raising the state pension age or cancelling accrued rights it is not only highly unjust but also likely to be largely ineffective. Allowing people voluntarily to postpone the age at which they choose to retire is fine; indeed it can be encouraged by a compensatory increase in the eventual pension. But obligatory raising of the retirement age fails to register that while there are some modest signs that employers are turning to older workers, there still remain many men aged fifty-five to sixty-four who are out of work in the OECD countries, ranging from 40 per cent in the US to 60 per cent in continental Europe, with the unemployed rates among women being much higher. So it is highly likely that depriving those in their mid-sixties of their public pension would simply swell the ranks of those applying for welfare or a 'disability' pension.

Raising the official retirement age is particularly unfair on manual workers, whose life expectancy is between three and five years less than that of managerial and professional employees; they therefore draw their eventual pension for an average of about thirteen or fourteen years instead of for eighteen or nineteen years.[41] Although life expectancy is rising the social class gap is not narrowing. Ethnic minorities, especially if concentrated in manual employment, also have higher mortality rates. The unfairness of class differentials is compounded by the fact that most manual workers, having missed out on further education, started work three or four years earlier than the more long-lived graduate employees, so that those with the longest contribution records receive fewer benefits. Any increase in official retirement ages will simply intensify these injustices. Such an increase is also likely to be highly unpopular because it conflicts with the value set on free time. In general the male age of exit from the workforce has dropped steadily since the mid-twentieth century. This is obviously not because of declining physical fitness. Instead it reflects the waning attractions of work in older age. If employers were willing to offer more flexible hours and higher remuneration then they might well be able to tempt more older workers back into employment. Legislative attempts to force people to keep working by withholding pension benefits are likely to be strongly resisted. And even if the necessary legislation is passed, it will either be ineffective because quite mild – raising the retirement age by a year or two in thirty or forty years' time – or it will seek to make a serious contribution to the looming shortfall, but require raising the retirement age to the mid-seventies, and finding some way to oblige employers to take on these probably unwilling toilers.[42]

The entry of young working-age migrants is another development that can raise income to Social Security systems and mitigate the ageing effect. However the amount of help afforded by immigration is limited. If migrants are legally employed they will accrue Social Security rights as

part of their employment; if they are employed illegally then they are
unlikely to be paying insurance taxes. In purely economic terms the
immigration of highly skilled workers will tend to yield a tax surplus,
while the legal entry of unskilled workers will make less of a contribution.[43]

In practice migrant workers play a vital role in plugging gaps in the
delivery of badly needed services and this is likely to continue, but it does
not fix the cost problem of ageing societies.

Existing population projections already assume the maintenance of
immigration at current rates (for example, annual net immigration of
between three-quarters of a million and a million, so far as the main US
projections are concerned). An increase in the numbers of immigrants
will be desirable in itself, allowing families to re-unite, helping to foster
multi-cultural societies and beginning to establish a universal human right
to freedom of movement. But immigration will have only a modest
impact on the ageing trend and cannot reverse it. New arrivals swiftly
adopt the demographic profile of the host populations, with their greater
longevity and lower fertility. This means that ever-larger numbers of
migrants are needed to lower the population's age profile. In order to
maintain the support ratio between pensioners and those of working age
constant at the 1995 level between 2000 and 2050 it would be necessary,
according to a UN study of *Replacement Migration*, for the United States to
admit 10.8 million migrants annually for a total of 592.8 million
immigrants by 2050 and to see the total population rise to 1.1 billion.
(For comparison, if all immigration halted then the US would have a total
population of 290 million in 2050, of whom 68 million would be over
sixty-five). The 'old' Europe of the pre-enlargement EU would need to
admit 12.7 million immigrants annually for a total of 700.5 million, and
would see its total population rise to 1.2 billion. The UK would need to
admit 59.8 million immigrants between 2000 and 2050 to maintain a
constant support ratio at 1995 levels, and would see its total population
rise to 135 million. Clearly such overall population increases would create
many more economic problems than they solved, requiring huge physical
infrastructure investments. But while declaring such a solution to be
unfeasible, the report by no means rules out significant levels of immigration − higher than at present but lower than these artificial,
'migration only' scenarios − as playing a helpful but modest role in
off-setting declining support ratios.[44]

The strains associated with 'old' Europe's serious ageing problem will very probably be partially alleviated by immigration, including from the new members in Central and Eastern Europe. Income per capita in the latter is only half that in the former. Twelve of the old member countries have supposedly retained control of the migrant flow until 2011, but most of these are already issuing large-scale permits. Polish plumbers have become legendary in France, while the Polish language is said now to be more widely spoken in Ireland than Gaelic. But the new member countries also have their own 'ageing' problem and are themselves in receipt of migrants from the Ukraine and Russia. The European Commission claims that there will be an EU-wide shortage of 20 million workers by 2020. Because the 'old' EU has been ageing for some time it is sometimes implied that this might have something to do with poor economic performance over the last three decades. But this poor performance had nothing to do with labour shortages – on the contrary, its main expression was high levels of unemployment. Until the EU shows a capacity to use its existing labour resources, warnings about the dire effects of labour shortages should be taken with a pinch of salt.[45]

While immigration can contribute something to meeting the costs of the ageing society in the advanced countries, we should also bear in mind the needs of the developing countries which will not wish to lose all their expensively educated and trained workforce. Most of these countries have ageing populations themselves, as we have seen. At the very least, much greater provision should be made for the remittance of immigrant earnings to their countries of origin, which have borne the costs of their upbringing and education. It is estimated that migrant workers to the United States already remit some $40 billion annually to their home countries. Some of the eleven million or so 'illegals' amongst them may not pay FICA contributions (the payroll tax), but many do, and hence contribute to financing Social Security and Medicare. The British and US governments bend to xenophobic hostility and set the 'illegals' a dangerous obstacle race, yet they convey a welcome to those with scarce skills. Hospitals in the UK and the US recruit highly skilled staff from countries like South Africa and Ghana, which paid for their training and badly need them. Of course if they subsequently return, having acquired extra expertise, then their compatriots would benefit. While large-scale migration will continue, and has many positive features, its contribution to meeting pension-funding problems will be modest.

Another way to boost the number of employees per pensioner is to raise the actual employment level of the working-age population. Any increase in the numbers of persons in paid work raises the amount received from payroll taxes, income taxes and consumption taxes. Exclusion from the world of work has bad effects on most people and it should anyway be a clear priority of public policy to eliminate involuntary unemployment. This is desirable for its own sake as well as to benefit public revenues. The reasons for persistent high levels of unemployment in continental Europe will be explored in Chapter 6. There can be no doubting that failure to provide work – especially to those under twenty-five and those over fifty-five – has weakened social solidarity, demoralized organized labour and furnished openings to the demagogic politics of the far right. An economic policy that boosted employment would also help provide needed finance for social programmes. But recent changes in these countries have moved in the wrong direction, cutting pension entitlements while maintaining regressive taxation which – in combination with the deflationary policies of the European Central Bank – reduce demand and hence perpetuate the low employment economy.

The problems of the United States and Britain are different. Their employment rates have been ten points higher than the core states of western Europe, and working hours are often extraordinarily long. There remains some scope for reducing unemployment in the United States and Britain, because unemployment has been masked by disability benefit and by women's disinclination to register for work when work is not available. However, the real challenge facing these countries is to improve the quality and security of employment, and the work/life balance. The need for more education and retraining, and the widespread desire for more free time, will set some limits on the scope for raising the overall employment rate for those of working age. It would also be good to discourage routine over-working ranging above 50 hours per week.

Better macro-economic management can help to promote higher employment levels. The British economy avoided recession in the period 2000 to 2005 partly due to counter-cyclical measures which raised public-sector employment by some 800,000. Given the need for continued investment in public infrastructure and services, and on measures to meet the problems of global warming, the overall employment rate can certainly be raised in both countries. Because higher employment generates more payroll tax revenue it helps to finance Social Security pensions in the US and a better public pension in the UK. Such neo-Keynesian policies are desirable in themselves, and will also contribute to meeting the costs of the ageing society. But over the medium or long run such a policy needs to be twinned with rising productivity and buoyant demand if it is to be sustained. British performance has been marked by stagnant productivity. Even where productivity yields a bonus, there will remain the question of what it should be spent on. Pensions would have a claim but so would education, health, child poverty, public infrastructure and research.

Both the US and the UK have only been able to sustain demand by promoting unhealthy levels of personal indebtedness. A further problem with these 'Anglo-Saxon' states is that their taxation systems have largely ceased to be 'progressive', in the technical sense of taking more from the rich than those with low or medium incomes. The traditional progressive taxes – income tax and corporation tax – are of reduced importance. In the UK the poorest actually pay tax at a rate higher than the richest tenth, while those in between are almost level. This is because Value Added Tax, and alcohol and tobacco duties, take their toll on the budgets of the poor. Some progressivity nevertheless returns to the system because of the pattern of expenditure, with state pension expenditures helping to alleviate what would otherwise be dire poverty. Nevertheless the overall result is increasing polarization of rich and poor, and heavily leveraged consumption patterns for those in the middle.[46] Public revenues fall short of what is needed, and ageing costs are so considerable that they are likely to suffer from any shortfall. It is a striking fact that the postwar boom in the Western economies was accompanied by high and progressive taxation, much greater equality and more generous welfare programmes. On the other hand, finding our way back to this storied 'golden age' is likely to require innovation and imagination rather than simply reliance on mechanisms of redistribution that have already encountered their limits or have been outflanked by the counter-measures of wealthy individuals and powerful corporations.

Raising the Birth Rate

Demography is not destiny, but a product of changing conditions and changeable human behaviour. An increased birth rate could produce more comfortable ratios of workers to the retired in several decades' time. In conjunction with the right institutions this could somewhat alleviate the pension-funding problem. The projections of an ageing population make assumptions about longevity and the birth rate that reflect current trends. Is it right simply to project these decades, or even half a century or more, into the future?

Life expectancy has been growing steadily for a long time and is likely to continue to do so. If epidemics, or a poisoned planet, pushed up mortality this would be very shocking and efforts would be made to restore healthy conditions. But the birth rate slump is not a simple negative, as it reduces burdens on women and will diminish the pressure on natural resources. As indicated in the Introduction, the well-established ageing trend is rooted in low fertility as much as increased life expectancy. Whereas women used to average three, four or five children each at the beginning of the twentieth century in Europe, North America, Japan and China, the number had dropped to less than the replacement rate of 2.1 by 2000 in all these areas. In Italy, Poland, Germany and Spain average lifetime fertility in 2000 was only 1.2 to 1.3 children per woman. In Scandinavia and France, where governments have made an effort to frame child-friendly policies, it was a little above 1.7. In Japan the ratio is only 1.4. The exact figure for China is not yet clear but as a consequence of the famous 'one child policy' is likely to be well below 2.0. In the United States the fertility rate has also fallen sharply but at 2.0 it is only just below the overall replacement rate.[47]

While much of the birth-rate decline represents the greater availability of birth control, and women's desire to escape from the burden of multiple child-rearing, most women would still like to have at least two children. Many don't manage this because they postpone having their first child until quite late and then run out of time. The rising cost of bringing up children and the special burdens which are faced by mothers after childbirth help to explain this pattern. In an economically insecure environment, and with higher expectations, young women find it more difficult to find the right partner and the right conditions to start a family. I have already cited the 1998 estimate that the cost of bringing up a middle-class child and paying for their education to the age of twenty-two was $1.45 million.[48] A British academic study looked not at the direct cost of having a child but at the income foregone by mothers as a result of childbirth – the withdrawal from paid work and the loss of seniority at the workplace. It found that a couple with a medium level of skill would lose £140,000 for one child and £257,000 for two.[49] Clearly these estimates reflect current arrangements which could be changed by more enlightened policies. But the changes involved would have to be rather large ones and would not be cheap.

While Göran Therborn offers a subtle account of the major global regional variations, which stresses that fertility declined where couples were better able to assert control of their lives, John Caldwell and Thomas Schindlmayr offer demographic transition and a brusque summary of the fundamental drivers of fertility decline that is implicitly less optimistic: 'consumerism, increasing need for dual incomes, a perception among many young people that raising children is simply too expensive, and a tendency for partnering rather than parenting to provide the family core are likely to reduce fertility. Better contraception and easier access to sterilization and abortion have provided the means for achieving any level of fertility, no matter how low.'[50]

If good child care was widely available and cheap, if men took on themselves more of the burden of child care, and if there were generous maternity and paternity leave, it could encourage women to have more children. Child-friendly policies also generate employment. Any package of measures that actually brought down the cost of having children would inescapably be quite expensive. The Scandinavian countries are closer to having child-friendly policies than other parts of the advanced world. They have a somewhat higher fertility rate than Germany (1.72 compared with 1.36), notwithstanding the fact that many more women go out to work than in Germany. France also has somewhat higher fertility rates. In the past this reflected a determined governmental natalism, inspired by a nationalist concern to boost a historically slow-growing population; more recently the introduction of the 35-hour week seemed also to have helped a bit (but by 2003 it was under attack). However, although such approaches should be pursued for their own sake as well as because they may somewhat moderate – but not reverse – the ageing trend. Federal authorities in the United States contribute $15 billion annually to child-care programmes but Suzanne Helburn and Barbara Bergmann urge that this needs to be raised to $30 billion.[51]

So long as having children is expensive, and so long as many women delay childbirth, families will remain small and the ageing effect will be pronounced. It is quite likely that the troubles of the European economies since the 1970s, including slow growth and high unemployment, have contributed significantly to women's inclination to delay having a child, and to not have a second child. These societies will certainly take measures to raise the birth rate and eventually, perhaps in the wake of an improved economic and social model, they may have some modest success. We come back to the fact that the last four decades of lowered birth rates already set a limit on the size of the affected cohorts which stretches down to, and beyond, mid-century.

Charting the interrelationship between demography, economic growth and capital accumulation, the birth-rate and the business cycle, is not easy. The advance of industrialization has coincided with a secular decline of the birth rate. Somewhat smaller families enjoyed a higher standard of living and this allowed for more investment in the education of each child. China's 'one child policy' of the 1980s and 1990s – whatever its future costs – repeated this conjunction in an even more intensive way, though the country's remarkable surge of growth now seems to favour some relaxation and a small increase in fertility rates. The broad, secular relationship between growth and a lower birth rate also corresponds to women's desire to escape the tyranny of domestic toil in the patriarchal family. Women's demand for education, paid employment and social rights have often accompanied economic development, a lower birth rate and smaller family size.

But within such a broad correlation there are also counter tendencies. The demographic buoyancy of nineteenth-century North America, in a context of abundant resources and capital inflow, helped to increase the supply of labour and expand the domestic market. Likewise, the strong growth of the immediate postwar period in North America and Europe, proved to be quite compatible with a 'baby boom' – fertility rates less than those of the nineteenth century (four or more children per woman) but, at three children per woman, still well above the replacement rate. More troubled economic conditions – in the 1930s, or again in the 1970s and after – saw depressed birth rates. The post-1970 decline to below two children per woman was unprecedented and no doubt reflected some mixture of women's greater ability to control their fertility, new social gender relations as well as the contraceptive pill and legal abortion. Whatever the exact explanation in each particular case, the consequences for the evolving age structure of the population are large. Yet the scope for 'demographic engineering', or pro-growth natalism, is very limited. French governments have long practised the latter but with modest results. In the end it is couples and women who will make the decisions and political leaders will have to adjust to the consequences.

Caldwell and Schindlmayr are convinced that fertility rates will not increase because their present state reflects the pressures of today's consumerist, post-welfare capitalism: 'One guarantee of that [low birth-rates] is the probable survival of liberal economies, seemingly necessary to provide the continuing economic growth expected by all societies, and the associated limitations placed on the welfare state and the consequent widespread feeling of insecurity among young adults. And young adults are not likely to be listened to by politicians as the fertility decline ensures that they are a diminishing proportion of the electorate.'[52] This conclusion still leaves room for a new socio-economic regime which would somehow combine more security and reasonable prosperity in such a way as to encourage a modest recovery of the birth rate in those countries where it is lowest, say from 1.3 or 1.7 to something nearer 2.0.

I have suggested that a global population which grows less rapidly, or begins gently to decline, is welcome since it will reduce the pressure of population on resources. But if it is consumerist pressures which drive the fall in fertility then this conclusion may be too optimistic. At all events there will still be a sizeable tab for ageing costs.

Pension Costs as a Share of GDP

As urged in the Introduction, a fifth of the US population, and a quarter of the EU population, will be over sixty-five within thirty years. A way should be found to address old-age poverty and to ensure that pension incomes as a whole keep abreast of national prosperity. At present pensioner incomes are around 70 to 75 per cent of average income. If this overall share is to be maintained then it would amount to around 15 per cent of GDP in the US, not including the cost of health care, and 18–22 per cent in the EU, not including health costs.[53] US health costs for the over-65s are already 5 per cent of GDP and are growing explosively. Senior health costs must be met whether basic health care is regarded simply as a free universal entitlement, which tends to be the European approach, or whether it is seen as a consumption good to be paid out of pensioners' incomes. The US government does cover much, but by no means all, of the medical costs facing the elderly through its Medicare programmeme. And European programmes also have co-payment provisions, so the contrast between the two approaches is not sharp.

It is only fairly recently that attempts have been made to measure overall pension needs against overall pension resources. Curiously enough, the mid-century gap between the one and the other that looms in such estimates seems to be around 4 per cent of GDP, whether one looks at Europe or North America, albeit that the respective contributions of public and private schemes is still rather different. While the emergence of this 4 per cent gap is largely accidental, it does signal a degree of convergence and a common problem with raising needed resources through given financing methods.

The UK Pensions Commission has estimated that if pensioners are not to suffer a decline in their relative income this will require, by 2050, that they receive 16.1 per cent of GDP, or 13.9 per cent if women's actual retirement age can be raised to equal that of men by 2020, in line with the raising of women's official pensionable age. On current trends the Commission estimated that public and private pensions will supply about 10 per cent of GDP in pensioner incomes in 2050. With means-tested supplements the state pension will supply 6.9 per cent of GDP, unfunded public-sector pension schemes 0.8 per cent, and funded pension schemes of all types between 2.1 and 2.6 per cent, for a total of 9.8 to 10.3 per cent, leaving a gap ranging around 4–6 per cent. [54]

The European Commission's estimates of the proportion of GDP required to fulfil the new scaled-down EU public-pension promises in the fifteen 'old' member states runs at 12.9 per cent of GDP by 2050, as was noted in the Introduction. At this level pensioner incomes were already 40 per cent less than they would be if the ratio of pensioner incomes to average incomes is held constant at the 2004 level. Nevertheless the Commission estimates that contributions set at prevailing rates will raise only 9.0 per cent of GDP, 3.9 per cent less than will be needed to pay the downsized pensions.[55] The Commission is unable to forecast, on present trends, the filling of this gap – still less the maintenance of relative pensioner incomes – by factoring in occupational and private pensions. In the Netherlands, Sweden and the UK there will be significant input from such schemes, but in those states public pensions are in any case 2.5 per cent of GDP lower than the EU average. Inclusion of the new member states leaves the picture substantially unchanged, with scaled-down outlays of 12.8 per cent of GDP and contributions of 8.9 per cent of GDP, for a 3.9 per cent gap.[56]

Public discussion of pension provision in the United States and Britain customarily focused on the goal of alleviating or removing poverty rather than on the overall proportion of national income or GDP required to ensure that the elderly will not be left behind by the rise in national prosperity. In the United States, Social Security entitlements are usually specified by a monthly figure – the average payment to a single pensioner being a little over $900 a month in 2004. In Britain the value of the basic state pension has long been reckoned in weekly amounts, as with children's pocket money. If these sums were reckoned in annual amounts, as would normally be the case with people in full-time employment, then their inadequacy would be clearer. The British state pension is currently just over £80 a week, or £4,000 a year, but many do not qualify for it. The average pension paid by Social Security is $11,000 a year but many fall below the average.

The US Social Security trustees report at regular intervals on the state of the programmeme's finances. In 1998 the UK government produced a strategy document, or Green Paper, on pensions which remained so besotted with commercial provision, and so fixated on weekly amounts, that it failed to assess the implication of its own goal that private schemes should supply 60 per cent of all retirement incomes by 2050. Rising public anxiety about pensions, the closing of good occupational schemes and the flop of its own attempt to encourage the financial services industry to supply a new individual savings vehicle – the 'stakeholder pension' – prompted the Labour administration to establish the Pensions Commission in 2002. Its members, generously interpreting their rather narrow mandate, decided to look into overall pension adequacy. The first report of the Commission not only calculated future annual state pension budgets, as has long been the practice of the trustees of Social Security in the United States, but also set a target level of pension provision in terms of its share of GDP. This was an important step towards a more realistic and research-based approach. In its first report in December 2004, the Commission came up with its previously cited conclusion that by 2050 there was likely to be a shortfall of at least 4 per cent of GDP, a sum equivalent to the entire public pension budget of 2004.

The annual reports of US Social Security trustees set out the pro-grammeme's revenue needs in terms of the proportion of GDP that will be required to meet them, but give no estimate of other retirement incomes. Their aim is to test the viability of a specific government programmeme not to arrive at a target for all types of pension provision once the 'baby boomers' are retired. The projections made by the Congressional Budget Office (CBO) are also focussed on the public programmes. In 2002 the combined outlays of Social Security, Medicare and Medicaid totaled 7.0 per cent of GDP, while in 2030, according to the CBO, they will total 11.1 per cent and in 2050 12.6 per cent. Receipts to these programmes, however, which were 7.0 per cent of GDP in 2002 are expected to rise to only 7.2 per cent in both 2030 and

2050 under present financing provisions.[57] The doubling in the size of the aged population largely explains the surge in outlays: Medicare is exclusively for the health-care of those aged sixty-five and over; Social Security outlays go largely to seniors (the balance going to survivors and the disabled), and older patients make significant claims on Medicaid (e.g. for nursing home provision). The total estimated shortfall is 3.9 per cent by 2030 and 5.4 per cent by 2050 but most of the deficit arises from the medical programmes, with the Social Security portion amounting to only 1.5 per cent in 2030 and 1.8 per cent in 2050, according to the CBO. While the CBO does not directly estimate future income from personal and occupational pensions it has recently estimated the tax revenue that will be generated by future private pension pay-outs. Debate on the probable size of this tax revenue suggests that private pension income will amount to between 1.5 and 2.5 per cent of GDP in 2035–50.[58] If the Social Security shortfall is somehow met or avoided then it will supply 5.0 per cent of GDP on sneior incomes by 2035. To this can be added 1.5 percent of GDP generated by public sector pensions and as much as 2 per cent of GDP represented by the earings of those over 65 for a total of 11 per cent of GDP by 2035, just 4 per cent short of the target 15 per cent of GDP neded to maintain relative senior incomes.

When a shortfall first appeared in the Social Security trust fund in 1981 it sparked a widespread discussion and eventually led to the establishment of the Greenspan commission, which recommended trimming some benefits and raising contributions. Richard Musgrave published a paper which argued that the fairest way to deal with the problem of differing cohort sizes was to share the burden by adjusting taxes and benefits so that the ratio of pensioner incomes to average income remained the same. John Myles has recently argued that this approach should guide pension provision in Europe.[59] The UK Pensions Commission has endorsed this shared-burden approach by agreeing that maintenance of average pensioner incomes relative to overall average income should be a goal of public policy. While there are specific conclusions reached by the Commission that I disagree with, and will later criticize, its decision to adopt a holistic and equitable perspective on future pension needs is commendable and in welcome contrast to much written on the subject that advocates drastic cuts and wholesale privatization, unsupported by any ethical argument and without any target for future provision.

Estimating the likely future revenues that will be supplied by funded pension provision in the United States is no easy task. Future chapters –

especially Chapter 3 – will make it clear quite how uncertain the prospects for private pensions now are. In the case of the UK the Pensions Commission estimated the figure I have cited above – 2.1 to 2.6 per cent of GDP. This amount was based on the assumption that the same percentage of funded pension income goes to normal retirement age pensioners in 2050 as it does today. The Commission estimated that funded pension schemes were generating 2.2 per cent of GDP in 2002, a figure quite close to that for the United States. The previously cited debate on CBO estimates of the tax yield from private pensions implies that the latter will be in the range 1.5 to 2.5 per cent of GDP, as we have seen. According to the 2005 trustees report Social Security is due to supply old-age pensions worth 5.43 per cent of GDP by 2030 and 4.77 per cent by 2050, assuming existing provisions. Non-funded public sector pensions would be doing well to supply 0.8 per cent of GDP in both years. If the implicit CBO estimate for funded income is adopted for the US then total pension incomes could be in the region of 9.0 per cent of GDP in 2030 and 8.3 per cent in 2050. The earnings of those who were over the new retirement age of 67 might add an extra 1 per cent of GDP. These rough and ready calculations will have to be revisited in the course of the book, and especially in the conclusion. For the moment they show a potential US pension income shortfall of at least 4 per cent of GDP.

The defense and improvement of public provision will play an important role in addressing the pensions deficit. Existing public pro-grammes are highly cost-effective and their most glaring coverage defects easily mended. Their resilience in the face of the privatization lobby is hugely significant. Even in 'Anglo-Saxon' economies where private provision has long enjoyed lavish subsidies, the most important source of the income of most retired people is the public pension. However in their prevailing form in the United States and Britain the public pension is modest. If the revenue shortfall for Social security is tackled – there are several ways of doing this, as we will see, without cutting benefits – it will still only supply 6.0 per cent of GDP at mid-century, a time when seniors will need to receive more than double that figure if they are not to fall behind. The British state pension and (means-tested) Pension Credit is on course to supply only 7.2 per cent of GDP to a larger elderly population and the 2006 government White Paper failed to raise this target.

It was pointed out above that average annual medical costs for the over-65s are four times those for the under-65s, and this has implications for the share of GDP that will be needed for medical care of the elderly.

In the United States health spending on the over-65s already comprises 5 per cent of GDP, with the figure coming in at around 3.0 to 3.6 per cent in Canada and Europe.[60] While from one angle this is money spent on older people, on the other it is income for those who work in the health sector and for corporations which supply that sector. Public health-care systems should have enough purchasing power to prevent themselves being exploited by pharmaceutical and equipment companies, but the fragmented US system is not in this position and similar problems threaten the UK.[61] Health spending in the US has been rising more rapidly than GDP growth, and more rapidly than health-care in countries with comparable health outcomes. Excess commercial costs and profits are certainly part of the problem. But so are justifiable increases due to ageing patterns, new treatments or the pressure to maintain the relative remuneration of medical staff. Following a report to the Medicare trustees by a technical panel it is now common to assume that medical expenditures will rise one per cent faster than per capita GDP growth. But since US health costs already comprise 20.6 per cent of US consumption, and 14 per cent of GDP, this soon creates problems, crowding out either non-health consumption or investment or both. One study finds that rising health costs are most likely to lead to 'declines in the real non-health consumption, particularly [for the] low income elderly' and extra calls on 'public sector financing'.[62] Finding extra resources will be harder because budgetary and trade deficits will also have to be tackled.

The European Commission's estimates of the future cost of health care, and long-term care of the elderly, assumes both more comprehensive entitlement and more rigorous cost control than prevails in the US Medicare and Medicaid systems. Assuming that medical costs will evolve in line with GDP growth and the age characteristics of the population, the EU sees public spending rising from 6.5 per cent of GDP in 2004 to 8.1 per cent of GDP in 2050, an increase of 'only' 1.7 per cent (the quote marks are there because that amount of the GDP of the full 25-member Union is not a modest sum). The Commission itself observes: 'the pure demographic effect of an ageing population is projected to push up health-care spending by between 1 and 2 per cent of GDP in most Member States. At first sight this may not appear to be very large when spread over several decades. However on average it would amount to approximately a 25 per cent increase in spending on health care as a share of GDP'.[63] The Commission also considers the possibility that improved overall health – notably lower morbidity due to advances in health care for the elderly – will reduce the 2050 figure to 7.9 per cent, a rise of 1.6 per cent from 2004, though it cautions that such an effect may be offset by other trends, such as people's propensity to favour more spending on health as they get more prosperous.

Estimating the future cost of long-term care for the elderly is particularly difficult. In the last decades of the twentieth century improvements in the fitness of the old and the policy of encourageing the frail to live at home was associated with a reduction in residential care. Such policies were pursued in different ways and with varying results. Where care homes are closed primarily as an economy measure the result can easily be anxiety and even earlier death. But where there are well-resourced community-care services and health provision a non-residential approach can, for many older people, be greatly preferable to institutionalization. What should be uppermost is concern for the health and autonomy of the older person, not a determination to minimize costs.

In 1997 Britain's newly elected Labour government established a Royal Commission headed by Sir Stewart Sutherland to investigate how best to provide for the costs of long-term care for older people. The government was concerned to contain costs by stipulating that social insurance would only cover medical costs, not 'personal care'. But the Commission warned against confining the notion of care to narrowly medical expenses: 'The most efficient way of pooling risk, giving the best value to the nation as a whole across generations, is through services underwritten by general taxation, based on need rather than wealth. This will ensure that the care needs of those who, for example, suffer from Alzheimer's disease – which might be therapeutic or personal care – are recognized and met just as much as those who suffer from cancer.'[64] But New Labour refused to accept this recommendation, which it said would cost nearly £1 billion a year. It also favoured, as we saw above, a continuing switch from public to private provision and a regulatory framework which tolerated poor wages and conditions in many care homes in receipt of public contracts, while those with private coverage are quite differently treated.[65]

In March 2006 the message that elder care was bound to cost much more in future was endorsed by Sir Derek Wanless, former chief executive of the NatWest bank and a man whom the British government had earlier engaged to review NHS finances. In a report for the Kings Fund, a think tank, he urged that if proper provision were to be made for elder care the government should anticipate spending much more on elder care in future and that it should abandon its existing means test.

Wanless saw elder care costs rising from about £10 billion in 2004 to £29 billion in 2026, or nearly 2 per cent of GDP. He urged that a common approach to all areas of care – care homes places, care at home, meals on wheels, help with bathing, toileting and nursing care – would yield 'better value for money' and would, where possible, restore to the elderly themselves a sense of control over their fate. He warned that the baby boom generation would not accept age discrimination in the provision of care but would demand good quality and reasonable choice. There should, he believed, be a 'core of free services' ensuring a dignified existence, with extra refinements available via a new, 'partnership' system, under which costs would be shared between the public programmeme and the older person where the latter could afford it.[66] The spectacle of a distinguished former banker recommending partial de-commodification of elder care, and of a Labour government resisting that advice, would certainly have shocked Aneurin Bevan, the architect of the NHS.

As the cohort of the over-80s doubles or trebles it will be quite possible for there to be both a growing proportion of fit elder persons and for there to be a need for to be a growing number of residential care home places. Over a period of three decades the number of the dependent elderly in the United States is expected to rise from 7 to 14 million, though with appropriate help many of these would not have to be fully residential. In 2002 the US Bureau of Labor Statistics calculated that 900,000 new paraprofessional, long-term care workers would need to be found between that date and 2012. Denmark and Sweden have shown that the best way of raising standards of elder care is to pay decent wages, encourage unionization and combine training with employment.[67] Often a willingness to spend generously on the support of the frail elderly while they are still at home can render the heavier costs of residential care unnecessary. When assessing costs in this area it is also necessary to be aware that the frail already receive a vast amount of free care from their nearest and dearest. As the numbers of the frail and elderly grow new approaches might include – as Roberto Mangabeira Unger has suggested – arrangements whereby all are expected to undertake some caring duties on an unpaid, or minimally-paid, basis. As he writes: 'Checks sent through the post are not enough: The principle must be established that every able-bodied adult will have a position in both the production system and the caring economy: part of a working life or of a working year should be devoted to the provision of care for the young, the old, the infirm, and the desperate.'[68] This helpfully reminds us that there is a non-commodifiable dimension to care. However, once again, such an approach would itself work best if backed by resources for training and technical or administrative support. It would not render redundant the provision of care homes and professional attention for those requiring them, and widespread acquaintance with the conditions in care homes would strengthen pressure to improve them.

Forecasting the cash needs of elder care is difficult and crucially depends on the anticipated health status of the over-80s. The EU Commission report observes in regard to existing provision: 'About 20 per cent of the estimated dependent population receives long-term care in an institution and about 30 per cent receives formal care at home: hence some 50 per cent of people considered dependent receive no formal care provided by the State and instead rely on informal or no care. Differences across Member States are wide.'[69] The countries that are deemed to have a good balance of community and residential care usually allot 1 to 2 per cent of GDP to this purpose, a proportion that is much more likely to increase than to diminish. The expense of privately furnished long-term care is such that it swiftly becomes too expensive for all but a favoured few. For home-owners, selling or remortgeing their dwelling can be a desperate expedient, as was noted above. And if they sooner or later do sell their home this contributes to feelings of isolation and loss of hope, deepening institutional dependence.

If there is a publicly organized system of social insurance covering both health and retirement, then there will be scope for some risk-pooling between these two. On average those with serious health problems will be less long-lived than the healthy and so will have less need of a pension – but will be in greater need of health care. The healthy will draw less on medical coverage but, if long-lived, will need economic support during their extra years of life. These partially offsetting risks are not as easily captured by commercial organizations because of their scale, which makes it advantageous to construct a comprehensive public system that offers both good pensions and good medical coverage.[70] But despite such risk-pooling the overall costs will still rise because the better the overall health of the elderly population the longer they will live. We are still left with the fact that meeting the livelihood and health needs of a population, at least a fifth or a quarter of whom are aged over sixty-five, is bound to absorb a big chunk of GDP, something like 15–22 per cent if serious poverty and destitution is to be avoided. Arguments about pension provision should start from such orders of magnitude. Existing systems of state provision in the United States and the United Kingdom were framed with far more modest goals in mind.

Having identified a gap, the next chapters consider the origins and actual workings of existing pension regimes to establish whether or not they will be able to meet the bill. The reader will have already gathered that I am sceptical about this. Succeeding chapters will, I hope, explain why. In this chapter I have sketched some of the major challenges – and, let's face it, costs – posed by the ageing society. I believe that those who wish to defend universal social protection from privatizing trends are right to do so. But in the twenty-first century they will need to find new sources of revenue for these programmes and new models of governance. The commodification of life stages may furnish financial houses with juicy public contracts; as we will see, however, it does not effectively meet ageing costs but rather exacerbates them. Public programmes are also showing signs of strain and will need extra help to meet their promises. We will also discover that traditional methods of delivering pensions can also create 'collateral damage', being bad for employment, fostering inequality or tolerating weak governance.

Notes

1 Jonathan Leake, 'Now Adulthood Starts at 30', *Sunday Times*, 1 August, 2004. The studies referred to were by Elsa Ferri of Britain's Economic and Social Science Research Council and Frank Furstenberg of the University of Pennsylvania.

2 There is ongoing research into these patterns being undertaken at the Institute of Social and Economic Research, University of Essex.

3 Roberto Mangabeira Unger, *What Should the Left Propose?*, London 2006.

4 Thorsten Veblen, *The Theory of Business Enterprise*, New York 1904.

5 'Out of the Mouths of Babes', *Economist*, 24 December 2005.

6 Hutton, *The World We're In*, pp. 154–5.

7 Marie Woolf and Stephanie Goodchild, 'Bankrupt', *Independent*, 29 January 2006.

8 Philip J. Longman, 'The Cost of Children', *US News and World Report*, 30 March 1998, cited Nancy Folbre, *The Invisible Heart: Economics and Family Values*, New York 2002, p. 109.

9 Miranda Green, 'Top Degree "May Not Reap Great Reward" ', *Financial Times*, 15 June 2004.

10 Patrick Collinson, 'Lunchbreak Sessions to Tackle Financial Skills' and 'Study Reveals Financial Crisis of the 18–40s', *Guardian*, 28 March 2006.

11 Ibid.

12 'Out of the Mouths of Babes', *Economist*, 24 December 2005. This report noted that the website of the Student Debt Yearbook had much information on the topic.

13 Jonathan Clements, 'Dodging the Hazards of Post-College Life', *Wall Street Journal*, 7 December 2005.

14 Ibid.

15 Linda Greenhouse, 'Student Debt Collectible by Social Security', *New York Times*, 8 December 2005.

16 Milton Friedmann, *A Theory of the Consumption Function*, Cambridge MA, 1957.

17 For a leading example of this approach, complete with citations of its use by some official bodies see J. Kotlikoff and Scott Burns, *The Coming Generational Storm: What You Need to Know about America's Economic Future*, 2nd edn, New York 2005. The authors do complain that the warnings of the 'generational accountants' are not always sufficiently heeded by officialdom and the media but their gloomy message has certainly received lavish coverage. For a critique of this work see Paul Krugman,'America's Senior Moment', *New York Review of Books*, February 2005. And for a critique of 'generational accounting' as such see Dean Baker and Mark Weisbrot, *Social Security: the Phony Crisis*, Chicago 2000.

18 Ellen Kelleher, 'Equity Release Schemes "High Risk" ', *Financial Times*, 6 January 2006. See also Patrick Collinson, 'Forget Release – You'll Get Punished', *Guardian*, 28 January 2006.

19 Elizabeth Warren and Amelia Warren Tyagi, *The Two-Income Trap: Why Middle Class Mothers and Fathers are going Broke*, New York 2003, pp. 50–1.

20 Jacob Hacker, 'Economic Risk has Shifted from the Government and Corporations to Workers and their Families', *Boston Review of Books*, vol. 30, no. 5, September–October 2005. Hacker notes: 'Although volatility could reflect increased economic mobility other studies show that long term economic mobility has not increased. In fact it may now be lower in the United States than in the traditionally class-bound nations of Europe.' Ibid.

21 Sara Arber, Kate Davidson and Jay Ginn, 'Changing Approaches to Gender and Later Life', in Sara Arber, Kate Davidson and Jay Ginn, eds, *Gender and Ageing*, Maidenhead 2003, pp. 1–14, p. 6.

22 Sara Arber and Jay Ginn, ''Ageing and Gender', *Social Trends*, no. 34, January 2004, p. 10.

23 Jenny de Jong Gierveld, ' Social Networks and Social Well-Being of Older Men and Women', in Arber, Davidson and Ginn, *Gender and Ageing*, pp. 95–110.

24 Kevin Phillips, *Wealth and Democracy*, New York 2002, pp. 345–6.

25 John Hills, *Inequality and the State*, Oxford 2004, p. 57,

26 Michel Houellebecq, *The Possibility of an Island*, London 2005, pp. 61–2.

27 William F. Bassett, 'Medicaid's Nursing Home Coverage and Asset Transfers', Federal Reserve Bank, Economic and Financial Working Papers, 2004-15, Washington DC, 2004.

28 Allyson Pollock, *NHS plc: The Privatisation of Our Health Care*, London 2004, pp. 157–90. For the US see also Sheryl Zimmerman, *Assisted Living: Needs, Practices and Policies in Residential Care for the Elderly*, Baltimore 2001.

29 Eric Klinenberg, *Heat Wave: A Social Autopsy of Disaster in Chicago*, Chicago 2002.
30 Klineberg, *Heat Wave*, p. 237.
31 Simone de Beauvoir, *Old Age*, New York 1972.
32 Margaret Morganroth Gullette, *Aged by Culture*, Chicago 2004.
33 Richard Sennett, *The Culture of the New Capitalism*, New Haven and London 2006, pp. 94–101.
34 In fact, Britain's Labour government in the 1960s had already established, in the shape of the Open University, an organization dedicated to making university-level education open to all, so long as they were prepared to take the requisite foundation courses. Its lectures are carried on public television. By the time Laslett wrote his book the Open University had already established itself as a great success, attracting hundreds of thousands of mature students – including early retirees, mothers whose children had grown up, and grandparents. The OU equipped them to acquire new interests or develop new skills. In Laslett's terms the innovatory courses of this institution catered to both the second and third ages, enabling its students to negotiate a new phase of life in ways they found fulfilling.
35 Peter Laslett, 'What is Old Age?' in Grazielli Caselli and Alan Lopez, eds, *Health and Mortality Among Elderly Populations*, 2nd edn, London 1996, pp. 19–38, p. 32.
36 Pater Laslett, *A Fresh Map of Life: the Emergence of the Third Age*, Basingstoke 1996, p. 249.
37 Uwe E. Reinhardt, 'On the Apocalypse of the Retiring Baby Boom', *Canadian Journal of Ageing*, Summer 2001, vol. 20, supplement 1, 2001, pp. 192–204, p. 193.
38 Despite real defects – cynicism, a fascination with magical fixes – the French Canadian movie *The Barbarian Invasions* (2002), directed by Denys Arcand, had the merit of raising this issue. In it an ageing leftist academic with terminal cancer finds himself lost in an overcrowded hospital. His oil-trader son flies in from London and is persuaded by his mother to help out, notwithstanding his low regard for his dad. The son's Blackberry and gold card swiftly ensure comfortable conditions, an expert diagnosis, a good supply of cocaine and a final gathering in his book-lined country cottage attended by family, estranged former lovers and long-lost friends. The film lampoons but also partakes in a culture which believes that young traders can perform miracles. Nevertheless, its dark humour scores some palpable hits and it's a challenge to come up with a better idea of a good death.
39 Melena Z. Ryzik, 'Moving to a "Don't Grow Old" Programme', *New York Times*, 6 October 2005.
40 This concept of de-commodification of pension provision is elaborated in a classic study by Gosta Esping-Andersen, *The Three Worlds of Capitalist Welfare*, Cambridge 1990, to be further discussed in the next chapter. For caution in using the concept see Viviana A. Zelizer, 'Circuits within Capitalism', in Victor Nee and Richard Swedberg, eds, *The Economic Sociology of Capitalism*, Princeton NJ, 2005, pp. 289–322.

41 These are the differentials for the UK. See Pension Commission, *A New Pension Settlement for the Twenty-first Century*, London 2005, pp. 90, 92.

42 The UK Pension Commission estimates that financing the British State Pension at the current credit guarantee rate in future decades means increasing the qualifying age for the pension to 68.3 in 2030, 71.4 in 2040 and 72.6 in 2050. The alternative of keeping the age of retirement constant but raising more money to pay it, would require ear-marking 6.5 per cent of GDP in 2030, 7.5 per cent of GDP in 2040 and 7.7 per cent of GDP by 2050. (Ibid., p. 101). However, as the Commission accepts, Britain should anyway be seeking to devote about double this proportion of GDP to pension needs.

43 For a discussion of these issues see the contribution of John F. Helliwell to the Jackson's Hole seminar organized by the Federal Reserve Bank of Kansas in 2003.

44 Population Division, United Nations, *Replacement Migration: Is It the Solution to Declining and Ageing Populations?*, New York 2001, pp. 27, 77, 89–91.

45 Sarah Laitner and Stefan Wygstyl, 'Freedom for the Workers: How Europe is Coming to Terms with a Westward March', *Financial Times*, 10 February 2006.

46 John Hills, *Inequality and the State*, pp. 167–8; Andrew Glyn, *Capitalism Unleashed: Finance, Globalization and Welfare*, Oxford 2006, pp. 165–71.

47 Göran Therborn, *Between Sex and Power*, London 2004, pp. 230–1, 285.

48 Philip J. Longman, 'The Cost of Children', *US News and World Report*, 30 March 1998, cited Nancy Folbre, *The Invisible Heart: Economics and Family Values*, New York 2002, p. 109.

49 Hugh Davies and Heather Joshi, 'Who Bears the Cost of Britain's Children in the 1990s?', Working Paper, 1998, Birkbeck College, University of London, cited Paul Johnson, 'Paying for Our Futures: the Political Economy of Pension reform in the UK', paper presented at the conference, 'Why Has It All Gone Wrong? The Past, Present and Future of British Pensions', British Academy, 15 June 2005, p. 42.

50 John C. Caldwell and Thomas Schindlmayr, 'Explanations of the Fertility Crisis in Modern Societies', *Population Studies*, vol. 57, no. 3, November 2003, pp. 241–64, p. 256.

51 Suzanne W. Helburn and Barbara R. Bergmann, *America's Child Care Problem: the Way Out*, New York 2002. See also the review of this book by Ruth Rose for interesting information on Quebec's child care programmes which cover three-quarters of infants aged one to four, *Feminist Economics*, vol. 11, no. 3, pp. 191–5.

52 Caldwell and Schindlmayr, 'Explanations of the Fertility Crisis', p. 256.

53 I use GDP because that is now becoming standard practice. However there is a case for saying that Net National Income would be a better benchmark. The broad target figures for proportions of GDP assume that allowance has be made for more resources to go to investment as well as a rising share for pensions.

54 Pensions Commission, *Pensions: Challenges and Choices*, p. 17. If early

retirement schemes are included private funded provision could rise to the range 3.4 to 4.2 per cent, which would still leave a 4 per cent gap vis-à-vis the projection for constant real retirement ages.

55 European Commission and Economic Policy Committee, *The Impact of Ageing on Public Expenditure*, Brussels, February 2006, pp. 71, 101.

56 Ibid. pp. 71, 101.

57 Douglas Holtz-Eakin, 'Testimony: Social Security and the Federal Budget', 1 August 2002. CBO website.

58 CBO, 'Tax Deferred Reitrement Savings in Long-term Revenue Projections', Washington DC, 2004; Michael J. Boskin, 'Deferred Taxes on the Public Finances', Hoover Institution, Washington DC, July 2003; Alan J. Auerlach, William G. Gale and Peter R. Orszag, 'The US Fiscal Debt and Retirement Saving', *OECD Economic Studies*, vol. 39, 2004, no. 2, pp. 10–23, p. 15. Boskin's projections are condensed in a figure on this last page and show a sharp spike in private pensions around 2018–20 followed by a steady drop. As we will see in Chapter 3 private pension coverage is declining and is often not properly indexed.

59 Richard A. Musgrave, 'A Re-appraisal of Financing Social Security', in *Public Finance in a Democratic Society*, Volume II, *Fiscal Doctrine, Growth and Institutions*, Brighton 1986, pp. 103–22. John Myles, ' A New Social Contract for the Elderly', in Gosta Esping-Andersen et al., *Why We Need a New Welfare State*, Oxford 2002, pp. 130–72.

60 Uwe E. Reinhardt, 'On the Apocalypse of the Retiring Baby Boom', *Canadian Journal of Ageing*, vol. 20, supplement 1, 2001, pp. 192–204, p. 193.

61 Allyson Pollock, *NHS plc: the Privatisation of Our Health Care*, London 2004.

62 Glenn Follette and Louise Sheiner, 'The Sustainability of Health Spending Growth', Federal Reserve Bank Working Paper, 2005–60, pp. 3, 16. These authors construct a scenario based on the 'assumption that society would not want to actually reduce real non-health consumption in order to finance increased health spending.' (p. 6). Yet the 1 per cent 'excess growth' model does lower the non-health consumption of 'some subsets' (the elderly) and only cushions the impact on the rest of non-health consumption by postulating a decline in investment from 16.4 per cent of GDP in 2004 to 11.8 per cent in 2030 and 10.7 per cent in 2050.

63 European Commission, *The Impact of Ageing on Public Expenditure*, pp. 128, 133.

64 Quoted in Pollock, *NHS plc*, pp. 173–4.

65 Ibid.

66 Nicholas Timmins, 'Scrap Means-Testing on Care of Old, Says Study', *Financial Times*, 25–6 March 2006.

67 Sophie Korczyk, *Long-Term Care Workers in Five Countries: Issues and Options*, Public Policy Institute, AARP, June 2004.

68 Roberto Mangabeira Unger, *What Should the Left Propose?*, London 2006, pp. 94–5.

69 Ibid, p. 152.

2

The Divided Welfare State
and the River of Time

The postwar Britain in which I grew up prided itself on being a 'welfare state'. The postwar Labour government had built on foundations laid by Liberals like Keynes and Beveridge, and Conservatives like Winston Churchill and Rab Butler. Roosevelt's New Deal, and its Social Security programme, were seen as kindred achievements. The construction of the welfare state was seen as the dawn of 'social citizenship'.[1]

The US Social Security programme was embraced by President Eisenhower and the Republicans, and the Social Security number became the badge of civic identity. Indeed the benefits it conferred reached a high point in the early 1970s with legislation signed by a Republican President, Richard Nixon. Likewise in Britain, Conservative Prime Ministers – Edward Heath as much as Harold MacMillan – not only accepted the welfare state but added new programmes, such as secondary pensions (MacMillan) and child allowances paid to the mother (Heath). This seemed to be part of a movement in all advanced countries to work towards universal programmes that would eventually cover all the costs of education, health and retirement. Poverty-relief programmes and means tests still survived at the edges, but these programmes were by no means aimed at the poor. The GI Bill allowed any veteran to go to college. In Britain the members of the 'New Labour' Cabinet not only had their university fees paid in their entirety but also received a substantial 'grant' towards their living costs. Those who planned the future of welfare liked to quote the warning, 'benefits for the poor soon become poor benefits'. This watchword is attributed in Britain to Richard Titmuss, one of Labour's most eminent welfare strategists, but in the United States to Wilbur Mills, a veteran Democratic Congressman. The 'welfare' offered by the 'welfare state' improved the life chances of all. It was not until much later, in the last decades of the century, that 'welfare' ceased to be something in which one could take a patriotic pride and came to be associated with a stigmatized minority. Yet pensions, because everyone was entitled to them and paid into them, were often not thought of as 'welfare'. Nevertheless they became a target of 'reform'. Being paid to nearly all members of a swelling age bracket, public pensions loomed large in the budget. They also came to be seen by an increasingly influential lobby as being in competition with independent suppliers, which was not the case when they were first introduced as social insurance for the mass of average wage-earners who could not then afford private coverage.

The apparent postwar consolidation of public programmes of welfare and pension provision gave rise to an impressive literature. Less noticed was the phenomenon of what some have recently called the 'hidden welfare state', or 'divided welfare state', or 'public–private welfare state', defined by public subsidy – in the shape of tax relief – underpinning commercial and private provision.[2] Elite educational and medical facilities were open to those with the money to pay. But private and corporate pensions were different – they were positively encouraged by tax relief to the full value of whatever the employee or employer paid in. It took longer for a small body of work to focus specifically on this and other features of what could be seen a 'residual' system of commercial provision, operating side-by-side with the new, almost universal, provision of rights to education, health and social insurance in old age. In a commanding work of synthesis Gosta Esping-Andersen measured the extent of 'de-commodification' achieved by the different variants of what he called 'welfare capitalism'. The essence of capitalism is generalized commodity production, with labour power also being a commodity. But, following Karl Polanyi, Esping-Andersen saw the capitalist labour market as embedded within a wider social order in which access to certain goods – education, health care and retirement security – was not wholly determined by what could be purchased out of current wages and salaries. In some cases this was the legacy of pre-capitalist paternalism, and in others it was the outcome of pressure from organized labour and other social movements. As he explained: 'The variability of welfare-state evolution represents competing responses to pressures for de-commodification. To understand the concept, de-commodification should not be confused with the complete eradication of labour as a commodity; it is not an issue of all or nothing. Rather, the concept refers to the degree to which individuals, or families, can uphold a socially acceptable standard of living independently of market participation.' [3]

When Esping-Andersen wrote of 'welfare capitalism' he meant that the entire capitalist order had been reshaped by powerful reform movements – and elite responses to those movements – to furnish to all decent levels of education, health care and income support in retirement. Up to around 1980 the trend still seemed to be towards an expansion of non-commercial – 'de-commodified' – public provision, albeit that formidable interest groups defended the tax privileges of private providers in a range of predominantly 'Anglo-Saxon' countries. In the United States the term 'welfare capitalism' referred not to an entire capitalist social order shaped by public welfare programmes, but to the willingness of many companies to offer health and retirement benefits to their own employees, a willingness greatly enhanced by legislation dating from the 1920s and 1940s which offered tax relief to such schemes. The term 'welfare capitalism' never caught on in Britain, but fiscal regulations dating back to the 1920s had long encouraged similar corporate schemes.

It is conventional to distinguish between 'defined benefit' (DB) and 'defined contribution' (DC) pension schemes, with the former guaranteeing a specific pension entitlement calculated in terms of salary and years of contribution while the latter offers only whatever pension can be purchased in the money markets for the sum in the pension pot at retirement. As we will see, public pensions generally offer a 'defined benefit' but, up to the early 1980s, so did most corporate schemes. The latter thus exhibited an element of apparent de-commodification, or insulation from market forces, though the promise was only as strong as the company offering it. Public employees generally obtained DB coverage, often as part of an implicit contract of public service whereby pay was modest but job security, and health and pension benefits, were good. The arrangements made for public sector workers served as a model for the more ambitious private schemes, and, where they were pre-funded, sometimes helped to establish an annuity market that could be used by private pension providers.

Esping-Andersen began the work of bringing the functioning of commercial and corporate pension regimes into a systematic common focus. His classification of welfare states ranged from high to low indices of de-commodification, with the implication that citizens denied good public provision would be driven to rely on private providers. While private health and education were of growing significance in the United States and Britain, Esping-Andersen's figures for private-pension provision in these states showed it to be quite modest, albeit above the level found in most of continental Europe. Thus in 1980, which he took as a benchmark year, public pensions in the UK supplied benefits worth 6.4 per cent of GDP, public sector schemes a further 2.0 per cent, private occupational schemes 1.0 per cent of GDP and personal pensions only 0.1 per cent of GDP. In the United States the public programme, Social

Security, supplied benefits worth 5 per cent of GDP, the public sector schemes 1.5 per cent of GDP, the private occupational schemes 1.4 per cent of GDP and personal pensions 0.2 per cent. It is true that US and UK public pensions lagged a few points behind France, Germany and Sweden (though not Italy), but they were still supplying more than 80 per cent of all pension income.[4] The weak performance of the private schemes was partly to be explained by their comparative immaturity – many corporate schemes had only been founded in the 1950s or later. But even if this adequately explained their weak performance at this point, the question of whether they were efficiently handling the stream of contributions and tax subsidies they received remained undecided. In seeking to quantify the contribution of the different pension methods, Esping-Andersen was showing the need for an integrated approach to assessing pension adequacy.

As it turned out, the year 1980 was a turning point, marked by Margaret Thatcher's successful attempt to weaken indexation of the UK's new system of basic and secondary, earnings-related pensions (about which more below). Reagan attempted to follow suit but was defeated. Paul Pierson was later to describe the strategy of cutbacks as tantamount to what he called 'implicit privatization' in his study *Dismantling the Welfare State* in 1994.[5] Modern welfare states had been born when visionary politicians responded to popular hopes for a better world. But actual welfare regimes have been shaped by state bureaucracies and business networks, and by economic constraints and religious traditions, as much as by politicians looking for popular support. The very idea of pension provision represented an attempt to colonize the future and circumscribe the workings of time, in the real or supposed interests of a group of beneficiaries. At its most generous this was an attempt to construct an overarching framework of 'social security' which would benefit all citizens. But this noble project has been strewn with pitfalls, some stemming from recalcitrant interests and structures, others from the unexpected logic of demography or political economy.

Recent writing has stressed the active or passive role of business leaders in shaping public systems of welfare provision, and has insisted that generous public subsidies to private providers are part of the welfare state too. In *Capitalists Against Markets* (2002) Peter Swenson argues that the extent and character of welfare provision has been determined at least as much by the disposition of employers and the structure of the labour market as by the pressure of class mobilization. Under some circumstances employers find that it makes sense to allow the state to organize the provision of welfare and pensions to all employees and citizens while, under others, they prefer to reach their own agreements with a fragmented – or as he puts it 'segmented' – labour force.[6] In *The Divided Welfare State* (2002), Jacob Hacker also brought business calculation into view by showing how public subsidies have created a thriving industry. He argued that the US and continental Europe have in effect devoted similar public resources to pensions and health care, but that the US has done so by means of massive tax breaks for private provision.[7]

A 'holistic' or integrated approach to the costs of pension provision in the ageing society must strive for a clear view of the combined impact of public and private provision, and of the overall likelihood that they will be able to furnish the needed incomes in retirement. In the last chapter I cited the estimate made by the UK Pensions Commission in 2004, when it warned that the over-65s would need between 13.9 and 16.1 per cent of GDP if they were not to fall behind.[8] This was the first official attempt to estimate such a figure. I also quoted a report submitted to the European Union by Commissioner Joaquin Munera which forecasts overall levels of ageing costs without proclaiming any target. In the United States a quasi-official body, the Employee Benefit Research Institute, also issues relevant, if less comprehensive, forecasts. (In Chapter 3 I draw on EBRI reports which warn of increasing pensioner poverty but do not actually specify a desirable proportion of GDP to be applied to ageing costs.)

There is now mounting uneasiness over the adequacy of retirement provision of all types. But until very recently private systems were believed by advocates of 'pension reform' to be doing very well in the United States and Britain, and were held up as a model for others to follow. One of the reasons why British governments opposed membership of the euro was that they believed that Britain had made appropriate provision for the *Age Shock* and that continental governments had instead lumbered themselves with hugely expensive and unfunded public systems.

Public pension systems were at their most generous in 1980 in most Western states. Around the same time governments saw it as their task to protect the rights of those who contributed to corporate schemes from bad management or hyper-inflation. But in the years 1986 to 1995 European governments began cautiously to explore cutbacks to public provision while promoting commercial, funded pension schemes. The British and US governments gave strong backing to tax-privileged personal pension plans while sending mixed messages to the corporate sponsors of defined benefit schemes. The corporations were urged to offer good quality coverage yet permitted to skip contributions to their pension funds.

Public and occupational pension schemes both have their weaknesses, as I will be explaining in detail. But they nevertheless represent historic attempts to anticipate the needs of ageing populations. Most schemes, whether public or private, offered a 'defined benefit' (DB), calculated with reference to previous earnings and years of contribution. The public systems are very efficient and cost effective. They simply need good benefit formulae and adequate revenue sources in order to deliver good results. The occupational schemes have problematic features and have become prey to financialized capitalism. Indeed the private DB schemes are now very vulnerable to what the financial press calls 'vulture capitalism' – corporate bankruptcies carried through with the aim of dumping pension liabilities. The devaluation of the pension savings of tens of millions of workers is very similar to what David Harvey identifies as 'accumulation by dispossession'.[9] Both public and private pensions systems have witnessed a veritable bonfire of entitlements just at a time when the ageing of populations means that they are needed more than ever before.

In order to understand what is being lost, and to explain the agony of welfare capitalism, I next supply a brief history of pensions, which looks at the origins of today's mixed regimes and asks whether principles which worked in the past still apply in the ageing society.

The Puritan and the Baroque

The first public pensions were conferred as privileges rather than rights, the recipients being soldiers or public servants who had rendered conspicuous service. The English Poor Law allowed that aged paupers should be given some relief, but local gentry and municipalities had great discretion in awarding it. Each parish was responsible only for its own, and relief could be refused, or administered only in the most humiliating way, to those deemed to be bad characters. Nevertheless, by the eighteenth century most English parishes did pay modest old-age pensions to those deemed 'past work', and it was not until the 1830s that residence in a poor house sometimes became a condition of receiving this stipend. Meanwhile the growing sophistication of financial markets made it possible for the wealthy to purchase life insurance and annuities for their spouses or favoured retainers. Relatively simple products of this sort, tailored to one customer or a small group of customers, were available in Renaissance Italy and the Dutch Republic of the seventeenth century. Advances in the calculation of life tables and risk enabled suppliers of life insurance like the Equitable Life Society, founded in 1762, to offer annuity products which enabled their clients to pool risk.[10] Life insurance and pension provision had complementary characteristics, with the former paying out to the survivors of the deceased, while the latter paid out a 'mortality bonus' to the long-lived. Providers often found it made sense to supply both types of financial product, and not infrequently did so on a mutualized basis, that is, the insurer was owned by its customers rather than shareholders. In the case of life insurance, known death-rate probabilities made it possible to pay out the capital sum when needed. Likewise with pensions, actuarial calculation would establish life expectancy, but was also assisted by the fact that only a minority would reach the pension age, and even fewer would claim it for any length of time.

The early United States inherited English approaches to poverty alleviation but was a somewhat richer, and – so far as whites were concerned – far more equal, society than the Britain of the late eighteenth and early nineteenth centuries. Many owned property by their thirties, and possession of a farm, workshop or business was the best source of old-age security. However, the minority without property or profession, and those unable to appeal to propertied relatives, had to throw themselves on a localized and stingy system of public charity. Aged paupers were viewed with distrust. Was not their poverty punishment for past improvidence? Giving them old clothes might be all right but cash would enable them to carouse in the taverns. Why should local taxes be raised to subsidize reprobates who would never repent? Some Protestant pastors openly argued that the 'frosts of old age' did not favour genuine conversions.[11]

There is a dichotomy between a 'Puritan' and a 'Baroque' approach to pension provision. The Puritan approach was individualistic and stressed the rewards of thrift, prudence and hard work. Not a few of today's large pension providers, whether in London, Edinburgh, Boston or New York, stress their roots in Protestant self-help and sport names such as Fidelity and Prudential. This strand of pension provision long preceded the universal public pension and was never entirely eclipsed by it. The

Baroque tradition had its roots in the claim of good monarchs to protect loyal retainers and deserving subjects, especially soldiers and key civil servants. At its limit the royal power was to extend to cover all. While the Puritan spirit famously appealed to indivial self-denial and asceticism, the Baroque beguiled the public with an aesthetic display.

The Elizabethan Poor Law had elements of both approaches, since it was centrally mandated but locally administered. It was later supplemented by special state-sponsored arrangements for old soldiers, who were housed in such imposing structures as London's Chelsea Hospital, itself inspired by Les Invalides, founded by Louis XIV. Meanwhile, in both Britain and France there were stipends for retired civil servants, notably the employees of Customs and Excise.

In France there were several proposals in the last years of the Ancien Régime to develop a universal system of old-age pensions. Condorcet argued that the risk-pooling pioneered by private insurance houses would be even more effective if carried out on a national scale by a public body. If applied universally such principles would enable the scourge of old-age poverty to be banished – because after all only a minority were going to survive much past 45 years of age. In April 1794 the Revolutionary National Convention enacted a decree influenced by this approach, also calling for old people's homes in every department and setting aside a special day every year to honour aged citizens and to invite them to impart to the young a hatred for tyranny. But the overthrow of the Jacobin republic a few months later doomed this attempt, and it was left to the Chancellor of the German Reich, Count Otto von Bismarck, to introduce the first national old-age pension in 1889. Bismarck believed that the legitimacy of the monarchy, challenged in different ways by the Social Democrats and the Catholic Church, would be strengthened if the Kaiser raised the aged out of poverty and prevented them from becoming a burden on their relatives. In Britain social reformers and trade unionists pressed for a similar programme leading, in 1908, to Lloyd George's Old Age Pension Act. These pension systems embodied a weak notion of pension rights – weak because the pensions were not that generous and were conditional on means-testing to prove poverty. Means tests actually reduce the attractions of private pensions or the schemes offered by some paternalistic employers.[12] However in the Anglo-Saxon countries the Puritan self-help approach, and commercial organizations and 'friendly societies' rooted in it, not only survived as a still-crucial component of the overall system, but were endowed with fiscal privileges. The trade unions had a stake in 'friendly societies', voluntary mutual insurance clubs run for their members, which they believed should be entitled to legal protection and favourable tax treatment. But the task of supplying old-age pensions to all of the growing numbers of the elderly proved beyond the capability of non-state institutions.[13]

Increases in longevity, industrialization and urbanization, and the rising numbers of the population without a claim on small property, made it seem more reasonable for the public authorities to furnish basic social insurance to risks like old age and disability. Social reformers and labour organizers campaigned for old-age pensions, or the 'endowment of old age' as they put it in Britain. Governments saw pension provision as a way of boosting their legitimacy and weakening opponents. The pension systems not only alleviated poverty but also tended to confirm patriarchy and the social hierarchy – there was an echo of the Baroque here, which could be seen in differential contribution/pay-out conditions, and special regimes for the military and key civil servants. Esping-Andersen detected a legacy from Absolutist monarchy in such arrangements, and this chimes in with what I have called their Baroque features.[14] Such an impulse was not entirely lacking even in the United States, where public pensions were conferred on Navy veterans in the early nineteenth century and, on a lavish scale for veterans of the Union army after the Civil War.[15]

The pressure for universal provision developed slowly. In the meantime many of the aged worked till they dropped, or were lucky enough to have a paternalist employer, or a profession, or just enough property (a farm or small business) to keep them going in old age and to ensure the help of their heirs. In the United States Puritan resistance to a public pension was greatly weakened when the Great Crash of the 1930s wiped out the savings of millions of hard-working Americans. The Social Security Act of 1935, responding to this crushing market failure, laid the basis for a national retirement pension scheme. Because the richer states had large numbers of workers living on average, or below average, incomes they could nevertheless be won to a programme which would, as part of a wider scheme of redistribution, also redistribute income from rich to poor states. At first the programme did not cover millions of farmers, small businessmen, women in domestic service and rural workers, especially Southern Blacks and itinerant whites. However it did cover those whose existence was most wholly dependent on wages and salaries, and it reflected a growth in national sentiment and class attachments. It was not until amendments adopted in 1950 and 1954 that Social Security

became nearly universal in scope.[16] Married women received entitlements based on their husband's contributions or their own, whichever
were the greater. Since women often had a broken contribution history
because of family responsibilities, they were rarely able to improve on the
pensions to which they were anyway entitled through marriage. This
meant that the contributions they made as employees brought them no
extra entitlement.[17] Men who contributed more because they were
better paid, on the other hand, received a slightly higher pension in
consequence.

Social Security nevertheless benefited both women and minorities.
Unlike commercial annuities, the pensions paid to women were not
reduced because of their greater average longevity. The programme
offered not only an old-age pension, but also survivor benefits to the
widows of men who died before reaching the age of retirement. While
the pension that women receive from Social Security only weakly reflects
the contribution they have made, the public pension became, as it
remains, more significant than any private entitlement most women
can build. Good occupational schemes, especially in the public sector, can
help women who have enough qualifying years. Many Blacks and
Hispanics lack the earnings power really to benefit from private pensions,
so they also depend on Social Security and, where they qualify, public-
sector occupational schemes. All those who nevertheless fall below a
certain threshold can appeal to a poverty-relief programme, which caters
to about 5 million people today, compared with the 44 million supported
by Social Security.

President Roosevelt insisted that, in order to safeguard Social Security
from future attacks, it should be financed by specific contributions rather
than from general taxation. Contributions took the form of a flat-rate
payroll tax paid up to a threshold set at about twice average earnings. It
was the contribution record that established the right to the pension, not
the mere fact of being a citizen or resident of the United States. By the
mid-1950s nearly all US citizens would be covered, with farmers and the
self-employed brought into the fold together with employees, their
spouses and dependents.

By the last decades of the twentieth century the majority of really poor
seniors were women, as we saw in the last chapter (Table 1.1). They were
women who had never married, or widows whose husbands had
inadequate contribution records and who received no recognition for
their own contributions. Male workers with long-term earnings signifi-

cantly below the median, or with many breaks in their contribution record, would also receive a Social Security pension that was below the poverty line. Nevertheless the Social Security programme was in principle both redistributive and universalistic – everyone paid in and everyone could claim. The contributory and universal approach helped to build both entitlement and public support. Because the Social Security pension was not means-tested it should not be seen as a safety net. It is true that, if private provision failed, most could count on Social Security to provide a basic pension. But a safety net will catch only those who fall. Because of the absence of a means test, Social Security was there for all, acting as a foundation upon which supplementary provision could be built.

The construction of the first public universal pension systems and the wider process of the 'invention of retirement' created a new status, but was itself the product of a mixture of civic and class struggle. Trade unions and social reformers accused employers and governments of either working older employees to death, or throwing them on the scrap heap. While willing to accept company schemes, they still usually insisted that governments alone had the scope to establish universal measures of social insurance. The political leaders who sponsored the first public old-age pensions – Bismarck, Lloyd George, Franklin Roosevelt and Truman – were bidding for votes at times of great social turbulence. They saw themselves as heading off class conflict and showing how a more enlightened policy could restore the authority of the established order. Moreover some business leaders could see the advantage of the state taking over aspects of social insurance that could become a cumbersome burden for the private employer. The Social Security amendments of 1950 were passed against a background of a showdown between unions and employers. Social reform and civic entitlement were often linked to national pride and patriotic mobilization. Many of those who pressed for the introduction of old-age pensions saw them as a way of rescuing fellow citizens from poverty and perhaps allowing them to escape fears for their own future.

The introduction of old-age pensions reduced the numbers of those still in work after the new retirement age. In the UK in 1931 over a half of men over sixty-five were in work; by 1961 this had dropped to a quarter and by 1981 to only one in ten. In the United States the proportion of men aged sixty-five or over who were still working was no less than 68.3 per cent in 1890, dropping to 55.6 per cent in 1920, 41.8 per cent in

1940, 30.5 per cent in 1960, 24.8 per cent in 1970 and 16.3 per cent in 1990.[18] This continuous decline, despite steady increases in fitness and life expectancy, can be seen as the 'invention of retirement'. While corporations were happy to lose less productive older workers, the retirees, if they had a decent pension, welcomed the free time they gained.

The old age pension, once obtained, was a lifetime civic entitlement, rather than a 'deferred wage' or a commercial contract. Precisely because public pensions have been a mechanism of de-commodification they became the target of very controversial 'reforms' that revise or cancel the gains and concessions they embody. The same has become true of collective pension rights in 'defined benefit' schemes conceded by public or private employers, who now try to renege on agreements made decades ago.

The Option for Pay As You Go

It is only across considerable stretches of time that it becomes clear who has gained from an inter-temporal bargain that can turn into a game of musical chairs in which, when the music stops, many retirees find themselves with nothing to sit on. Another dimension stems from the arcane logic and complex rules of many schemes and the disappearance of the funding that was to sustain them. During the postwar boom and for a while longer the resources flowing into pension schemes, whether public or private, were generally considerably in excess of outgoings.

The appearance of sizeable pension reserves was the inevitable concomitant of contributory pension systems combined with economic growth and varying cohort sizes. This posed the question of what types of asset it would be appropriate for publicly controlled pension trust funds to hold, and who should be given the responsibility of managing these funds. In the United States and Britain, leading businessmen, politicians and bank officials urged that there could be no question of public trust funds owning corporate stock. If they did they might acquire leverage over the investment process and be tempted to meddle in business affairs. Reflecting such anxieties, US and UK Treasuries issue IOUs to the pension and Social Security trust funds that are barred from holding other assets. In consequence surplus cash that flows into the public offers as pension contributions is actually used to defray any urgent need that presents itself. If such funds were earmarked only for public infrastructure investment, as in Japan, their investment would at least be contributing to future economic strength, and hence pension provision. As it is, trust fund surpluses give more latitude to the public authorities, whether they use it well or ill.

Such fears have also surfaced in other countries whenever pre-funding seemed advisable. They were behind the huge controversy which erupted when the Swedish Social Democrats pressed for pre-funded secondary state pensions in 1958–9; in deference to this outcry elaborate precautions were added to the trust fund to prevent it from meddling in the world of private business. In Germany and Italy another solution was adopted. Corporate boards were themselves entrusted with the custodianship of pension reserves. In Singapore the Provident Fund was permitted to take stakes in a wide range of assets but this was organized under the aegis of a state elite which enjoyed the confidence of the island's fledgling business and financial community, and which was insulated from democratic control.

As the new, supposedly universal, pension systems were established the contribution requirement was only loosely applied. Older male workers were usually credited with contributions they had not made, or which they had made to a system that had been destroyed by hyper-inflation and economic collapse. This 'blanketing in' was possible because these schemes all make great use of the pay-as-you-go financing system. Over time benefits were increased, contributions raised and the contribution record came to determine the precise entitlement. As in the US, wives who did not work full-time derived rights to a pension according to their husband's contribution record, conditions which left many older women with a weaker entitlement even in the more generous pension systems. The 'pay-as-you-go' system of pension finance was adopted because it enabled fairly good pensions to be paid out quite quickly, using the blanketing- in of notional contributions. The stream of income to the system was used to pay current pensions, with any surplus going to a trust fund, which was invested not in the stock market but in low–interest public bonds.

The pay-as-you-go system can only be used by a public authority, which is able to count on its ability to tax future generations to pay the entitlements accrued by current workers, since the latter's contributions are going to pay current pensioners. Indeed this system, as Paul Samuelson pointed out in a classic article, only balances its books by counting on contributions from the unborn.[19] There are, of course, a great many social arrangements which the 'unborn' find in place – their family, the language they speak, reigning political institutions and so forth – all of which most individuals are happy to inherit and which are scarcely a matter of choice. A well-functioning pay-as-you-go system is easily seen as an asset and worth supporting. In postwar conditions in Europe and the United States, pay as you go worked particularly well because the income to such systems is determined by what is happening to wages and employment. If these are rising steadily – as was the case in 1950–72 – benefits and entitlements can rise commensurately. The workforce was growing and so was productivity.

The language of pension rights or entitlements applies in somewhat different ways to public pension schemes and personal-pension plans, and, since both are linked to past contributions, prevailing legislation and uncertain future conditions, neither is unqualified. It is true that well over 90 per cent of the population will have rights in the public-pensions systems, but there remain significant numbers of older women who are not fully covered, because they didn't marry, or their husband failed to make contributions, or because they did not have formal employment, or some combination of the foregoing. In the UK women's unpaid labour in the home has only very recently been given some recognition, with the Pensions Commission urging that this be made a much stronger strand of entitlement to the second state pension. Likewise members of immigrant communities often do not have the prescribed length of contribution record – say thirty-nine years for a full UK pension for a woman. There are currently proposals in several European countries for the introduction of 'citizen pensions', which would only require a record of residence.

Pension systems are very expensive and the tremendous boost which war gave to the taxing capacity of the state – especially World War II – played a key role in showing that it was possible to pay for expenditure on this scale. The connection of welfare regimes to wartime experience was, however, complex as well as close. One of the most successful and long-lived welfare regimes, the Swedish 'national home', arose in a non-combatant country and, like all other welfare regimes, it reflected a peculiar mixture of class struggle and class collaboration. While the terms of the compromise were proposed by trade union economists – Gösta Rehn and Rudolf Meidner – the employers found that the 'solidaristic' wage-bargaining round secured advantageous conditions for Swedish large-scale industry, regulating their wage costs and enabling exporting corporations to seize favourable postwar openings.[20] It was only in future decades that tensions surfaced when trade union plans encroached on the Swedish life insurance business, or threatened to break up the ownership of the main industrial groups (on which more below).

In Germany and Japan, the starkness of defeat and the urge to reconstruct shattered national economies allowed plenty of scope to public authorities in devising systems of social security that would dovetail with industrial recovery. Banks participated in this process as leaders of industrial groups rather than as providers of financial products. The French haute bourgeoisie was sufficiently discredited to allow the Council of the Resistance great scope in devising the postwar social security and pension system. The Communists, Socialists and Gaullists all agreed on a corporatist and republican structure in which unions and employers collaborated as trustees and managers of the solidaristic, pay-as-you-go pension regimes which the Council established. The term used to describe this settlement was 'repartition', or sharing, and it did permit both the incorporation of older workers lacking contributions and an element of cross-subsidy between different occupational schemes.[21]

Pension coverage became steadily more generous throughout the Western world during the postwar boom, as wage growth boosted receipts to the pay-as-you-go systems. This happy scenario was interrupted in the 1970s not by any demographic shock, as is sometimes implied, but by economic shocks and a subsequent rise in unemployment in the later 1970s and after.[22] From the mid-1970s welfare regimes came under strong pressure to cut back pension benefits and to extend commercial coverage and subsidies. The parties of the Left failed to consolidate and extend welfare gains, or to come up with effective answers to the 'stagflation' which brought an end to the postwar boom in the 1970s. Trade unions were greatly weakened. Their bargaining power was reduced by three simultaneous developments which expanded the available labour force. First by the coming of age of the baby-boom generation, secondly by the entry of more women into the labour force; and thirdly by the outsourcing of jobs to newly industrialising lands. The reappearance of unemployment reduced labour's bargaining power. In the US hourly wage rates remained stagnant for over two decades despite increases in productivity. Household incomes rose modestly only because there were more homes with two earners. Pay-as-you-go financing was by no means a crushing burden during the last decades of the twentieth century; in fact such programmes were taking in more money than they were paying out. However, by weakening demand these programmes could, if this imbalance was not counteracted, also weaken employment, an effect that was most pronounced in continental Europe because of the scale of its public-pension systems.

Despite economic woes, public-pension regimes in most countries other than the UK proved quite resilient down to the last years of the twentieth century. The French, German and Italian pension systems have delivered, and despite cut-backs still deliver, a more generous pension than do those of the US or the UK. The US Social Security system delivers a better, non-means-tested, pension than the UK's basic state pension (BSP), and has so far withstood all attempts to dismantle it. British pensioners who are poor enough to qualify for a Pension Credit, and willing to claim it, receive a total pension which replaces 30 per cent of average earnings – the Social Security pension is set at around the same replacement rate, but goes to every former employee or their spouse. The UK Pension Credit is a new programme, but early indications suggest that more than a fifth of those entitled to significant payments failed to claim them. These pension systems – the US included – are based on the principle that all those who contribute receive a benefit, as of right. In Britain too, everyone who has the appropriate contribution record receives the BSP, but a means-test limits the right to the more generous Pension Credit. To this extent the Pension Credit really does operate as a safety net – it is only paid to those who have inadequate provision for retirement – and not a platform on which other provision can be built. If the UK government's 2006 White Paper is embodied is legislation the proportion of pensioners covered by the Pension Credit will remain at about a third rather than rising sharply. This strategy document envisages linking the state pension to earnings not prices, beginning in 2012 or a little later. But the newly-indexed state pension will still be rather modest and the Pension Credit a needed supplement for many. The persistence of means-testing gives many of the low paid a disincentive to save.

The Divided Welfare State

Even during the heyday of postwar collectivism, private pensions survived and thrived in some key states. In countries with a historically strong stock market – especially the United States and Britain, but also Switzerland and the Netherlands – finance houses continued to offer pension products such as annuities to the better off, and paternalistic large corporations still sponsored their own plans. The financial-services industries in the UK and the US had the greatest success in securing state support on their own terms. Wall Street and the City of London successfully argued that personal and corporate saving should be independently and commercially managed, but subsidized by generous tax breaks. In contrast, the Swiss and Dutch finance houses were induced to participate in pension regimes that were nearly universal, and the Dutch was quite closely regulated.

US and British corporations and their managers have had a variety of reasons for offering their employees participation in a pension or health-care plan. One study summarizes the case as follows: 'bargained fringe benefits continued to serve many of the old purposes of stabilising the employee population of the plant, and increasing its attachment, if not to the work, at least to the job. Reducing labor turnover of prime adult males, and increasing the seriousness of the threat of disciplinary discharge (which came to mean loss of accrued seniority and welfare entitlements), increased management's control of the workforce.'[23] However, as this author concedes, the unions were usually happy to accept the proffered benefits, or even pressed for them. Legislation of 1940, which was subsequently greatly extended, meant that the sums contributing to pension and health benefits were free of tax, an arrangement that was particularly prized at a time when tax rates were high. And while managers hoped to discipline labour, they also used benefit packages as a way of competing for scarce workers. There was a steep hierarchy of such packages, with the best usually offered by companies that dominated their domestic or export markets. This was, as Swenson puts it, the fruit of a 'segmented' rather than 'solidaristic' market structure, and it steadily undermined and replaced the dramatically egalitarian 'wage compression' of the wartime years.[24] In the 1950s and 1960s the employees at large, well-placed companies enjoyed better benefits than most of those at smaller concerns, but in more recent decades entitlement differentials between 'insiders' and 'outsiders', core and casual or part-time employees, have grown. Trade unions are tempted to salvage what they can by defending the entitlements of the existing core workforce while allowing new recruits or part-timers to be excluded. As we will see, this turns out to be a short-sighted and self-defeating approach, striking at the very basis of trade-union bargaining power.

Although Anglo-American managers might stress such issues as labour retention, they themselves were also beneficiaries in these schemes. The difficulty of defending tax-privileged 'top hat' pension schemes for bosses, while denying them to employees, led to legal stipulations that pension schemes must be open to all employees. Although there were legal limits on what a manager could contribute to a scheme, these limits were quite generous, and as higher-rate payers they gained more from the tax breaks than anybody else. In recent decades the richest 10 per cent of households have been the recipients of over half of all pension-related tax relief in both the UK and the US.[25] Leslie Hannah rightly stressed that managerial self-interest was a powerful element in the setting-up of occupational schemes.[26] This 'tax relief' is sometimes referred to as 'deferred' tax because tax will be payable on the eventual pension when it is paid out. But pension income is usually taxed at a lower rate, and some of the accumulation in the pension pot, or some of the eventual payout, will be tax free.

Down the years fitful attempts have been made to reduce tax concessions that deprive treasuries of huge revenues – recently around $120 billion each year in the United States and £19 billion annually in the United Kingdom. The US Tax Reform Act of 1986 was initially intended to claw back such concessions in order to help restore public finances at a time of spiralling deficits. But Robert Packwood, the Republican chair of the Senate Finance Committee, stopped this initiative in its tracks. As Hacker explains: 'Packwood's hardline stance was backed by a powerful coalition of insurance companies, business groups and labor unions bent on preserving the tax-subsidized private welfare system that had been firmly institutionalised in the postwar era . . . eliminating the tax exemption for private benefits would have imposed immediate and traceable costs on all Americans covered by the pension plans.'[27]

In Britain, Labour and Conservative administration found pension-related opt-outs and tax privileges extraordinarily difficult to remove or reduce. In the late 1960s, then pensions minister Richard Crossman was warned by joint delegations of employers and unions that that they must be able to retain their ability to opt out of any state second-pension scheme.[28] When Labour came to legislate on pensions in 1975 it respected this injunction. In the following decade Nigel Lawson, the Conservative Chancellor of the Exchequer, was anxious to phase out the tax-free lump sum which British pension scheme members can claim at retirement. In his memoirs he explains that the outcry which followed showed the 'awesome power of the pension fund lobby' and recalled: 'at the boardroom lunches I attended at this time all talk of the state of the economy, or of their own businesses, was suspended, as directors turned the conversation to the all-important question of their pensions.'[29]

The privileged position of tax-favoured pension and health care provision thus created a 'divided welfare state', supported both by business lobbies and by beneficiaries with a record of contributions.[30] The scheme members saw their own money go into the plan and saw their promised 'defined benefit' pension and health care entitlements as an integral part of the labour contract. There is even a certain collective logic in the DB schemes, since they usually employ risk-pooling as well as asset-pooling among participants. 'Defined Contribution' (DC) plans can also be sponsored by an employer but the latter no longer guarantees any particular pension. The DC plan became more widespread in the 1980s and it also attracted tax relief. Such instruments as the US Individual Retirement Account (IRA), the 401(k) – named after a chapter of the US Internal Revenue service code – and even the British 'Stakeholder Pension' have all been especially attractive to higher-rate payers (in the UK the higher paid have been able to purchase Stakeholders for their spouses).

Most DC pension schemes and personal pension plans have the logic of a commercial transaction. Those who contribute have the right to be fairly and honestly treated, but no specific pension promise is being made. In the DC scheme market risk is entirely borne by the contributor. If the market slides then the pension will follow it. Governments in a growing list of countries now give tax relief to such plans, and employers in the US and the UK have increasingly switched to offering them over the last two decades. On the other hand the 'Defined Benefit' occupational pension schemes cannot easily be wound up, however anxious employers may be to get rid of them. Indeed just as the last decade has seen a concerted assault on the more generous 'defined benefit' public pension schemes in Italy, France and Germany, so the corporate DB schemes have become the target of 'vulture capitalism', a phenomenon that will be explored in the next chapter.

As Hacker stresses, pension regimes tend to be 'path dependent'.[31] Once citizens or employees have vested rights in a pension system, whether public and universal or private and segmental, they will be disposed to defend them. Powerful as this path dependence undoubtedly is, it can be disturbed by shocks, whether internally generated or externally imposed, which allow 'regime change'. This happened around mid-century in the United States, where Depression and war allowed a 'Puritan' regime to be significantly qualified by the construction of a universal public pension. Likewise in Sweden there have been major regime shifts, at mid-century and again in the 1990s, the first stemming from broad popular mobilization and the second from the economic crisis of 1992. A pension system which seems no longer capable of delivering on its promises will be vulnerable. In different ways both existing public and private pension systems now experience that vulnerability, as successive chapters will show. They remind us that there is something distinctly ambitious about any attempt to guarantee flows of economic resources many years in the future.

Generational Arbitrage

Many ways of thinking about inequality and social division assume a continuous present. They seek to identify who gains and who loses, who is included and who excluded, by core social institutions and practices. Age cohorts can be isolated and identified in this way too. Their relative size, situation, cultural resources and historical experience lay the basis for generational identities and projects. Thomas Jefferson observed that each generation is a new country. As individuals bid for self-expression, recognition, responsibility and rewards they will appeal to, or help constitute, that generational identity or project. Hence such well-known constructs as the 'Great Generation', those born in around 1900–25, or the 'baby-boomers', born in the period 1945–65, who partake of a certain generational as well as class or gender experience. On the other hand each generation is bound to its predecessors and successors by the life course. All individuals acquire a primary identity from their long period of dependence as infants and children. Later many will seek and support the parental role. The maturation curve allows new generations to assert themselves but also perpetuates a cycle of inter-generational dependence applying to the young and the old.

Generations are trapped in a one-way flow of time, posing a challenge to the market's rules of simultaneous exchange. However the life course still offers scope for a cycle of delayed reciprocity, whereby the debt to parents is repaid in old age. In pre-industrial societies kinship systems furnished a mechanism for meeting the needs of dependent young and old, while charity dealt with those without kin or in poverty. National 'cradle to grave' welfare regimes sought to end poverty and to use risk-pooling both within and between generations, congruent with modern aspirations to equality, liberty and solidarity.

Pensions are devices for conferring rights to future streams of income. Capitalism is also such a device. Profits, rent and interest are also claims to future income streams rooted in the ownership of assets. (As noted above, capital is the discounted present value of the anticipated stream of earnings from an asset.) That capitalism can generate conflict between employers and employees is well known – such conflict ebbs and flows, but in 2004–5 management at Wal-Mart and Boeing found that it can still easily flare up. Sadly, there can also be conflict between different age groups within the same workforce, especially where they enjoy different entitlements to non-wage benefits (Chapter 3 will supply examples). But over and above such antagonisms there is also the implicit conflict between devoting some future tax or asset income to pay pensions, or allowing it to go to other recipients, whether deserving or otherwise. In different ways fiscal systems and property systems both seek to determine future income flows, and their intimate interdependence and rivalry plays a large role in determining pension provision.

The pensioner's rights have traditionally been built up through public or private service, or financial contributions. Usually such rights take many years, or even decades, to acquire. The power to confer a pension exercised by a sovereign or government, or by a private institution or wealthy individual, is a reflection and confirmation of their power and their recognition of service. But however sincere they may be, and authoritative they may seem, pension-givers have to be able to deliver many decades after the promise has been made – like they say, the opera is not over until the fat lady sings. Pensions have to be understood by means of a kind of longitudinal or inter-temporal political economy or sociology. The latter registers today's social arrangements, but understands that the final shape of the deal that has been struck – whether it be between sovereign and subject, government and citizen, employer and worker, master and servant, customer and financial supplier, husband and wife – will only be known when the last payment is made due under the pension agreement.

These days the great majority can expect to live to long past retirement age – in most developed countries, on average, about an extra twenty years once they've reached sixty-five. Of course, students and young people generally – very understandably – don't give any thought to this. Indeed they often believe that they'll live forever – exactly how, they're not sure. Ageing is something that happens to others. We all tend to discount ageing as something that happens to one's body, but not to the core self. Today's employee accepts a wage or salary, and establishes pension rights essentially by making contributions, whether to a government or private scheme. However the link between present contribution and future benefit is at best indirect, if not entirely fictitious.

Political leaders exploit voters' tendency to focus on the present and disregard the future, the result being a sort of longitudinal arbitrage, in which immediate comforts hide future losses. In 1994 the first Berlusconi government in Italy collapsed, largely because it had attempted a deeply unpopular pension reform. The parties of the Left then supported the centre-left Dini government, which brought forward its own 'compromise' proposals in 1995, that rapidly passed into law. Any worker who had contributed into the pension system for eighteen years or more was guaranteed to retain full benefits under the existing scheme. Those with less than eighteen years of contributions will still be entitled to benefits at the old rate on any contributions already made. The new, much reduced, entitlement rules will only fully apply to those who began employment after 1995. It is estimated that half of Italy's pensioners in 2050 will still be enjoying some benefits accrued under the old system. Nevertheless, the effect of the Dini reform is to achieve a reduction in pension expenditure from about 2014, becoming even sharper after 2025. Likewise, the Swedish reform enacted around the same time will not reduce pensions until 2020 and will not be fully implemented until 2040, yet shrinks the pension bill just when it was due to surge.[32] Neat as this is, it ignores the fact that the cost of pensions was due to rise, not because pensioner incomes were going to rise more rapidly than average income but because there are going to be more older citizens in need of it. The new regime will also involve a transition period when younger workers are paying high contributions to a pension system which will pay them very modest pensions, falling well short of what will be needed to maintain their relative position.

Another, milder, exercise in postponed disentitlement was the 1983 US National Commission on Social Security Reform headed by Alan Greenspan. The Commission was invited to save the scheme from an imminent deficit. This it did partly by raising contribution rates. But it also recommended that the retirement age should be raised by two years –

but this would not be phased in for over twenty years, pushing this potentially unpopular change well into the next century.

The formula dubbed 'implicit privatization' by Paul Pierson was pioneered by the Thatcher government in Britain in 1980.[33] The change was seemingly quite small and attracted little notice. It stipulated that in future the basic state pension (BSP) would be upgraded each year in line with the increase in prices – not, as had formerly been the case, the increase in earnings. Between 1980 and 1997 this reduced the value of the BSP from 20 per cent of average earnings to less than 15 per cent. In 1987 the Thatcher government also scaled back the newly established second-state pension, or State Earnings-Related Pension (SERPS). To drive home the message that people should, in future, look to the private sector if they wanted a decent pension (the essence of 'implicit privatization'), employees were encouraged to take out personal pension plans and to opt out of any enhanced state pension; indeed, the campaign even encouraged employees to leave good occupational schemes. It was subsequently found that one and a half million people had been 'mis-sold' private pension plans which were inferior to either SERPS or to their previous occupational plan. Notwithstanding this scandal Margaret Thatcher believed that the pension cutbacks were one of her most daring achievements. She wrote: 'Because we controlled public expenditure effectively in the 1980s – particularly by limiting the basic retirement pension and other long term benefits to prices rather than incomes and scaling back SERPS – Britain already enjoys an advantage over other European countries which failed to take such action.'[34]

Tony Blair's New Labour government, elected in 1997, refused to restore the earnings link, despite the fact that Britain's state pension was by then one of the meanest in Europe. In 1998 Blair endorsed a government Green Paper, which looked forward to a continuing decline in the public contribution to pension incomes (a drop from 60 to 40 per cent) to be offset – supposedly – by a dramatic increase in private provision (which was meant to rise from 40 per cent to 60 per cent over the same period). The Green Paper was subtitled *A New Partnership for Pensions*, with the partners supposedly being the financial services industry. However the latter did not like the government's new pension product, the Stakeholder pension, because it established a one per cent annual cap on charges. The Stakeholder flopped, the private contribution to retirement incomes stubbornly refused to rise and the commercial sector was dogged by a succession of mis-selling scandals and defaults (notably Equitable Life in 2001 and Federal Mogul in 2002). It was against this background that the Pensions Commission was eventually set up in 2002.

The US Social Security old-age pension is set at a better level than the UK basic state pensions, but is still not very generous at around 27 per cent of average earnings. Unlike the British pension supplement (the Pension Credit) it is not means tested. However it has been a target for both explicit and implicit privatization. Reagan's budget director tried to slash the value of benefits in 1982 but was stopped in his tracks by a popular outcry led by the many-million-strong AARP (American Association of Retired Persons), the AFL/CIO, and such passionate figures as Congressman Claude ('Red') Pepper of Florida. The Senate passed an unanimous motion condemning the plan. This opened the way to a bi-partisan Commission under Alan Greenspan, which raised the payroll tax or FICA, thus boosting income to the system while also trimming benefits. In 1997 President Clinton set up a White House task force to study the introduction of private accounts. Under Larry Summers, it had made considerable headway until the eruption of the Monica Lewinsky scandal changed the president's priorities and he declared, in a successful bid to rally Democratic support, that the budget surplus should be used to 'Save Social Security First' establishing a Social Security 'lock box'.[35] Albert Gore helped himself by strongly backing the programme, but John Kerry inexplicably downplayed the issue in 2004. George W. Bush set up a Presidential Commission to explore ways partially to privatize Social Security in 2001 but its report failed on two counts: first the members of the Commission could not agree on a common approach, and second they could find no way of tackling the problem of transition to the new regime of personal accounts, other than to raise a loan of over $1 trillion. The president has failed to make any headway with privatization but he continues to recommend it and even to incorporate it into his budget proposals. In their annual reports the Social Security trustees continue to warn that the programme will not be able to pay the pensions it promises some time around 2041. So long as a query remains over the future funding of the programme it will face a more insidious danger than 'explicit privatization' in the shape of benefit cuts that will be tantamount to 'implicit privatization'. This could include raising the retirement age and weakening the indexation of benefits. Such a combination could be presented as 'rescuing' the programme and might attract bi-partisan support – but not in an election year. In Chapter 6 the options will be more fully considered.

Even if Social Security survives unscathed – and this may very well be the case as it is still a very effective and popular programme – there is still good reason for US employees to look for a second pension to boost their expected retirement provision. Unlike many other advanced countries, including the UK, the United States has never had a publicly organized second pension – except for public employees. Instead it has occupational and personal schemes which enjoy generous tax relief. But US retirees are increasingly worried about shortfalls. Social Security pays no more than a subsistence stipend and is not designed to furnish a really satisfactory, still less comfortable, existence. Millions of older workers in the US have seen their hoped-for retirement provision eroded by depressed markets, by lowered rates of return on safe assets, by the closing of 'defined benefit' occupational-pension schemes and by increased medical costs (the destruction of such entitlements will be detailed in the next chapter). To counteract these trends the savings rate should have risen if retirement prospects for the 77 million post-1945 baby-boomers were to replicate those of their parents.

It's not only pensions which can be subject to longitudinal massage. In 2001 President Bush secured passage of a swingeing programme of tax cuts which will eventually deliver huge savings to the wealthy. By 2010 the richest 1 per cent of American households will garner nearly 60 per cent of the gains from the new tax regime, while the bottom 80 per cent will receive about a quarter. But in the first year of the cuts the richest 1 per cent obtained less than a tenth of the gains, while 60 per cent of those gains were garnered by the bottom 80 per cent. Indeed, shortly after passage of the legislation the majority of voters received refund cheques worth a few hundred dollars. Another aspect of the legislation was 'sunset clauses' which restore the status quo ante after ten years. While this might seem an example of legislative restraint it has a different logic. The existence of the sunset clauses allows for comforting future projections of revenue despite the tax cuts. But future legislators, so it is calculated, will not in practice find it at all easy to restore the old tax rates.[36] The overall result is a likely constraint on public revenues just when they will be badly needed.

Frailty and Free Time

Bryan Turner maintains that pensioners and the elderly are stigmatized by their lack of function and their economic dependence.[37] The past is the past, with a shrinking claim on the present and even less on the future. Hedonism and the culture of celebrity have little space for old age. Life is there to be enjoyed by those who have the requisite energy and fortune. Those who were dumb enough to believe their employers' and/or greedy enough to extract an unrealizable promise, deserve their fate. Even apparently respectful terms such as 'pensioner' or 'senior citizen' can easily acquire negative connotations. The supposed tedium of pension discussions may also reflect a devaluing of the old. But Turner, writing in Margaret Thatcher's Britain, underestimated the potential strength of support for public pensions in countries where they had been more strongly and visibly entrenched in the institutions of the welfare state. In the UK the flagship programme of the welfare state was the National Health Service but in the United States it was Social Security. Both programmes survived Thatcher and Reagan and may even survive their successors.

Public pensions replace, or at least supplement, reliance on the family, or one's own savings, as the prop of old age. They also enable the different generations to preserve a degree of autonomy that both parents and children valued. The older person possessed of an adequate pension was less likely to become a burden on their children. At the limit most adults did not want their parents living with them, while still feeling a keen obligation towards them. This intense cluster of sentiments marked out pension provision from other species of social insurance and probably helped to lend it special support. With the ageing of populations the generational spread widens. Not only does the average citizen have more parents than children but they also must expect their grandparents – perhaps even great-grandparents – to be around for longer. A public pension system may find this a bit of a strain but the new 'beanpole' family cannot be looked to as an alternative.

Bryan Turner has also argued that the bestowal of social rights is a device for protecting human frailty and, beneath the complicated contributory formulae, pensions have often been awarded for this purpose.[38] The construction of rights to pensions has certainly been about a duty of care to the frail elderly. But with people looking forward to living well beyond retirement, the pension becomes not so much an insurance policy as a promise of happiness and even self-fulfilment. It is about the opportunity to enjoy life after retirement, to have more free time and to be able to command a modicum of respect from friends and relations. Those who are frail have a claim on the public which is sometimes achieved at the cost of a dependent, supplicant status. The right to a pension in retirement has been seen precisely as a far preferable alternative to being demeaned by acceptance of poor relief. Many older Britons or Americans who readily claim the old-age pension as their due, proudly decline means-tested assistance.

Research by Peter Townsend in the UK and Michael Harrington in the United States showed there to be widespread old-age poverty in the 1960s, a poverty that could prompt guilt, pity or contempt, or a mixture of these.[39] The improvement in the relative position of many pensioners in the last decades of the twentieth century, began to change attitudes towards the growing number of more affluent and assertive retirees. This phenomenon can lead to notions of 'greedy geezers', hiding the persistence of pensioner poverty, especially amongst elderly women, and preparing the public to accept a steady decline in pensioners' relative incomes in future. Today we have a very unequal pattern of pension provision, closer in shape to a pyramid than to an hourglass but with the substantial middle that this implies. As many as two-fifths of those approaching pension age have good coverage in 'defined benefit' and 'defined contribution' schemes but those below the top tenth are nevertheless quite insecure, as we will see in Chapter 3. Meanwhile a similar number hover a little above or below the poverty line. By 2020 and 2030, on present trends, the pensions shortfall will be extending the base of the pyramid.

The baby-boomers have not had a good press, often being portrayed as feckless and fun-loving, self-absorbed and materialistic. These abusive generalizations fail to register that the baby-boomers might have grown up in the halcyon days of the postwar boom, but their adult lives have been lived in the post-1973 world of increased insecurity, sporadic unemployment, slower growth, welfare cuts and increasing polarization. In the United States hourly wage rates were largely flat from the mid-1970s onwards, and household incomes grew because the labour-force participation ratio of the baby-boomers shot up. Many were forced to accept low-paid service or unskilled jobs with minimal health and pension benefits. Others thought themselves lucky because they found a low-paid public sector job, but with reasonable health and pension coverage. But today the deal is being challenged and such workers – whether teachers, janitors, bus drivers or care workers – find their promised benefits the target of 'reform'. The neo-Puritan scapegoating of such people devalues the integrity of the public sphere and of the labours that sustain it.[40]

Of all forms of welfare, pensions have enjoyed the highest degree of legitimacy. We all have parents and we all face the 'risk' of old age. Sarah Irwin challenged Turner's warning by pointing to opinion-poll evidence that the aged are seen as deserving recipients of public funds, in contrast to the unemployed and 'welfare scroungers'. She cited reasons to believe that the fact of intergenerational dependence can and does generate solidarity rather than conflict. [41]

However, Turner is not wrong to point to the corrosive effect of market-based perceptions, which can indeed eclipse a sense of reciprocal obligation between young and old. Modernity itself requires the young to throw off the tutelage of the old. It nourishes a cult of youth that associates ageing with manifold negative traits. Against this there remains an awareness that renewal and self-respect are themselves rooted in a trans-generational human condition. Human beings are distinguished from other animals not only by neotony (lengthy childhood) but also by the greater relative importance they attribute to their forebears in nourishing fundamental identity. The widespread marking of graves characterized the appearance of homo sapiens. But today geographical mobility, social mobility and the longitudinally extended family of four or five generations puts greater strain on the norms of generational solidarity than ever before. Above all, institutions which have been established to provide for the needs of the aged are themselves frail, and subject to constant erosion.

Notes

1 T. H. Marshall, *Citizenship and Social Class*, Cambridge 1950.
2 Christopher Howard, *The Hidden Welfare State: Tax Expenditures and Social Policy in the United States*, Princeton 1997; Jacob S. Hacker, *The Divided Welfare State: The Battle Over Public and Private Social Benefits in the United States*, Cambridge 2002, and Jennifer L. Klein, *For All These Rights: Business, Labor and the Shaping of America's Public–Private Welfare State*, Princeton 2003.
3 Gosta Esping-Andersen, *The Three Worlds of Welfare Capitalism*, Oxford 1990, p. 37.

4 Ibid., p. 84.

5 Paul Pierson, *The Dismantling of the Welfare State: Reagan, Thatcher and the Politics of Retrenchment*, Cambridge 1994.

6 Peter A. Swenson, *Capitalists Against Markets; the Making of Labour Markets and Welfare States in the United States and Sweden*, Cambridge 2002.

7 Jacob S. Hacker, *The Divided Welfare State: The Battle Over Public and Private Social Benefits in the United States*, Cambridge 2002.

8 Pensions Commission, *Pensions Challenges and Choices, The First Report of the Pensions Commission*, London, November 2004, p. 17.

9 David Harvey, *The New Imperialism*, Oxford 2003, pp. 13, 71, 137–82, 205.

10 Gareth Stedman Jones, *The End of Poverty?*, London 2004.

11 An expression used by the Reverend Albert Barnes quoted in Thomas R. Cole, ' "Putting Off the Elderly" ', Middle Class Morality, Ante-bellum Protestantism, and the Origins of Ageism', in David van Tassel and Peter N. Stearns, eds., *Old Age in a Bureaucratic Society*, Westport CT, 1986, pp. 49–65, 60.

12 Blackburn, *Banking on Death*, pp. 31–56.

13 In the first chapter of *Banking on Death* I gave a broad-brush account couched in terms of the Puritan and the Baroque, with the latter reflecting what Esping-Andersen saw as the 'Absolutist' and hierarchical strand of welfare and pension provision. For a far more systematic exploration of how different religious traditions helped to define the character of welfare regimes, see Philip Manow, 'The Good, the Bad and the Ugly: Esping-Andersen's Regime Typology and the Religious Roots of the Western Welfare States', Working Paper 04/3, Max Planck Institute for the Study of Societies, Cologne, September 2004. See also Matthieu Leimgruber, 'Achieving Social Progress Without State Intervention? A Political Economy of the Swiss Three-Pillar Pension System, 1890–1972'. To be published by Cambridge UP in 2007.

14 Campaigns for pension provision in the United States initially focused on state-level provision for mothers as well as Federal provision for veterans. They invoked familistic and patriarchal notions as well as patriotic or nationalistic sentiment, but growing commodification of labour and the spread of mass consumption also fostered class identities. See Theda Skocpol, *Protecting Soldiers and Mothers: the Political Origins of Social Policy in the United States*, Cambridge MA, 1992; Ann Shola Orloff, *The Politics of Pensions: a Comparative Analysis of Britain, Canada and the United States, 1880–1940*, Madison WI, 1993. The growing significance of class identities is traced by Lisabeth Cohen, *Making a New Deal: Industrial Workers in Chicago, 1919–1939*, Cambridge 1990.

15 This widening is traced in Alice Kessler Harris, *In Pursuit of Equity: Women, Men and the Quest for Citizenship in Twentieth Century America*, Oxford 2001, pp. 117–69; Robert C. Lieberman, *Shifting the Color Line: Race and the American Welfare State*, Cambridge MA, 1998, pp. 67–117; and Daniel Béland, *Social Security: History and Politics from the New Deal to the Privatization Debate*, Lawrence KA, 2005, pp. 97–140. Béland points out that location in the socio-economic system explains the initial coverage of the programme,

and argues that Social Security advanced because, unlike public health, it did
not have a vociferous lobby opposing it. The Social Security pension was not
set at a level where it rendered complementary private coverage redundant.
And because it was not means tested it did not inhibit anyone from taking
out private coverage.

16 Nancy Folbre, *The Invisible Heart: Economics and Family Values*, New York
    2002, pp. 96–104.
17 John Macnicol, *Age Discrimination: an Historical and Contemporary Analysis*,
    Cambridge 2006, pp. 210, 257.
18 Paul Samuelson, 'An Exact Consumption-Loan Model of Interest, With or
    Without the Social Contrivance of Money', *Journal of Political Economy*,
    December 1958.
19 Peter Swenson, *Capitalists Against Markets*, pp. 121–66.
20 The details are explained in Tony Lynes, *Paying for Pensions: The French
    Experience*, London 1985.
21 The causes of this downturn are complex but are not to be explained by any
    shrinkage of the labour force since the 'baby-boomers' were only just getting
    their first jobs. See Robert Brenner, *The Economics of Global Turbulence*,
    London and New York 2006, for a penetrating account of the fundamental
    imbalances at work.
22 Howell John Harris, *The Right to Manage: Industrial Relations Policies of
    American Business in the 1940s*, Madison 1982, p. 170. Quoted in Swenson,
    Capitalists Against Markets, p. 47.
23 Swenson, *Capitalists Against Markets*, pp. 47–70, 167–90.
24 Gerard Hughes and Adrian Sinfield, 'Financing Pensions by Stealth: the
    Anglo-American Model and the Cost and Distribution of Tax Benefits for
    Private Pensions', in Gerard Hughes and Jim Stuart, eds., *Reforming Pensions
    in Europe: Evolution of Pension Financing and Sources of Retirement Income*,
    Cheltenham 2004, pp. 163–92, p, 171.
25 Leslie Hannah, 'Why Employer-Based Pension Plans?', *Economic History
    Review*, vol. 45, no. 3, June 1985, pp. 347–54. See also Leslie Hannah,
    Inventing Retirement, Cambridge 1986.
26 Hacker, *The Divided Welfare State*, p. 161.
27 Richard Crossman, *The Diary of a Cabinet Minister*, vol. 3, *Secretary of State for
    Social Services*, London 1977, pp. 176, 206.
28 Nigel Lawson, *The View from Number 11*, London, 1992, p. 368.
29 Hacker, *The Divided Welfare State,* pp. 124–78.
30 Ibid., pp. 9, 26–7, 52–8, 303–11.
31 Antoine Math, 'The Impact of Pension Reforms on Older People's In-
    comes', in Gerard Hughes and Jim Stewart, eds., *Reforming Pensions in
    Europe: Evolution of Pension Financing and Sources of Retirement Income*,
    Cheltenham 2004, pp. 109–62, 111.
32 Paul Pierson, *The Dismantling of the Welfare State: Reagan, Thatcher and the
    Politics of Retrenchment*, Cambridge 1994, pp. 64–9, 71.
33 Margaret Thatcher, *Preparing for Power*, London 1995, p. 573. I have a full
    account of this in *Banking on Death*, pp. 285–94.

34 The miserable BSP was subsequently supplemented by a means-tested Pension Credit which, for those that apply for it successfully, raises their income back to about 20 per cent of average earnings. But such a device, as noted in the previous chapter, removes the incentive for lower-paid employees to save.

35 I recount the little-known story of how Monica Lewinsky saved Social Security in Chapter 6 of *Banking on Death*.

36 Jacob S. Hacker and Paul Pierson, *Off Center: The Republican Revolution and the Erosion of American Democracy*, New Haven 2005, pp. 58–62.

37 Bryan Turner, 'Ageing, Status Politics and Sociological Theory', *British Journal of Sociology*, December 1989, vol. 40, no. 4, pp. 588–60.

38 Bryan S. Turner, ' Outline of a Theory of Human Rights', *Sociology*, vol. 27, pp. 485–512.

39 Michael Harrington, *The Other America*, 2nd ed., New York 1972 and Peter Townsend, *Poverty in the United Kingdom*, London 1979.

40 For a more balanced picture, see Paul Light, *Baby Boomers*, New York 1988.

41 Sarah Irwin, 'Age Related Distributive Justice and Claims on Resources', *British Journal of Sociology*, vol. 47, 1996, pp. 69–82. See also the contributions by Ted Benton, Diane Elson, Miriam Glucksmann and Lydia Morris, to Lydia Morris, ed., *Rights: Sociological Perspectives*, London 2006.

3

Commercial and Corporate Failure

We have seen that the Anglo–American formula has been based on giving enormously generous tax breaks to encourage the financial services industry to supply and manage old-age pension products, costing US Treasury over $120 billion a year in lost taxes (more than five times the size of farm subsidies); and costing the UK Treasury a net £13 billion annually. In the US employers can also offset health insurance for their employees against tax. Jacob Hacker has pointed out that the 'divided welfare state' absorbs almost as much public revenue as the publicly administered welfare arrangements of Germany and France.[1] Unfortunately such arrangements are both less efficient and less egalitarian. The results of public subsidy of private provision have been mediocre or worse, whether we look at delivery, coverage, or the impact on savings rates. The US tax-favoured 401(k) and IRA programmes have grown rapidly over the last two or three decades, and the UK's New Labour government tried to emulate this success, but its Stakeholder pensions failed to take off and the first report of the government's Pensions Commission in 2004 identified a huge savings shortfall, affecting at least 7 million people on low and medium incomes, with women being particularly at risk.[2]

In the United States the commercially successful 401(k) or IRA schemes only cover about half the working population, and many of those with nominal coverage will benefit little, as we will see. Traditional 'defined benefit' (DB) occupational pension schemes, which promise a pension linked to salary and years of membership, still have over 40 million members, but so many of these are under threat of closure or default that it has cast a deep shadow over the whole sector. The performance of the relatively new types of 'defined contribution' (DC) pension is not strong enough to compensate for the slow but relentless decline of traditional DB coverage. DC pensions make no specific pension promise but instead furnish a savings vehicle which will pay out a pension which reflects market return; in the years 2000–4 these returns were negative or low. Official pension policy seeks to stave off collapse by raising the retirement age, by re-engineering pension products and by shoring up the traditional schemes with additional insurance. Matters have not been helped by the fact that most debate has focused on public pensions when so much of the real crisis is to be found in the private sector.

Edward Wolff of New York University has established that already in 1998, before the stock market crash and before the closure of so many schemes, the US pension regime was not in good shape. He found that 18.5 per cent of households heading for retirement in that year would receive incomes below the poverty line, while 42.5 per cent would not be able to replace 50 per cent of their pre-retirement income.[3] But Wolff's snapshot of 1998 showed that a larger number – a sizeable majority – would then experience income erosion in retirement. Wolff traced the remorseless decline of the income of the median household – that is, the household at the mid-point in the distribution – at successive ages after 47–52. The median income of US households ranked by the age of the main income recipient in 1998 was as follows:

Table 3.1: *The Decline of Income after 52 Years of Age*

Age of Main Recipient	Median Household Income
47 to 52 years of age	$49,000 a year
53 to 58	$43,000
59 to 64	$35,000
65 to 70	$26,000
71 to 76	$21,000
77 and above	$16,000

Source: Edward N. Wolff, *Retirement Insecurity: the Income Shortfall Awaiting the Soon-to-Retire*, p. 65.

After peak earnings in the age band 47–52, ageing leads first to income erosion and then to a toboggan slide. Pensions of various sorts are not good at replacing earnings because of poor coverage, lack of inflation-proofing and heavy transactional costs in private schemes. Women have weak coverage yet let live longer, so decreasing income matches in-creasing feminization at higher ages. Blacks and Hispanics have low coverage and entitlement – their mean retirement wealth per household at sixty-five, including Social Security, is only $141,500 compared with $372,900 for non-Hispanic white households. But because of lower life expectancy among Blacks and Hispanics, the relatively poorer, most elderly age group is disproportionately white as well as female. The figures are for 1998 so those for older ages will also reflect past coverage, though figures for 1983 and 1989 showed a similarly steep decline.[4] The 'median' income figures I have quoted highlight age and race differences, which are clearly very significant, but do not illuminate sex and class differences within each category, which are also very striking. Another study finds that in 2000, 45 per cent of women aged sixty-five or over , and 20 per cent of men of this age, received less than $10,000 a year, while 18 per cent of men aged sixty-five or over, and 6 per cent of women of this age, received over $40,000 a year.[5]

A later study by Edward Wolff found that, despite a huge savings effort and a big jump in share prices, the majority of US employees were little better off in 2001 than they had been in 1983. He also observed: '[P]ension wealth inequality grew sharply as well. In fact counting total wealth (including pensions), the average household was somewhat worse off in 2001 than in 1983.'[6] Wolff found that the proportion of households where at least one member had a Defined Benefit (DB) pension plan fell from 69 per cent to 45 per cent between 1983 and 2001, while the proportion with a Defined Contribution (DC) plan rose from 12 per cent to 62 per cent. Overall, 'Private Accumulation' (the sum of net worth and pension wealth) fell by 2 per cent.

In April 2006 the Employee Benefit Research Institute issued a report which suggested that the big swing to DC schemes was having rather modest results. 56 per cent of employees had less than $50,000 in savings, and 66 per cent had less than $100,000, a sum that would yield a pension of perhaps $5,000 a year, probably less. Around a half of workers aged 45–54, and fifty-five and over, had less than $50,000 in savings, with over a third having less than $10,000. Only 22 per cent of employees had over $250,000, the size of pot that might generate an income to compare with the Social Security cheque.[7] The implication of these figures is that the United States had a very inefficient savings system. As we will see below, this inefficiency relates more to exorbitant costs than to rocky stock markets, though the latter certainly takes its toll.

Wolff's studies and the EBRI report reveal the weakness of today's and tomorrow's pension assets in the world's largest and richest economy – and in a society that relied greatly on private retirement provision. They did not seek to capture the prospects of pensioners the *day after tomorrow*, which now appears likely to be much worse. In this context, the day after tomorrow may be 2030 or 2020 or it may be sooner than that. The years after 2001 brought more 'unravelling', as DB sponsors reneged on their promises, DC plans wilted and more households faced poverty in retirement. An earlier study of pension adequacy by the EBRI sought to estimate future income from all sources – occupational schemes, personal plans and Social Security. It concluded: 'America's elderly face an income shortfall between 2020 and 2030 of at least $400 billion – including at least $45 billion in 2030 alone – just in their ability to cover basic living expenses and any expense associated with care in a nursing home or from a home health care provider.'[8] Robert Reynolds of Fidelity concurred: 'By 2030, the system is on track to provide low income workers with only about a quarter of their pre-retirement incomes.'[9] This disturbing conclusion – 25 per cent of a 'low income' is a real pittance – was not much alleviated by his further observation that: 'This "replacement rate" does rise to 56 per cent for the most highly-paid workers.'[10] In twenty or thirty years time more older women will have some work-related entitlement and pension wealth, reflecting the rise in female participation in the workforce in previous decades. But because much of this employment was part-time or lower-paid work the effect will be reduced – as will be shown below, the lower the savings the less efficient the private pension system. Women's spousal entitlement to the Social Security pension – today still an important factor in female entitlement – will diminish as a result of lower marriage rates and higher divorce rates (divorced women need to have been married for ten years to claim the spousal pension). African American women will be worst affected by weak spousal entitlement.[11]

British data tell a similar story. A 2002 study focused on those aged 50–64 found that one half of this group were in households that had pension assets and entitlements ('pension wealth') that would yield an income of less than £11,000 a year from all sources. The cohort selected should be among the best provided for, having had a long accumulation period in relatively benign economic conditions and with prospects buoyed by the fact that they are close to peak earnings. While this is certainly the case with the upper deciles the overall picture is quite polarized. A couple with the indicated level of income would be just above the poverty line, defined as 60 per cent of median income. A quarter of this age group had no private or occupational coverage at all. The UK's very modest state pension comprised more than half of all income for the poorer half–that is the bottom five deciles, and was the major source of pension income for the bottom seven deciles. Overall the state pension comprised 35.2 per cent of all pension wealth, with current Defined Benefit pensions supplying 30 per cent and current Defined Contribution pension plans accounting for only 7.4 per cent of pension wealth, despite the fact that 33 per cent of men and 20 per cent of women had such plans. Just over a quarter of pension wealth came from 'past pensions', most of which were also DB schemes, some already paying a pension and disproportionately benefiting the top deciles. Women's pay lags behind men's pay by 17 per cent in the UK and expected pension income in retirement closely reflects this inequality, with 26 per cent of both sexes receiving a pension that is less than 50 per cent of their former income, a further 23 per cent receiving between a half and two-thirds of their former income and 50 per cent receiving over 67 per cent.[12]

While state pension entitlements are fairly evenly distributed, private pension wealth is very unequally concentrated, and is highly correlated with non-pension wealth. The richest tenth of this cohort approaching retirement had pension wealth and overall wealth that was more than twice as great as the next decile. This richest decile had total wealth of over £1.6 million and pension wealth of around three quarters of a million pounds. The researchers add a note explaining: 'the mean levels of each form of wealth . . . are inflated by a small number of extremely wealthy individuals (about the top one per cent of the whole distribution)'.[13] However, they add that even excluding such individuals, the outcome is polarized with the richest tenth doing very well. The fact that half of UK tax relief goes to the richest tenth of households helps to explain their impressive accumulation of pension wealth. But the benefits of the now-threatened Defined Benefit approach to occupational pension provision, and the meagre contribution made by the so-called Defined Contribution schemes, also make a striking contrast.

By 2005, the Anglo-Saxon pension regime was in deep trouble on both sides of the Atlantic. Addressing the long-term impact of crumbling occupational schemes, weak securities markets and exorbitant costs resembled trying to measure the meltdown of a glacier in a heatwave. Pension promises – solemn contracts that helped to constitute the 'pension wealth' which Edward Wolff already found inadequate in 2001 – were seemingly there to be broken. Even those who were comfortably middle class could not escape pension collapse. In November 2003 the *New York Times* cited the following example: 'Robert M. Bowden retired from his job as accounts manager for a large trucking company with a plan to travel for himself. But his company's pension plan collapsed this year, and his annual pay-out was cut to $24,000 from

$48,000. Mr Bowden and other retirees of the company, CNF, see a culprit. In a lawsuit they accuse the company of failing for many years to set aside enough money in the plan.'[14] Mr Bowden's disappointment left him well clear of the poverty line, but sore nonetheless, and, even taking Social Security into account, living on less than a half of his former pay. Millions of members of corporate schemes have done considerably worse. The promised pensions of steel workers, airline workers and auto workers have been, as we will show, victims of sabotage and chicanery.

The quality of overall pension coverage declined steadily in the period 1995–2005 and this will show up as lower future retirement income. Total enrolment in Defined Benefit occupational schemes remained high but by 2005 there were more retired than contributing members, with many schemes frozen or closed to new members, and others threatened by the bankruptcy of their sponsor. The private sector DB schemes have 36.4 million members, about 17 million still contributing and the others drawing a benefit or hoping to do so. These schemes supposedly offer a pension linked to salary and years of employment. When schemes approach maturity their link to a single employer is revealed as a major source of weakness, as some employers encounter difficulty and seek to shed commitments. The DB pension promise is enshrined in a legal contract and corporate financial officers have to take these liabilities seriously, sometimes with dire consequences for current employees. Later we will examine the protracted agony of the DB pension schemes and explain why it has given openings to a new breed of 'vulture capitalist', who makes a killing by finding a legal way to offload, or wreck, the Defined Benefit pension plan. In the next section I analyze the 'defined contribution' (DC) plans whose rise has been so meteoric over the last two decades.

DC Plans as Leaky Buckets

Employers in the US and UK now much prefer DC schemes because they eliminate a future risk, and allow them to fix and reduce their contribution. Employees may grumble, but the DC scheme is portable while most corporate DB accounts are not. In the DC scheme the future pension will be simply whatever the accumulated sum in the fund will purchase at retirement, with no link to final salary. While some large employers operate their own DC scheme, others make available a menu of savings options offered by the large commercial suppliers. In the US the tax-favoured 401(k) envelope has attracted a huge inflow over a period of two decades. The UK has had a succession of tax-favoured savings schemes since Gladstone's 1853 budget, but until the introduction of the Stakeholder in 1999 employers were not obliged to offer them to all employees. Yet neither in the UK nor the US has employer provision solved the besetting problems of DC schemes, namely uneven coverage, high charges and weak employer commitment.

Employers generally contribute fewer resources to their DC plans than were characteristic of the traditional DB schemes. In the US, employers are allowed to contribute their own shares to pension schemes, and find this convenient. The employee contributing to a 401(k) plan is often able to claim equal amounts of company stock, producing an unhealthy concentration of risk in the portfolio. Aside from employer contributions, employees with 401(k)s are signing up to make a stream of contributions to one of the large finance houses, such as Fidelity, Barclays, Merrill Lynch, Putnam and so forth. The employer who sponsors a 401(k) makes no commitment to guarantee its value and has transferred all market risk to the employee. The employee has a 'portable' pension fund, free of either sponsor risk or sponsor guarantee. The advantages to employers and employees alike led to the numbers of those with 401(k)s rising from zero in 1980 to over 55 million by 2005. But charges are high and their prospects as a retirement vehicle reduced by the fact that holders of 401(k)s who get into difficulties prior to their retirement can make draw-downs from their accounts.

High charges also drag down the rate of return achieved by those who establish an Individual Retirement Account (IRA) with the commercial supplier of their choice. And, once again, the individual bears the market risk, moreover he or she does so without being able to draw on the type of risk-pooling which allows those who die earlier to subsidize those who live into their nineties. Because women are more long-lived than men they suffer more from this constraint on risk-pooling. Where a good annuity can be purchased on retirement some risk-pooling can be achieved, but good annuity products are very difficult to find in the US and are becoming rarer in the UK as well. Partly this is because of the decline in long-term interest rates, but it is also because suppliers do not like being exposed to 'adverse selection'. Unless the purchase of an annuity on retirement is compulsory, those taking up the option are thought likely to have better insight into their probable life expectancy than the supplier. Commercial pension suppliers are not averse to 'asymmetric information', as we will see – so long as it is not they who are skewered by it. If all tax-favoured savers have to take out an annuity at retirement then the peril of what the supplier will see as adverse selection is less but is difficult to remove altogether without moving to some universal, non-commercial model. Whatever their weaknesses, the traditional DB schemes at least embodied the risk-pooling of classic insurance principles. As we will see below, the annuity problem is just one reason why the transition from DB to DC will show up in two or three decades' time as a rise in pensioner poverty.

If pension coverage is to be effective it should move away from, not towards, the commercial and individualized form. Pension provision is a field where commercial provision has been tested and found wanting. After nearly fifty years during which more than half the working population has paid into such schemes – and during which they enjoyed, as we have seen, vast subsidies – the modest (US) or miserly (UK) public old-age pension is still the most important source of income for 60 per cent of those in retirement in those countries. One reason for the comparative success of the public systems in generating incomes from contributions is that *their costs are low*. There is no expensive customization and marketing. Contributions are handled as part of payroll and the public employees who administer the schemes do not earn the exaggerated salaries of those in the financial sector. The *longevity of the public provider* is also an asset. As people are urged to insure themselves against the major risks of life by applying to commercial organizations, we should recall Richard Titmuss's famous observation that while we can be fairly confident that there will be a government of some sort in fifty years time we cannot say the same about any particular company or financial provider. Even the most up-to-date and glamorous corporation can collapse, as Enron's employees and investors, including many pension funds, discovered in 2001. Likewise, even the oldest and most respectable financial house can be obliged to close its door, as nearly a million policyholders with Britain's venerable Equitable Life (founded in 1762), discovered to their cost around the same time.

During the boom years of the 1980s and 1990s many of those paying into private pension schemes did quite well. Awareness of this fact has encouraged those with scheme membership, or the beginnings of a pension pot, to bask in unwarranted optimism. Even in the heyday of booming exchanges, plan charges still absorbed much of the generous tax subsidy. During three years of negative returns in the stock markets in 2000–2 the high charges were still there, but not the high returns to cover them. US fund values fell by about a half over these three years. The millions who reached retirement age at this time, or were forced into early retirement, paid a stiff price for the market slide. Even the more comfortable holders of 401(k)s, the most widespread savings vehicle, mournfully quipped that they had turned into 201(k)s. The subsequent stock market recovery ran out of momentum before many stocks had returned to previous levels. The bubble and its aftermath leave a long shadow and it will require a very strong and sustained recovery to repair the damage. (Instead of which there was a graver crisis and heavy share price falls, see preface p. xxvi.)

The problem of depleted funds is compounded if, as has been the case recently, there is a sharp drop in the returns on the sort of safe assets – notably bonds – which best suit a retirement portfolio. Declining bond yields stem from deep-going shifts in the economic environment, but the problem of low yields can be compounded by the sheer scale of pension-fund demand for such assets as the 'cult of equity' characteristic of the 1980s and 1990s is condemned by new accounting standards and results in a flight to security. Corporate pension funds that approach maturity can be obliged to sell their equities and buy government bonds, however modest the yield. By the end of 2005 UK long-term bond yields net of inflation were less than one per cent annually. In the United States new accounting standards create similar pressure in a financial marketplace that has never been very hospitable to purchasers of annuities.

All this reduces the revenue in retirement that can be generated for a given sum. Those clicking on MSN's financial advisor in 2004 were informed that a couple who wished for a retirement income of $40,000 a year would have to accumulate a savings pot of $1 million. Proper health coverage required a similar sum. In other words, to obtain a decent middle-class pension you needed to be a millionaire! A rise in interest rates might lower the bar a little, but here is another risk the individual saver will find difficulty negotiating. The corporation or super-wealthy individual can turn to a hedge fund, and iron out interest rate fluctuations by means of a swap, but such procedures don't work for small sums.

The wealthier holders of 401(k)s and IRAs did very well out of them in the 'roaring nineties' and often quite reasonably in later years. This is because they were able – up to stipulated income limits – to claim back higher rate income tax at 35 per cent or more, and because the size of their portfolio spread the cost of management charges, so that they were lower as a proportion of the fund value. In the US the richest 10 per cent of tax payers received 62 per cent of the tax relief granted on pension and health coverage in 1988, while in the UK the corresponding figure was 51 per cent in 1996.[15] The subsequent lowering of the top US rate of tax will still leave the top 10 per cent of tax payers sitting on their past gains and claiming rebates worth around $60 billion a year, while their UK counterparts do likewise and pocket over £6 billion of foregone taxes annually.

But for the majority of US employees their 401(k) savings have furnished a poor return because of heavy administrative and marketing charges. One source of high charges is the fragmentation and proliferation of small schemes. The *Wall Street Journal* reports an industry survey which found that: 'Investors in 50-person plans pay an average of 1.4 per cent of their assets in fees or about $14 for every thousand dollars invested – assuming an average participant balance of $40,000 – according to a new study by HR Investment Consultants in Baltimore. That compares with 1.17 per cent for investors in 1,000 person plans. But investors in small plans pay as much as 4 per cent or more according to HR. That could mean a significant difference to participants over time. Over twenty years, a 1 per cent increase in fees on a $100,000 investment can reduce the portfolio's ultimate gain by $66,254, assuming annual investment returns of 7 per cent. And fees can take a particularly large bite out of an investor's annual return when investment returns are low . . .'[16] According to this report of the 400,000 companies with 401(k) plans nearly three-quarters are plans with fewer than fifty members. These small-company-sponsored plans held a total of $192 billion of assets in 2004, which would generate annual management fees totalling $8 billion or more at the indicated expense ratios.

A major source of high charges is intense competition for business. The employers, who have their own businesses to run, are likely to think they have done their duty by their employees if they selected a well-known supplier. Almost without exception the better-known suppliers are those who advertise a lot. They do so, firstly, to promote their brand, and, secondly, to promote particular funds. Most suppliers maintain scores of funds with somewhat varying strategies. On the one hand they can cater to different investment styles and, on the other, their range of funds should have some with above average performance to brag about. A company that spends a lot on its brand is sometimes said to be signalling confidence in its product to consumers, but multiple product lines and lengthy maturation periods mean that the signal is very misleading in this case. A further complication is the cost of exit and the dearth of alternatives.

There is great inertia in this market – people will stay for years with their first supplier. Since there are often penalties for switching to another, this is quite rational. But it traps the policy holder in sub-standard provision. It also supplies a strong reason for providers to spend lavishly to attract customers to their schemes. Each customer is pledging to pay a stream of cash over many years to a total value somewhere between that of a house and a luxury car. So a huge marketing effort is in order. The same logic applies to other personal plans, leading to a marketing 'arms race' amongst providers. Moreover, according to rule 12 (b)-1, the money managers can legitimately charge the cost of attracting new members against the accounts of existing members of their schemes. Contributions to 401(k)s and to IRAs are often used to buy stakes in mutual-funds (similarly in the UK, tax-favoured 'stakeholder pensions' are invested in 'unit trusts', which, like mutual funds, assemble a diversified portfolio of securities). The mutual funds have their own significant costs and, as we will see in the next chapter, have sometimes allowed hedge funds to game their customers.

DB schemes, being occupational, incur little or no marketing charge, and administrative costs of 0.5 per cent or less of the fund each year; DC schemes typically incur costs of at least an additional one or two per cent of fund value each year. The 401(k)'s compounding-charge drain, noted above, is very much shared by other types of plan – over forty years, an extra 1 per cent charge is likely to reduce the size of the pot by around 20 per cent. Employees often lack the information they need to make good choices and usually pay a penalty if they decide to switch schemes. The choice the employee is able to make is anyway constrained by the fact that employers limit that choice to a handful of funds, often from a single manager. This practice helps to keep down administrative costs but gives leverage to the suppliers, who are well placed to lock their customers into profitable savings contracts, with the latter having only their employer to root for them. This practice not only rewards relentless advertising but also can help the employer to build a relationship with a financial concern. Academic research showed that mutual fund charges were high but, in what seemed a competitive market, most clustered around the average. An industry–wide study of mutual fund performance between

1970 and 1999 found that there was a 2.3 per cent difference between gross and net performance.[17] The mutual funds seemed to outperform the market in gross returns but to fall behind it once charges were taken into account. Operating on a large scale they had the opportunity to secure lower trading costs, but their overall costs and profits were taking a big bite – around $130 billion a year by 2002. Economists have established several ways in which suppliers have the advantage over their customers.

E. Philip Davis, in his authoritative study of pension funds, explains that 'personal defined contribution plans are particularly vulnerable to agency problems vis-à-vis financial intermediaries'.[18] The financial supplier has the upper hand, in his view, because of 'the information asymmetry between seller and buyer, the one-off nature of the transaction, and the lack of purchasing power of the purchaser . . . as well as the ability of the seller to impose high commissions on the purchaser.' He added that 'there are also economic reasons for high costs, such as the need to construct individual contracts, as well as the need for expenditure on advertising, marketing and public relations.'[19] The eruption of the US mutual fund scandals in 2003–4 (to be considered in Chapter 5) was to bear out several of these general points and to add others. But long before this, it became clear that DC schemes and personal pension plans were often highly unsatisfactory savings vehicles and hence that employers who simply channelled contributions to a widely advertised supplier were not protecting their employees' interests.

In *Banking on Death* I cited a host of studies conducted in the 1980s and 1990s showing reductions in yield on DC plans of between 20 and 55 per cent.[20] In 2001 two *Business Week* journalists published a book entitled *The Great 401(k) Hoax*, which highlighted their dismal performance during the great bull market. Two former Treasury officers reached the same conclusion in a book published the following year, entitled *The Great Mutual Fund Trap*.[21] Another former regulator added to the picture. In an autobiography published in 2002, Arthur Levitt, the former chairman of the Securities and Exchange Commission (SEC), spent two dozen pages itemizing 'The Seven Deadly Sins of Mutual Funds', his unsuccessful attempts to correct them in the heady atmosphere of the 1990s, and the formidable lobbying power of the financial services industry. One of the abuses he identified was the well-known practice of so-called 'soft dollars', whereby fund managers give business to traders and receive free business services – Bloomberg TV screens, company research – in return. The cost of these services is wrapped up in the trading charge. In consequence the clients' gross returns are understated and a part of the fund manager's profit concealed. But, as Levitt explained, 'soft dollars' might confuse the investor but they were a 'legal kickback' nevertheless, and he had not been able to do anything about them. Levitt put fund-management profits at the considerable sum of $50 billion a year.[22]

An even more devastating indictment of the industry appeared in 2005 when John Bogle published *The Battle for the Soul of Capitalism*. Bogle is the founder and former CEO of the Vanguard group, the only major fund group to be organized on non-commercial, genuinely 'mutual' principles, with no shareholders. As an insider, and rival of the commercial suppliers, Bogle knows where the bodies are buried. He points out that while total assets of the equity funds run by the money managers grew from $2.5 billion in 1950 to 4,034.5 billion in 2004, expenses grew from $15.2 million to $37,117 million. In other words assets multiplied by 1,595 while expenses multiplied by 2,445. This might look quite bad but Bogle supplies a further breakdown. He points out that from 1945 to 1960 charges fell, as managers achieved economies of scale and passed along the savings to customers. But since 1960 the movement has been very much the other way, with the industry leaders raising average annual ratio of assets to charges by 169 per cent.[23] However, he urges that it is misleading to measures charges as a percentage of assets and himself prefers to specify their total in dollars and to measure these against dividends earned by the fund assets. 'The Investment Company Institute [ICI, an industry association] of course strongly objects to measuring fund costs in dollars. (They're enormous.) It prefers ratios (they're tiny).'[24]

I have cited the ratios in the industry-standard format. Bogle helpfully gives not only the dollar total (for example, $37.1 billion in 2004, as cited above) but also calculates these amounts as a proportion of fund earnings in the same period: 'Tiny numbers like 0.92 per cent or even 1.56 per cent [these were the industry's total weighted and unweighted expense to asset ratios in 2004] seem relatively trivial. Yet when we examine expenses as a percentage of a fund's dividend income . . . the numbers take on a more ominous cast. Indeed with today's yield on stocks at about 1.8 per cent, a typical 1.5 per cent equity fund expense ratio consumes fully 80 per cent of a fund's income.'[25] In better years an equity fund might earn a total return – including capital gains – of 6 per cent so the expense ratio would be 25 per cent, still a hefty cut.

Note that the total expense figures given here are only for equity funds. The fund management industry also offers other savings vehicles, including bond funds, real estate funds and a variety of diversified hybrids. People investing for their pension will be encouraged to lean increasingly to bonds as they approach retirement, since they involve less capital risk. However fund charges for bond funds are broadly similar to those for equity funds. If we discount for inflation, bonds are likely to offer a return of no more than 2–4 per cent and charges will take a big bite from this and sometimes wipe it out. Those who save with IRAs in the US, or personal pension plans in the UK, usually talk to a financial consultant who will also charge a fee, often on a recurring annual basis.

The former employee of a large corporation with a DC scheme who meets the vesting conditions will be able to claim the assets in their pot and convert them into a pension when they retire. Such plans are portable but in principle more risky, as well as vulnerable to fee erosion. Market risk rests with the employee who will suffer if a lowered market coincides with their retirement. Another problem is that employers themselves contribute little to DC plans, usually only a half, or less than a half, of the contribution they make to a DB plan. The employers' contributions to DC funds often have 'vesting' conditions which mean that they are worthless unless the employee stays with the company for, say, five years, or reaches the age of fifty. It is also common practice, notwithstanding its notoriety at the time of the Enron collapse, for the employers' contribution to take the form of company shares. While it is easier for employers to issue new stock than pay cash, it concentrates the employee's risk. A survey of one and a half million 401(k) plans by Hewitt Associates showed that 28 per cent of their assets at the end of 2002 were shares in the employer's stock.[26]

In the two decades after their legality was confirmed in 1983, 401(k) schemes grew to the point where they cover 22 per cent of US employees. About half this number have an IRA, a type of DC vehicle. Employers contribute cash or shares to 401(k)s, and help to administer them, while beneficiaries organize their own IRAs. The growth of 401(k)s was encouraged both by employer sponsorship and by a raised tax-free contribution threshold. By 2004 some 60 million DC accounts together contained $2.6 trillion of assets, of which $1.6 trillion were equities. However, DB schemes, covering nearly forty million public and private employees, are still larger in value, with total assets of $4.9 trillion, including over $2 trillion in equities – private schemes hold $1.8 trillion in assets and public schemes $3.1 trillion of assets.[27] The DB funds are still large because, having been founded in the 1950s and 1960s, they have had time to build up large holdings and because even those schemes which are closed to new members need to be able to pay pensions for many decades ahead. One way or another two thirds of US households have a member enrolled in either a DC or a DB pension scheme, or both. But this figure is less impressive than it sounds because the extent of participation can be very modest. Employees who work for a company with a DB scheme for the minimum vesting period – say five years – and then leave, will be owed money once they reach the specified retirement age. But normally this will not be protected against inflation – it will simply reflect the salary they were actually paid and could be very low. The simple fact of having a 401(k) or IRA can mean even less. In 2002, 42 per cent of all 401(k)s were worth less than $10,000. 401(k)s can be drawn down earlier, to cover an emergency, though this may mean loss of the tax relief. This flexibility weakens the instrument's contribution to retirement provision.

With the collapse of the share bubble, fund values dropped by nearly a half over the three years following March 2000. In 2001, at midpoint in the decline, 42 million savers held a total of $1.8 trillion in their 401(k) accounts. The average holding was around $50,000, but, as we have seen, 42 per cent held less than $10,000.[28] While new accounts are bound to be small, at least three quarters of these micro-accounts were depleted because of collapsing stock prices and/or emergency draw-downs. Holders of 401(k)s and IRAs lose if they sell when the market is down, and pay a charge if they transfer funds to a new scheme.

Many suspect they don't get a good deal from the fund managers and everyone knows that the stock market is risky. The historic rationale for DB funds was their greater security and cost-effectiveness. But, of late, the apparently greater certainty of these schemes has too often turned out to be an illusion.

The Agony of 'Defined Benefit'

Those who belonged to the Defined Benefit schemes, the classic mid- and late-twentieth-century occupational arrangement, generally did quite well if they retired before the dawn of the twenty-first century. Employers saw these schemes as a good way to attract and keep the best workers. They were offered to individual employees but also loomed large in negotiations with unions. They were thought to be the 'gold standard' of retirement coverage. Following legislation in 1974 – the Employee Retirement Income Security Act (ERISA) – the future benefits they offered seemed assured. ERISA established the Pension Benefit Guaranty Corporation (PBGC), an insurance scheme to which all corporations running DB schemes had to belong. At their high point, in the early 1980s the majority of workers belonged to such schemes but they became unpopular with some managers and many shareholders around this time as it became clear that the new arrangements could erode shareholder value. The total number of such plans offered by corporations declined from 112,200 in 1985 to 29,700 in 2005.[29] The ERISA pension regime was more onerous for employers, with mandatory disclosure and contributions. The quest for maximum shareholder value was stimulated by takeovers, mergers, bankruptcies and successful attempts by employers and investors to avoid pension obligations that would weigh on the balance sheet. In the early days future pension obligations did not figure in the main accounts. By the 1980s regulators and investors took a keen interest in pension disclosure. During the share boom, boards were happy to oblige as pension fund gains could be used to strengthen the bottom line. But the collapse of the share bubble in 2000 and after revealed large deficits. Corporations also found retiree health care benefits an increasingly awkward burden, withdrawing them where they could. The number of large companies offering such benefits dropped from 66 per cent to 36 per cent between 1988 and 2004, according to the Kaiser Family Foundation.[30]

On 6 December 2005 the *New York Times* reported that Verizon, the telephone company that serves 50 million lines in twenty-eight states, was to freeze the DB pension plan it offers to its 50,000 managers, with effect from the end of June 2006, and that it would replace this with a 401(k) plan. The company increased by 1 per cent of salary the amount it would match in contributions to the 401(k), but its former contribution to the DB scheme otherwise disappeared. Those with less than 15 years employment were no longer to receive promised health benefits in retirement. So long as the company stays in business, it will continue to honour already-accrued benefits under the DB scheme but no further benefits can be accumulated. These cuts were expected to save the company $3 billion over the next ten years. The company had made a fat profit of $1.9 billion in the previous quarter, so it was not financial desperation which prompted the move.[31] The company's cynicism was lampooned on the 'Colbert Show' on that day's comedy channel. But even the satirists could not match the full-page ad placed by the company itself in the next day's *New York Times*. Under the banner 'Our People, Our Network', it supposedly quoted one of its local managers as declaring: 'a job at Verizon comes with great benefits that encourage me to get and stay healthy and help me to save for the future . . . This is a special time for all of us. Future generations of Verizon men and women will make the network faster and more powerful . . .'. The advertisement, scheduled by a promotional department unaware of the impending freeze, was accompanied by a smiling photo of the hapless manager, arms comfortably folded.

Notwithstanding plan closures, the remaining DB schemes still had large assets and a rising number of participants, that is, retirees and contributing employees. At the end of 2004 DB funds held $3.8 trillion of assets, up from $1.7 trillion in 1990. The DB form is widespread in the public sector and DB funds in this sector held $2 trillion of assets in 2004 compared with $0.8 trillion in 1990. The total number of participants in private sector plans has continued to grow even while the number of those plans had dropped. At the end of 2004 there were 44.4 million participants in private sector schemes, over a half of them now retired and drawing pensions. Though many have been closed or frozen, the process takes a long time to complete because of obligations already incurred. A 'closed' scheme is closed to new members, but existing members continue to build their entitlement. In a 'frozen' scheme existing entitlements are preserved but can no longer be built upon. Someone who was part of such a scheme from 1980–2000 may have twenty years to go before they can claim a pension and will then draw it for twenty-five years, so the frozen scheme should still be active for half a century. And, of course, there are still successful companies, with well-funded schemes, who remain true to their promises. Assuming no legislative or economic earthquake – these systems are built on a fault-line, so this would be optimistic – paying out pensions will eventually run down the size of such funds and death will eventually reduce their participant numbers. The members of these schemes will still be able to claim a pay-related pension, but if they left the sponsoring company ten or twenty years before retiring, the pension they get will lose value because it will reflect neither seniority nor promotion. [32]

Despite their supposed statutory protection, the recent vicissitudes of DB schemes show them to be vulnerable to employer negligence or even

deliberate sabotage. The funding formula laid down by the PBGC and
the Financial Accounting Standards Board (FASB) made it too easy for
the employer to skip contributions. During the boom years of the
business cycle employers can take contribution holidays – GE went
for thirteen years in the 1980s and 1990s without making any contribution to its pension fund. Over these years many steel companies, telecom
operators, airlines and auto companies also skipped contributions or
minimized them by means of unrealistic accounting. United Airlines
made no cash contributions to any of its four employee plans between
1996 and 2002, years when the fragile condition of the company should
have made this a priority. When the PBGC took over its liabilities in
2005, the schemes were found to be underfunded by $1.4 billion.[33]
British legislation stipulated a target amount for contributions but also
allowed this to be offset against any rise in the value of the pension fund.
In 2003 the Inland Revenue calculated that UK companies subsequently
found to be running a deficit had skipped contributions worth £27
billion between 1988 and 2001.

In both the US and the UK the law seeks to prevent employers using
the pension fund as a place to store tax-free profits, so it insists that the DB
schemes should not be over-funded, sometimes making a contribution
holiday compulsory. But after a stock market downturn the annual audit
is likely to show that future liabilities are not adequately covered by the
depressed assets in the fund. Just when it is most difficult to do so, the
employer is forced to stump up cash to ensure that the scheme does not
menace the corporation's good financial standing. Employers who then
make substantial contributions to the pension fund have fewer resources
for maintaining investment and employment. Alternatively their financial
officers were drawn to anticipate quite unrealistic rates of return to the
assets in the fund, thus obviating the need for anything other than a token
contribution from the sponsor.

At many leading companies the pension fund long ago grew to be
worth more than the company itself. Indeed at such companies as Boeing,
Ford, General Motors or Colgate/Palmolive in the US – or BT, GKN or
Unilever in the UK – the pension fund was worth several times the equity
valuation of the sponsor by 2000, if not long before. Financial analysts
began to describe GM as a hedge fund on wheels and United Airlines as a
pension fund with wings (of lead as it turned out). Companies that had
happily booked pension fund surpluses as profit, encountered a more
awkward logic when the stock markets slumped. Because the company

stands as guarantor to the DB pension fund, it has to make good any shortfall that may arise. Matters can be disguised by fancy accounting but following the collapse of Enron and Andersen, and the advent of tougher reporting standards, auditors became less inclined to indulge their clients' wishful thinking. Once under-funding is admitted, the corporation has to put in place a programme of payments to restore its solvency, with results that weaken earnings or investment or both. At the end of 2002 the majority of corporations in the Standard & Poor 500 in the US, and FTSE 100 in the UK, had under-funded pension schemes, with the total deficit being around $300 billion in the US and, supposedly, £55 billion in the UK.[34]

The overall pension deficit continued to grow in both the US and the UK during the modest recovery of the years 2002-5, because of the difficulty of making up for three lost years and because of accountants' greater stringency . . . In October 2003, after a sustained share rally, the director of the Pension Benefit Guaranty Corporation (PBGC), told the US Congress that the corporate pension fund deficit stood at about $350 billion.[35] By mid-2005 the PBGC estimated the same deficit at no less than $450 billion. Deficits relating to 'other post-employment benefits' (OPEBs), mainly retiree health-care coverage, ran at an extra $300 million.[36] In the UK a newly established Pension Protection Fund (PPF) estimated the shortfall in DB private sector schemes in June 2005 to be £134 billion.[37]

The estimated deficit is sensitive to discounting assumptions. If a higher discount rate is employed then it will produce a lower 'present value' of the future pension obligation, making deficits more likely and higher. The FASB and PBGC had traditionally prescribed a rate of interest that would be 85 per cent of the rate on thirty-year Treasury bonds, the rationale being that the return on a safe asset was the right match for pension saving. But in 2003 this was changed by Congress to the full T-bond rate and then, in 2004, to 85 per cent of good corporate bonds, raising the discount rate still further. Chief Financial Officers (CFOs) could now discount their obligations by nearly 5 per cent annually instead of by less than 3 per cent.[38] Special legislation allowed airline companies even easier calculations. While Congress was indulging corporate fantasy by notionally shrinking their pension obligations, many corporations were helping themselves, by similar means, to inflate the future value of their fund assets. Despite three dreadful years on Wall Street, CFOs were still blithely anticipating long-term rates of return on their pension fund holdings of 8, 9 or even 10 per cent annually. Though the SEC was to investigate some egregious cases of make-believe, blind optimism was often indulged by regulators and legislators alike because of the implications for jobs.

The accounting rules governing corporate sponsors allow them both to bring in the income of their pension funds and to engage in legal 'smoothing' of their overall earnings. A study of 3,000 companies over eleven years undertaken at Harvard Business School and MIT is reported to conclude: 'companies tended to ratchet up their assumption of pension fund returns, padding their profits just before certain corporate events, like acquisitions, secondary stock offerings or the exercise of stock options by executives – all times when a higher stock price is desirable.'[39] David Zion, an analyst with Credit Suisse First Boston, investigated the reported earnings of all companies in the Standard and Poor top 500 with a DB fund in the years 1999–2003 and showed the widespread use of phantom pension fund earnings to conceal real losses. The CFOs were permitted to come up with a figure for anticipated pension fund earnings at the beginning of the year and then to book those earnings at the year's close even if the real performance had been much worse. Zion likened this practice to 'depositing a paycheck for what you think you should be paid instead of what you were actually paid'.[40] The result was to raise aggregate earnings of these companies from $73 to 221 billion in 2002, and from $81 to 247 billion in 2002. At many companies the changes made the difference between a profit and a loss: in 2003 FedEx reported a profit of $830 million, but with pension fund earnings stripped out this became a loss of $87 million, while at Boeing the same procedure turned a $713 million profit into a $158 million loss.[41]

There is such latitude for make-believe in corporate pension funding that it is easy to come away with the idea that fund liabilities are infinitely fungible. But that is not the case. This is partly because employees do eventually retire and must be paid their pension. It is also because of the increasing nervousness of accountants, regulators and shareholders. Many older companies now have more retirees than they do current workers; if there is not enough in the fund then pensions become a charge on cash-flow. In late 2004 GM floated a bond specifically designed to help pay pensions – it has around a million pensioners. The damage to the overall credit-worthiness of the auto giant led its bonds to be downgraded to junk status within months. Pension woes have also damaged Ford. At the time these companies still had cash surpluses, but should they wish to raise capital in future it will be more expensive.

In considering the impact of DB funding it is necessary to bear in mind that a company's pension obligations have a contractual force that cannot be magicked away by fancy accounting, or the fiat of a CFO. On the other hand, and partly in consequence, DB pension entitlements remain very vulnerable – corporate leaders come to hate them, and are willing to consider almost any desperate expedient if it promises relief from the nightmare of pension liabilities. Theoretically legislators could openly tear up the pension contract, declaring it null and void. In practice this is most unlikely because it would be too unpopular and because there are less blatant ways of achieving the same result – encouraging workers to agree to 'give-backs' in order to save their job. The threat of bankruptcy has come to haunt many large sponsors. While threats sometimes suffice, real liquidations are messy and costly, removing employee entitlements but involving real losses and risks for the existing managers and owners. A bankrupt company can shed pension obligations but many existing owners and managers find such a cure worse than the disease, with the former losing value and the latter their jobs. So some corporate managers decide to reduce their pension deficits by giving this a belated priority and seriously paying down their deficit. In the UK the introduction of more stringent rules for calculating pension fund deficits – FRS 17 – led companies to pay £25 billion in contributions to their DB pension funds in 2004, twice what they had contributed in the previous year.[42]

Jobs versus Pensions

Paying down a pension deficit can hurt employment. It leads companies to avoid hiring and to shed labour. Accounting practice confers an extra bonus for the balance sheet. Every worker off the books means that the accountants henceforth only need to count the ABO (Accrued Benefit Obligation) rather than the PBO (Projected Benefit Obligation). Because the ABO does not incorporate future raises and seniority, it is generally only about two thirds of the PBO. So a policy of firing workers helps the employer in two ways; it reduces current outlays and it reduces future liabilities. This logic helps to explain why about 2.8 million workers lost their jobs in the US in 2000 to 2003.[43] In Britain, manufacturing industry lost jobs at the rate of 5,000 a week in 2002–4 but overall employment remained high thanks to the creation of hundreds of thousands of jobs in the public sector. While the overdue rehabilitation of public services was welcome, the losses to manufacturing are likely to be permanent. By March 2006, unemployment had crept up to 1.5 million, with a further 2.7 million claiming disability pensions, up from 0.4 million in 1990.

The conjuncture of 2001–3 echoed that of the early 1990s when an orgy of downsizing – especially at DB-sponsoring companies like the US steel corporations – put hundreds of thousands on the scrap heap with a reduced pension. 'Pension deficit disorder' thus contributed to the debility of US and British manufacturing, since enterprises in this sector typically had mature DB schemes and often found themselves starved of funds just when investment should have been boosted. The logic of DB funding was 'pro-cyclical', encouraging weak contributions during the good years (because the fund goes up anyway) but helping to accentuate job loss in a recession, and to slow recovery thereafter. For some time joblessness has been lower in the US and UK than in continental Europe (to be considered in Chapter 4), but its composition is different. In Europe employers were discouraged from creating low-paid service jobs by weak demand and high payroll taxes, even though they were allowed to put some of the latter into company reserves. But strong manufacturing concerns – with strong productivity and reserves accumulated in the good times –were able to sustain the sort of permanent, skilled employment which was destroyed by the 'Anglo-Saxon' pension regime.

The basic design flaw in the DB schemes is that they carry the guarantee of a single corporate sponsor. Over the three or four decades it takes for a pension scheme to mature, the sponsor can go from being a blue chip to a basket case. Comparing the US or UK stock exchange stars of the 1950s, or even the 1970s, with those of 2005, the overlap is small. The oil companies, the banks, and GE, still loom large in the NYSE but much else has changed – Microsoft, Wal-Mart, Intel, Google, and eBay are quite new. IBM and Coca-Cola are still there but have shrunk in size. The UK FTSE 100 is likewise dominated by newcomers like Vodafone, while famous names like ICI, Marconi and Unilever are shadows of their former selves. In this changeable corporate environment it would have made far more sense to have a multi-employer structure to guarantee pension provision. In Europe many large employers understood this and supported state-sponsored collective provision with different variants in Germany, France and, combined with national wage negotiations, Sweden.[44] Some leading US manufacturers also understood this, but the temptations of a segmented approach in such a large country had proved too strong for many employers. The managers who pushed company-specific schemes in the 1950s saw it benefiting labour retention and did not recognize the liability in the corporate accounts. And perhaps it made them more comfortable with the generous coverage they enjoyed themselves. In the 1990s some corporations backed the Clintons' complex health care reform, but not vigorously enough to prevent its defeat by the private medical and pharmaceutical lobbies. Given the huge pressure of health care costs and pension costs on US employers evident by 2005, it is not surprising that when Toyota opted to raise its output capacity in North America in that year it sited the new plants in Canada because of the latter's more collectivized health care and pension arrangements. Under such arrangements the employee gains security and is also able more easily to move from one employer to another, something the good employer does not have to worry about. Presumably Toyota sees itself as a premium employer, without need of pension handcuffs.

The Pension Benefits Guaranty Corporation (PBGC) furnishes a measure of insurance to DB schemes, but in case of default beneficiaries generally get about 75 per cent of their pension and none of their retiree health care benefit. Corporations have to pay an annual premium calibrated according to the size of their liabilities. So long as the company remains solvent it cannot invoke the insurance, so scheme members' expectations of full benefit are still dependent on the fate of a single company. US companies that enter Chapter 11 'bankruptcy protection' ask the court to pass over their liabilities to the PBGC, with the latter now becoming responsible for the future payment of reduced-rate benefits. The courts are likely to agree if it is the only way to save the company as a going concern. Employers with large obligations have used the threat of receivership to obtain union agreement to benefit cuts and to pressure the PBGC into granting further contribution holidays. The PBGC has proved no better at resisting extortion than the unions. However much store workers may set by their pension entitlement, they need and value their job even more. In mid-2003 the PBGC identified chronic pension deficits at 270 large corporations, but was itself over $5 billion in deficit and therefore in no position to alleviate the situation. As companies filed for Chapter 11, they called in their insurance coverage and the PBGC was obliged to extend it. Thus in 2001 it took responsibility for Bethlehem Steel's obligations and in 2005 accepted $6.6 billion in unfunded liabilities

from United Airlines.[45] The agency's deficit grew to $23.5 billion by
2004. The deficit here is the gap between its current assets – over $39
billion of securities in 2004 – and anticipated income, on the one hand,
and the present value of its future liabilities, on the other. While it can
expect future income to cover some of the shortfall the sharp rise in its
deficit makes a general default all too possible, no doubt triggered by the
collapse a few major schemes. The PBGC is not covered by any Federal
guarantee, but some suppose that the Treasury would have to step in to
prevent actual bankruptcy should that loom.

While an insurance system in certainly needed, that currently offered by
the PBGC is neither convincing nor appropriate. UK DB schemes had no
insurance available to them at all until 2004, a year marked by some high
profile bankruptcies which prompted the government to come up with a
remedy. Because of the US agency's well-advertised difficulties, the British
government's Pension Act of 2004 significantly modified the PBGC model.
The UK Pension Protection Fund (PPF) was to be funded in a way that, it
was hoped, would avoid two defects that have shown up at the PBGC:
firstly that companies in difficulties blackmail the agency into forgiving
contributions, and secondly that the very existence of the insurance scheme
encourages corporations to award over-generous pensions secure in the
knowledge that the insurer would pick up the tab ('moral hazard' in
economists' jargon).[46] The PPF was mandated to rank all participating
corporations according to ten degrees of risk and then oblige the more risky
to contribute at a higher level. In this way weaker companies would be
required to contribute more, not less. A 2005 bill before the US Senate
sought to enable the PBGC to adopt the same approach.

However, this tougher species of insurance will further weaken already
troubled companies because they will have to pay at the highest rate,
subtracting from the resources they need for survival. Awareness of this
awkward fact has pushed judges and regulators to an interesting expedient, requiring corporations that have defaulted on contributions to
issue shares to the insurer in lieu of cash. As the *Wall Street Journal* reported
in November 2005: 'The US government is on its way to becoming a big
shareholder in the nation's airline industry and possibly in the auto
industry. The Pension Benefit Guaranty Corporation . . . recently was
awarded 7 per cent of US Airways Group Inc. by a federal bankruptcy
court handling the company's Chapter 11 reorganization . . . The agency
got the shares as compensation for the under-funded pension plans it
assumed when the company filed for bankruptcy. The agency is likely to

get an even larger stake – between 15 and 25 per cent of new shares – of UAL Corp.'s United Airlines . . . And it is likely to get sizeable chunks of Northwest Airlines, Delta Airlines and Delphi Corp. – if, as expected, the companies ask the bankruptcy courts to dump their pension plans on the insurer.'[47] In the UK the newly established Pensions Regulator found himself in exactly the same situation in June 2005, when he allowed the Pension Protection Fund (PPF) to accept one-third of the shares in a recently reorganized company. He explained his decision by saying that it would both permit the PPF to garner an asset and protect jobs at the company concerned. [48] While there is a strong case for moving to a new system of second pensions which is not company-specific, those employees who have already built up entitlements will wish to see them better insured. Allowing an insurer such as the PBGC or PPF to accept shares in lieu of cash could make sense, but not confining this policy to weak companies. (If companies could contribute in shares as well as cash this would ease the pressure on cash-flow yet still produce a diversified portfolio – and the value placed on publicly quoted shares would measure the strength of the company. I return to these possibilities in Chapter 7.)

'Turn-Around Kings' or 'Vulture Capitalists'?

The problems of the DB pension schemes have produced a new breed of financier dubbed the 'vulture capitalists'. They specialize in extracting value from firms burdened by large pension and medical liabilities by shedding the latter. Robert S. ('Steve') Miller has appeared on the scene of a string of corporate wrecks. At Chrysler in the 1980s, he used threats from the company's creditors and bankers to extract concessions from the unions and the PBGC. As CEO of Bethlehem Steel in 2001 he closed down the company's pension plan, leaving $3.7 billion of unfunded liabilities to be inherited by the PBGC. Wilbur Ross stepped in to buy Bethlehem and four other dying steel companies, putting them into bankruptcy in order to wind up their pension plans and then selling the newly viable concerns for a profit of $4.5 billion. The employees, by contrast, were left with shrunken benefits.[49]

Steve Miller went on to become chief executive of Federal Mogul, a car parts maker with factories in the UK as well as the US. In July 2004 the UK subsidiary of this company went into receivership and successfully shed pension obligations for over 20,000 employees, with losses for a further 20,000 in an associated company.[50] The British government protested (and felt obliged to bring forward their own scheme for a Pension Protection Fund). But Carl Icahn bought up Federal Mogul paper at 20 cents on the dollar in a bet that bankruptcy plus liability-shedding would succeed. Filing for bankruptcy protection used to be a rigorous process allowing the company an interval to get its affairs in order. It was meant to protect employees, among others, from a precipitate and perhaps unnecessary liquidation. But the specialists in 'distressed assets' use the pause for their own, very different, ends.

By the late summer of 2005 Steve Miller was CEO at Delphi, another company sinking under the weight of the pension and medical insurance promises it had made to its employees. Delphi, previously a division of GM but spun off by it in 1999, was the world's largest auto-part maker with 50,000 employees in the US and 180,000 worldwide. Miller's sign-on fee was $3 million with an annual salary of $1 million (after an outcry he renounced the annual pay and kept the sign-on fee; the value of any options package was not revealed). Miller also paid off twenty executives with comfortable retirement packages while urging the great mass of employees to accept huge cuts – of 50 per cent or more – in their wages and health care and pension entitlements, saying that only this would save their jobs and help Delphi to avoid bankruptcy. He spoke of workers earning $65 an hour, though average wages were in fact $27 an hour, and proposed that instead they should be around $10–12 an hour.[51] The $65 figure might refer to a sub-group and included the cost of making up overdue pension and health care contributions as well – the latter being steep because the company had skipped contributions for so long. When his appeal for such savage reductions was turned down by the UAW – as he must have known it would be – the company filed for bankruptcy protection under Chapter 11 on 8 October 2005. Miller continued to urge huge cuts in benefits and the UAW continued to resist them. Because Delphi is a concern that was spun off from GM, the auto-maker still had residual responsibility – estimated at at least $4 billion, perhaps much more – to honour commitments to its former employees. In this case GM rather than the PBGC would have to come up with a rescue plan, but employees lose out whichever route is taken, because GM will not cover the post-1999 entitlement. This allowed Miller to seek credit from GM in order to keep Delphi afloat – and such moves scared thousands at both GM and Delphi into accepting a reduced buy-out package rather than hold out for their full promised benefits.

Miller explained: 'Under the bankruptcy law, we are required to bargain with our unions in good faith, and to supply sufficient information to establish our case for reduced labor costs. This will take a number of months. In most cases management and unions arrive at an equitable settlement. If we should fail, however, then we can appeal to the court to allow a rejection of the current labor contract. If granted the result is a free-for-all, wherein management can impose whatever terms it chooses, but the union is free to strike. Nobody wants to end up there which is why a settlement is reached in almost all cases . . . We have about a $5 billion shortfall in our [pension] plan assets to our plan liabilities . . . The big question will be whether we can formulate a plan of reorganization over the next few months that can generate sufficient capital to support continued funding of such plans . . . Globalization is a fact of life these days. What has been brought into sharp relief is the differing value the global market places on knowledge workers versus basic manufacturing workers.'[52]

The *Wall Street Journal* flanked this interview with a table showing that Delphi's labour costs in China were $3 an hour while in the United States they were $65 an hour (presumably including fund costs, as noted above). Miller seemed not to have noticed that many knowledge workers – from computer programmers to financial services personnel – also face the pressure of outsourcing. A table further indicated that Delphi sales were $19.6 billion in the United States and only $1.1 billion in Asia. This geographical distribution might help explain why Miller was keeping production in North America at all. The Delphi factory in Lockport, upstate New York, is reasonably close to major auto plants, notably GM's. Wage costs are only about 10 per cent of total costs. Locational advantages in the epoch of just-in-time production help to explain why Miller was bargaining to keep the Lockport, NY plant working, when he could have simply moved everything to the factories which Delphi already has in the cheap labour zones.

Wilbur Ross once again expressed interest in the 'distressed asset' and was already positioning himself to acquire it by buying up other auto-parts companies. As a reporter who had interviewed him explained: 'Mr Ross concedes that "the industry model is broken" but says he can fix it. Some of his plans are obvious: buy flailing companies at rock bottom prices . . . But some are less intuitive. He plans to pump a lot of money into product research. W. L. Ross recently teamed up with Masters Capital, a hedge fund . . . Mr Ross is also certain that a huge [auto-parts] company has a better chance of locking in its prices for raw materials, and of exerting influence with its automotive companies.'[53] Indeed in an age when rapid response to changing conditions is essential to success, the automobile manufacturer needs suppliers who can modify what they produce at a week's notice. There are high entry costs to these lines of production because 'tools and processes cannot be quickly replicated' and because of the previously cited locational advantages: 'the parts themselves are bulky, which makes it uneconomic for auto-makers to buy parts that must be shipped long distances.'[54]

While in some interviews Steve Miller held out the hope that Delphi's pension plan could be saved, in others he took a rather different, but no less disingenuous, tack. He presented his moves as a quest to prevent self-centred and greedy retirees from destroying their grandchildren's jobs: 'Delphi is simply a flashpoint, a test case for all the economic and social trends that are on a collision course in our country and around the globe. I fear something like intergenerational warfare, as young people increasingly resent having their wages reduced and taxed away to support social programmes for their grandparents' income and health care concerns.'[55]

Miller was here playing on a division within the workforce that had been set up by prior labour contracts which gave better benefits to established workers than to new hires. Unions can easily be tempted by such contracts because they don't appear to harm their existing members – they hope gradually to bring the new hires into the fold but the right moment never arrives. A policy of allowing the 'core' labour force to enjoy benefits on terms that will never be available to newcomers introduces caste division into the union ranks – and it's even worse if the newcomers are kept out of the union. But whether or not the union's past strategy could be faulted, it still did not justify Miller's attempt to throw the blame for the pension fund deficit on the workforce rather than where it belonged, with the company management.

In road haulage and construction US unions co-sponsor multi-employer pension funds. But the standard formula in corporate DB schemes is for the pension fund to be run by the financial officers of the sponsoring company. All trustees are nominated by the board of the sponsoring company which decides how much money to contribute as part of its wider overall strategy. If the company fails properly to fund such a pension scheme then the primary fault is that of the officers whom the shareholders have chosen to run the company for them, and some transfer of value from securities holders to pension beneficiaries would be in order. A key assumption here is that the pension promises made to workers under DB schemes are a contractual obligation comparable to any other legal engagements it makes. In the limbo of Chapter 11, workers find that their legal claims are sacrificed to those of new owners.

The rationale for Chapter 11 is to allow potentially viable companies some relief from creditors and banks, giving them an opportunity to reorganize for the benefit of shareholders and employees alike. But it has become a device for degrading some corporate obligations to the benefit of others – often new owners or creditors who negotiate priority at the expense not only of pre-existing shareholders – who are ultimately responsible for a company's management – but also of the pension plan members, who have no such responsibility. If the company was genuinely bankrupt and had no value as a going concern then the plight of the workers cheated of their pensions would still be tragic. But Delphi still had valuable contracts and leverage. Commenting on the move by Wilbur Ross, Miller was quoted as saying: '"Wilbur likes to invest industries that are out of favor, and auto-parts are certainly in that category . . . But he wants assets that have gone through bankruptcy, had the barnacles stripped off and liabilities resolved.'[56]

John Gapper, a financial journalist, finds corporations' ability to use Chapter 11 to dump their commitments to their workers shocking. He writes: 'They say that you should not visit a sausage factory if you like sausages and in this case the ingredients being ground up for profits are health and (perhaps) pension rights. It does not take a union activist to be disturbed by the prospect of Delphi workers losing benefits that they dedicated their lives to gaining by working there.'[57]

Corporate management is, of course, fully responsible for the substance and shape of existing pension and benefit programmes. Even though unions happily negotiated the detail, employers proudly took the initiative in the 1950s and 1960s in devising schemes which they saw as promoting employee retention. Writing about parallel UK developments Martin Wolf offers the following devastating verdict: 'The implosion of private sector defined benefit pension schemes accelerates . . . Predictably as the schemes disappear, the supply of self-serving, self-exculpation from managements and those who speak for them soars . . . What we are watching is the unwinding of what was – in effect, if not in intention – a confidence trick known as "bait and switch": offer something attractive and then switch it for something else when the customer comes to collect. Pension provision provides attractive opportunities for such a game. The aim was to hold on to valuable staff, encourage them to acquire company-specific skills and pay them less than their market wage. A clever way to do this is to promise pay far in the future. That, after all, is all pensions are – deferred pay. Companies have played the bait and switch game: now comes the switch.'[58]

The manoeuvres at Delphi are part of the softening-up process for what will happen elsewhere, including the auto companies themselves, led by GM with its million-strong army of retirees. Ten days after Delphi went into Chapter 11 the UAW accepted cuts in health benefits at GM worth $15 billion. GM and Ford remain hugely important companies. Because of large pension and health liabilities their share price does not reflect their true value. Thus in October 2005 GM was valued by the stock market at no more than $15 billion according to its share price, while its pension and health-care liabilities had been reduced from $77 billion to $62 billion.[59] In broad terms what this means is that the stock market would value GM at $77 billion if it had no pension and retiree health-care deficit. This is still a net value because of outstanding loans and bonds but it does show that GM is still thought to have assets of great value. In 2004, a bad year, GM was still the world's largest car maker with Ford not far behind. Both have valuable plant, equipment, patents, research, brands and marketing networks. GM, the weaker of the two, was not short of cash, having $24 billion of liquid assets in October 2005. Indeed the real downside at the company was a board of directors which had failed to invest in R&D and had bet the bank on unending demand for gas-guzzling SUVs while neglecting electric cars, hybrids and fuel economy.[60] Finally, it is worth underlining that the pension benefits that GM workers were due to receive, after at least thirty years of gruelling assembly-line work, averaged only $18,000 a year, or half of average earnings. GM is heading for Chapter 11 for reasons that have everything to do with benefit-shedding; if it succeeds in offloading its obligation this average pension will decline to about $13,000 if the PBGC is still around, and would be weakly, if at all, indexed.

The plight of major employers should have persuaded US legislators to introduce public-health coverage such as is enjoyed by auto-workers in many other countries; if they were really imaginative they could also press for decent secondary pension coverage for all. As it is, each of the big three US auto companies have relocated production to Canada, because Canada, with its public health system, absolves them of the need to pay for health insurance on top of wages.[61] As noted above, Toyota also announced in 2005 that it would be opening a major plant in Canada. Other US companies have a less progressive solution to the health-cost problem. An internal Wal-Mart memo which surfaced in October 2005 revealed that the company was hiring more workers on temporary, non-insured contracts, and that it was planning to introduce a health screen for those who would still be covered.[62]

Instead of introducing universal public-health coverage, US legislators continued to devise loopholes to allow companies to underfund their health and pension plans. US Congressmen, highly dependent on corporate campaign contributions, gave corporate DB sponsors all the contribution holidays they wanted and a similarly constrained White House went along with it; only in 2005 did the President's officers, worried at the threat of PBGC collapse, threaten to veto further ruinous indulgence.[63] More contribution holidays can offer only a short-term fix. As larger numbers reach retirement age, or are laid off because of difficult trading conditions, the hollowness of unrealistic projections of pension fund growth will be exposed.

The owners of the large airline companies also played the Chapter 11 card, notwithstanding the fact that they are rather implausible victims of globalization – they can buy fuel virtually tax free and on their major routes they do not face competitors paying Third World wages. Auto will be next, with telecom companies not far behind. In October 2005 Northwest Airlines, having already availed itself of bankruptcy protection, asked the court to allow it to repudiate its pension obligations. With the services of eight law firms and two bankruptcy consultancies it was likely legally to outgun its own employees. Delta took the same path, hiring seven law firms and four financial advisory firms. The *Wall Street Journal* commented: 'Bankruptcy has long been lucrative for lawyers, but the airline industry is providing an unusual bonanza. This week's fourth annual forum on airline re-structuring in New York, sponsored by the American Conference Institute think tank, serves as a summit about how lawyers can make money out of the turmoil – or, as they put it, "partnering with your clients to capitalize on opportunities in the distressed airline industry".'[64]

Even if all this is hugely expensive, and hugely unfair, surely such reorganizations of 'distressed assets' deliver results in the end? The fact that they do deliver value shows, firstly, that erroneous conclusions are too often drawn from the facts of globalization and, secondly, that these enterprises could have contributed more to honouring their pension promises. Take the case of Bethlehem Steel, which entered Chapter 11 in 2001 with 11,000 US workers. By 2005 Bethlehem was part of a thriving international consortium, Mittal Steel, with facilities all over the world and 8,200 employees at the profitable US subsidiary producing high-quality steels tailored mainly, but not exclusively, to the huge local US market. Because of surging productivity, pay and benefits for the employed worker had grown, not shrunk. By 2004 it took a US worker two hours to produce a ton of steel compared with eight hours in 1980. Steel-industry operating profits ran at $4 billion compared with total labour costs of a little over $2 billion.[65] But neither Bethlehem retirees, nor the PBGC that supplies their pensions, had any benefit from this recovery. It would have been perfectly possible for the PBGC to have been granted stock in the reorganized enterprise in partial compensation for the contributions it had not received. If the PBGC had stakes of this sort in all the companies whose liabilities it insures its deficit would be lower and – with this extra help – it might pay something closer to the full promised pension, rather than the three quarters it currently supplies. If companies paid much of their PBGC contribution in shares rather than cash this would remove unwanted strain from their cash-flow and the market, via share price, would assess the strength or weakness of the company's prospects. (In Chapter 7 I argue that such contributions should be compulsory for all private employers above a certain size, in order to obtain the most advantageous risk-pooling.)

The specialists in distressed assets like to operate through closed, private-investment vehicles that do not have to obey the standards of disclosure and reporting of the normal public company. In this way they avoid signalling their moves in advance and keep rivals guessing. But the closed company can also be a source of vulnerability to its owner, exposing him or her to the liabilities of entities in which they have a controlling stake. In 1992 the financier Carl C. Icahn had a controlling stake in Trans World Airlines when it filed for bankruptcy protection. The PBGC, aware that it was about to be stuck with the airline's pension obligations, took out a claim against Icahn's assets, including his favorite racehorse and ocean-front residence. Icahn eventually agreed to pay $30 million a year for eight years to help cover TWA's pension deficit.[66]

This episode was recalled in February 2006 when the PBGC sought to attach the assets of another financier specializing in distressed assets: Ira L. Rennert. Rennert's holding company Renco is the owner of WCI Steel, a company reorganized after bankruptcy in the early 1990s. In 1995 the company's employees went on strike and won a new pension agreement. Prior to this the company had issued bonds worth $300 million, redeemable in 2004. However, by this date WCI's 2,000 employees and retirees were alarmed to learn that the company was in bad shape again and that, in case of bankruptcy, the pension fund would have a deficit of $189 million. Repeating its earlier tactic the PBGC responded by taking a lien on Rennert's other assets which, as the insurer well knew, were impressive. In 1992 Rennert had purchased AM General for $133 million, selling a 70 per cent stake for $930 million in 2004. AM General is the manufacturer of the Humvee military vehicle and the civilian Hummer, distributed by GM. With the fruits of such investments Rennert had built a palatial estate, 'Fair Field', situated in Sagaponeck, the Hamptons, Long Island. This beach-front estate comprises five buildings with twenty-nine bedrooms and thirty-nine bathrooms and according to a report '[i]ts inlaid floors, its frescoes and other splendors have an asset value of $185 million, uncannily close to the $189 shortfall that the WCI actuary found [in the company's pension fund]'.[67] The PBGC claimed that Fair Field could be attached because Renco was its beneficial owner, holding over 80 per cent of Blue Turtles, the entity that directly owned the estate.

However, a spokesman for Renco, a former counsel with the PBGC, explained that his client was not the villain of the piece and had no intention of short-changing the pensioners. The attempt to stick the pension liabilities on the PBGC was the work of a group of Wall Street firms who had acquired the company's outstanding bonds and who saw the pension fund as a rival claim on the company's assets. 'No matter how big and valuable Mr Rennert's house is, Mr Ford said, the agency should instead be setting its sights on a group of Wall Street firms that, he said, were really the ones trying to dump the pension fund. "They are the ones driving this", said Mr Ford.'[68] However, the judge of the bankruptcy court was evidently unimpressed by Rennert's offer to respect the pension-fund obligations. She deemed him not to be a person who could be relied upon to behave in 'the most economically reasonable manner'. While the judge criticized the Wall Street financiers she had no confidence in Rennert: 'She cited a deposition in which Mr Rennert said that he did not know who sat on the Renco group board, where the company kept its records or what its ownership structure was.'[69] I offer these details simply as an illustration of the Byzantine complications of corporate finance and pension funding. They also show the PBGC as willing to take a tough line with those they believe to be delinquent owners.

While the PBGC has made a vital contribution to the reorganization of hundreds of companies it has usually received nothing in return; its recent receipt of weak airline stock is far too limited to have made any difference. By contrast former shareholders and directors, who must have borne some responsibility for the mess, were compensated. Former shareholders either sold out for cash to the new owners, or received stock in the reorganized concern. And Wilbur Ross, who had been the 'distressed asset specialist' for Bethlehem, made several billion dollars for himself and his backers by arranging the transfer from the old to the new owners, something which a public agency like the PBGC could also have supervised.

The PBGC has been an unacknowledged – and largely unrewarded – instrument of industrial reorganization and industrial policy. Partly in consequence its future is in doubt. Further large-scale defaults will drag down the PBGC and lead to calls for a Federal bail-out. Those who now depend on the PBGC will find their shrunken pensions further reduced and the US tax payer will underwrite the 'barnacle removal' of the distressed assets specialists. The UK's Pension Protection Fund, which opened for business in April 2005, finds itself facing very similar problems. These are disasters waiting to happen.

As noted above, it was the junking of Federal Mogul's UK pension plan that prompted the setting up of the PPF in 2004, but the British government took care to exclude from the latter's remit compensation for the 85,000 workers who had lost almost the entirety of their pension assets in the years 2001–4, notwithstanding the fact that the government itself had strongly advised employees to subscribe to these schemes if they were provided. This reckless advice, plus the refusal to compensate those affected, earned the government a stinging rebuke from the Parliamentary Ombudsman when she reported on the matter in 2006. Around the same time it emerged that Britain had its own home-grown 'vulture capitalists'. In March 2006 the *Financial Times* carried the following report concerning a property group which had acquired a controlling stake in the Allders retail chain: 'Minerva, which owned a 60 per cent stake in Allders when it went into administration in January last year, has always insisted the 3,500 pensioners in the group's pension scheme were not its responsibility. But the circumstances surrounding the collapse of Allders, with a pension deficit of £68 million are still being examined by Kroll, the insolvency practitioners. Minerva paid £49 million for Allders' flagship Croydon store just months before the retailer's collapse. It is expected that Allders will soon be put into liquidation, at which point the pension trustees can ask for help from the government's Pension Protection Fund . . . Minerva has endured a turbulent 18 months, with . . . the Allders collapse and the the replacement of chairman Sir David Gerrard with Andrew Rosenfeld, former chief executive. It emerged last week that the two men had lent a total of £3.3 million to the Labour Party. Mr Hasan [the chief executive] yesterday denied suggestions that Minerva may have won planning permission for its unbuilt Minerva Tower in the City as part of this loan.'[70] In a peculiarly British twist to the vulture capitalist scenario, Downing Street had also nominated Gerrard for a peerage. While in the US the party donors get to influence legislation, in the UK they can actually become legislators as well − though in this case untoward exposé of the secret loans was to upset the calculation.

Public Sector Pension Schemes

So far, I have dwelt on the private sector schemes because they are most at risk, but public sector schemes have severe problems too. Many such schemes are meant to be pre-funded, but all are ultimately backed by the revenue-raising powers of the local authority concerned, whether municipality, county or state.[71] The promises they embody often have legal force. Voters generally value the contribution of firefighters, teachers, nurses and other public workers. They know that their pensions often compensate for modest pay and that they help retain experienced personnel. When Arnold Schwarzenegger, the newly elected Governor of California, was unwise enough to take on teachers' and nurses' benefits in 2005 he soon found that he had was losing public support. The 'Terminator' backed down and was heavily defeated in subsequent 'reform' referenda.

Nevertheless a strengthening of the finances of public-sector employee schemes is badly needed. Even the funded schemes can be in difficulties because of cutbacks in social budgets which have sometimes led the sponsoring authorities to skip proper contributions. On other occasions, pensions have been given priority but services and employment have been slashed. Public schemes are spared some of the Byzantine complications of their corporate counterparts and their management is generally entrusted to boards of trustees that include some elected officials. The cost structure of public schemes is invariably far more modest than those in the commercial sector and – so long as privatization is kept at bay – such schemes should be protected from 'vulture capital'. Members of such schemes generally have the opportunity to move within the public sector without loss of pension rights. They also enjoy a measure of legal protection. The courts prevented the City of San Diego from using threatened bankruptcy to slough off pension commitments to its own employees – instead it has had to pledge 8 per cent of future revenues to this purpose. In the UK the government of Tony Blair announced a later retiring age for municipal workers, but found it advisable to back down just before the 2005 general election.

Notwithstanding their claim on future revenues, US public-sector retirement schemes have run into difficulties and are sometimes said to be 'heavily under-funded'. The problem is usually the soaring cost of retirement health-care promises rather than the pension promise as such. Since 1965 the Medicare programme has supposedly offered basic health coverage for those over sixty-five, but enough is excluded from this coverage – the cost of medicines, certain operations, emergency care and so forth – that local authorities can attract employees to public service by offering to cover these supplementary medical costs for their retirees. By 2005, forty-one US states offered some medical coverage to their employees on retirement but only eleven states had established pre-funding to cover the cost. The remaining thirty states planned to cover such costs on a pay-as-you-go basis. At municipal and county level there were similarly uneven arrangements. In 2005 the Governmental Accounting Standards Board announced the phasing-in of a requirement for each authority to estimate the total value of its pension and medical promises across a thirty-year horizon and to explain how it planned to meet them. Already in 2005 there were 5.5 million retired public employees with such coverage. The combination of growing numbers of retirees and ballooning medical costs leads to actuarial estimates of future liabilities that reach scary numbers. One report put the liability at $1 trillion. But it also added: 'The numbers can vary wildly by locality, depending on how rich its benefits are, what assumptions the actuary uses about future demographic and investment earnings, and that great unknown, the cost of health-care 30 years in the future.'[72] In the public as in the private sector the runaway costs of health care would be best tackled not by pre-funding but by a move to a public health care system. The removal of retiree health costs would then leave a more manageable pension problem.

The state of Alaska estimated a pensions and health care 'deficit' of $5.7 billion using the new accounting approach. At the prompting of the governor and conservative legislators, the state introduced reduced benefits for new employees (the state constitution forbids changing the entitlements of existing employees). In the case of a company going out of business such an accounting method is quite appropriate, but it is too crude when applied to public authorities which can count on future revenues and which can, at least to some extent, adjust outgoings to fit them. To suppose that the state of Alaska has no scope for raising extra revenue is scarcely realistic. Of course the purpose of treating a public authority like a failing business is to encourage benefit cuts, budget cuts, the sub-contracting of public services to commercial suppliers or even full privatization. And if budget cuts take the form of driving a wedge between old and new workers, then the result will be fragmentation of the workforce and generational tension. In the Alaskan case the White House put pressure on local Republicans to replace 'defined benefits' by private accounts.[73] The plight of the US public sector supplementary pension schemes, no less than that of those in the private sector, points up the need for a secure, universal and independent system of second pensions. If there is a problem of paying for decent pensions in the public sector it will not be overcome by adoption of the commercial model.

Thumbs Down for Private Pensions

The commercial pension-fund regime, whether DB or DC, fails on many counts. The extent and quality of coverage is poor. Corporate DB schemes are increasingly risky, and can be bad for investment and jobs. Public DB schemes seem to be living on borrowed time. DC schemes are plagued by marketing costs and hidden charges. They are vulnerable to unscrupulous intermediaries, and their flexibility is achieved at too high a cost. They consequently do not build adequate funds or yield good returns to contributions. All this robs pension arrangements of their raison d'être but does not exhaust their problems. In the next chapter we consider some of the structural defects of pension finance which further contribute to its dismal record and to such spreading economic distempers as the aggrandizement of CEOs, grotesque inequality, heavy personal indebtedness, and opaque financialization.

I have suggested that there might be ways of strengthening the finances of the schemes which contribute to the PBGC and the PPF because it seems only fair to salvage as much as possible from pension arrangements to which many millions have contributed for so long. But the real lesson of the great insecurity of private pensions – and of US employer-supplied health benefits – is the need for universal public coverage. Arrangements that depend on the financial health of particular corporations or providers will always be risky. The US economist and columnist Paul Krugman was moved by the showdown over Delphi to write: 'American workers at big companies used to think they had made a deal. They would be loyal to their employers, and the companies in turn would be loyal to them, guaranteeing job security, health care and a dignified retirement. Such deals were, in a real sense, the basis of America's postwar social order . . . What went wrong? An important part of the answer is that America's semiprivatized welfare state worked in the first place only because we had a stability that – along with any semblance of economic security for many workers – is now gone . . . [I]nstead of trying to provide economic security through the back door, via tax breaks designed to encourage corporations to provide health care and pensions, we should provide it through the front door, starting with national health insurance.'[74]

Notes

1 Jacob Hacker, *The Divided Welfare State: The Battle over Public and Private Social Benefits in the United States*, Cambridge 2002, pp. 93–5, 149–50, 161–2, 185, 294–5.
2 The Pensions Commission, *Pensions: Challenges and Choices*, London 2004, p. 86.
3 Edward N. Wolff, *Retirement Insecurity: the Income Shortfall Awaiting the Soon-to-Retire*, Economic Policy Institute, 2002.
4 Ibid., pp. 79–80.
5 Timothy Smeeding and Susanna Sanderstrom, 'Poverty and Income Maintenance in Old Age: a Cross-National View of Older Women', *Feminist Economics*, vol. 11, no. 3, November 2005, pp. 163–86, p. 176.
6 Edward N. Wolff, 'The Unravelling of the American Pension System, 1983–2001', paper delivered at a conference on 'Pension Fund Capitalism', New School For Social Research, New York, September 2004.
7 Employee Benefit Research Institute, *Will More of Us Work Forever? The 2006 Retirement Confidence Survey*, Washington DC, April 2006, p. 7.

8 Jack VanDerhei and Craig Copeland, *Can America Afford Tomorrow's Retirees?*, Employment Benefit Research Institute, November 2003, p. 1.
9 Robert L. Reynolds, 'The Next Generation', *Wall Street Journal*, 28 November 2005.
10 Ibid.
11 Madonna Harrington Meyer, Douglas A. Wolf and Christine L. Hines, 'Linking Benefits to Marital Status: Race and Social Security in the United States', *Feminist Economics*, vol. 11, no. 2, July 2005.
12 James Banks, Carl Emmerson, Zoe Oldfield and Gemma Tetlow, *Prepared for Retirement? The Adequacy and Distribution of Retirement Resources in England*, London 2005, pp. 18, 25.
13 Ibid., p. 31.
14 Mary Williams Walsh, 'Failed Pensions: A Painful Lesson in Assumptions', *New York Times*, 12 November 2003.
15 Gerard Hughes and Adrian Sinfield, 'Financing Pensions by Stealth: the Anglo-American Model and the Cost and Distribution of Tax Benefits for Private Pensions', in Gerard Hughes and Jim Stuart, eds, *Reforming Pensions in Europe: Evolution of Pension Financing and Sources of Retirement Income*, Cheltenham 2004, pp. 163–92, p. 171.
16 Christopher Oster and Karen Damato, 'Big Fees Hit Small Plans', *Wall Street Journal*, 21 October 2004.
17 Russ Wermers, 'Mutual Fund Performance', *Journal of Finance*, vol. 55, no. 4, August 2000.
18 E. Philip Davis, *Pension Funds: Retirement Income Security, and Capital Markets*, Oxford 1995, p. 236.
19 Ibid.
20 Robin Blackburn, *Banking on Death or Investing in Life: the History and Future of Pensions*, London 2002, Chapter 2.
21 William Wolman and Anne Colamosca, *The Great 401(k) Hoax*, New York 2001; Gregory Baer and Gary Gensher, *The Great Mutual Fund Trap*, New York 2000.
22 Arthur Levitt, *Take on the Street: What Wall Street and Corporate America Don't Want You to Know*, New York 2002, pp. 41–64.
23 John Bogle, *The Battle for the Soul of Capitalism*, New Haven and London 2005, pp. 154–5
24 Bogle, *Battle for the Soul of Capitalism*, p. 154.
25 Ibid., p. 156.
26 Gretchen Morgenson, 'Lop-sided 401(k)s All Too Common', *New York Times*, 5 October 2003.
27 Federal Reserve Bank, *Flow of Funds Accounts of the United States*, 2004.
28 Levitt, *Take on the Street*, p. 257.
29 Pension Benefit Guaranty Corporation, 2004 Annual Report, Washington DC, 2004, p. 14; Donald L. Bartlett and James B. Steele, 'The Broken Promise: The Great Retirement Rip-Off', *Time*, 21 October 2005.
30 Quoted in Bartlett and Steele, 'The Broken Promise', p. 38.

31 Ken Belson and Matt Richtel, 'Verizon to Halt Pension Outlay for Managers', *New York Times*, 6 December 2005.

32 Employers have also sought to replace DB coverage with so-called 'cash-balance' plans which greatly devalue the obligations to long-service workers in DB schemes. Because this severely cuts the entitlement of older workers the courts ruled that they need scrutiny and sanction from the Treasury Department, but the latter has sought to side-step responsibility. See Ellen Shultz and Theo Francis, 'Treasury May Delay Pension Rules', *Wall Street Journal*, 16 October 2003.

33 Roger Lowenstein, 'The End of Pensions?', *New York Times Magazine*, 30 October 2005; Michael Shroeder, 'UAW Fuels Logjam on House Pension Bill', *Wall Street Journal*, 8 December 2005.

34 A meticulous assessment of pension fund and health care deficits for companies in the S&P 500 was presented by Adrian Redlich of Merrill-Lynch, in a thorough research paper dated 5 November 2002. He expected the deficits to reach the range $184–323 billion by year end, with health benefits raising the overall deficit to the range $458–638 billion. The higher estimates assumed future annual returns of 9 per cent, the lower estimates even better rates of return than this. The President, House and Senate were all anxious to be seen to be helping. Avoiding an open Treasury bail-out, Congress instead brought forward legislation which allowed pension fund trustees to discount future liabilities more deeply by using a higher discount rate. But this number-massaging approach condones under-funding and exempts companies from needed contributions. It stores up problems for the future. See Norma Cohen, 'Senators Seek to Square Circle on Pension Relief', *Financial Times*, 16 September 2003; Mary Williams Walsh, 'Senate Panel to Vote on Bill to Aid Pension Plans', *New York Times*, 16 September 2003 and 'Senate Committee Votes to Give Pension Relief', *New York Times*, 18 September 2003.

35 Norma Cohen, 'Court Case Raises Fears for Solvency of US Pension Schemes', *Financial Times*, 27 October 2003.

36 'Corporate America's Legacy Costs', *Economist*, 15 October 2005.

37 'Out of Pocket', *Economist*, 5 November 2005.

38 Pension Benefit Guaranty Corporation, *2004 Annual Report*, p. 15.

39 Marty Williams Walsh, 'A Pension Rule, Sometimes Murky, is Under Pressure', *New York Times*, 8 November 2005. The study, conducted by Mihir A. Desai, Daniel B. Bergstresse and and Joshua D. Ruah was, according to this report, scheduled to appear in *The Quarterly Journal of Economics*.

40 Ibid.

41 Ibid.

42 'Out of Pocket', *Economist*, 5 November 2005.

43 I have more on this in 'The Great Pension Crunch', *The Nation*, 16 February 2003. See also Joseph Stiglitz, *The Roaring Nineties: a New History of the World's Most Prosperous Decade*, New York 2003, pp. 115–27.

44 Peter Swenson, *Capitalists Against the Market*, Cambridge 2003.

45 'Corporate America's Legacy Costs', *The Economist*, 15 October 2005.
46 There is much evidence concerning the first danger (employers using the threat of closure to obtain contribution holidays). The second supposed flaw ('moral hazard' generosity) has been rare because companies have to declare bankruptcy in order to shed pension liabilities, something managers are often loath to do. However, Lowenstein cites as an example of such undue generosity the United Airlines decision to increase the value of its pension by 40 per cent prior to entering Chapter 11 in 2002. Lowenstein, 'The End of Pensions?', *New York Times Magazine*. This decision was made after it was already clear that the company was about to enter Chapter 11. Its effect was not to raise pensions by the stated amount because the PBGC does not pay full promised pensions; overall it was designed to safeguard the level of existing pension promises following their assumption by the agency. By this time employees held a large chunk of UA stock and had representation on the board. This, together with a union promise to cooperate, explains why the usual restraint on management did not operate.
47 Michael Schroeder, 'Big Stakes in Ailing Airlines Raise Questions for U.S. Pensions Agency', *Wall Street Journal*, 3 November 2005.
48 The UK Pension Regulator, David Norgrove, explained his decision in a letter which was published in the *Financial Times* correspondence columns on 14 June 2005.
49 Mary Williams Walsh, 'Whoops! There Goes Another Pension Plan: Retiree Benefits Turn Into Gold for Wall Street', *New York Times*, 18 September 2005.
50 Editorial, 'Pension Crisis Comes to the Boil', *Financial Times*, 26 July 2004.
51 Paul Krugman, 'The Big Squeeze', *New York Times*, 17 October 2005.
52 Jeffrey McKracken, 'Reassembling Delphi', *Wall Street Journal*, 17 October 2005.
53 Claudia H. Deutsch, 'Got an Ailing Business? He Wants to Make it Right', *New York Times*, 26 October 2005.
54 Ibid.
55 Dan Roberts, Bernard Simon and James Macintosh, 'Delphi Flash-Point Between Generations', *Financial Times*, 11 October 2005.
56 Claudia Deutsch, 'Got an Ailing Business?', *New York Times*, 26 October 2005.
57 John Gapper, 'The Danger of Rewriting Chapter 11', *Financial Times*, 13 October 2005.
58 Martin Wolf, 'A Shameful Pensions Confidence Trick', *Financial Times*, 1 July 2005.
59 Danny Hakim and Jeremy Peters, 'Union Offers Details of Health Deal With G.M.', *New York Times*, Business Section, 21 October 2004.
60 This was the verdict of analysts of quite different persuasions: see, e.g., Greg Easterbrook, 'The GM Lesson', *New York Times*, 12 June 2005 and John Schnapp, 'GM Needs an Extreme Makeover', *Wall Street Journal*, 24 October 2005.
61 'Corporate America's Legacy Costs', *The Economist*, 15 October 2005.

62 For an article that addresses GM's plight, the Wal-Mart memo and the case
    for introducing a single-payer, public-health insurance system in the US see
    Paul Krugman, 'Pride, Prejudice and Insurance', *New York Times*, 7 No-
    vember 2005. Krugman, citing a *Health Affairs* study, points out that the US
    spends far more on health care per person than Canada or Germany or the
    UK for health outcomes which are broadly comparable. While surgery
    waiting times were shorter in the US than in the UK or Canada this was not
    true of Germany and on many other metrics the US underperformed the
    other states. He also points out that Taiwan, by switching from a US to a
    Canadian style system, raised health care coverage from less than 60 per cent
    to 97 per cent.

63 Mary Williams Walsh, 'Veto Threat As Senators Approve Pension Bill', *New
    York Times*, 17 November 2005.

64 Susan Carey, 'Bankruptcy Lawyers Flying High', *Wall Street Journal*, 21
    October 2005.

65 Eduardo Porter, 'Reinventing the Mill', *New York Times*, Business section,
    22 October 2005.

66 Mary Williams Walsh, 'Pension Battle May Entangle Mogul's Home', *New
    York Times*, 3 February 2006.

67 Ibid.

68 Ibid.

69 Ibid.

70 Jim Pickard, 'Pensions Regulator "Will take No Action" Against Minerva',
    Financial Times, 28 March 2006.

71 The above-quoted, and generally excellent, *Time* magazine survey of US
    pensions gave figures for public sector pension deficits as if they were wholly
    comparable to those in the private sector. But not all of these schemes aimed
    to be wholly pre-funded, as a company scheme should be. While there is no
    guarantee that any given company will be around in 40 years' time this is not
    the case, as was pointed out above, for San Diego, Philadelphia or Illinois,
    three cases of pension deficits cited by the report. Donald Bartlett and James
    Steele, 'The Broken Promise', *Time*, 21 October 2005. Local authorities
    probably should try to pre-fund a significant portion of the pensions they will
    owe their employees for reasons to be explored in Chapter 5, below, but
    their fiscal powers allow them to use local taxes or bond sales to meet them as
    well. Indeed a mixed approach could well be optimal.

72 Milt Freudenheim and Mary Williams Walsh, 'The Next Retirement Time
    Bomb', *New York Times*, 11 December 2005.

73 Ibid.

74 Paul Krugman, 'Age of Anxiety', *New York Times*, 28 November 2005.

4

The Murky World of Grey Capital

The US and UK pension funds control huge assets but the ownership rights of plan members are very unclear, enabling either corporate sponsors or fund management companies to wield – or abstain from wielding – the proxy power of the underlying owners. The pension fund can be thought of as a species of 'grey capital' because the property rights it embodies are a twilight zone or grey area. There are, in fact, multiple levels of ambiguity and uncertainty, depending on the type of pension fund, and it is these that I explore in this chapter. Some economic sociologists have taken to using the word 'ambage' to describe a world where the oscillations in meaning are embedded in the phenomena they are studying, not simply a trick of perception. More generally, the process whereby workers' 'deferred pay' is siphoned off by pension contributions and handed to financial managers who funnel it to exotic new settings, far removed from workers' own life world, is a new dimension to the alienation which Karl Marx thought defined capitalism. Some find that their savings are invested in shopping malls or shiny office blocks in distant lands, while their own community suffers neglect and decay. Others find that shares in their pension portfolio are being rented out to hedge funds that have targeted the companies in which they or their neighbours work.

While private sector DB pension funds in the United States are supposedly held for the benefit of plan members, they are controlled by trustees appointed by the corporate sponsors. Recent regulation in the UK has required a minimum number of the trustees in such schemes to be employees of the company, but there remains the problem that there are essentially two types of trustee, either well-informed and financially sophisticated personnel appointed by the Finance Director, or lay trustees who lack the expertise needed to chart a significantly different path. In the case of most DC funds, whether in the US or the UK, the plan members are equally removed from direct control of their savings, which are entrusted to a fund manager who undertakes and manages the direct investment process. In both types of plan the agents are formally required to give priority to the financial interests of the plan members, but the evidence assembled in the last chapter shows how empty this injunction can be. Nevertheless, prosecutions for breach of this 'fiduciary duty' are very rare (some exceptions will be considered below). In addition to private-sector DB plans, and the variety of DC plans, there are also public-sector DB plans which do give some representation to plan members through trade union representatives and local elected officials. There are also some US multi-employer funds where the trade unions play a coordinating role. Potentially the management of public-sector and multi-employer funds could be different from those of the private sector, but in practice the criteria by which they discharge their duties have been rather similar. While there are a number of quite well-run public-sector schemes which delivered good returns and have encouraged plan members to have some input, the record of the multi-employer schemes has been very mixed, with some cases of fraud.

A Double Accountability Deficit

When private sector DB schemes were established in the 1950s, the obligations were distant – they did not even appear in the company accounts – yet the advantages were immediate, encouraging employee retention and furnishing a new link to the world of finance. The last chapter stressed how burdensome DB schemes have become to many sponsors in recent years, but in their early years, and in buoyant conditions, they were widely embraced by management. The flow of contributions to the fund could be advantageously coordinated with the company's overall financial planning. Seen from one standpoint the assets in the fund were simply there to ensure that the company could deliver on its promises, and to that extent belonged to the corporation. But when the law relating to DB funds was tightened up by the Employee Retirement Income Security Act (ERISA) of 1974, it was made clear that sponsors could not simply draw down the pension funds as if they were company reserves, and were instead obliged to maintain enough assets in the fund to cover the likely liabilities. British law was also tightened up in 1995 following the Maxwell scandal. (The British press magnate Robert Maxwell stole £400 million from pension funds sponsored by the companies he owned, using the cash to prop up the share value of his companies. He was probably breaking British law, but he committed suicide and the trustees who executed his instructions were never convicted. Goldman Sachs, his brokers, paid compensation to the pension funds.) Legislation reserving pension assets for use in paying employee pensions strengthened employees' claims but did not make such assets their property or mandate any employee role in the management of funds. One legal interpretation has urged that pension assets in a DB scheme are 'non-private property' that are entitled to 'protected storage', as is the case with corpses, or body parts – though the wishes of the deceased are more likely to be consulted than are those of the member of a pension plan.[1]

The trustees of a DB scheme are bound by a rule which holds that the fund must be managed as a 'prudent expert' would manage it. According to a circular logic, the standards of the prudent expert are those observed by the financial services industry itself. The immense sums raised by pension funds of all types have hugely increased the importance of institutional investment. In the 1940s and early 1950s nearly all pension money was invested in government bonds, on the grounds that their future value was guaranteed and that this was therefore the safe and prudent thing to do. But before long pension fund trustees were invited to consider adding private securities to the portfolio. It was urged that corporate shares and bonds would earn a higher return over the long run; the sponsor could either economize on contributions, or use better benefits to attract key workers. The higher return to shares was, of course, a reward for risk but it was urged that a pension fund that had well-diversified shareholdings would, over the long-run, reduce that risk as the under-performance of some companies was compensated for by the out-performance of others. To this evolving debate over portfolio theory there was added the implications of a rising inflation rate. The government bonds in which pension fund managers had invested proved a poor hedge against inflation. Other things being equal, a fund with tangible assets, such as shares or property, would be able to keep abreast of rising prices. After about 1982, the cult of equity carried almost all before it and even quite cautious fund managers would happily contemplate corporate securities comprising 80 per cent of fund assets. Finally, in the dawning epoch of financialization, attention has focused not just on the right mix of assets but on financial products and treatments – swaptions and the like – which give one type of asset some of the characteristics of another. By the early twenty-first century the fund manager or board of trustees who are worried about inflation risk, or interest rate risk, can purchase a product that will hedge it. It would also be common for fund managers to earn a little more on their holdings by lending stock to hedge funds who would employ them in short-selling operations (i.e. selling the borrowed shares in the hope that this will drive down the share price, so that they can then repurchase the shares at a profit prior to returning them to the lender – on this more below). It will readily be grasped that such procedures have the effect of complicating and weakening ownership rights. There is also the problem that the trustees who permit or encourage the use of financialized techniques are more concerned with saving the sponsor money than they are with fortifying the pension promise.

Whatever the new sophistication of fund management, it remains the case that the nominal owners or beneficiaries of the assets in a pension fund have no say in how their savings are managed. The shareholding power of pension funds is used – or neutralized – in ways which sponsoring companies and fund managers find mutually convenient. In 2005, pension funds owned a big chunk of publicly quoted shares, amounting to a quarter of UK public securities and a fifth of US quoted securities. The holding of any one fund would not comprise more than a few per cent of the shares in any given company. Nevertheless the outlook and concerns of 'institutional shareholders', sometimes coordinated by bodies such as the Council of Institutional Investors (CII) in the US, or the National Association of Pension Funds (NAPF) in the UK, was something that managers were bound to take into account. Large companies have an executive whose job it is to keep in touch with the institutional investors and when major announcements are made the CEO will be available to answer the fund managers' questions.

Nevertheless there is a double accountability deficit, with fund managers not answerable to plan beneficiaries and corporate management only sporadically answerable to shareholders. Indeed the now widely admitted crisis of corporate governance – several symptoms of which are to be considered below – has its roots in the failures of pension funds, and other institutional investors, properly to represent the interests and views of the ultimate owners, namely the plan participants. The evidence suggests that capitalism works better if its stewards are answerable to someone other than themselves.

The typical outlook of the corporate executive assigned to the job of looking after the pension fund has been evoked in a pioneering study by two US anthropologists, William O'Barr and John Conley. They report the following exchange with one corporate pensions executive: ' "*Do you have any contact with the beneficiaries of the fund?*" "None whatsoever." "*It never happened?*" "None whatsoever." " *What kind of reporting is done to the beneficiaries every year?"* "The legal requirement under ERISA." *"What does it look like on paper?"* "I'm trying to remember." "[2] In contrast to this distant relationship, the pensions executive will be in close and daily contact with the Chief Financial Officer (CFO) of the sponsoring company – indeed in some cases he will be the CFO.

In earlier decades sociologists used to debate what they called the managerial revolution.[3] The atomization of share ownership, it was said, had permitted business leaders to establish undisputed sway over the corporations entrusted to them. In the 1960s and 1970s I was inclined to question this, since the exposure of management to the risk of takeover gave the owners real leverage, the power of 'exit' (selling their holdings) if not 'voice' (a say in company policy). The ambitions and share-stake of corporate managers also inclined them to share the concerns of large shareholders. And anyway the competitive context obliged them to follow a certain logic of accumulation whatever their private inclinations.

The rise of employer-sponsored pension funds created a new type of owner and potentially strengthened their hand, overcoming fragmentation and furnishing them with a knowledgeable agent. This was particularly the case with DC schemes but applied to DB schemes that are sponsored by an employer. And even pension products that are individually purchased and held, such as the contents of many IRAs (Individual Retirement Accounts) in the US or Stakeholder Accounts in the UK, are supposedly geared to the needs of the future retiree – this is how they are advertised and why they attract tax relief. The fund managers are offering those who participate in such schemes access to information, expertise and operational economies that are superior to those available to the individual small-scale investor. The price they charge for this may be exorbitant but they do offer market power.

In 1974, Peter Drucker, the doyen of management studies, published *The Unseen Revolution: How Pension Fund Socialism Came to America.* In it he argued that the American working class was becoming the real owner of US industry and would soon be able to ensure that management did its bidding. The events of the following decade showed this prophecy to be wide of the mark. Fund managers operated in two modes, neither of which was dictated by any concern for the workforce. The mass of pension-fund money was conservatively managed in ways that avoided challenging existing corporate leadership. The boards of the sponsoring companies chose the pension trustees, and through them, the pension fund manager. The relationship between fund managers and corporate officials could be cosy, or it could be distant, but in either case it was not antagonistic or even engaged, and in neither case was there any input from employees. If it was convenient for the corporation to skip a contribution, then the trustees would normally fall into line, with the consequences considered in the last chapter. Nevertheless, the managerial horizon was still the enterprise and its future, in a pattern that had been established during the postwar boom.

But there was a second mode in which the dynamics of corporate finance became detached from any given enterprise or workforce. Some sponsors, trustees and fund managers were anxious to boost returns, and realize 'shareholder value', even if it meant jeopardizing cosy relationships. If a more aggressive policy was pursued – for example lending support to takeover specialists – it would typically endanger the jobs of employees at target companies. If returns to a DB pension fund were consequently increased it might be thought that this would benefit those expecting to receive their pension from that fund. But, strictly speaking, this was not the case because the entitlement of each plan member would reflect their service in the company and their final salary, not returns to the pension fund. On the other hand good returns did help sponsors because it enabled them, to reduce, or skip, their own contribution to the fund.

There were thus occasional jousts, with fund managers backing attempts to reorganize corporate assets. In the 1980s pension funds and other institutional money was made available to corporate raiders like James Goldsmith and financial engineers like Michael Milken who successfully sought to boost the importance of share value in corporate affairs. As Michael Useem observed: 'The challenge to the managerial revolution came with a novel twist. Ownership was resurgent, but not from the original founder entrepreneurs . . . The new ownership muscle came instead from major institutional investors, take over specialists and financial professionals.'[4] The financial professionals and take over specialists organized a wave of mergers and acquisitions that boosted the share price of the target companies but often brought little lasting benefit to the shareholders in the predator company. Looked at from the employee's standpoint, the pain was felt by those who lost their jobs in the post-merger reorganization. Teresa Ghilarducci charged that pension funds aided and abetted the downsizing of the late 1980s and early 1990s. She wrote: 'the stewards of labor's capital, used pension funds in speculative investment activity, which closed plants and strangled communities.'[5] The supposed justification for this takeover activity was that it promoted the efficient reallocation of capital. But pension funds discovered that the majority of takeovers did not, in fact, benefit them overall. A study of 700 takeovers in 1996–8 by the accountants KPMG found that in 86 per cent of the cases studied the acquisition either added no value to the predator, or had lost it.[6]

Fund managers can gang up to remove CEOs who do not succeed in sustaining shareholder value. In the early 1990s CEOs at a string of underperforming giants were removed thanks, in part, to shareholder pressure – such exits were seen at, among many others, such important companies as GM, IBM, Westinghouse, American Express, Xerox and Coca-Cola.[7] In other cases institutional shareholders pressed for corporate reorganizations that broke up historic companies like AT&T and ITT. Concern for shareholder value was the driving force in these dramatic developments.[8]

But so long as the share price was buoyant the fund managers would tolerate much by way of high-handed behaviour from CEOs, including actions that did nothing for the long-term interests of the companies' stakeholders. Moreover the CEO can only be removed by the board of directors so that institutional investors only prevailed where they could find allies on the board, as well as a convincing alternative candidate for the top job. The wave of takeovers led CEOs and their boards to insulate themselves from shareholder pressure by such devices as staggered board elections (e.g. only a third of directors needed to be elected in any one year). By 1990 two-thirds of large companies were protected by 'poison pills' – in case of a takeover the pre-takeover shareholders would have the right to purchase additional stock at below-market prices, thus nullifying the predator's gain. But if a company needs to raise new capital then it often finds that investors will require a dismantling of such defences. Management can also bolster its position by promoting employee stock ownership, since employees are known as loyal shareholders.[9] (When the full scale of pension fund deficits became visible in the early years of the new millennium, it emerged that perhaps the best 'poison pill' of all was a generous, but underfunded, pension scheme).

Though some pension funds lent to the corporate raiders, the normal stance of privately run pension funds has been to support the existing leadership of a business. As Useem puts it: 'private-fund managers know that their bosses look unkindly on overt challenges to other corporations'.[10] The fund managers are naturally attentive to the interests and viewpoint of the sponsoring board, which has nominated the trustees who will renew or drop their mandate to manage the fund. The fund managers are often themselves divisions of large financial concerns like Barclays, State Street, Citigroup, Merrill Lynch and Morgan Stanley, which hope to make fat fees from supplying other services to the corporations – rights issues, initial public offerings (IPOs), mergers and acquisitions (M&A) and so forth. This gives them a further reason to ingratiate themselves to the sponsoring CEOs and boards of directors. When the money managers come to vote the shares they hold in trust at AGMs, they will defer to the board and often disregard poor governance. Sometimes the trustees themselves will mandate such a policy. Simple shareholder passivity is usually enough to allow the board a free hand. John Bogle, the veteran money manager, writes: 'No mutual fund, pension manager, bank, or insurance company has ever sponsored a proxy resolution that was opposed by the board of directors or managers.'[11] (The way this is phrased allows for a rare action of this sort taken by a public-sector pension fund.)

Managers of actively traded funds who are unhappy with the way a company is being run will sell its shares rather than openly challenge its managers at an AGM. But for reasons of diversification large funds have to own nearly all publicly quoted companies. Passively managed index funds, accounting for roughly half of all pension money, cannot respond to concern by selling shares. At the limit index- tracking funds may use abstention in board re-election votes at AGMs to express unhappiness, or may join informal representations to a failing corporate leadership warning of such action. In a takeover situation even index funds usually have some leeway for adjusting their portfolio.

Over the 1990s the investment banks, in their eagerness for extra business, became the handmaidens of executive aggrandizement. Business leaders, increasingly free from public regulation, found their most cherished schemes for expansion and enrichment cheered on by finance houses who made huge fees from mergers and acquisitions, IPOs and rights issues. This situation damaged the interests of policy-holders and bred many of the business scandals and disasters of the last few years. Shareholder 'democracy' has never been very robust but 'classified boards' (staggered elections), cumulative voting and poison pills have further weakened it at many companies. In good times CEOs urge that their sole duty is to deliver shareholder value; in bad times they urge patience. They doubt that shareholders, especially institutional share-holders, have the commitment and far-sightedness needed to pursue a long-term strategy.[12]

When fund managers feel unhappy with a corporation they simply sell its shares. Indeed shares are typically held for months not years – hence the common complaint of 'short-termism'. Today the logic of financia-lization can add a further twist. The pact between boards and fund managers is eroded as the latter turn to hedge funds in a desperate attempt to boost returns. The hedge funds specialize in aggressive shorting operations, that is, they borrow shares in order to sell them, so an employee's assets might well be used to drag down his employer. Even if the pension fund does not itself invest in the hedge fund, the latter still generally rely on institutional investors when borrowing shares to carry out the short selling operation.

The large companies are subject to regular audit, with the resulting audited accounts supposedly enabling shareholders to judge the effec-tiveness of managerial stewardship. But part of today's crisis of governance has been the realization that corporations can capture the apparatus meant to invigilate their workings – examples will be given in the next chapter. Furthermore there are now only four accountants of truly global scale – Deloitte, Ernst and Young, Pricewaterhouse Coopers and KPMG – and this 'big four' operate a discreet cartel.

Among the signs of the indulgence extended to corporations by accountants and auditors are the fact that more than 700 large companies were forced to re-state their accounts between 1999 and 2003. Profes-sional advisers allowed companies to issue so-called 'pro-forma' accounts which supposedly reported 'underlying' performance and earnings, while omitting 'exceptional' costs or write-offs. Corporations which were meeting very demanding quarterly earnings targets were nevertheless barely recording a profit when the tax-sensitive annual accounts were filed.[13]

Like the financial groups, the auditors wanted to curry favour with business leaders because these people could award them lucrative non-audit work. Auditors earned rich fees from the tax advice and consultancy they proffered to clients. And senior accountants have taken jobs with companies they had audited. Auditors are nominally appointed by the shareholders at AGMs, but in reality they are chosen and paid by the CEO and board, arrangements which by themselves compromise their independence. In 1999–2000 the Securities and Exchange Commission

(SEC) and the Financial Accounting Standards Board (FASB) sought to make auditors more independent of corporations, but they were defeated by tenacious lobbying from the accounting industry, with support from the Democrat Senator Joe Lieberman and the Republican Senator Phil Gramm.[14]

The allocation of pension fund mandates is arbitrated by a tightly knit structure similar to audit and insurance. Prior to renewing a pension fund mandate the trustees will engage one of the handful of consultants – Watson Wyatt, William Mercer and Hewitt being the largest – who, in their turn, have a network of relationships with the large financial houses. William Mercer also has its own fund management arm. The recommendations and endorsements of the pension fund consultants are deemed to satisfy the trustees' fiduciary duty towards fund beneficiaries. While the structure is questionable, the pension fund consultants accumulate a formidable body of information on fund performance and can draw on the best actuarial, economic and accounting expertise.

A good summary of the implications of the existing 'institutional investor' model has been laid out by John Bogle, founder and former CEO of Vanguard: 'The failure of investment America to exercise its ownership rights over corporate America has been the major factor in the pathological mutation that has re-shaped owners' capitalism into managers' capitalism. That mutation in turn has been importantly responsible for the gross excesses in executive compensation, as well as flaws in the investment system itself that emerged in the late twentieth century . . . Whatever the reasons for turning a blind eye, the record clearly shows that investment America largely ignored corporate governance issues. Using Pogo's formulation, "We have met the enemy of corporate governance and he is us".'[15] It remains to explore the consequences.

Passive Investors and CEO Enrichment

The 1980s and 1990s witnessed the eclipse of corporate man and the rise of the superstar CEO, who trampled on employees, pensioners and, eventually, shareholders too. Leading financial economists such as Michael Jensen and Kevin Murphy argued that a device was needed to reinforce the priority of shareholder value and to align executive interests with those of the owners. They recommended that CEOs and directors should have a much larger equity stake in the companies they ran.[16]

While it would be good if directors could buy at least some of this stock with their own money this was not always practical and the stock option achieved nearly the same result. The public should not be squeamish about rewarding executives, they argued, so long as they had an equity stake: 'By aiming their protests at compensation *levels*, uninvited but influential guests at the management bargaining table (the business press, labor unions, political figures) intimidate board members and constrain the types of contracts that are written between managers and share-holders.'[17] The fear that boards would shrink from properly rewarding CEOs was to prove laughably misplaced, with Jensen's own expert recommendations playing a modest role in loosening all restraint.

In a presidential address to the American Finance Association in 1993 Jensen argued that capitalism was undergoing a new revolution as far-reaching in its consequences as the industrial revolution of the nineteenth century. In his view, CEOs and boards of directors should no longer think it their task to come up with bold plans for investment or product improvement. They should be just as willing to consider downsizing, returning value to the shareholders by means of buy-backs, and preparing their company for 'exit'. Jensen even had a kind word for those unfairly demonized figures, the corporate raiders, who were simply promoting a more rational allocation of capital.[18] In fact Jensen was lending his own gloss to a financial revolution that was already well underway. Executives were already learning to love share options as a powerful supplement to salary, and began to see possibilities in combining them with share buy-backs and the pursuit of shareholder value.

Stock options gave an option to buy at the prices current when issued, giving senior executives an interest in ramping up share values. If their company's shares rose they could make millions by exercising their options, and immediately selling the cheaply acquired shares. CEOs and CFOs boosted share price in a way that did nothing to serve the long-term interests of shareholders. Between 1994 and 1999 they borrowed $1.2 trillion from the banks, supposedly for the purpose of strengthening their investment programmes. But instead they used most of this money – 57 per cent – to buy back shares in the companies they ran.[19] This naturally boosted shares prices. The CEOs and CFOs then sold their share options for a massive profit. Men like Jack Welch of GE, Charles Wang of Computer Associates and Ken Lay of Enron became multi-millionaires. Huge inequalities opened up. By 2001 the chief executive of one of the top US 500 companies earned 224 times the annual salary of the average employee. In most cases the cost to the company of employee options did not appear on the books even though it amounted to 19.5 per cent of profits in 2000. Some of this total related to options given to employees in new tech start-ups, but the lion's share went to senior executives in large companies.

Nomi Prins writes: 'According to a Fortune Magazine study one thousand corporate executives siphoned off $66 billion between 1998 and 2001, with $23 billion going to insiders at the top twenty five firms . . . Quest led the Top 25 club with $2.3 billion transferred from the pensions of its workers to the pockets of its leaders. How did this happen? Workers' pensions were invested in their own company's stock. When the senior circles cashed out at the peak just before the crash, they reduced the value of the shares and thus the value of the workers' pensions.'[20]

The years following the collapse of the share bubble saw no abatement in the exorbitant payment of chief executives. Boards were even willing to re-price share options that were under water (i.e. below the strike price and hence not yet 'in the money'). Research by the Corporate Library of Portland, Maine, found that overall executive compensation rose each year from 1999 to 2004 at 1,522 of the larger US companies, with the median payment (i.e. the payment at the mid-point of the distribution from largest to smallest) rising from $1 million to $2.5 million annually over this period.[21]

Chief executives of the top companies were likely to receive total compensation worth $25–35 million a year, as were CEOs of major finance houses. Indeed at the latter, in a good year, such largesse reaches quite far down the organization chart. In 2005 Goldman Sachs, with 22,425 employees in the US, paid average compensation of $521,000, with senior staff receiving between $1 million and $25 million.[22]

The enrichment of senior executives, whether corporate or financial, was so great that it can be seen in national income statistics. Over the last thirty years the income of the top 10 per cent of US tax-paying households has grown significantly at the expense of that of the remaining 90 per cent. But this statistic exaggerates the benefit to some of the top 10 per cent. In fact all the gains have accrued to the top 5 per cent, and 80 per cent of these gains have been reaped by the top 1 per cent of incomes. Furthermore, even this is misleading since within the top one per cent most of the gains went to the top 0.1 per cent.[23] To qualify for the top 1 per cent in 2000 a household had to be receiving at least $313,500, but the real winners were the top 0.1 per cent of households who had to be gaining at least $1.6 million in that year. There were 129,000 households in that category and together they earned $505 billion – as much as the other nine tenths of households in the top 1 per cent.[24]

The foregoing figures may understate the recent growth in income inequality, because they are based on IRS returns and because they do not reflect wealthy tax-payers' growing sophistication. Tax planning, as we will see, is central to the financialized world and leads to a multiplicity of devices for hiding income from the tax authorities, either by directing it to an off-shore tax haven or disguising it as something else. Partially offsetting this would be the lowering of top tax rates after about 1982, which somewhat reduced avoidance incentives – though the top rate after the Bush tax cuts was still 35 per cent in 2002, and many of the rich found this high enough to be worth avoiding. Whatever their imperfections, the IRS records do register the growing significance of 'partnership' income at the top end of the income scale. Gérard Duménil and Dominique Lévy have shown that those earning over $200,000 in 2001 received just over a half of this as wages, 29 per cent as capital income and capital gains and 14 per cent as partnership income. Tax-avoidance strategies are likely to be more effective at 'disappearing' capital income than at hiding salary or partnership income. Large investment banks or law firms earn revenue within the tax jurisdiction and need to pay it out as salary or partnership income if they are to avoid paying tax themselves. Duménil and Lévy report that partnership income relating to 'core finance' and the pay of CEOs were two key factors behind the galloping momentum of inequality. 'Core finance represents 59.2 per cent of total partners' capital accounts. This industry comprises 33.7 per cent of the total net income, and 57.8 per cent of the total net portfolio income distributed to partners.'[25] They add: 'The scale of this should be emphasized: the $2,216 billion of partners' capital accounts amounts to 23 per cent of the total net worth of US non-farm, non-financial corporations, and just over the total net worth (104 per cent) of all financial corporations.'[26] Whereas the US CEO with the tenth largest salary in 1970 earned 47 times the average salary of an employee, by 1999 the tenth best rewarded CEO earned 2,381 times the average salary, and the average of the top 100 CEOs was over 1000 times the average salary of an employee. Duménil and Lévy add: 'By 1999, salaries represented only 9.7 per cent of the total pay of CEOs (although note that the salary of the tenth [highest paid] CEO was $10 million); stock options accounted for 58.5 per cent, and other shares 31.8 per cent of the total pay. This rise of top "remunerations" was so concentrated at the apex of the hierarchy, and so accentuated, that it can hardly be interpreted as a reward for improved managerial skills – or for rising "marginal productivity", in the neoclassical jargon, measured by the hike in stock prices. Rather, what is at stake is a privileged device to channel surplus towards a fraction of the ruling elite.'[27]

It might be thought that during the share bubble the fund managers would have seen the warning signals and would have curbed executive aggrandizement or at least tried to dampen the speculative fever of the late 1990s. But they did not. They were playing with other people's money and the incentives they were offered encouraged irresponsibility. Managers usually receive a bonus related to the performance of the funds they manage over the previous year. In a prescient 1992 article entitled 'Churning Bubbles', two financial economists, Franklin Allen and Gary Gorton, warned of the design flaw in fund manager incentive schemes, encouraging them to join a speculative bandwagon even if they knew that it would eventually run into a ditch. As they explained: 'The call option form of portfolio managers' compensation schemes [exposing them to upside gains but not downside losses] means they can be willing to purchase a stock if there is some prospect of a capital gain even though they know with certainty that its price will fall below its current level at some point in the future.'[28] And beyond such calculations there was the fear of losing mandates, and even losing their jobs, if they carried out a rigorous assessment of company worth. In the late 1990s the analysts retained by the big banks joined the throng with 97 per cent 'buy' or 'hold' recommendations on the stocks they tracked.

Another trial lying in store was that of dubious business practices that might help a company over a bad patch but which could prove lethal if the bubble burst – as it inevitably would. J. K. Galbraith pointed out in *The Great Crash – 1929* that there is always a bit of 'bezzle' around even when things are going well.[29] When the bad times arrive the bezzle can no longer be hidden, and embezzlement leaps to view. We were told that Enron and kindred organizations were companies of the future, with their complex derivative products that could hedge everything from the price of oil to next year's weather. Yet scrutiny of the malpractices at Enron and other collapsing giants reveals that most of them were ancient ruses dressed up in the language of up-to-the-minute financial engineering. The bankers and professional advisers should have been highly suspicious of revenue boosted by hollow swaps and sham transactions, of the booking of current costs as capital assets, or the hiding of liabilities in Special Purpose Entities (SPEs). When Citibank and Morgan Stanley helped the energy company to devise SPEs, they would have gained enough knowledge to smell a rat. Merrill Lynch, in a sham transaction designed to boost Enron's profits, become the temporary owner of three energy barges off the coast of Nigeria. The bank had a commitment from Enron that it would buy back the barges as soon as the new reporting period had arrived. Citibank and Morgan Stanley lent large sums to Enron but they then constructed so-called 'credit derivatives' chopping up the loan into many pieces each carrying a different level of default risk. These were then sold, in a game of pass the parcel, to pension funds and other institutional investors. When Enron went bust many fund managers had to pick up the bill on behalf of their clients.

The banks subsequently agreed with the SEC and the attorney-general of New York that they would pay $1.4 billion in fines and compensation, though insisting that they do not admit that they were in any way at fault.[30] In several cases the banks, so far from being duped by their corporate customers, had actually themselves devised and sold obfuscatory or fraudulent devices to the deliquents.[31] Many fund managers fell over themselves to acquire what were touted as glamorous new financial products. Despite the 'deal' between regulators and banks, and the latter's protestations of future good behaviour, the accountability and regulatory deficits which allowed the scams to happen have not been remedied.

The Sarbanes–Oxley Act (2002) – to be considered in the next chapter – focused on corporate governance, not the role of the banks. Leading executives at Worldcom, Enron and dozens of other failed corporations were prosecuted and sentenced to between eight and twenty years in jail. The banks' role in helping to construct opaque – or even fraudulent – financial instruments was deemed less culpable. As already noted, the banks never admitted any guilt. However the fund managers, institutions and individuals who had lost tens of billions of dollars pursued, and sometimes won, private suits alleging malpractice, neglect and absence of due diligence on the part of their financial advisers and brokers. The banks' 2003 settlement with the regulators involved a penalty totalling $1.4 billion, as we have seen. However they paid out much larger sums in settlement of private suits brought against them by investors – by the end of 2005 they had paid $6.9 billion to settle Enron-related suits and $6.0 billion to settle Worldcom-related suits. In each case the total losses stemming from the collapse were about ten times as great as the indemnity paid out. However inadequate, Wall Street seemed to accept that it owed some compensation. But their insurers discovered that even this expiation was not what it appeared. As a *Wall Street Journal* report explained: 'The banks . . . are battling to recover a portion of the more than $13 billion they paid in fines for settlement and regulatory actions related to the frauds. They say insurance policies they bought during the 1990s should cover payments the banks made to settle class action suits over their roles in advising Enron and Worldcom. The Swiss Reinsurance Co. and some other large insurance companies are balking.'[32] One of the banks concerned, Bank of America, had taken out insurance to provide coverage of up to $100 million for claims 'arising out of any wrongful action committed by the insured'.[33] Insurance of this sort exacerbates representational problems by insulating the agent from the most likely sanction for malpractice, a fine.

The business scandals were partly explained by pressure to produce results at a time of underlying deterioration in the profitability in the provision of non-financial goods and services in the major western economies.[34] The wave of deregulation in the 1990s made its own contribution, with scandals proliferating in sectors where controls had been most thoroughly abandoned – finance, energy, communications. The Litigation Reform Act of 1995 shielded from legal challenge the claims and promises made by CEOs and company promoters.[35] Repeal of the Glass–Steagall Act in 1999 meant that investment banks were no longer constrained from going into the brokerage or retail business, even though this would mean that their brokers would be trading, and their analysts assessing, stock their bank had itself underwritten. But the scope and nature of the scandals also pointed to underlying 'agency problems', namely the betrayal of policy-holders by their own representatives, the hallmark of what I have called 'grey capitalism'. Financial concerns were helping CEOs out of a tight spot at the expense of millions of small savers. While the CEOs were anxious to conceal poor results, the banks were expecting and demanding double digit annual returns. The fund managers were flattered to have their business solicited by swanky 'bulge bracket' investment banks, even though they struggled to understand the nature of the credit derivatives and 'collateralized debt obligations' (CDOs) that they purchased. Much of the money lost in speculation was being handled by agents who were not responsible to plan members and pension policy holders.

In a study of the corporate-scandal wave Abraham Gitlow, a former

Dean of the Stern School of Business at New York University who has served on the boards of several public companies, pinpoints the overweening power of the CEO as the single most disastrous factor, seeing this as a reflection of tame boards and marginalized and comatose shareholders: 'The corporate accounting scandals . . . involved more than the separation of ownership and management control. They involved a massive concentration of power in the hands of the chief executive officer. Many CEOs achieved complete dominance over their boards thereby neutralizing their board's power over them. Once that domination was achieved it was not difficult to find professional people retained by the corporation to do its audit and perform other services . . . And, in a feedback symbiosis, significant numbers of those professionals became, with time, active initiators of schemes that helped misbehaving executives.'[36] Overcompensation as well as fraud was the consequence.

The 'managerial revolution' model is more useful that I used to suppose − it is a striking fact that it appeals to so many who have been close to the investment process like John Bogle, Allen Sykes and Robert Monks.[37] But it has the weakness that by focusing on owners and managers so tightly it fails to grasp the way that corporations are shaped by the environment in which they compete. The legal charter of the corporation has given them and their owners extraordinary privileges. They have the rights of persons while being exempt from many of their responsibilities. The limited liability of the corporation encouraged shareholders to make their investment secure in the knowledge that their potential loss was limited to what they put in. However imperfect, the competitive environment encouraged corporations to seek the rewards of specialization and of scale. This could favour rationalization and rising productivity of labour, though particular enterprises would always seek to corner the market or establish a cartel. Even Karl Marx saw the joint stock corporation as the expression of an attempt to overcome the limitations of private property and to reach new levels of co-operation.[38] Marx did not believe that after socializing the means of production working people would have to remake the world entirely anew, they would instead be able to salvage what was positive in the capitalist organization of productive processes. Today's corporate critics sometimes narrow their concerns to particular corporate malpractices without tracing the ways in which these really spring from the wider context of capitalist accumulation. Of course campaigners against corporate abuse are up against formidable, and quite amoral, antagonists but they should be aware that there can be functions fulfilled by companies which its employees, customers and suppliers will value. Likewise they should be aware that even welcome changes in corporate practice may have little or no overall effect if the competitive environment is not changed, and that even the appointment of the most progressive chief executive could leave many problems still unresolved. The admirably hard-hitting documentary film *The Corporation* (2004) sometimes failed adequately to reflect the contradictory yet systematic character of today's corporate capitalism, but the accompanying book by Joel Bakan, despite occasional psychologization of the corporate entity, nevertheless made a whole series of important and valid criticisms.[39] Naomi Klein's *No Logo* fully deserved its huge success and its stress on the coercive character of branding was accompanied by recognition that brands can increase corporate vulnerability.[40] But important as the cultural promotion of corporate products may be, it should not be allowed to hide the ultimately financial imperatives of capitalist accumulation. It is not household names like Nike or Coca-Cola which are the capstones of contemporary capitalism but finance houses, hedge funds and private equity concerns, many of which are unknown to the general public. In the end even the largest and most famous of corporations have only a precarious and provisional autonomy within the new world of business – ultimately they are playthings of the capital markets. The pension fund is very much a (subordinate) part of this world which is why I am seeking to place it in this context. This fact has been underlined by the advance of financialization, a development dating from the last two decades of the twentieth century, which is profoundly reshaping the corporate world.

Financialization and the Disposable Corporation

The distribution of power within corporations and financial networks has been shifting and unpredictable because of the growing exposure of all institutions and arrangements to the opportunities of financialization, as well as to the more familiar pressures of globalization. The term financialization refers to the growing and systemic power of finance and financial engineering in all spheres of life. In 1948 the profits of financial concerns comprised 7 per cent of all US profits; by 2004 the proportion had grown to 34 per cent.[41] These profits can arise from merging two or three corporations and then, a little later, breaking them up again. Money is made not only by those who garner the direct M&A fees but by others who practice risk arbitrage, buying and selling the newly merged or separated entities. Underwriters earn good fees from initial public share offerings (IPOs) and rights issues even though Google has shown, by successfully launching itself as a public company, that those fees are often excessive. Financial returns can also be earned by managing consumer debt, by commodifying the life course, or from the sale and use of financial products such as lease-backs, derivatives and hedging techniques. Financialization involves the eclipse of the realm of production by that of circulation, though with real effects on future production.

Financialization affects even the most powerful corporations because the banks and the ratings agencies determine their credit-worthiness and hence the cost of their capital. They may be able to finance all the investments they wish to undertake from their own resources, but this will not mean that they are free from the pressures of financialization. In drawing up their investment plans they will have to show that they will achieve the benchmark or 'hurdle' rates of return established by the financial sector.[42] Even the largest corporations have to submit to the inspections and interrogations of the ratings agencies – Standard and Poor's, Moody's and Fitch Ratings – if they wish to reassure investors and ensure cheap access to capital. Making a good profit is no longer enough; a triple A rating is also needed.[43]

The competitive process, and the changeable state of the company's outstanding obligations and assets, all exercise a constant pressure. From the standpoint of the pure investor, the corporation itself is an accidental bundle of liabilities and assets which is there to be rearranged to maximize shareholder value, which in turn reflects the fickle enthusiasms of other investors. The corporation and its workforce are, in principle, disposable. In the 1980s hundreds of thousands, if not millions, of employees discovered this, and in the 'downsizing' of the early 1990s swathes of middle and upper management discovered that they too were surplus to requirement. By the turn of the century Enron's managers became famous for a managerial regime in which each employee knew that one tenth of the staff, those who failed to reach trading targets, would be sacked each year, no matter how good or bad the overall performance. Wal-Mart, with over a million employees, occupies a quite different niche but it too ensured the malleability of its workforce, by specifying physical norms to its recruiters, by instilling a corporate ethos of emulation and by rigorously monitoring performance. Paradoxically, the disposable workforce went hand-in-hand with a new corporate doctrine of 'human relations', which celebrates 'flexibility', innovation and learning. The worlds of rhetoric and reality neatly dovetailed when the HR department of PGE, an Enron subsidiary, offered grief counselling to employees who had lost both their jobs and their savings, the better to enable them to adjust to what was happening.

Financialization's lack of commitment to employees or communities is supposedly dictated by the pursuit of the efficient allocation of capital. But because financialization is not embedded in a macro-policy or strategy it often plays a part in strangling growth. Booms lose their way if they are channelled into short-term speculation and arbitrage, rather than long-range investment. Sustained growth requires infrastructural and educational investments that may not pay off for decades. While arbitrage can help to spot and eliminate excess costs, if unregulated it will wipe out all long-range projects. While previous booms saw the construction of railroads or interstate highways the stock market thrills and spills of the 1980s and 1990s lacked the sort of commitment and foresight displayed by Henry Ford, and other founders of industrialism, or John Maynard Keynes, and other architects of the postwar boom. The managers of pension funds were part of the problem since they wanted investments that yielded immediate returns and which could easily be turned into cash. This was, in part, the result of accounting methods which required that assets be 'marked to market' every year.

In the mid-1990s Kevin Phillips and Giovanni Arrighi warned that the profits of financialization would have the further defect that, unlike advances in manufacturing, communications or trade, they tend to enrich only a small part of the population and do not create a broad basis of sustainable mass demand.[44] For a while this can be concealed by a 'wealth effect' as millions of small investors see the nominal value of their assets – whether shares or the homes they live in – climb, but once the bubble bursts demand plummets. From 2000 to 2005 consumer confidence was shored up by a house-price boom, borrowing and tax cuts, but ballooning debt, rising interest rates, and a weak recovery, stored up problems for the future and created a difficult climate for manufacturers. In the speculative process large-scale finance has the edge over the small saver and the cash-strapped corporation. In the past the large banks were able to grow at the expense of the savings of the small man, because they had larger reserves and better information.[45] Today the small savers' holdings in pension, insurance and 'mutual' funds play this role. The mass of employees may own a significant slice of productive assets but they do so in ways that render them vulnerable to hedge funds and other finance houses, which are better informed and more nimble.

In the 1990s and after, the small investors with holdings in mutual funds, 401(k)s or unit trusts reacted to the exorbitant cost of 'actively managed' funds by steering their money towards passive 'index tracking' funds. The latter came to comprise half or more of funds held for retirement. While fees are certainly lower in such funds there are other problems with this investment approach. The funds which really do mimic the big liquid indices, like the S&P 500 or FTSE 100, find that they are buying dear and selling cheap – when companies enter the index they are already doing well, while by the time they exit problems will have long been apparent. The hedge funds charge heavy fees but are able to exploit the clumsy and predictable movements of a market heavily influenced by index funds. The trading desks of the investment banks service the hedge funds, and are well placed to seize arbitrage possibilities opened up by bids and counter-bids. On large transactions these concerns will be able to spread trading costs until they leave a handsome profit.

High Finance and Distressed Debt

In another dimension of financialization, companies that were having difficulty making a profit from selling goods found that it was sometimes easier if they offered finance too, from the humblest consumer credit network to complex deals where a company sold its product to a subsidiary which then leased it to the customer. Not infrequently the transaction passes through a tax haven. GE Capital has long helped the company's customers acquire its aero-engines and other machinery using tax-efficient lease-back arrangements. GE Capital soon diversified into consumer credit because of the attractive return this generated. By 2003 42 per cent of the group's profits were generated by GE Capital. In the same year GM and Ford registered nearly all their profit from consumer-leasing arrangements, with sales revenue barely breaking even. When these two auto giants encountered real difficulties in 2005 and after, they came under pressure to sell their profitable leasing divisions as a way of raising badly needed resources. In 2004 the General Motors Acceptance Corporation (GMAC) division earned $2.9 billion, contributing about 80

per cent of GM total income. GM hoped that GMAC would be valued at
$11 billion or more and that it could retain a major holding even while
selling a 51 per cent stake. The company's creditors, including the PBGC,
were said to be scrutinizing all such proposals, ready to make a claim on
behalf of the company's own employees and pensioners should they
deem that necessary.[46]

In a kindred development it was striking to see the eagerness with
which gigantic financial concerns like Citigroup and HSBC sought to
acquire consumer finance operations and even 'sub-prime' lenders ('loan
sharks') which they would have previously regarded with disdain.
Citigroup acquired Associates First Capital, and HSBC bought Household Finance, blazing a trail others were to follow. Finance houses have
teamed up with retailers to shower so-called gold and platinum cards on
all and sundry with the hope of ratcheting up consumer debt – running at
over 110 per cent of personal annual disposable incomes in the US in
2002, rising to 130 per cent by 2005 – and subsequently charging an
annual 18 or 20 per cent on money for which the banks were paying
three or four per cent. It was the hot rates of return which attracted the
banks to seamy lending. They believed that they could repackage the
debts in ways that allowed them to slough off the risk while retaining
most of the high return that was supposedly the risk premium.

With direct access to sub-prime mortgages, the banks and hedge funds
could then bundle together and divide up the debt into tranches, each of
which represents a claim over the underlying loans or securities but with
the lowest tranche representing the first 5 per cent to default, then the
next 25 per cent to default, leaving 70 per cent in the supposedly safe
'senior' tranche. Borrowers who can only negotiate a sub-prime mortgage have either poor collateral or poor income prospects, or both, and so
are required to pay over the odds. Of course the bottom tranche –
designated the equity – has very weak prospects but can still be sold
cheaply to someone as a bargain. The top tranches, and even many of the
medium tranches, will be far more secure yet will pay a good return. The
chief executive of a mortgage broker boasted: 'Sub-prime mortgages are
the ideal sector for the investment banks, as their wider margins provide a
strong protected cash-flow and the risk history has been favourable. If the
investment bank packages the securities bonds for sale, including the
deeply subordinated risk tranches, it can, in effect, lock in a guaranteed
return with little or no capital exposure . . . Generally investment banks
do not like lending money but they are good at measuring risk, parcelling

this up and optimising its value.'[47] This statement captures the hubris of the fianancial sector at the time. The banks brought up mortgage portfolios and bundled, tranched and insured millions of subprime mortgates, turning them into Collateralized Debt Obligations (CDOs). Ratings agencies were paid a handsome fee to award them a tripe A grade, after which they were sold to other financial institutions or stored away in a Special Investment Vehicle (SIV). These were 'over the counter' transactions, using 'model', rather than market, prices. In the years 2001–6 sub-prime CDOs grew into the main asset base of a fabulous, off-balance-sheet – hence unregulated – 'shadow banking system'.

The credit derivatives boom enabled the banks to achieve record profits in the years up to 2006. However, the increasingly indebted households turned out to be unrealiable debtors for those who now held their debt. For a while a continuing housing bubble kept alive the illusion of expanding wealth but by 2006 US consumers had to spend 18 per cent of their earnings simply to service their debts. As millions fell behind in their mortgage payments it became a source of systemic risk. Even banks which had sold on the CDOs before they soured could not escape exposure to the consequent disaster. (For the latter see the preface).

Perilous Ways of Hedging Risk

I have already drawn attention to hedge funds and their ability to outwit large institutional investors. The years 2000–6 have witnessed a mushrooming of thousands of hedge funds – by mid 2006 the total was thought to be around 8,000 controlling $1.5 trillion of assets (this compared with $7 trillion in US mutual funds of all types). The hedge funds started out as the preserve of the really wealthy investor, though eventually several pension funds gave them a small slither of their holdings. In the bear market of 2000–2 the hedge funds often made positive returns when most conventional funds, especially index funds, made heavy losses. Conventional funds, whether actively managed or index-linked, were 'long only', which is to say that they bought and sold stocks but did not short them. Hedge funds also offer and employ 'derivatives', investment products like options which allow the purchaser to place a bet on the movement of sections of the market. Spotting price discrepancies, hedge funds made money by arbitrage, rapid trading and the novel use of credit derivatives, which would repackage corporate debt. Investment banks and the treasury departments of large corporations also engage in large-scale hedging of currency and interest rates but hedge funds have the greatest latitude and are closest to the unbridled spirit of financialization.[48]

Banks and mutual funds are lightly regulated, but the hedge funds do not have to reveal their holdings at all, and effectively escape all regulation. They charge fees that are often 2 per cent of the money invested plus 20 per cent of the annual rise in capital value. Their charging structure usually allows them to make a lot of money when they do well, but not to forfeit these gains if the returns then collapse. The hedge funds do have higher costs than other fund managers because of heavy trading, but claim that this will enable them to outperform the market and to generate positive returns during a downturn. Many have performed very well for particular clients, encouraging pension-fund managers to take a lively interest in them, an interest generally encouraged by regulators and consultants on both sides of the Atlantic.

While hedge funds may deliver the consistent, double-digit returns which justify their fees for special clients, can they pull off the same trick for the entire class of pension funds, given that the latter constitute such a large component of the market? A shorting operation can deliver results to its practitioner but it does not directly benefit all investors, as does a rising market.[49] And while a 'long' investment can rise and rise, the price of a share cannot drop below zero, limiting the profits of shorting. The pension funds which invest in hedge funds usually do so by purchasing a 'fund of funds' vehicle, yet in doing so lose the edge which the best hedge-fund managers will be able to offer. A diversified stake in the sector may offer a little more security but also lowers the return, since it will include poor performers and perhaps even those that go bust. Between 1998 and 2003, 1,800 hedge funds closed their doors, yet most statistics on the performance of the sector will display 'survivor bias' by failing to include their losses.[50]

Due to their modus operandi the hedge funds were to have a starring role in the mutual funds scandals. The large finance houses which sponsor mutual funds discovered that they could earn extra fees from hyperactive traders, on top of the good fees they were already earning from the mass of their investors. They granted hedge funds privileges not extended to other investors. They even gave the hedge funds credit to enable them to take advantage of their clients' funds still valued at 'stale prices' (on which more in the next chapter). This way the finance house can charge interest as well as earn a transaction fee. Furthermore, trades do not have to be only in already-existing shares. If new issues are imminent then hedge funds and other punters can purchase sell and put options on the not-yet-existing shares on what is called, appropriately enough, the 'grey market'. Shorting shares in the grey market can lead to extraordinary complications and the embarrassment of 'naked shorts', where the short-seller is discovered to have no stock, whether borrowed or not.[51] Another problematic issue is where hedge funds use the voting power of borrowed stock to endorse takeover bids, especially where shareholders in the target stand to lose, but the hedge fund will gain because of other positions it has taken on the outcome of the bid.

The hedge-fund manager uses derivatives to unpack bundles of property rights or claims on flows of income, and to reassemble them in a supposedly more advantageous configuration. They may be guided by a hunch as to what is the next big thing but they don't aim to take responsibility for running a business. On the face of it, 'private equity' concerns are quite different. They specialize in taking over under-capitalized and underperforming businesses, with the aim of reorganizing management and relaunching the business. This may take three or five years, during which money is borrowed, loss-makers are spun off and the core business overhauled. Investors – including pension funds – are invited to back these operations. Most pension funds will only be able to set aside a small slice of their funds for such ventures because they are usually required by consultants and fiduciary regulations to invest in 'liquid' assets, while a private-equity stake has to be held for a few years and is difficult to value. The private-equity fund is really a sort of collective entrepreneur, and may deliver a good return to the large-scale investor, but the relaunched business will have been loaded with debt. Like hedge funds their charges are higher than those of ordinary fund managers and normally comprise both a standard annual fee of 2 per cent together with a portion of the eventual pay-off, or 'carried interest', once the reorganization and refloat is complete.[52] The investor thus contributes not to the private-equity organization as such but to a specific fund which it will launch. It will raise a given sum – from as little as £10 million to several billions of dollars or pounds – which will be used to make acquisitions in a given sector. When the Texas Pacific Group announced a $15 billion fund in April 2006 this was a record, but the scale of private equity had grown over the previous decade, albeit with a dip in 2001. The private-equity concern will have real costs, such as legal 'due diligence', insurance and staff, but as the size of funds grows the annual management fee will tend to become more interesting than the entrepreneurial profit, which itself will be spread over several years. Private equity 'club deals' enable different concerns to aim at larger targets, pool costs and increase their funds under management.

The combined effect of such trends is to bring private equity closer to a generalized fund-management logic where the real goal is to boost the size of the funds under management, because this in turn will boost the fees.[53] The capital raised, and the loans issued, may exceed the good investment opportunities that are available. Those engaged in a range of takeover and buy-out possibilities will tend to have advance knowledge of market events, with those whose bid fails being most likely to talk or seek compensation by acting on the information in their possession – in February 2006 London's Financial Services Authority pointed to evidence that suspicious trading activity preceded about one-third of all major deals.

Just to round out the picture of the triumph of financialization, mainstream fund managers, in a bid to retain mandates, are also now prepared to abandon their 'long only' approach and make some use of 'shorting' and derivatives.

Criticism of the new world of finance should avoid the mistake of treating finance itself as necessarily a domain of delusion and chicanery. The financial techniques employed by hedge funds or the finance departments of large corporations are not all designed for some dubious purpose. The use of derivatives to hedge currency or interest-rate swings can aim simply to reduce uncertainty. It may make sense to offset other, similar, risks to achieve a balanced portfolio. But hedge funds, finance houses and accountants invariably go far beyond such tame procedures. They don't limit themselves to a plain 'vanilla swap' – say to replace fluctuating by fixed interest rates – but will sell clients a lease-back within a sale within a swap in order to thoroughly befuddle regulators, tax authorities and shareholders alike. Likewise they often use leverage (borrowed money or assets) to increase their profits on a transaction, but in so doing also increase the exposure of their clients. Those who buy an asset stand to lose what they have paid. Those who buy a derivative can be exposed to unlimited loss. The barely contained collapse of Long Term Capital Management in 1998 – patronized by central banks and staffed by brilliant minds – illustrated several of these dangers.[54] More generally, as Edward LiPuma and Ben Lee urge, the use of derivatives in contemporary financialization aims at short-term gains that short-circuit flows of production and trade, garnering an immediate gain at the expense of what might have been a long-term social surplus. [55] Private equity aims to be different but operates in a financialized context which can subvert any longer-term, constructive purpose.

The techniques of the financial revolution – derivatives, hedging, SPEs, CDOs, etc. – can be used simply to insure a corporation against hazard. But several of these devices lend themselves to manipulating a firm's basic numbers (a case in point, 'finite insurance', will be considered in the next chapter). The cult of shareholder value and financial engineering could seem to conjure immediate gain out of any merger or acquisition. Companies which perfected the art of growth by acquisition – GE, Vodafone, AOL, Worldcom and so forth – became the darlings of Wall Street. Sometimes this corresponded to real growth and a more logical business. But it could also betoken 'aggressive accounting' and herald future share-price tumbles. The willingness of the old-fashioned type of investor to accept the consequences of ownership vanishes in the hedge fund world. As a recent survey notes: 'The hedge funds' case has not been helped by behaviour such as that of Perry Capital which in 2004 bought shares in Mylan Laboratories only in order to vote in favour of its acquisition of King Pharmaceuticals in which Perry was a big shareholder. Perry hedged its exposure to movements in Mylan's share price and was thus able to exercise its voting rights without having any apparent exposure to the consequences.'[56]

In the 1980s and 1990s GE took over scores of companies and reduced its US workforce by more than two-thirds. Earnings predictions were met with clockwork precision. By 2001, 43 per cent of its earnings came from financial activities, ranging from consumer credit to aircraft leasing operations which encouraged airlines to buy GE products. In 2001 the European competition commissioner ruled against a proposed merger with Honeywell because of the belief that it would create monopoly power in some markets. Faced by earnings decline, in 2003 GE acquired Amersham, a large medical company with products that complement GE's: analysts wrote that 'revenue synergies' and 'cross-selling' opportunities should help share price, since GE sells imaging machines to hospitals while Amersham supplies the injection agents. A hospital procurement officer explained: '. . . most hospitals regarded large medical equipment like M.R.I. machines as a capital expense, which is not directly billable to patients, while the injectable agents are charged to patients or their insurers. The company could begin providing deep discounts on the equipment while increasing the price of the agents.' An industry consultant commented: 'Will everyone pay more? That would be their goal. They are not missionaries.'[57] The report carried a denial from GE that it would behave like this. But the possibility conjured up shows the need for new types of regulation, backed up, if possible, by a new type of owner.

Fooling the Tax Man

The wish to outwit the tax system plays a large role in the spread of financial engineering. In 1965 corporate taxes accounted for 4 per cent of US GDP; by 2002 they comprised only 1.5 per cent of GDP. Already in 1985 the *Wall Street Journal* published an op-ed by two students at Harvard Business School. In it they explained: '[We] have discovered that a large portion of the school's curriculum is devoted to preparing us to both understand and "beat" the U.S. tax system'.[58] They added that, after a typical class, 'We might have learned how to be more successful businessmen and wealthy individuals, but certainly not through any creation of wealth. We had merely spent another day learning how to beat Uncle Sam. As we looked at our real estate homework for the next day, with its tax shelters, sale-leasebacks, and depreciation rules, we realized that tomorrow would be more of the same.'

This article is cited by Myron Scholes and Mark Woolfson in an influential book which triumphantly codified the achievements of finan-cialization, *Taxes and Business Strategy: A Planning Approach*, first published in 1991. According to Scholes and Wolfson, who quote the article, the two students had flunked the test. The purpose was not to beat the US tax system or to minimize taxes. The purpose was to arbitrage the tax systems of all countries and to maximize profits and shareholder value, which might require paying some taxes, since countries where profitable openings were to be found often had the capacity to tax. In their view businessmen should accept that the taxing authority was an 'investment partner' in their firm, who should be cut in where necessary but who couldn't really know what you were up to. The 'tax planning' approach sought to 'repackage ownership rights', through the use of derivatives and swaps, with the aim of switching income or assets from high-tax to lower-tax periods, locations or monetary forms. As they explain: 'With financial engineering, many different combinations of assets, securities and "synthetics" [a contract that duplicates the financial effect of an underlying asset] can lead to economically similar cash-flows. Yet taxing authorities often impose different tax treatment across the economically similar bundles.' Thus a US tax-exempt entity might wish, for the sake of diversification, to invest in Europe while a European tax-exempt entity might want for the same reason to invest in the US. Both face the problem that their tax-exemption applies to home and not overseas markets. They therefore have an incentive to reach a swap agreement, such that each makes an investment in the home market and pledges all returns to their foreign partner. Prior to the 1980s such swaps were unknown, but since then they have been almost infinitely elaborated. Likewise if there is differential taxation of dividends and capital gains a financial device can turn the more highly taxed into the less taxed. Scholes and Woolfson explain: 'The market typically does a better job than the taxing authority in sorting out the economic characteristics of securities. At first blush it might appear sensible to decompose a transaction into its component parts and tax each part accordingly . . . The decomposition approach, however, faces practical difficulties. It is not always obvious how to decompose a contract into its constituent parts. Assets can be decomposed into multiple ways that are equivalent except for taxes . . . Should the taxing authority adopt a more conceptual approach, wherein it attempts to determine whether a particular set of transactions is motivated solely by tax purposes and re-characterize such transactions to afford a less tax-advantageous outcome for the tax payer? Probably so, but as a practical matter, the taxing authority can only guess what is behind a complicated string of transactions. What is the authority to do? For the most part it has given up in the financial innovation market.'[59]

These authors do not argue that such considerations entirely nullify the powers of taxing authorities, since the latter can impose uncertainty. Finance houses which discover a new tax avoidance device are encouraged to register it with the authorities, thus earning brownie points. But as accountants found an ever-widening market for tax avoidance products the inducement to register was weakened. In the case of one such product marketed by KPMG an internal memo noted: 'The rewards of a successful marketing of the OPIS product (and the competitive disadvantages that may result from registration) far exceed the financial exposure to penalties that may arise.'[60] The tax-shelter business is huge. Deutsche Bank furnished $10 billion of credit over a three-year period to

clients who purchased just one of KPMG's tax shelter products. Testify-
ing before a Senate committee, a former 'structured finance executive' at
Deutsche Bank admitted that the loans involved no risk – they were
backed by 100 per cent collateral – and that they were repaid within two
months. He denied they were sham loans or simple tax shelters, preferring
to describe them as investment deals with 'significant tax benefits'. [61]

Companies do not want to undergo the hassle of a special investigation,
even if they know their tax-planning strategies to be impregnable. But
the IRS is just one organization, with a limited staff; it can, for example,
only check the returns of one partnership in 400, with 'partner' being the
designation of choice for those on very high incomes. Companies also
have to worry about shareholders, who are thought to favor proper tax
planning. Thus in Fall 2003 Citigroup announced a record quarterly
profit of $4.7 billion, but was concerned that it was paying tax at the rate
of 31.3 per cent of its profits while GE was only paying at the rate of 23.5
per cent. At this point Citigroup already derived 40 per cent of its revenue
from outside the US. Todd Thompson, chief financial officer, promised
analysts and shareholders that the tax rate could be lowered: 'There are
possibilities to manage that number down through some of our international operations.'[62] A study of 250 major US companies in 1996–8
found that they were paying an average of 20.1 per cent of their profits in
tax, instead of the official rate of 35 per cent.[63] A study of the 50 largest
UK companies in the years 2000 to 2004 found that they paid corporation tax at an average rate that was 5.7 per cent less than their earnings
seemed to warrant. It calculated that the likely 'expectation gap', or
shortfall below official rates, amounted to £9.2 billion a year, or 28 per
cent of corporation tax receipts in 2004–5.[64] (When citing such statistics it
is important to note both that tax avoidance is on a large scale and also
that, if we assume that these companies would prefer to pay nothing, that
large sums are nevertheless raised by corporation tax. The implication is
that, notwithstanding globalization, companies can be made to pay taxes.)

The strategies adopted to fox the tax authority are also capable of
confusing the shareholder. The taxing authority and the shareholder have
different sources of information and leverage, but both can be bamboozled by a complex maze of financialized transactions. Fund trustees
and managers have sought to tackle these problems by focusing relentlessly on shareholder value, but long-term prospects for the latter have
frequently been eroded, by a combination of executive willfulness,
inappropriate gambles and financial sleight of hand.

In most American states the electrical utilities are allowed to charge customers a tax that legislators intended should be handed on to the fiscal authorities. But many utilities are now part of business groups which can claim these taxes to offset losses in other operations so that the money meant for the state or municipality never reaches its destination: 'many utilities have expanded into unregulated businesses such as energy trading or aircraft leasing, while others have been acquired by companies that own other businesses. When those other businesses lose money or create artificial losses through tax planning, those losses can be used to offset income earned by the utilities. As a result the parent company owes less in tax than their electric customers paid. Sometimes these companies owe nothing or receive large tax refunds. By not remitting taxes [paid by customers], the companies effectively save more money to invest in their operations or pay to shareholders in dividends. The ability to intercept tax payments is not limited to electric utilities. Natural gas, water and telephone utilities can use the same techniques.'[65] This report quoted Mike Hatch, the Minnesota attorney general, as commenting: 'Essentially the utilities customers pay the tax twice, once through the utility bill and again through the lost revenue to the government that means higher taxes for them or less government services.'[66]

The sums involved run into many billions. In ten Western states, Xcel Energy managed to hold on to $723 million which a utility stand-alone would have had to hand over to the government. Another utility owner, Pepco Holdings. held on to $546 million in 2002–4. Enron acquired Portland General Electric in order to absorb tax-enriched revenues of $900 million and offset them against losses in 881 companies registered in the Cayman Islands and Bermuda. To allow an enterprise to offset its own losses against profits in a later period is one thing, but to extend this concession to other unrelated entities has the economic effect of giving free insurance to the loss-makers involved, and of offering a windfall to those who tie up the deal. A spokesman for Pepco saw matters very differently: 'Utility customers did not bear the risk of that business, and they should not benefit either'.[67] But the owners of the other, loss-making, business should not be compensated at the expense of taxpayers for their own mistakes.

During the 1950s US corporations accounted for 28 per cent of federal revenues; by the first years of the twenty-first century this contribution had fallen to 11 per cent, and 61 per cent of all US companies paid no tax whatsoever. And many whose income was drawn from the United States had learned how to re-route it via Bermuda, with the Bermuda 'head office' receiving lavish and untaxed payment for management services, use of copyright, and interest on loans. While US banks and insurance houses would explain to customers how to exploit such schemes, their European counterparts were certainly no slouches and are believed to have devised off-shore funds for wealthy individuals holding about $2–3 trillion of assets, compared with perhaps $1.6 trillion held for wealthy Americans.[68]

But tax havens, with their often flimsy safeguards, are problematic places to stow assets. Many wealthy corporations and individuals simply send their profits on a round trip to be laundered in a haven but then return to some more secure locale. The wealthy require havens with some security and for this reason opt for territories that are dependencies of an EU state or the United States – Bermuda, Cayman Islands, Monaco, the Isle of Man and so forth. The US and European authorities are beginning to monitor these financial hidey holes more closely and could do a lot more. The desire for security without onerous regulation is also seen within the US, with companies flocking to Delaware because of its corporate-friendly regulatory regime.

The financialized world girdles the planet with transactions worth trillions of dollars, euros and pounds, yet there comes a time when the deal has to be registered, and perhaps enforced, or cash handed over, or trades settled. And many of these elaborate transactions still depend on trust, personal contact and a certain density of well-regulated and reasonably transparent financial institutions. It is striking that even the hedge funds tend to cluster their operational HQs not in some tropical tax haven but in locations not so far from the old financial districts – London's Mayfair or Greenwich, Connecticut. Of course this is just the tip of the iceberg. The main offices of banks and funds are located in or near London, New York or Tokyo, but the financial device or analysts' report will often be drawn up overnight in branch offices in India.

I am not arguing here that such financial institutions are today either transparent or well-regulated. The next chapter will show that this is still far from being the case, notwithstanding new legislation in both the US and Europe, and a new vigilance from international agencies. My point is rather that even in the supposedly borderless world of globalization some territories are very much more secure and advantageous for corporations and wealth-holders than others, and that this offers considerable scope to a determined regulatory authority.

Financialization is defined by the use of sophisticated mathematical techniques to distribute and hedge risk, so it might be thought that these instruments are themselves a major part of the problem of what I have called 'grey capitalism'. But this would be an error. It is true that the collapse of Long Term Capital Management in 1998 was deemed to pose a systemic threat, leading to a bail-out coordinated by the Federal Reserve Bank of New York and the major Wall Street institutions. In today's highly financialized world such a threat could easily reappear but this is likely to be the result of poor institutional structures than of faulty calculations. The collapse of Enron and Worldcom was a disaster for the pension funds and employees who had invested in the shares and financial instruments offered by these concerns. But the tangled mass of derivative contracts unwound with much less pain. In the second half of 2005 Refco, the largest US futures trader, was forced to declare bank-ruptcy after revealing that an entity owned by one of its key executives had owed the company $300 million since 1998. The individual in question had, it is true, used a small hedge fund to help conceal this debt. But the financial manipulation he used was of breathtaking simplicity – the debt was simply rotated around three accounts with different reporting periods, one of the hoariest scams known to financial history. What permitted the fraud to succeed was the willingness of highly respected lawyers and accountants to prepare and endorse the rotating payments. The errant executive acquired his colleagues' trust because of his access to funds held for an Austrian workers' pension fund, which suffered a heavy loss. On the other hand the complex mass of the company's derivative and futures contracts were settled by counter-parties who had freely entered into them.

Soviet planners learnt long ago that managers who are told to maximize one number – say tonnage of output – will have an incentive to bend the whole enterprise to that end regardless, even if it means goods that are heavier than consumers want. Linking executive compensation to shareholder value will, over time, have similar distorting results. It will encourage the massaging of the numbers that influence share price and this over-riding concern with today's quote may very well undermine longer-term reputation, and hence value. The critique of Soviet planning by Friedrich von Hayek stressed that owners spread throughout the economy could be aware of many local opportunities that were invisible at the centre. And they would therefore be willing to exploit them at their own cost. The regime of 'grey capitalism' fails to control the managers or to give the ultimate owners any responsibility. The Soviet Union produced vast quantities of steel, cement and electricity but failed to meet its people's needs. The financial engineering regime produces vast quantities of financial products but leaves people more insecure, poorer and less in control.

Just as the Soviet system produced its *nomenklatura* so financialized and grey capitalism has thrown up an extraordinarily privileged social class of over-compensated CEOs and financial 'partners'. When I wrote *Banking on Death* I compared this layer to the nobility of France's Ancien Régime. I had in mind such echoes as that the estates of the pre-1789 French nobility had been formally exempt from taxation, that the Régime financed itself by bringing in private contractors to collect the tolls on the poor (the 'tax farmers') and its recourse to lotteries to plug holes in the royal revenue. The wealth of today's financial aristocrats is held in the form of corporate securities. For most ordinary citizens the home they live in is their most valuable possession and they have to pay a tax on it. But those who own property in the form of shares and bonds pay no tax for so doing. They are only liable to capital gains tax when they realize the gain and, if they use a tax haven, not even then.

The financial aristocrats live lives as far as possible removed from those of the common herd. No facility is more prized than the private jet, usually paid for by the corporation. While all this is scarcely a secret it is nevertheless gratifying to find the picture – and the historical parallel – confirmed by the following e-mail to colleagues sent by Conrad Black (Lord Black) at a time when control of his media empire was slipping from his hands: 'There has not been an occasion for many months when I got on our plane without wondering whether it was really affordable. But I'm not prepared to re-enact the French Revolutionary renunciation of the rights of nobility. We have to find a balance between an unfair taxation on the company and a reasonable treatment of the founder-builders-managers. We are proprietors after all, beleaguered as we may be. Care must be taken not to allow this to degenerate into decadence, as it did with the old Argus. But nor should we allow the agitations of shareholders, amplified by certain of our colleagues discountenanced by the performance of their stock options, to force us into a hair shirt, the corporate equivalent of sackcloth and ashes.'[69]

Black retained control of Hollinger, the company which owned the *Chicago Sun Times*, the UK *Daily Telegraph* and *Sunday Telegraph* and the *Jerusalem Post* by means of special voting rights that conferred over 73 per cent of the votes on a share stake that comprised only 30 per cent of the outstanding stock. Black used his position as CEO, and his leverage over the board, to extract from Hollinger some $300 million, which he then used both to fund an extraordinary extravagant lifestyle – his wife Barbara Amiel confessed that she was a hopeless shopaholic – and to fund a string of right-wing causes. Among the directors of the holding company that channeled many of these funds were Henry Kissinger and Richard Perle. Some of the long-suffering shareholders, led by the institutional investor Tweedy Browne, sued Black and his colleagues for violating their fiduciary duty. They succeeded first in removing Black from his post as chief executive, and then winning full control of the company in the Delaware courts in February 2004. The humbling of Black was a signal from the courts of Delaware – where so many US companies are registered – that there were limits to the extent to which imperial CEOs could trample on the interests of shareholders. Delaware is popular with the corporate community precisely because its regulations are not too onerous – Ireland and the Netherlands play this role in Europe. However the Chancery Court of Delaware evidently believed that Black had gone too far, that a proper respect for the duty of care owed by boards to shareholders had to be upheld and that underlying ownership counted for something after all. This conflict was part of a larger battle, to be considered in the next chapter, in which a small band of regulators sought to check abuse and in which the political authorities also sought to shore up the comprised structures of the business community and to curb some of the more outrageous privileges of the new financial aristocracy.

Notes

1 J. W. Harris, 'What Is Non-Private Property?', in J. W. Harris, ed., *Property Problems from Genes to Pensions*, London 1997, pp. 175–89, 185. I have further discussion of these issues in *Banking on Death*, pp. 125–8.

2 William O'Barr and John Conley, *Fortune and Folly: the Wealth and Power of Institutional Investing*, Homewood IL, 1992, p. 107.

3 The term derived from James Burnham, *The Managerial Revolution*, New York 1944, but the evidence for a fragmentation of ownership was laid out in Adolf A. Berle and Gardiner C. Means, *The Modern Corporation and Private Property*, New York 1932, and the argument was further developed by Ralph Dahrendorf in *Class and Class Conflict in Industrial Society*, London 1959, and by J. K. Galbraith, *The New Industrial State*, New York 1965. I

presented a critique of the concept in 'The New Capitalism', in Robin
Blackburn, ed., *Ideology in Social Science*, London 1972, pp. 164–86. The cult
of sharcholder value in the 1970s and after was to make it clear that owners
still had great leverage and provoked some reassessment of the classic
argument for the eclipse of ownership by control (see, Robert Hessen,
'The Modern Corporation and Private Property', *Journal of Law and Economics*, vol. xxvi, June 1983.) J. K. Galbraith urged that the managerial
'technostructure' had acquired a degree of immediate control, or relative
autonomy, as a result of share dispersal in *The New Industrial State* in 1965 and
in this he was right. But the strong professionalism he believed was
restraining use of this leverage has been less and less evident in recent years
amongst senior executives. Across the last decades of the twentieth century,
and into the twenty-first, there is evidence of a tug of war between owners
and managers, with the balance tipping first one way and then another,
according to the sector and period. My concern here is the impact on this
balance of networks of institutional ownership which were in their infancy
when the managerial revolution thesis was first elaborated. For a cross-
national study of such new networks see John Scott, *Corporate Business and
Capitalist Classes*, Oxford 1997. And for a review of the 'managerial
revolution' debate, see Mark Mizruchi and Linda Brewster-Stearns, 'Money,
Banking and Financial Market' in Neil Smesler and Richard Swedberg, eds,
The Handbook of Economic Sociology, Princeton NJ, 1994, pp. 313–41, and
Thomas Clarke, ed., *Corporate Governance Critical Perspectives*, vol. 2, *Anglo-
American Corporate Governance*, London and New York 2005.

4 Michael Useem, *Executive Defense: Shareholder Power and Corporate Re-
   organisation*, Cambridge MA, 1992, p. 243.
5 Teresa Ghilarducci, *Labor's Capital*, Cambridge MA, 1992, p. 130.
6 KPMG, *Unlocking Shareholder Value, the Key to Success*, January 2001.
7 See Robert Reich, 'Look Who Demands Profits Above All', *Los Angeles
   Times*, 1 September 2000, and Robert Reich, *Success*, New York 2000.
8 Michael Useem, *Investor Capitalism: How Money Managers Are Changing the
   Face of Corporate America*, New York 1996, pp. 1–3, 108–9, 126–7. This
   outstanding study, drawing on interviews with senior officers at twenty large
   financial and non-financial corporations, is an essential reference point for
   understanding the impact of institutional investors. It brings out vividly the
   managerial 'culture of resistance' to shareholder pressure, but it does not yet
   fully register the cult of the superstar CEO which was to burgeon in the later
   1990s, nor does it foreground the conflicts of interest that were to erupt
   spectacularly in 2001–3. For the latter see the remarkable insider's account:
   John C. Bogle, *The Battle for the Soul of Capitalism*, New Haven 2005, pp. 3–
   46. John Bogle is the founder and former CEO of Vanguard, the third-
   largest money manager in the United States.
9 Useem, *Investor Capitalism*, pp. 28–9, 110.
10 Ibid., p. 57.
11 Bogle, *The Battle for the Soul of Capitalism*, p. 90.
12 Useem, *Investor Capitalism*, pp. 70–106.

13 Bogle, *The Battle for the Soul of Capitalism*, pp. 36–7.
14 Arthur Levitt, *Take on the Street, What Wall Street and Corporate America Don't Want You to Know*, with Paula Dwyer, New York 2002, pp. 192–4, 241. Levitt was the chairman of the SEC at this time. See also Bogle, *The Battle for the Soul of Capitalism*, p. 39 and Abraham L. Gitlow, *Corruption in Corporate America*, Lanhan MD, 2005, pp. 51–68.
15 Bogle, *The Battle for the Soul of Capitalism*, pp. 92–3.
16 Michael Jensen and Kevin J. Murphy, 'CEO Incentives: Its Not How Much You Pay, but How', *Harvard Business Review*, May–June 1990, pp. 138–53. See also Kevin Murphy, 'Top Executives Are Worth Every Nickel They Get', *Harvard Business Review*, March–April 1986.
17 Jensen and Murphy, 'CEO Incentives', p. 139.
18 Michael Jensen, 'The Modern Industrial Revolution, Exit and the Failure of Internal Control Systems', *Journal of Finance*, 1993, pp. 18–36, p. 33.
19 Robert Brenner, 'The Boom and the Bubble', *New Left Review*, no. 6, November–December 2000, pp. 5–44, 24. See also Robert Brenner, *The Boom and the Bubble*, New York and London 2002, pp. 150–1.For an account of how these options operate, and how attempts to make them more visible were frustrated, see Joseph Stiglitz, *The Roaring Nineties: a New History of the World's Most Prosperous Decade*, New York 2003, pp. 115–27. See also Andrew Glyn, *Capitalism Unleashed: Finance, Globalization and Welfare*, Oxford 2006, pp. 58 63.
20 Nomi Prins, *Other People's Money: The Corporate Mugging of America*, New York 2004, p. 1. Prins is a former managing director at Goldman Sachs. The article from which her data were drawn was Mark Gimein, 'You Bought, They Sold', *Fortune*, 11 August 2002. Gimein's totals are less than are implied by Brenner's account quoted in the previous footnote. This is because they concern fewer people and a shorter period, ending with a downturn.
21 Joann S. Lublin, 'Another Boost for the Boss', *Wall Street Journal*, 12 December 2005.
22 Jenny Anderson, 'Profit at Goldman Sachs Rose by 37% in Fourth Quarter', *New York Times*, 16 December 2005.
23 The data here is drawn from Thomas Picketty and Emmanuel Saez, 'Income Inequality in the United States, 1913–1998', *The Quarterly Journal of Economics*, vol. cxviii, no. 1, 2003.
24 David Cay Johnston, 'Top 1% in '01 Lost Income, But Also Paid Lower Taxes', *New York Times*, 27 September 2003.
25 Gérard Duménil and Dominique Lévy, 'Class and Income in the US', *New Left Review*, no. 30, November–December 2004, pp. 105–33, 112.
26 Ibid., p. 112.
27 Ibid., pp. 117–8.
28 Franklin Allen and Gary Gorton, 'Churning Bubbles', *Review of Economic Studies*, vol. 60, 1993, pp. 813–36, p. 832.
29 J. K. Galbraith, *The Great Crash – 1929*, Boston 1954, p. 138.
30 Kurt Eichenwald, 'Merrill Reaches Deal with U.S. in Enron Affair', *New York Times*, 18 September 2003.

31 This is the contention of a very slightly fictionalized 'novel' written by an English banker directly involved in these events. See Robert Kelsey, *The Pursuit of Happiness*, London 2000. Note that this book, describing how an English bank helped to devise fake revenue for a Texas energy trader called 'Hardon', was published a year before the collapse of Enron.

32 Charles Fleming and Carrick Mollenkamp, 'Insurers Balk at Paying Wall Street's Penalties', *Wall Street Journal*, 23–26 December 2005.

33 Ibid.

34 Robert Brenner , 'Afterword', *The Boom and the Bubble*, paperback edition, New York and London 2003.

35 A point stressed by Nomi Prins, *Other People's Money: the Corporate Mugging of America*, New York 2004.

36 Abraham L. Gitlow, *Corruption in Corporate America*, Lanham MD, 2005, p. 13.

37 See Allen Sykes, *Capitalism for Tomorrow*, Oxford 2000 (which I drew on in *Banking on Death*) and Robert A. G. Monks and Neil Minow, *Corporate Governance*, Cambridge 1995.

38 Karl Marx, *Capital*, vol. 3, London 1991, p. 567.

39 Joel Bakan, *The Corporation: The Pathological Pursuit of Profit and Power*, London 2004. While I would like to have seen more attention to systematic economic forces, the author's concluding checklist of reforms remains very useful.

40 Naomi Klein, *No Logo*, London 2002.

41 For a wide-ranging account which focuses on the 1980s and early 1990s see Greta R. Kippner, *The Fictitious Economy: Financialization, the State and Contemporary Capitalism*, Ph.D. awarded at the Sociology Department of the University of Wisconsin-Madison, 2003. See also Andrew Glyn, *Capitalism Unleashed*, pp. 5–76.

42 John Grahl, 'Globalized Finance', *New Left Review*, no. 8, March–April 2001, pp. 23–48.

43 See Timothy J. Sinclair, *The New Masters of Capital: American Bond Rating Agencies and the Politics of Creditworthiness*, Ithaca NY, 2005.

44 Kevin Phillips, *Boiling Point: Republicans, Democrats and the Decline of Middle Class Prosperity*, New York 1993, p. 197; Giovanni Arrighi, *The Long Twentieth Century*, London 1994, pp. 314–15.

45 The ways in which big capital bullies and battens on small capital has been a theme of socialist and progressive writing from Marx's *Capital* to Rudolf Hilferding's *Finance Capital*, and from Jack London's *Iron Heel* to Naomi Klein's *No Logo*.

46 Dennis K. Berman, Henry Sender and Ian McDonald, 'GM Auction Won't Be Simple', *Wall Street Journal*, 9 December 2005.

47 Jane Croft, 'Banks Pile into Sub-Prime Lending', *Financial Times*, 21 December 2005.

48 Edward LiPuma and Ben Lee, *Financial Derivatives and the Globalization of Risk*, Durham NC, 2004, pp. 90–2.

49 Shorting is not all bad. It can boost liquidity, or help to uncover inflated assets

(as did the Ursus Fund in the case of Enron) but better regulated and more modest hedge funds could do this. Or these functions could be better fulfilled by other institutions.

50 Bogle, *The Battle for the Soul of Capitalism*, pp. 120–1.

51 In the UK, short-selling of 'grey market' shares in Room Service in November 2003 led to a situation where there were more trades than shares to fulfil them. The short sellers were exposed as 'naked' because a promised rights issue stalled. When the authorities suspended trading, and cancelled some prior trades, this damaged many who had not knowingly been involved in the shorting operation. Elizabeth Rigby, 'Room for Change on Short-Selling', *Financial Times*, 29 November 2003.

52 Richard Freeman, 'Venture Capitalism and Modern Capitalism' in Victor Nee and Richard Swedberg, eds., *The Economic Sociology of Capitalism*, Princeton and Oxford 2005, pp. 144–67.

53 Notebook, 'Why Take Risks When You Can Take Fees?', *Guardian*, 4 April 2006. See also Matthew Bishop, 'Capitalism's New Kings', *The Economist*, 25 November 2004.

54 Donald MacKenzie, 'Long Term Capital Managemenbt and the Sociology of Arbitrage', *Economy and Society*, vol. 32, no. 3, August 2003, pp. 349–80; and Brenner, *The Boom and the Bubble*, pp. 171–2. For informative material on the use and abuse of derivatives see Randall Dodd, Derivatives Study Center, at financialpolicy.org. See also Henwood, *Wall Street*, pp. 28–41.

55 LiPuma and Lee, *Financial Derivatives and the Globalization of Risk*, pp. 9–10, 125.

56 'Battling for Corporate America', *The Economist*, 11 March 2006.

57 Melody Peterson, 'G.E. to Buy British Medical Company', *New York Times*, 11 October 2003. See also Lex, 'General Eclectic', *Financial Times*, 12 October 2003.

58 'What *Do* They Teach You at Harvard Biz?', *Wall Street Journal*, 23 December 1985.

59 Myron S. Scholes and Mark A.Woolfson, *Taxes and Business Strategy: a Planning Approach*, Englewood Cliffs NJ, 1991, pp. 410–11. Scholes, who went on to win the Nobel prize for his work on pricing options, may have been unwise to speak so confidently of the incomprehension of the tax authorities. He became a partner in Long Term Capital Management – the hedge fund which collapsed in 1998 – where he devised tax-planning vehicles. For the past few years the IRS has been prosecuting LTCM in an attempt to prove that one of its devices – a swap involving sale-lease-backs and preferred stock – was illegal since it lacked 'economic substance' and existed only to allow tax to be be evaded. Scholes was alleged to have helped devise similar products. See Kara Scannel, 'Meriwether Provides Glimpse into LTCM at Tax-Shelter Trial', *Wall Street Journal*, 3 July 2003.

60 Cassell Bryan-Lowe, 'KPMG Didn't Register Strategy', *Wall Street Journal*, 17 November 2003.

61 Joshua Chaffin, 'Deutsche Bank "Provided Tax Shelter Funds"', *Financial Times*, 21 November 2003.

62 Gary Silverman, 'The "Healthy" Pursuit of Reduced Tax', *Financial Times*, 1–2 November 2003.
63 Institute on Taxation and Economic Policy, *Corporate Income Taxes in the 1990s*, October 2000.
64 Tax Justice Network, *Mind the Tax Gap*, February 2006.
65 David Kay Johnston, 'Many Utilities Collect for Taxes They Never Pay', *New York Times*, 15 March 2006.
66 Ibid.
67 Ibid.
68 Lucy Komisar, 'Profit Laundering and Tax Evasion', *Dissent*, Spring 2005, pp. 48–54.
69 Quoted Sandor Joo, 'Is Hollinger Deal a Sale?', *International Herald Tribune*, 30 March 2003.

5

The Limits of Reform
and Shareholder Activism

The years 2001 to 2005 were marked by a rolling succession of corporate and financial scandals, which provoked calls for tougher regulation, corporate governance reform and rigorous ways to call insiders to account. I have urged that the accountability deficit of 'grey capitalism' and the new formulas of financialization were deeply implicated in the scandals. However, there were other factors. In the 1990s, deregulation had rendered the financial system more vulnerable. The share bubble showed that the supposedly sophisticated new financial structures were as prone to delusion and speculative excess as those who had participated in the seventeenth-century Dutch tulip mania, London's eighteenth-century South Sea Company or Charles Ponzi's coupon scheme. The bubble burst when poor returns and revenues could be hidden no longer, and this helped to trigger major corporate collapses. The scandals were not confined to US business but involved a number of major European concerns – Vivendi, Parmalat and Ahold – who were seeking to emulate Anglo-Saxon business practices.

Washington, once famed for gridlock, moved with unwonted speed. The Sarbanes–Oxley Act was on the statute book by July 2002, before most of the corporate malefactors had even been indicted and, as it turned out, before the real scope of the scandals was clear. This Act tightened up corporate reporting but did not tackle abuses in the financial sector itself. Yet between 2001 and 2005 corporate scandals were soon eclipsed by the revelation that core financial institutions – the major investment banks, mutual funds and insurance houses – had colluded with corporate crime, and were themselves awash with insider-dealing, kick-backs and techniques for skimming their own customers. The revelation of these abuses was deeply embarrassing and led to settlements in which the financial sector paid out billions of dollars in fines to regulators, and reimbursed some clients. The regulatory regime was supposedly tightened a bit but no further legislation was forthcoming.

When the corporate scandals first broke President and Congress sought to demonstrate their concern to the broad mass of investors and pension-fund holders, and regulators also strove to demonstrate their relevance. It almost goes without saying that a well-functioning investment system needs to be embedded within an effective and honest system of regulation. Those who strove to ensure this, like Eliot Spitzer, the New York attorney general, should have become heroes, worthy of admiring profiles in the *Wall Street Journal*, and subject only to the carping of a few special interests. The scams were revealed to harm all types of investor. While some mainly targeted individuals, others stripped value from huge pension funds. But, as it turned out Sarbanes–Oxley was to be the end as well as the beginning of the correction process and any further reforms – touching on mutual funds, hedge funds or derivatives disclosure – turned out to be highly controversial.

Traditionally a species of self-regulation has been the norm in the financial sector, with senior, superannuated figures being nominated to a toothless oversight role. Wall Street, the City of London, the Swiss banks, have traditionally preferred it this way. Such mechanisms use peer pressure to sanction errant individuals, but they are no barrier to the abuses that have been common practice. Indeed they protect rather than police the cartel-like characteristics of the financial system. The failings of unadulterated self-regulation have repeatedly led to scandal, leading eventually – but not without heavy external pressure – to the setting up of more independent regulators. The creation of the Federal Reserve system in 1913, or the Securities and Exchange Commission (SEC) in 1934, or the passage of the Glass–Steagall Act in the same year, were all designed to ensure the professional regulation of vital financial institutions. In the UK, the City of London was always averse to outside regulation but was freed from irksome restrictions by Margaret Thatcher in her 1987 deregulation measure known as the 'big bang'. Nowhere were the hazards of deregulation to become more apparent than in the field of pension products. High pressure salesmanship produced the 'pensions mis-selling' scandal in which, it was subsequently established, two million employees had been persuaded to abandon good pension schemes and purchase inefficient personal products instead. This was followed by similar scandals concerning 'endowment mortgages' and 'split-level trusts' in more recent years. The exposure of extravagant and unwarranted promises forced the venerable Equitable Life insurance house to close its doors after 240 years. Against this background the incoming Labour government established the Financial Services Authority in 2002, largely replacing the old structures of self-regulation and endowed with powers analogous to those of the SEC in the US.

Elsewhere in Europe malpractice has compromised the leadership of Credit Lyonnais, the Bank of Italy, Deutsche Bank and several Swiss banks, leading to demands for sterner regulation. The European authorities believe that they have something to learn from the long history of business regulation in the United States. At the same time the International Accounting Standards Board, with strong European representation, maintains that it sets even more rigorous standards than the US Financial Accounting Standards Board (FASB). However, in the wake of Sarbanes–Oxley many companies have chosen to launch IPOs (Initial Public Offerings of shares) in Europe rather than the United States, because of the former's less demanding reporting requirements.

This chapter will look at the new financial landscape and new problems in the savings regime which have been brought to light by US regulators. It will also consider whether recent reforms – and a new spirit of 'shareholder activism' – are likely to be effective in protecting pension savings and restoring shareholder power. The United States may be the land of individualism and free enterprise but it has long given business regulators more power and resources than their European counterparts. If US regulators are frustrated nevertheless, it suggests that stronger medicine is needed – on both sides of the Atlantic.

Popular pressure prompted the move to tougher regulation in the US even though subsequent implementation was invariably milder. The Federal Reserve system was set up after more than two decades of Populist and Progressive agitation against the 'Communism of Combined Wealth' and the 'money monopoly'. The commercial banks were subjected to new rules regarding reserves, disclosure and the scope of their permitted business.[1] Wall Street was further invigilated by the terms of the state of New York's Martin Act of 1921. This gave the state's attorney general the right to bring criminal prosecutions against finance houses and, prior to this, the right to search the premises of suspects without warning and impound their documents.[2] This stringent measure – which was to play a crucial role in uncovering financial misdemeanours and crimes in 2002–5 – was adopted after hundreds of thousands had lost their savings in Ponzi's pyramid scheme – and after a million had voted for Eugene Debs, the Socialist candidate, in the presidential election.

The crash of 1929, and the speculative excesses which preceded it, discredited Wall Street and showed the need for the regulation embodied in the SEC and Glass–Steagall Act. However the powers of the SEC were limited and much of the work of overseeing accountants, brokers, bankers, and mutual fund managers was still left to professional bodies, or to institutions deeply beholden to the financial community, like the

New York Stock Exchange (NYSE). Moreover presidents generally took care to nominate senior businessmen, or cautious professionals, to the boards of the Federal Reserve Bank and SEC. The Glass–Steagall Act barred the large investment houses from owning or controlling retail banks and brokerages. If an investment house acted as an underwriter for the issuing of a corporate security, then under the terms of the Act it would not be able to use a retail arm to urge its own customers to buy that security. The large finance houses chafed at this barrier to expansion but it was not until 1999, in the midst of a veritable bonfire of regulations, that they persuaded president and congress to repeal Glass–Steagall.

Deregulation made possible a wave of mergers between investment banks, brokerages and retail banks inspired by the convenient doctrine that every conflict of interest was really a 'synergy'. By 2002 the absurdity of the claim was evident.[3] As we have seen, the large banks had abetted the aggressive growth of Enron, Worldcom and Tyco, growth that was fuelled by accounting fraud and financial legerdemain. The embarrassing fact that Bush was an intimate of Kenneth Lay ('Kenny Boy'), Enron's CEO, that one of Bush's Cabinet officers had recently been a senior officer at that company, and that Enron was a donor to both parties, help to explain why the president was so keen to be seen tightening the law and the regulatory regime.

Americans were shocked to see Enron's workers losing not only their jobs but their savings too. Half their 401(k) holdings took the form of Enron shares. And while the company's senior executives scrambled to sell their stock while it was still worth something, the members of the 401(k) plan found that they were barred from doing so as it was closed for an accounting review. The shock of Enron's collapse was so great because it was an admired, as well as large, company, its accounts scrutinized by supposedly the most rigorous auditors and its debt handled by the leading banks. Citigroup and Morgan Stanley, as we have seen, had created 'credit derivates' that gave many large institutional investors perilous exposure to the Houston company. The company's financial statements had been audited by Arthur Andersen, one of the then 'Big Five' world accounting firms. Following the revelation that Andersen had sought to destroy incriminating documents the audit concern began to disintegrate.[4] The subsequent collapse of Tyco, Global Crossing and Worldcom revealed a similar pattern of corporate malfeasance and financial or professional collusion.[5] Against this background Congress introduced, and the president signed, the Sarbanes–Oxley Act, setting new standards of disclosure and accountability.

Before the reforms could begin to be implemented Eliot Spitzer opened up a new flank when he revealed abuses in brokerage practices, investment advice and fund management services offered to investors by the finance houses. By seizing and publishing the internal records of leading Wall Street concerns, especially e-mails, he shone a spotlight on the dubious practices of the financial community. Old Wall Street hands knew that analysts were prone to boost the shares of companies with which their bank did business. But the public was less aware of this and certainly not ready for the cynical boasts and macho confessions with which the internal e-mails were replete. Stocks derided in e-mails as 'crap', 'a piece of junk' or POS (a piece of shit) were being recommended enthusiastically to clients. Subsequent and more serious scandals also turned on the availability of e-mail evidence, as the intimate new medium betrayed traders' assumptions and practices. In the early days of such electronic communication it was sometimes urged that the rapidity and profusion of e-mailing would make the task of the regulator impossible. Instead a harvest of e-mails began to illuminate the real workings of the financial system.

Proving securities fraud is extraordinarily difficult – it is necessary to demonstrate an intent to deceive or defraud – which is why so few are ever convicted of it. But the e-mails were a different matter. A memo sent in late 1999 by Jack Grubman, a star analyst at Salomon Smith Barney, to his boss Sanford ('Sandy') Weill, chief executive of Citibank, eventually helped to clinch the settlement in which the Wall Street giants paid $1.4 billion in fines and compensation. The financial damage revealed by the e-mail was minor in comparison with many later revelations but it put the CEO on the spot and shed a sidelight on the trading of favours which defines the governance style of the new elite. The heading of the message was 'AT&T and the 92nd St. Y'. Jack Grubman was a leading analyst for AT&T, the telecom giant, at the time and had rated its prospects as very poor. He was invited by Weill to take a 'fresh look' at the stock. Grubman later explained in an e-mail to a friend that a positive assessment of AT&T would help Weill in a boardroom battle. Weill wanted to secure the support of the AT&T chief, Armstrong, because he also sat on the Citigroup board. It also later transpired that Citibank was bidding for business from AT&T. Grubman duly reconsidered his view of AT&T and removed his 'sell' recommendation. Armstrong was gratified. Weill won his boardroom dispute with help from Armstrong and Citibank secured the business it coveted. Grubman had done his boss's bidding at the cost of misleading those who trusted his recommendations. Why had he done this? On his own account it wasn't simply a matter of ingratiating himself with his boss.

In an e-mail to a friend in 2001 Grubman explained that he was eager to make sure that his twin infant daughters gained entrance to the exclusive Upper East Side nursery known as the 92nd St Y. The Citigroup chairman was friendly with board members at the Y. In the memo, helpfully headed 'AT&T and the 92nd St. Y', Grubman informed Weill of a 'good' meeting with Armstrong and then proceeded seamlessly to ask a favour. He wanted Weill to put in a good word for the twins with the people at the Y. As Grubman explained to his friend in the 2001 e-mail this nursery was 'more difficult to get into than Harvard'. In the event Weill arranged for Citibank to make a donation of $1 million to the 92nd St Y and Jack Grubman's 3-year-olds gained admittance. This instructive exchange of favours captured in the memo's title was, together with the boast to the friend, the sort of smoking gun which Spitzer was looking for to force Citigroup to come to terms. (Institutional investors should not have been too deceived by Grubman's miscalls. If Grubman was the archetypical insider then the institutional investor would be a semi-witting half insider; indeed the girl friend to whom Grubman was boasting worked for the Singapore Provident Fund.)[6]

In a profile of Sanford Weill entitled 'Laughing All the Way to the Bank', the *New York Times* reported in September 2005, on the eve of his retirement, that his total compensation from the companies that he had run amounted to no less than $953 million. His desk was adorned by a large sign with the word 'e-mail' crossed out in red ink. On the wall was a plaque headed by his name and with a roll call of his major deals; underneath was the inscription 'The Man Who Shattered Glass–Steagall'. (The reporters from the *Times* also noted a photograph of Sandy with Clinton aboard Air Force One around the time of the repeal of that famous law).[7]

The Grubman affair, piquant details apart, was by no means the most serious instance of inappropriate behavior and misuse of power at Citigroup. The *New York Times* profile of Weill noted a highly problematic pattern: 'Regulatory enquiries in the United States and overseas laid bare serious problems . . . like the gauging of low-income borrowers, continued even after the regulators warned the bank to stop such activities. There were also glaring conflicts of interest which analysts said derived in part from Mr Weill's relentless desire for Citigroup to produce double-digit financial returns . . . Citigroup became a focal point of nearly every investigation that examined such conflicts, most notably in relation to its role in the collapse of WorldCom and Enron.' Had it still been operative, many of these conflicts would have been prevented by Glass–Steagall.

In 2003 Weill handed over operational control of Citibank to Charles Prince and a younger team, himself remaining as group Chairman. His successors strove to restore the group's reputation, but this was made difficult by continuing evidence of a reckless corporate ethos and pressure to generate sky-high returns. The Japanese regulatory authorities came close to banning Citigroup in 2004. The bank made financial restitution, promised future good behaviour and made a grovelling apology – offered in person, with a deep bow, by the bank's new chief executive officers. In the summer of 2004 it was the turn of the European regulators to be shocked by Citigroup's cynicism. The bank's European Eurobond trading desk dumped $17 billion of securities on the market within as many seconds in a massive assault on bond price levels – only to buy them back the same day once their price had dropped. It transpired via a leaked electronic memo that this smash-and-grab raid was a response by the European-bond trading desk to promptings from New York, which urged the former to raise the profitability of its trades. The memo pointed out that bond-trading was more profitable in New York because there were fewer players. The giant Euro-bond sell-off was designed to force the smaller bond traders out of the business and raise future trading margins.[8]

Citigroup also continued to be troubled by the retirement plans of its former chief executive, now Chairman. These raised new issues of propriety and conflict of interest. In early 2005 he proposed that he would buy the bank's underperforming asset-management arm, but the board ruled this out on the grounds that he could not direct a sale to himself without a conflict of interest. He then suggested that he contact his friend Legg Mason with a view to arranging a swap of the Legg Mason brokerage for the Citigroup asset-management operation, allowing him to eventually run the latter post-retirement. Weill's colleagues shot down this idea as they did a subsequent one according to which he would retire earlier and set up his own asset-management fund. The board said that if he did this he would no longer be able to use Citigroup facilities, including the executive jets. The report notes: 'Mr Weill says he ultimately decided not to pursue the venture because he didn't want to do anything that would be seen as competitive [to Citi], not because he might lose some perks.'[9]

Gaming Your Customers: the Emptiness of Mutuality

Eliot Spitzer, the New York Attorney General, continued to open new windows on the malpractices of Wall Street. With his tiny staff, Spitzer uncovered Wall Street activities that put the small and institutional investor at a serious disadvantage. His first batch of revelations had brought to light 'spinning', the practice whereby banks underwriting an initial public offering (IPO) would allot a tranche at the offer price to senior executives in companies whose business they wished to attract. The initial share price is usually set somewhat, or even considerably, below what the underwriters think the market will bear. They do this to ensure the issue sells out and to furnish an impressive price rise in the first weeks and months.

During the bubble, being allotted shares at the offer price was hugely lucrative – 309 IPOs during this period generated a total of $50 billion in first-day trading profits.[10] The banks did this either as a personal favor to the CEO or as a favor to his company; in either case they expected a quid pro quo. Since share allocation is or should be arbitrary it can be difficult to prove collusion. But e-mails brought into evidence at later trials left little doubt. The staff of Frank Quattrone, a banker at Credit Suisse First Boston who made $200 million in fees and salary in 1999 and 2000, kept a file called 'Friends of Frank' who were to receive allocations. In July 2000 Quattrone e-mailed Dell CEO Michael Dell as follows: 'my team has gotten word to me that you are personally interested in having dell ventures receive a meaningful allocation on the ipo of corvis, the optical networking company . . .'. Dell replied: 'We would like 250K shares of Corvis. I know there have been efforts on both sides to build the relationship and an offering like this would certainly help.'[11]

In September–November 2003 Eliot Spitzer turned his attention to the $7 trillion mutual-fund industry. Most employees fill their 401(k) with mutual funds, usually from a short menu of such funds selected by their employer. The mutual-fund concern is nominally owned by the investors, but in reality is simply a creature of the sponsoring financial corporation. The finance house sets up the fund and selects its directors. Supposedly these directors then choose the sponsoring company to run the portfolio (no other suppliers are considered), when in reality the sponsors select the dummy directors, who will be allotted a figurehead role at dozens, sometimes as many as a hundred, funds. Directors are often former political or business leaders and receive fees irrespective of performance. From the sponsor's point of view it makes sense to have a large number of funds since some must outperform and these can be touted in promotional material, of which there is a lot. In 2002, a year when most mutual funds recorded heavy losses, they nevertheless maintained the value of directors' fees: Fidelity's funds paid out $2.8 million, Putnam's $4.9 million, Merrill Lynch's $4.5 million and Morgan Stanley's $4.4 million.[12] Directors supposedly represent the interest of investors but have never been known to expose abuses or dump managers. Indeed with fund managers themselves acting as directors the notion of independent mutual fund boards is simply a charade.

The real money is made by the fund managers who earn six- or seven-figure salaries. John Bogle of Vanguard, one of the few true 'mutuals' (that is, really owned by the members), comments: 'Don't pay any attention to surveys that show the average is around $350,000 a year. This industry takes in revenues of $70 billion a year [Bogle is here referring to mutual-fund management, not to trading costs, which are borne by the fund, but do not show up as revenue to the fund managers]. Of that only $4 billion to $5 billion is spent on investment management or research. Of the total about 40 to 45 per cent is profit to the managers. I know some managers at one large firm who make $5 million a year.'[13]

Spitzer was able to establish that a broad swathe of leading mutual-fund managers were engaged in stunningly unethical practices, prompting a Republican Senator, Peter Fitzgerald of Illinois, to describe the industry as 'the world's largest skimming organization'.[14] They had allowed favoured clients the privilege of 'late trading' at the expense of 'stale prices', whereby these customers, mainly hedge funds, would be allowed to trade mutual funds after the 4 pm market close at the 4 pm price, thus being able to take advantage of breaking news in the US and on the European and Far Eastern stock exchanges. Spitzer also focused on the widespread practice amongst mutual funds of allowing 'market timers' to buy just before the close with the aim of selling the next day. In some cases 'late traders' and 'market timers' were given details about the composition of the funds, enabling them to estimate the impact of developments affecting companies which loomed large in their holdings. The fund managers gained partly by earning fees on the trades and partly by earning a good rate of interest on the money they lent to the market timers – since the latter did not even use their own money to despoil the underlying investors but borrowed it from the latter's supposed guardians. Some of the more unscrupulous fund-management chiefs did not bother with a middleman and arbitraged their own funds. While some of these activities violate the law, all of them would be a breach of trust. Mutual funds claim to cater to the long-term investor. The activities of the 'market timers' have nothing to do with long-term investing. The traders profits come at the expense of the mass of investors in the 'mutual'.[15]

Spitzer cited research from Stanford Business School showing that the activities of the market timers at some of the affected funds was reducing fund value for long-term investors by 1 to 2 per cent of their stake each year.[16] In fact it was academic research as well as incriminating records that put Spitzer onto the skimming scandal. As previously mentioned, researchers had been puzzled by the extent of poor returns in the mutual-fund industry. Eric Zitzewitz of Stanford subjected a huge mass of data concerning the mutual funds to rigorous economic analysis. Specialist consultants and analysts accumulate comparative information on the industry. Using data from Trimtabs, one of these consultancies, Zitzewitz devised a formula which would match price movements to the volume of sales.[17] His conclusion was that there was regular, large-scale trading taking place on the basis of 'stale prices'. After mentioning several possible, but unlikely, legitimate explanations of this bizarre result, he concluded that – as a last resort – it might be necessary to ask whether fund personnel were abetting trades at the expense of the funds they were meant to be protecting. One of Spitzer's aides rang him to explain that, very likely, this was exactly what was happening. When Spitzer brought his charges he cited Zitzewitz's work.

The SEC and the Secretary of the Commonwealth of Massachusetts announced their own sweeping investigations of the mutual-fund in-dustry. The SEC was subsequently to state that one half of the 88 mutual-fund groups it had questioned, together responsible for 90 per cent of all mutual-fund business, allowed 'market timing' while one quarter of brokerage firms that sell mutual funds had allowed certain customers to make late trades.[18] The mutual-fund managers' keenness to persuade the brokers to recommend their funds led even supposed pillars of Bostonian probity to allow them late-trading or market-timing privileges.

Among the renowned finance houses under investigation were industry leaders such as Fidelity, Richard Strong, Putnam, Merrill Lynch, Morgan Stanley, Janus, Charles Schwab, and Salomon Smith Barney, the brokerage arm of Citigroup, where three brokers were sacked.[19] As in the case of the earlier Wall Street revelations, the mutual-fund probe was not limited to a few 'bad apples', but revealed a compulsion to seize every opportunity for arbitrage, no matter how large or small. In the phenomenon known as 'millionaires diving in the sewer for pennies', Richard Strong, owner of a fund-management concern with a personal fortune of $600 million, nevertheless engaged in trades at the expense of his own customers that netted him $600,000 between 1998 and 2001.[20]

No doubt a determination to exploit every advantage explains where Strong's fortune came from in the first place. The multiple sources of gain were highlighted by the compensation package of Lawrence J. Lasser, CEO of Putnam Investments, the country's fifth-largest fund manager: 'In the past five years Mr Lasser has earned $5 million in salary and a nice, round $100 million in bonuses. He received restricted stock options worth approximately $12 million over the past five years. And at the end of last year he had $5.8 million in unexercised stock options. There's more. Mr Lasser signed a new employment contract in 1997 that earned him a special retirement benefit valued at $15 million "in consideration for a non-competition covenant and post-employment consulting arrangement", according to the company . . . Interesting that the company would confer a retirement benefit on Mr Lasser years before he retired and in consideration for his agreement not to compete with the company he was still working for. That's creativity . . . Finally Mr Lasser got $200,000 for his work as a trustee of various Putnam mutual funds. And why not? You can't expect him to work for free. Add the figures up and you see that Mr Lasser has pocketed $163 million. Oh and one other thing; on his investments in private equity limited partnerships . . . Mr Lasser is not expected to pay a management fee.'[21] With pension funds withdrawing mandates from Putnam, Lasser was fired the day after this report. It was alleged that he had condoned self-dealing as well as market-timing when these had been discovered by the firm's own compliance people three years before the mutual scandals became public.

Spitzer's conclusion, as explained to a congressional hearing, was that the root of the problem was the fake structure of the mutual funds, with their phony boards of directors. ' "The larger issue here is board governance," Mr Spitzer said. "The common threads that runs through the mutual fund industry . . . and all the scandals of the past year has been board complacency . . . The attorney general also said that, had mutual fund directors put in even a minimal amount of effort, they would have spotted abuses that are now likely to cost the funds dearly in fines and penalties . . . [H]e blames the fund directors for the inflated fees paid by mutual fund shareholders. By his own estimate, mutual fund shareholders pay $10 bn more than [corporate] pension funds each year for comparable advisory services." '[22] (Individual retirement holdings are often invested in these mutuals.)

While Spitzer was able to shame the main Wall Street banks and mutual-fund managers, he has little power to extract structural transformation. The SEC had climbed aboard his Wall Street investigation and helped to broker the deal whereby the banks paid $1.4 billion in fines and compensation, and pledged future good behaviour. The banks promised to establish firewalls between underwriters and analysts but both remain within the same firm, dealing with the same clients. Boosterism has not disappeared.[23] Some of the undertakings made by the banks were extraordinarily ad hoc. Weill, the chief of Citibank, undertook that he would only meet with the bank's own analysts if in the presence of a lawyer. (As noted above Weill moved to the position of chairman in October 2003 before stepping down in 2005).

It is likely that the free business services which banks give to fund managers to reward them for giving them trading business ('soft dollars' or, in the UK, 'soft commission') will be reformed or abolished. The managers pass on to their clients inflated brokerage fees because of the 'free' research they receive from sell-side analysts. The pension plans should be large enough to establish their own research departments, but outside the public sector this is very rare. Under the terms of the settlement the investment banks agreed to help set up independent research boutiques, but it is unclear how this will be paid for in future and the banks themselves have not ceased supplying both research and brokerage services.

The mutual-fund revelations show how distant they are from principles of mutuality, even-handedness, accountability and investment for the long term. In an effort to staunch withdrawals some chiefs withdrew – Strong stepped down on the same day as Lasser at Putnam – and scores of miscreant employees were dismissed. New rules tightening regulations against late trades and market timing were announced. Spitzer called for fund managers to return to investors all management fees they had charged while condoning abuse. This time the fines may be even larger

than those in the Wall Street settlement, and there is a demand that
employers should be more vigilant in selecting schemes and fund directors
more independent of the fund managers.[24] But there was no sign of the
sweeping new legislation required to properly regulate the industry and
render it accountable to policy-holders will be forthcoming.

As glaring 'agency defects' were exposed, rival representatives began to
stir. Trustees don't like to appear to be easily bamboozled and trade
unions understandably saw the corporate scandals as an opportunity to
reassert themselves. The public sector funds are keen not simply to act in
members' interests, but to be seen to do so. The mutual-fund business
itself needs public confidence – it is its stock in trade. In the past it has
been able to buy and intimidate politicians. But today it needs to
ingratiate itself with a troubled public. Selective withdrawals aside, the
absence of a mass exodus from the funds points not to confidence in the
system but to the investors' quandary and bemusement; they know that if
they sell they may lose entitlement to compensation and, unlike the
market timers, face penalty charges. And anyway, where else are they to
put their money? So they stay put.

The financial services industry made large contributions to both
political parties in the run-up to the 2004 election. George W. Bush
already had a war chest of $170 million by October 2003. The Demo-
cratic national organisation was looking to get backing from the same
quarter. The issue of corporate tax avoidance briefly surfaced, but was
then quickly dropped. Sarbanes–Oxley was held to have restored integrity to US business and Eliot Spitzer was kept at arm's length from the
Kerry campaign. The *Wall Street Journal* was happy to report that the
Democratic contender's multi-millionaire wife herself only paid tax at
half the rate paid by ordinary tax-payers, on declared income which, at $5
million, was less than 1 per cent of her net worth. Bush himself urged that
it was useless to raise taxes on the rich because they would simply instruct
their accountants to avoid them.[25]

In the future, support for real reform could receive a fillip from the
new sensitivity of many pension funds to issues of governance and
corporate responsibility. Naomi Klein argued in *No Logo* that the giant
corporations are vulnerable because they invested so much in promoting
their brands and corporate image. Some objected that this was not so true
for large concerns which did little business with the individual consumer.
But the collapse of Andersen, one of the erstwhile 'Big Five' accounting
companies, has been a striking case of how reputational damage can bring

low even the mightiest and, in this case, a concern whose clients were businesses not individuals. The investment banks are prone to behave as if their resources and technical prowess make them impregnable. But their efforts to involve themselves in consumer finance, retail banking and the business of the mutual funds will increase their vulnerability.

The Scope of the New Regulations

The flood of revelations – which were soon to lap around the foundations of the immensely wealthy and respectable insurance industry – owed nothing to Sarbanes–Oxley. This Act, framed by a Democratic Senator, embodied rules of disclosure which the audit and financial lobby had previously opposed. But although it placed restrictions on the ability of auditors' to earn fees by performing consultancy services to their audit clients the elaborate new rules on disclosure were to prove a boost for their core earnings. Indeed the Sarbanes–Oxley Act imposes costs on companies, not their advisors. CEOs faced stiffer penalties for non-compliance and were to be asked to swear an oath to affirm the accuracy of their accounts. A Public Company Accounting Oversight Board, under the authority of the SEC, was to establish new rules for corporate governance – though mutual funds successfully lobbied to be exempted from these.

The new arrangements did not get off to a good start. The SEC was charged with implementation of the new measures yet its Chairman, Harvey Pitt, had been notorious as a Washington lobbyist for the financial services industry, playing a key role in blocking the attempt to rein in accountants in 1999–2000. Pitt was eventually forced to resign but not until after he had appointed William Webster to be the chair of the new Public Company Accounting Oversight Board. Webster also had to resign. It turned out that he had headed the audit committee of a company whose senior executive was under investigation for criminal fraud (the company, a private prison contractor, valued Webster for his official contacts).

More than a year after Webster's replacement the board still only had 50 inspectors and its new head declared: 'The approach I'm taking is to help accountants help themselves. We are much more likely to be effective that way than if we are combative.'[26] The new regulations on disclosure will generate more work for accountants and auditors. They are exhorted to restore 'primacy' to audit work and have been barred from doing some types of consultancy for the companies they audit. Many of the scandals occurred at companies – Enron, Worldcom, Tyco, HealthSouth – where the same accountants had performed the audit for ten years or more. Under the new regulations the senior partner assigned to an audit will have to change every five years. With Andersen down, the remaining 'big four' accountants audit 99 per cent of the large corporations. They still make a lot of money from consulting work even if, in the US, much of this work can no longer be done for an audit client.[27] However, the big four are not out to make trouble for one another – and anyway each is part of an international network.[28] Relations between auditor and auditee remain very cosy, and the accountancy firm doing the audit will tend to endorse advice tendered by a rival – after all, the roles could be reversed when they move to the next client. It is still boards which appoint auditors. We don't think it right for exam takers to select and pay exam markers, or for customs officials to be employed by importers, because we know that this would be a bad system. Yet that is still how audit works.

Sarbanes–Oxley did give some new powers and responsibilities to the SEC. The man chosen to replace Pitt, William Donaldson, was very much an industry insider but one who believed that the time had come to clean the stables. Donaldson had been a founder of DLJ, a renowned 1980s brokerage house (now part of Credit Suisse). He was to prove a knowledgeable as well as a quite tough regulator. During his comparatively short tenure (he was forced out in 2005) he could usually count on the support of two Democratic appointees to the SEC board. However he was consistently opposed by the two Republican appointees, notwithstanding his own Republican affiliation. Many of his reform measures were awkward compromises: the more radical ones attracted the ire of the Treasury and corporate interests were irked by what they saw as costly and intrusive new compliance procedures. Donaldson announced new rules allowing for the possibility of independently elected directors, but only after a two-year process that few might bother to pursue. Many boards will still be able simply to ignore resolutions passed at AGMs if they want to.[29] In a much-attacked proposal, Donaldson declared that hedge funds should be required to register as financial advisers and reveal more about their holdings. He also urged that only those with a net worth in equities of over $1.5 million should be allowed to invest in hedge funds. Despite the unpopularity of these measures with the financial community their implementation proved an anti-climax.[30]

Donaldson was not intimidated by Wall Street grandees; after all he was one himself. If he detected arrogance or insouciance he was prepared to denounce it. When the CEO of Morgan Stanley urged that the scandals and the settlement did not contain anything that should alarm the small investors or pension funds, Donaldson took the highly unusual step of sending him a public rebuke: 'Your statements reflect a disturbing and misguided perspective on Morgan Stanley's alleged misconduct. Your reported comments evidence a troubling lack of contrition and lead me to wonder about Morgan Stanley's commitment to compliance with the letter and spirit of the law and the high standards which all investors have a right to expect from their brokerage firms.'[31]

But Donaldson could not go beyond the remit given him by Sarbanes–Oxley and other legislation. Looking at the larger picture one year after the new regime was installed *The Economist* wrote: 'New federal laws, such as the Sarbanes–Oxley act, have created a dense thicket of rules prescribing good behavior in the boardroom. But the system's essential features – weak boards, muted shareholder participation and sweeping power for the boss – so far remain intact.'[32] Subsequent developments were very much to bear out this judgement.

On the second anniversary of the Act the chairman of KPMG was full of praise for a new audit regime which had obliged the firm's clients to spend more. He thought corporate leaders were wrong to complain at the cost of compliance, and he felt that the oversight board's inspections were notable for quality if not quantity: 'In KPMG's experience the inspection teams were qualified, experienced, able professionals. Their reports will indicate some issues to be addressed by the accounting profession. We shall take those reports to heart and respond robustly.' Satisfactory as all this was governance improvements were, he gushed, just as impressive: 'Boards generally, and especially the independent directors who con-stitute audit committees, are taking seriously their heightened responsi-bilities to shareholders. Audit committee meetings, once short briefings, now focus on reputational issues, transparency and risk management.'[33] (As noted in the last chapter, KPMG was itself soon engulfed by reputational issues of its own, concerning its marketing of tax-avoidance products.)

The Sarbanes–Oxley Act had passed so quickly because the accounting industry, burying the reservations of its more hidebound members, had helped to ensure that it contained the right sort of reforms. It obliged large companies to establish new internal controls and to disclose more relevant information. Clause 404 established stiff sanctions for deliberate misreporting.[34] However neither accountants nor auditors were to be held co-responsible for the veracity of company accounts. Such measures were not unwelcome to the investment industry, and accountants were happy at the extra business that came their way. The Act did not require the expense of executive or staff options to be recognized, nor did it lay down procedures for the determination of executive compensation. It was made no easier for shareholders to bring boards to account. The Act was focused on corporate reporting and corporate finance, including share issuance, but not on the financial services industry as such. Mutual-fund management was exempted from several of its key provisions. Hedge funds were not subjected to registration or regulation. By 2004 and 2005 CEOs might try to justify their huge pay rises by pointing to a recovery in stock prices, but even when these were at their lowest executive pay was irrepressible.

Insurance Lost in the Bermuda Triangle

Spitzer's next target was the insurance industry and, once again, he went for the really big fish rather than the minnows. In October 2004 the New York attorney general charged that 'on numerous occasions' officers of Marsh & McLennan, the world's largest insurance broker, had encouraged counterparts at American Insurance Group (AIG), the largest US commercial insurer, to submit a fake bid, pricing it up so it would then appear that Marsh, in steering its clients towards a slightly cheaper bid from another (pre-arranged) insurer, was vigorously forwarding their interests. On occasion the Bermuda-based insurer ACE was involved. Spitzer called this bid-rigging, which assumed an elaborate variety of forms, 'a scheme to defraud'. His indictment focused on the pay-off Marsh & McLennan received from insurers who won their clients' business, known as 'contingent commissions' or 'market service payments'. These were essentially kick-backs paid by those who were allowed to win the fake bidding process. The *Wall Street Journal* noted: 'Mr Spitzer's allegations indirectly touch three members of what might be called the first family of finance. The chairman and chief executive of AIG is Maurice H. ("Hank") Greenberg, while his eldest son Jeffrey W. Greenberg, a former AIG executive, is chairman and CEO at Marsh. Another son, Evan Greenberg, is president of Bermuda-based

ACE . . .'.[35] However Spitzer made it clear at a press conference that he was aiming much wider than this: 'The insurance industry needs to take a long, hard look at itself. If the practices identified in our suit are as widespread as they appear to be then the industry's basic business model needs major corrective action and reform.'[36]

The fact that Marsh & McLennan was at the centre of the bid-rigging investigations cast a shadow in the pension fund industry, since this broker owns William Mercer, one of the leading pension fund consultants – these consultancies are paid by trustees to evaluate their choice of pension fund manager and, if necessary, recommend alternatives. The SEC announced that it would investigate this aspect of matters.

The subsequent months saw the enquiry widen. Sweeping charges of malpractice were announced. Jeffrey Greenberg was quickly ousted from Marsh & McLennan but his father struggled to remain a force at AIG, using his control of a large group of shares which were held by the Bermuda-based Starr investment trust.[37] Far from rushing to some out-of-court settlement, 'Hank' Greenberg was to use his media contacts to strike back at the regulators.

The widespread use of insurance by a great variety of businesses gave extra significance to the unfolding investigation. Spitzer was able to document the practice of so-called 'finite insurance', by which companies entered an agreement with an insurer to guarantee a top-up payment in case they proved unable to meet an earnings target. Such insurance prevented investors from being able to assess the true state of the company. Not only would it make it hard for shareholders to assess company performance, but it was also likely to be very expensive. Both Spitzer and the SEC pursued investigations of insurance concerns, including Ace and General Re, the insurance arm of Warren Buffet's Berkshire Hathaway, which were believed to have offered offer clients this product.[38] Indeed General Re was said to have sold a product to AIG which allowed it to overstate its own reserves by $500 million in 2000 and 2001.[39]

While insurance oversight is a state-level affair the use of insurance instruments, or loans masquerading as insurance, are practices within the remit of the SEC. The latter body indicted AIG for an ambitious campaign to market deceptive 'loss mitigation' products, and off-balance sheet 'special purpose vehicles' which could hide non-performing loans and other liabilities. According to the SEC indictment, an internal AIG 'White Paper' was sent out to 32 managerial-level employees explaining how to draw up these products, complete with verbal clarifications not to be committed to paper.[40]

Putting the Brooms Back in the Closet

The limited clean-up operation being undertaken by Spitzer and Donaldson was very much in the interests of the future smooth running of the US financial system. The whole accounting and audit machinery is a device for generating legitimacy and securing trust. Wall Street and the City of London still need to re-establish confidence in their regulating, reporting and audit procedures. To this end they were, in principle, willing to accept more regulation than had been seen before. Spitzer and Donaldson could crack the whip and they could indict practices which, although 'common practice', could not withstand scrutiny by customers. But the legal changes embodied by Sarbanes–Oxley were limited – they did not focus on the perilous complexity and opacity of hedge funds and 'credit derivatives', or the booming 'shadow banking system' of which they were a part.

Donaldson certainly believed that he would be able to shame the financial services industry into self-reform, and that if this failed he would be able to impose it from above. He inveighed against what he called 'a fundamental betrayal of our nation's investors', declaring to a Securities Association meeting: 'The securities industry has found itself stuck in a legal and ethical quagmire, but I am confident that the industry will work together to pull the industry out of the muck and live up to a higher ethical standard. You can be sure that if you don't, those of us in government will.'[41]

This proud declaration was made at the end of 2003. Over the next eighteen months Donaldson was to find it increasingly difficult to live up to this promise. He and Spitzer both became the target of attack. In late October 2004 the *New York Times* reported that the SEC was 'deeply divided' over the policy of registering hedge funds. Its chairman's initiatives on those issues had attracted powerful opposition: 'In recent months, Mr Donaldson has come under pressure to reconsider the measure, from Treasury Secretary John W. Snow and some Republican members of Congress who have been recipients of donations from the [hedge fund] industry.'[42]

The next day a headline in the *Wall Street Journal* offered another straw in the wind. Splashed across three columns on the front page of its investing section it read: 'Spitzer Accused of Bully Tactics'.[43] 'Hank' Greenberg was one of the accusers. Editorials and op-ed pieces developed the theme that the attorney general was a danger to the financial community. The New York attorney general, it was claimed, was guilty of a cowardly failure to press his allegations through the courts. Unfairly intimidating businesses and unquestioned by 'media that live off his news leaks', Spitzer was trying to 'usurp the legitimate roles of elected officials and federal regulators'.[44] Spitzer had already announced that he would be a candidate for the Democratic nomination for Governor of New York, so he could also be attacked as a crowd-pleasing populist. (Spitzer won this nomination and went on to win the gubernatorial election. However, after a year in the post Governor Spitzer felt compelled to resign when it was revealed he had used the services of a prostitute.)[45]

In the early months of 2005, following the withdrawal of a Democrat-leaning member of the SEC board, the Bush administration indicated that it would keep this place vacant for a while, thus depriving Donaldson of the support he needed to press his reform agenda. Donaldson decided that the time had come to resign. In June 2005 Bush announced that he was appointing Christopher Cox, a Republican Congressman from California, to succeed Donaldson. One of Cox's few notable acts as a legislator, it was reported, 'was a 1996 bill sponsored by Mr Cox that significantly raised the burden of proof for investors who claim to have been defrauded.'[46]

Notwithstanding the very indifferent results of the spate of 'reform', the issues raised by the scandals will not go away. Many institutional investors are unhappy at executive arrogance and the weakness of shareholder rights, while many pension plan members are angry at the fund managers' lack of professionalism, ethics and accountability. Indeed fund managers comport themselves as leaders of society, patrons of the arts and of good causes, all the while treating fund members as Ancien Régime aristocrats treated the peasants on their estates, as sheep to be fleeced.

The dilemma facing those in charge of the financial system is as follows. For capitalism to work properly, the interests of owners vis-à-vis agents need to be asserted. But in the case of institutional funds the real owners are a hundred million or more pension plan contributors. The backlash against Spitzer and Donaldson reflected business concern that more transparency, and greater shareholder democracy, would unleash a dangerous wave of populism.

Michael Useem concluded his landmark study of institutional investing with the following pointed observation: 'Finding strength in numbers, conscious of their asset power, and experienced in the art of influence, institutional investors have joined the fray on behalf of the millions of individuals they represent. Yet in that mobilization lies the seeds of another revolution. The millions of ultimate owners . . . may come to question the policies of the new powers that be. Then the questions may expand from whether the professional managers are achieving maximum private return to whether they are fostering maximum public good.'[47]

Shareholder Activism and SRI

Even before the eruption of the corporate scandals, there were signs of restiveness with the imperious rule of the CEOs and their financial helpmeets. Two significant expressions of this have been the increased willingness of 'shareholder activists' to focus on poor governance, and the movement for Socially Responsible Investment (SRI). The pursuit of 'shareholder value' stimulated the first phase of 'shareholder activism' in the 1980s and early 1990s with attempts, some of them successful, to remove underperforming CEOs or to insist on ruthless cost-cutting. With the collapse of the bubble and the eruption of business scandals, several pension funds and fund managers began to broaden their definition of good corporate governance, demanding, for example, scrutiny of executive compensation – something rarely seen as an issue in the epoch of the corporate raiders.

The main exponents of the more radical approach to shareholder activism have been public sector pension funds, and these bodies have also recently begun cautiously to commit themselves to SRI. Public sector funds such as CALPERS – the California Public Employee Retirement System – or TIAA-CREF, the fund for US college teachers – have trustee boards which shield them from the crude pressures exercised by corporate sponsors. CALPERS and TIAA-CREF are huge, each having assets of well over $100 billion under management. This makes them larger than the great majority of non-financial corporations – indeed only Microsoft and GE are larger. These funds often manage their own money rather than entrusting it to commercial managers. And where they do engage money managers, they bargain to secure low costs. Indeed the administration charges of the public-sector schemes are strikingly lower than those achieved by commercial money managers: around 0.2 or 0.3 per cent of the fund each year, compared with between 1 and 2 per cent. However the investment strategies of the public sector funds have generally been quite conventional, with their trustees ever-mindful of their fiduciary duty to emulate the so-called prudent experts of the financial-services industry.

For the large pension fund – and there are hundreds of these in both the public and private sector – the very size of their holdings, and their need to hold a broad range of shares across the market, impels them towards 'voice' (playing an active part as shareholder) rather than 'exit' (selling the company's shares). Because of low administration charges, funds based on index tracking (owning all the stocks in an index) are now popular with trustees. Those invested in such a fund can no longer threaten exit. Michael Useem explains: 'Financial investors now turn their attention to corporate governance in part because their great holdings prevent them from readily selling their stake in under-performing companies.'[48] While public-sector funds blazed the trail, commercial fund managers have also begun to display concern over poor governance.

Following the market downturn, press comment on executive excess became far less tolerant. Even CEOs who had really delivered results could show embarrassment when their packages were inadvertently revealed. A case in point was the retirement package received by Jack Welch, the former CEO of GE. In addition to a pension of a quarter of a million dollars a month, it transpired that Welch was to enjoy free executive travel for life, with a chauffered limousine and the company jet at his command. He was to be supplied with opera seats, tickets to Wimbledon and a season ticket to the New York Knicks. The company was to pick up the tab for the rent of Welch's New York apartment and the wages of his domestic staff. Details of this extraordinary pampering of a man who was already a multi-millionaire filtered into the public realm only because Welch's wife sued him for divorce.[49] Welch's embarrassment stemmed, it seems, from a perception that such treatment could no longer be defended on the grounds that it helped him do the job – and also from the fact that he was dodging tax on favours-in-kind. Welch declared that he wouldn't be needing some of these perks and that he would pay tax on others.

Some public sector funds attacked extravagant executive compensation packages, especially where they were not linked to performance. In Britain the board of Vodafone awarded Chris Gent a bonus of £10 million for acquiring Mannesman without waiting to find out whether the merger would be a success – in fact Vodafone's share price was subsequently to slide steeply. Following objections by public-sector funds, even the commercial fund managers began to pipe up with their own criticisms of corporate self-indulgence. In several cases compensation packages have been trimmed. Chris Gent vowed to use his bonus to buy the company's shares and subsequently stepped down because he found the new atmosphere disagreeable. Stung into action by complaints at their prior passivity, some fund managers and trustees have taken up the struggle publicly at AGMs. On some occasions other fund managers have deemed it wise to join with the 'activists'. At the April 2003 AGM of the pharmaceutical giant GlaxoSmithKline the generous proposed compensation for the CEO was voted down. US pension funds played a key role in the ouster of the Chairman of the New York Stock Exchange, Richard Grasso, in September 2003. Grasso had accepted remuneration totalling $180 million from a hand-picked compensation committee despite the fact that the NYSE was, in its capacity as regulator, expected to exemplify best practice. The CALPERS Treasurer, backed by other large pension funds, urged that Grasso should resign.[50] He did so the next day – but kept the bulk of his package.

The public sector pension schemes usually allot some trustee representation to policy-holders and to elected office holders. This marks them off from the bulk of occupational schemes in the private sector (though there are some trade union-sponsored schemes, usually catering to a specific industry or sector, which also have such representation). Public-sector schemes also have a good record of keeping costs down and delivering returns to plan members. These plus points, and their turn to activism in the cause of good governance, do not mean, however, that they are always wholly free of the problems associated with private-sector schemes. The problem here can lie in the nature of the rules under which they operate. Where local or state authorities are obliged to maintain a balanced budget, then any pension shortfall – say in the value of a fund – will have to be made up by making cuts somewhere in the budget.[51] As with private corporations, flawed structures of this sort can offer a double incentive for employers to sack employees since, with one act, they reduce their future liability and their current expenditure. And, as might be expected, in some cases public-pension funds have become the tool of political and patronage machines. However, the scale of this has been limited by quite stringent audit and rules against self-investment.

But such structural constraints, for which they are not responsible, do not detract from the positive aspects of public sector pension funds. They too have begun to take an interest in socially responsible investment or SRI. Following a trade union campaign, CALPERS adopted SRI in 2002, saying that it would monitor its domestic and overseas investments to make sure that the companies in which it invests comply with basic labour rights and standards. It pulled out of a string of investments in Indonesia and Thailand where these criteria were not met. However, standard SRI procedure is not to boycott the shares of delinquent companies but rather to engage with them, by putting down resolutions at the AGM and proposing changes to the board of management.

How effective is SRI? The weak rights available to shareholders make it more difficult for investors to press their case with managers. Companies are still frightened of the reputational impact of a campaign against them and don't like to see large shareholders supporting critical motions at Annual General Meetings, even if such motions have no binding force. The adjustments made by corporations are often purely cosmetic. Even if they respond in good faith, the mechanisms of market competition may mean that others will pick up, and profit from, the bad practice which had been targeted. Already it is possible to invest in a Vice Fund which buys shares in all those activities shunned by ethical investors – armaments, gambling, alcohol and tobacco – but interestingly enough its portfolio doesn't seek to capture returns to those who promote sex tourism or drug dealings . The Vice Fund was reported to be defying the general gloom of the markets in 2002 and to be bounding ahead in 2003.[52] Could pension-fund trustees who refused to invest in the Vice Fund be deemed to be flouting the prudent expert rule and thus violating their duty of care to plan members? Trustees today have considerable latitude in interpreting their fiduciary duty. Short-term out-performance is characteristic of new funds. Pension fund trustees are meant to be investing for future decades and from that standpoint momentary out- or under-performance is not significant. In practice trustees can now take account of social and ethical issues when they invest so long as fund assets are properly diversified.

Given the huge size of the pension funds and their growing commitment to SRI, nearly all large companies pay some attention to the issues they raise. In conjunction with the campaigns of social movements, SRI representations have led some companies to examine their plants, subsidiaries and supply chains to defend themselves against charges that they foster sweat-shop conditions, child exploitation or dangerous industrial processes. Trade union-sponsored funds have, in some cases, used appeals to pension fund votes at AGMs to strengthen their case for trade union rights and recognition.[53] By itself shareholder SRI has inherent limitations, but together with other types of civic action it can be useful.

As long-term investors, pension funds should be particularly concerned that corporations avoid risks to their reputations. And as investors across the economy as a whole, anti-social practices that shift costs from one company onto the human or natural environment will not benefit their members. While there are special investment funds which might believe they have a stake in some seemingly profitable abuse, the broad spread of the investments of a large pension fund, and its long time horizon, may give greater scope for enlightened self-interest. Whether or not plan members understand matters in this way is of course another matter. But at least campaigners can plead that a socially responsible course does not jeopardize the best interests of plan members.

The popularity of SRI and ethical investing can be seen as an attempt to regain influence over a public sphere eviscerated by the pressures of globalization. As political parties make their pitch to dominant business interests and offer less choice to the voters, the latter seek to reshape the environment in other ways. The business scandals have made pension fund trustees and fund managers more inclined to proclaim their adherence to rules of responsibility and good governance. In the UK fund managers are required by law to state whether they take social issues into consideration or not when deciding which shares to hold. In the US there is pressure on fund managers to make public how they vote the shares they control at AGMs. The large financial groups resist such disclosure since they are keen not to advertise their passivity in the face of executive arrogance – but plan members demands for information will continue.

Given the scourge of 'vulture capitalism' it is not surprising that retirees have themselves become a major shareholder activist group. In 1995 Bill Jones, a former middle manager at Bell Atlantic, formed a group known as Bel Tel retirees which grew to have 165,000 members by 2002. Keeping a close watch on the management of the pension fund, they found that pay-outs to retirees were not keeping pace with executive compensation or with fund surpluses and they used publications, a website and a PR company to agitate for better treatment. There are many such groups and they use shareholder representations as part of the full gamut of ways of applying pressure on their former employers and on the government. The National Retiree Legislative Network (NRLN) declares on its website: 'We can help anyone with a burning desire to keep predatory executives from running through your pension money or taking away promised health-care benefits.'[54]

The SRI movement is hampered by the fact that shareholder powers are quite weak and only a small minority of shareholders take it seriously. The main leverage possessed by a large private shareholder is that they can sell their holdings. This is more difficult for the large institutions since they need to hold stocks in every company to achieve diversification. A few key investors like Carl Icahn or Kirk Kerkorian take strategic stakes with a view to fostering takeovers or mergers. But this is beyond the remit of the institutions. Anyway only a minority of public-sector pension funds are strongly committed to SRI. Though several are very large they remain a small minority of all shareholders. For SRI to become more effective there would need to be larger changes in the corporate landscape and in the modus operandi of pension funds. At present members of DB pension plans are a dwindling category. To make even a modest contribution to building democratic governance of corporations there would need to be a measure of workplace participation and universal membership of pre-funded secondary pension plans. It would also be necessary to dethrone the banks and to disperse the shadows in the 'shadow banking system'. (See Chapter 7 and the preface.)

Notes

1 Steven Weisman, *The Great Tax Wars: Lincoln to Wilson*, New York 2002, pp. 284–6.
2 Charles H. Mills, *Fraudulent Practices in Respect to Securities and Commodities, with special reference to the Martin Act*, Albany NY, 1923.
3 See, in particular, Nomi Prins, *Other People's Money: the Corporate Mugging of America*, New York 2004, pp. 71–112.
4 I have much more on all this – including the impact on Californian energy supplies, the role of credit derivatives and the reasons why Bush did not come to Enron's rescue – in Robin Blackburn, 'The Collapse of Enron', *New Left Review*, 14, May–June 2002 (available from the magazine's website at newleftreview.org). as well as in *Banking on Death*, pp. 188–97.
5 Abraham L. Gitlow, *Corruption in Corporate America: Who is Responsible? Who Will Protect the Pubic Interest?*, Lanham MD, 2005, pp. 61–8, 85–103.
6 The most detailed account of this affair was an article by John Cassidy in the *New Yorker*, April 2003.

7 Timothy O'Brien and Juliet Cresswell, 'Laughing All the Way to the Bank', *New York Times*, 11 September 2005.

8 David Ibison, 'Citigroup Apologises to Japan', *Financial Times*, 26 October 2004. 'Citigroup Faces Record FSA Fine', *Financial Times*, 1 June 2005.

9 O'Brien and Cresswell, 'All the Way to the Bank'.

10 Joseph Stiglitz, *The Roaring Nineties*, p. 347, n. 9.

11 'Offering Help', *Wall Street Journal*, 13 October 2003.

12 'Who's Watching the Manager of Your Mutual Fund?', *New York Times*, 14 September 2003.

13 Kenneth N. Gilpin, 'How Scandal Can Help the Fund Industry', *New York Times*, 2 November 2003.

14 John Plender, 'Broken Trust', *Financial Times*, 21 November 2003.

15 Floyd Norris, 'How to Beat the Market: Easy. Make Late Trades', *New York Times*, 5 September 2003 and Floyd Norris, 'Can Confidence be Restored?', *New York Times*, 5 October 2003.

16 Karen Damato, ' "Timing" at Mutual Funds Can Cost 2% a Year', *Wall Street Journal*, 19 September 2003.

17 Eric Zitzewitz, 'How Widespread is Late Trading in Mutual Funds?', Stanford Graduate School of Business, Research Paper no. 1817, September 2003.

18 David Wells and Adrian Michaels, 'Spitzer Warns of Huge Fines for Funds at Heart of Probe', *Financial Times*, 4 November 2003; Stephen Labaton, 'Extensive Flaws at Mutual Funds Cited at Hearing', *New York Times*, 4 November 2003.

19 Tom Lauricella, 'For Staid Mutual-Fund Industry, Growing Probe Signals Shake-Up; Widespread Abuses Hurting Small Investors; Unfair Pricing for Big Players', *Wall Street Journal*, 20 October 2003; John Hechinger, 'Putnam Says it Will Replace Fund Mangers', *Wall Street Journal*, 24 October 2003; Ellen Kelleher, 'Putnam to Face Fraud Charges in Funds Probe', *Financial Times*, 22 October 2003.

20 David Barboza and Riva Atlas, 'Some Call Fund Chief a Contradictory Man', *New York Times*, 31 October 2003; Jason Zweig, 'The Great Mutual Fund Rip-Off', *Money*, October 2003.

21 Gretchen Morgenson, 'At Putnam, The Buck Stays Put in a Pocket', *New York Times*, 2 November 2003.

22 Joshua Chaffin, 'Spitzer Blames Directors for Scandals', *Financial Times*, 4 November 2003.

23 'Proving that the more things change the more they remain the same Wall Street analysts have their pompoms out again. Yes, cheerleader analysts are not quite as prevalent as they were in 2000. But as the Intel earnings conference call last Tuesday showed, too many analysts seem to think it is part of their job to high five the companies they are supposed to be assessing for the benefit of their clients.' Gretchen Morgenson, 'Fawning Analysts Betray Investors', *New York Times*, 19 October 2003. See also, John Coffee, 'Wall Street's Conflicts Cannot be Settled', *Financial Times*, 29 April 2003.

24 The employers who make available 401(k)s to their employees may start

offering advice to them as well, to help them choose the right product. But the hiring-in of advice for this purpose will add a layer of charges.

25 Robin Blackburn, 'Why Kerry Lost', *Constellations*, June 2005.

26 Stephen Labaton, 'US Auditing Oversight Board Begins Policing Role by Settling on Procedure', *New York Times*, 8 October 2003.

27 Andrew Parker, 'Consulting Fuels Deloitte Revenue Rise', *Financial Times*, 1 October 2003.

28 'Still Counting the Cost, the auditing profession has still not put its problems behind it', *Economist*, 18 October 2003. The 'big four' – Ernst and Young, Deloitte, KPMG and PricewaterhouseCoopers – like to boast that they are global concerns able to offer a global service. But at any hint of trouble they insist that the partnerships in each country enjoy autonomy.

29 Floyd Norris, 'A Modest Proposal by the SEC', *New York Times*, 9 October 2003. The Business Roundtable, representing large corporations, nevertheless announced that it would oppose these modest measures, Deborah Solomon, 'SEC May Boost Holders' Power to Nominate, Elect Directors', *Wall Street Journal*, 9 October 2003.

30 Gregory Zuckerman and Deborah Solomon, 'Now the Hedge Fund Business Can Exhale', *Wall Street Journal*, 30 September 2003; 'Hedge Funds: Rules for the Unregulated', *Economist*, 4 October 2003.

31 Adrian Michaels and David Wells, 'SEC Censure for Morgan Stanley Chief', *Financial Times*, 2 May 2003.

32 'Worldcom's Revenge', *Economist*, 30 August 2003. Warren Buffet had earlier doubted the effectiveness of the corporate reforms. See Andrew Hill, 'Buffet Hits Out at Cosiness in Boardrooms', *Financial Times*, 10 March 2003.

33 Gene O'Kelly, 'Happy Second Birthday, Sarbanes–Oxley', *Financial Times*, 29 July 2004.

34 See Gitlow, *Corruption in Corporate America*, pp. 97–101, 133–61.

35 Theo Francis, 'Spitzer Charges Bid Rigging in Insurance', *Wall Street Journal*, 15 October 2004. Bermuda also hosted many AIG affiliates who, dating back over half a century, have received special privileges there, making it the 'risk capital of the world'. See Glenn Simpson and Theo Francis, 'In Bermuda, AIG Helped Shape a Legendary Corporate Haven', *Wall Street Journal*, 20 September 2005.

36 Francis, 'Spitzer Charges Bid Rigging'.

37 The Bermuda-based C.V. Starr and Starr International held huge sums in trust for an elite of employees and former employees. See Ianthe Jeanne Dugan and George Anders, 'Exclusive "Club" Lifted Greenberg's Power', *Wall Street Journal*, 12 April 2005. According to this report the Starr companies held large amounts of AIG stock. It was supposed to use its holdings to pay bonuses and pension supplements to the companies' 92,000 workers but apparently the lion's share of these disbursements had gone to about 800 senior executives.

38 Ellen Kelleher and Andrea Felsted, 'AIG Probe Draws in Buffet', *Financial Times*, 30 March 2005.

39 Timothy O'Brien, 'U.S. Case on Insurers is Expected', *New York Times*, 2 February 2006.
40 Michael Schroeder, 'AIG May Pay Up to $90 million', *Wall Street Journal*, 24 November 2004. The fine mentioned in this headline later appeared greatly to underestimate the damages for which the insurer was liable.
41 Stephen Labaton, 'S.E.C. Chief Vows to Act on Mutual Funds', *New York Times*, 8 November 2003.
42 Stephen Labaton, 'Divided S.E.C Likely to ask Hedge Funds for More Data', *New York Times*, 26 October 2004.
43 Ann Davis, Kara Scannell and Charles Forelle, 'Spitzer Accused of Bully Tactics', *Wall Street Journal*, 26 October 2004. The *WSJ* did publish a defence of the attorney general by John Bogle but its editorials were consistently hostile. John Bogle, 'The Spitzer Effect', *Wall Street Journal*, 18 November 2004.
44 'Spitzer in Court', *Wall Street Journal*, 23 September 2005.
45 In addition to his high-profile attacks on miscreant financiers he has also drawn attention to the miserable pay and negligible job rights of cloakroom attendants at Manhattan's upscale hotels, restaurants and clubs. However those who criticized Spitzer for his willingness to accept settlements rather than to press prosecutions did have a point.
46 Deborah Solomon and Michael Shroeder, 'Bush Heralds a Change in Regulatory Terrain with Pick to Lead SEC', *Wall Street Journal*, 3–5 June 2005.
47 Useem, *Investor Capitalism*, p. 267.
48 Michael Useem, *Investor Capitalism: How Money Managers Are Changing the Face of Corporate America*, New York 1996, p. 6.
49 With his keen eye for assets Welch wrote of Lord Weinstock, an English business associate: 'He had racehorses stabled with the Queen's thoroughbreds, had elegant homes, and had a spectacular wife.' Jack Welch, with John A. Byrne, *Jack: What I've Learnt Leading a Great Company and Great People*, New York 2001.
50 Vincent Boland and Andrei Postelnicu, 'Pension Funds Call on Grasso to Quit', *Financial Times*, 17 September 2003.
51 Peronet Despeignes, 'US States Face Long Term Budget Shortfall', *Financial Times*, 29 May 2003; for the consequent havoc in municipal and state budget prospects, see Mary Williams Walsh, 'States and Cities Risk Bigger Losses to Fund Pensions', *New York Times*, 12 October 2003.
52 'Virtues of Vice', *Economist*, 1 November 2003.
53 See the ICEM website for ongoing information concerning the campaign centred on Rio Tinto.
54 Quoted Prins, *Other People's Money*, pp. 294–5.

6

The Need for Strong Public Pensions

In the first chapter I urged that pension provision should aim to continue supplying about 70–75 per cent of average incomes to all those over sixty-five and that this will require between 15 and 22 per cent of GDP in most advanced countries by the middle decades of this century, with Europe being at the top end of this range. In the recent past the core continental European states, especially Italy, France and Germany, had public programmes in place that were on course to furnish such a chunk of GDP, in some cases with a little to spare. But this is no longer the case. On current plans the level of public spending on pension provision is set to lag way behind the ageing of the population. Ageing will also raise the need for spending on health and elder care.

Supposedly the citizens of Europe will be able to compensate for lost public pensions by taking out private-pension coverage, yet we have seen how inefficient and vulnerable this can be. Those who reach retirement age around 2030 are headed for a double short-fall. Firstly, their promised pension has shrunk and secondly, existing finance does not cover remaining pension promises. Despite huge inducements private pensions have never managed to achieve such levels in the United States or Britain, and are not on course to do so in the future. The siren song of privatization is now muted in these countries and the concern is to strengthen and enhance public provision. However it would be foolish to suppose that schemes of implicit or explicit privatization will not again be pressed as solutions to the pensions crisis. Such proposals are backed by powerful lobbies and will not disappear until the underlying pension challenge has been met. This chapter will explore the essential contribution which public pensions using the pay-as-you-go system of finance make to a good pension regime, but I will also address the limitations on current financing methods and the need to diversify and supplement them.

The 'privatizing' thrust of social and pension policy has had a global character, with a grandiose attempt to match the privatization of public assets to the privatization of public liabilities, in ways that would offer lush new grazing grounds to banks, insurance houses, fund managers and stock exchanges. To call this a recipe for wild capitalism would not be wholly fair since it would critically depend on a new regime of publicly mandated, publicly organized and publicly subsidised contributions from the mass of

employees. Governments were not only to offer lavish tax incentives but
were often expected to turn public bodies into collection agencies for
commercial concerns. Even the magic of financial engineering finds some
difficulty in conjuring a profit out of a mass of financial obligations.

Privatization Proves a Hard Sell

The privatizing offensive had traction in Europe because of a widespread
and persistent sense of malaise. The landmark World Bank report of 1994,
Averting the Old Age Crisis: Policies to Protect the Old and Protect Growth,
argued that pension regimes with a 'dominant public pillar' were
responsible for slow growth and high unemployment and urged that
they be cut right back and replaced with the compulsory enrollment of all
employees in private savings schemes. Though it was easy enough to map
the Bank's criticisms and recommendations onto pension problems in the
core European Union states, the report's arguments were couched in
general terms. They applied quite explicitly to emerging economies and
post-socialist states, but they also echoed themes dear to neo-liberals and
neo-conservatives in the United States and Britain.

   The cause of social security or pension 'reform' was attractive to financial
lobby groups but inspired great reservations amongst those who had
already built up entitlement in an existing public regime. In the former
Communist states inflation and 'shock therapy' largely destroyed the value
of public pensions, opening the way in several Eastern European states to
legislation replacing these systems by obligatory private provision, just as
the World Bank recommended. But in Western Europe there was still
much support for generous public pensions, so that the first attempts to
weaken the public programmes led not simply to massive demonstrations
and strikes but to the downfall of centre-right governments in the mid-
1990s – the governments of Silvio Berlusconi in Italy, Alain Juppé in
France and Helmut Kohl in Germany. Even in Britain, pension scandals
and disappointments contributed to the downfall of John Major's government in 1997 and disenchantment with Margaret Thatcher's legacy.[1] The
centre-left coalitions which replaced these governments acted with great
circumspection. They sought to avoid a head-on clash over most existing
pension commitments and entitlements but nevertheless harped on the
need for 'reform'. They singled out a few instances of apparently excessive
pension generosity and generally blamed Europe's stagnation and unem-

ployment not on the policies of central banks obsessed by monetary union, and the fiscal austerity established by the Maastricht treaty of 1992, but on the burden of pension and welfare provision. The Dini administration in Italy, as noted in the introduction, successfully negotiated a major install-ment of reform in 1995 when it downsized future entitlements while respecting those of workers aged forty and above. This formula of long-itudinal 'reform' was eventually adopted, notwithstanding much resistance, by the Schroeder government in Germany and the Raffarin centre-right administration in France. The failure of the centre-left governments to come up with an effective response to mass joblessness undercut and demoralized opposition to successive doses of 'implicit' privatization, often accompanied with legislation offering tax relief to those who signed up with a private supplier.

Already in 2001, prior to a new wave of cuts in the next four years, projected public expenditure per person aged sixty-five and over by EU states was on course to shrink dramatically from its 2000 level. In terms of expenditure per head as a percentage of GDP per head, the drop was to be from 72.0 per cent in France in 2000 to 57.5 per cent in 2040; in Italy from 72.3 per cent in 2000 to 45.9 per cent in 2040; in Germany from 67.4 per cent of GDP per head in 2000 to 54.8 per cent in 2040.[2] This was simply a first installment of downsizing with more to come from Raffarin, Berlusconi, Schroeder and Merkel.

The European retreat from public insurance of the risks of the ageing society is commonly regarded as a success for pension reform, with public expenditure being severely curbed. The report by the European Com-mission and its Economic Policy Committee presented in February 2006 predicted declining 'benefit ratios', that is, a decline in the ratio of per capita pension benefits to per capita output, for 2030 and 2050. As we saw in the introduction, its figures showed that, in per capita GDP terms, public-pension income per aged citizen is expected to drop year by year until by 2050 it will be only a little over half its level in 2004. In absolute terms public spending on old-age pensions, elder care and health creeps up but numbers of the aged nearly double. The EU-wide projections, covering 25 countries and some 450 million people, show overall public-pension spending growing even more slowly despite a rapidly increasing aged population.[3] Most of the new member states switched from public to private provision with haste and the portents, so far, are not good.

The public discussion on pension prospects that led to the cut-backs focused on pension outlays rather than on pension needs – which were bound to grow as the aged population grew. Even the more generous pension systems were geared to furnishing no more than 72 per cent of average GDP per head, while the 'reforms' were to bring them down to 45 per cent or less. These figures can be compared to estimates that cash benefits for the over-65s comprised 4.1 per cent of GDP in Britain and the United States in 1998.[4] Of course US Social Security and the British state pension were designed to offer a basic pension, leaving private provision to add comfort and a margin for emergencies. As we have seen, the private systems have performed badly and may do much worse. By contrast the public systems have proved to be efficient at turning contributions into pensions and effective in reducing pensioner poverty – even if over a tenth of pensioners still need extra help.

In Social Security the United States has a limited but very effective public pension programme. It offers nearly universal coverage, with the middle class grateful to the element of insurance it provides. It raises over 13 million older people out of poverty and furnishes the largest single source of support for the majority of retirees. Two-thirds of the over-65s rely on Social Security for more than half of their income, a figure that rises to three-quarters or more for women, Hispanics and African Americans. Over a fifth have no other income at all. Social Security's budget for retired workers topped $400 billion a year in 2004, with a further $150 billion in other social insurance benefits for the disabled and for those who had lost a bread-winner. The Social Security administration employs 65,000 people – about the same number of people as one of the larger Wall Street investment banks, but on much lower salaries. The political resilience of the programme testifies to the fact that the great majority of US citizens value it and count on it.

Public pension provision also now enjoys wider support in the UK. In 1998 the Blair government, as noted in Chapter 1, looked forward to a time when private pensions would supply 60 per cent of all retirement income by 2040, but this is now generally acknowledged to be a quite unreal hope. In response to pensioner unhappiness, the government introduced a Pension Credit guarantee in 2003 that raised the value of the state pension for those who applied by nearly a third, so long as they met the criterion of need it established. In 2004, 35 per cent of pensioners had an income sufficiently low that they qualified to receive the Credit. The government claims that this targeted benefit is cost-effective, removing many from poverty while avoiding the expense of supplying every pensioner with the Credit guarantee level – a cost that, at current rates, would be around £8 billion annually. However the effectiveness of this targeting exercise is expected to decline and the government's Pensions Commission estimated that by 2050 about 75 per cent of all pensioners are likely to qualify for the Credit, if they submit to the means test. While some were likely to find the means test demeaning, others would see it as a disincentive to their own saving. The government's own Pensions Commission recognized both the weakness of private provision and the disincentive effect of the Pension Credit in its first report, which appeared in December 2004.

The Commission's eventual recommendations, issued in November 2005, urged a new 'enhanced state pension', indexed to earnings rather than prices from about 2010. The cost of doing this was to be met first by raising the women's pension age from sixty to sixty-five (in 2010–20), and then by raising the pension age of both sexes, by stages, from sixty-five to sixty-eight by 2050. Indeed the Commission was able to show that its 'enhanced state pension' would cost the government no more in 2050 than did the existing pension arrangements. Somewhat surprisingly the Commission's proposed reform, designed to reduce means-testing, would still leave some 35 per cent of pensioners in 2050 being subject to a means test.[5] These two unexpected features of the British reform proposal show that enhancing public pensions and banishing the means test may be popular goals but they encounter strong resistance, emanating from the Treasury. (The measures proposed in the 2006 White Paper were to follow suit.)[6]

Linking the state pension to earnings rather than prices was a measure which the Blair/Brown government had long opposed. The Commission also suggested that all those aged seventy-five and over, regardless of contribution record, were to be granted the full basic state pension, a relatively inexpensive measure but helpful to older women with weak entitlement. Side-by-side with these arrangements there was to be a National Pension Savings Scheme in which everyone would be enrolled, but with the right to opt out if they wished. Those employees who stayed in the scheme would be required to contribute 5 per cent of salary, and their employers would thereupon be required to contribute 3 per cent.[7]

An unconditional public pension, such as Social Security supplies in the US, furnishes security while serving as a basis upon which other savings can be built. The effect of means-tested benefits is also to raise the implicit tax rate, so that an older worker who draws down savings, or takes a job, not only pays any tax due but also suffers loss of benefit, to create a combined implicit tax well above the rate paid by high earners.

Raising the official age of retirement helps to make public-pension systems cheaper but is difficult to justify, especially when older workers so often suffer unemployment and disability. As was noted in Chapter 1, manual workers in the UK have a life expectancy that is three to five years below that of professionals and managers. On the other hand manual workers have usually entered the labour force two or three years earlier than professionals or managers, so that those who have contributed for longer receive less benefit. Raising the age of retirement aggravates this injustice.

The Greenspan Commission of 1983 raised the normative retirement year of receipt of Social Security to sixty-seven albeit that implementation was to be delayed – phased in – over several decades and US workers would retain the right to retire earlier – at sixty-two – if they accepted a lower benefit. Class differences in mortality in the US are similar to the UK, with those in subordinate, low-paid positions having poor life expectancy, so the same objection applies.[8] Of course the real source of the injustice is the differential mortality rate but raising the retirement age makes matters worse, reducing a manual worker's average years in retirement by a larger proportional amount. There is also evidence that by the age of sixty-five many have used up their 'health capital' and that work beyond that age prevents the improvement in health prospects experienced by most retirees.[9]

Despite its successes, the universal, public, not-for-profit character of Social Security, and the large transfers it organizes, have made it a bugbear of US neo-conservatives and neo-liberals. Attempts have been made to weaken or part-privatize the programme, under Reagan, Clinton and George W. Bush, but each has failed.[10] George W. Bush opened his second term by declaring that he would use his 'political capital' to further partial privatization of Social Security. He went on the stump in more than thirty town meetings in the early months of 2005 but somehow the message did not catch on, even in the 'red' (Republican) states. The frustration of this privatizing bid joins the roll call of other defeats that have been inflicted on those who dared to menace the 'third rail' – Reagan's plan to downsize the programme in 1981, and the Clinton/ Summers plan abandoned in the wake of Monica Lewinsky. Bush's last hopes of making a start before the mid terms were dashed by Hurricane Katrina. Bush could not convince his own supporters that it was wise to reduce the contributions going to this national safety net and hand over the money to Wall Street instead. It was also significant that Social

Security redistributes from rich to poor states, with many of the latter being 'red'. While New York, New England and California are large net contributors to the scheme, Mid-Western and Southern states are significant net gainers.[11] The European Union possesses no programme of similar scope, capable of redistributing from rich to poor regions. While Social Security comprises over 4 per cent of US GDP, the existing EU budget for all purposes is only 1 per cent of its GDP.

While US Social Security may be secure for a while against attempts at outright privatization, it still needs to be defended from sneaky attempts to 'strengthen' it by reducing benefit levels or targeting them on the poor. The benefits it now provides are quite modest and any reduction – say through weaker indexation or a raised retirement age – would inevitably increase old-age poverty. Indeed benefits need to be improved to strengthen the coverage enjoyed by women and minorities. The British government still has something to learn from the superior US system. The Social Security Administration has its own dedicated source of revenue, and its own administrative staff, complete with economists and actuaries. In Britain, pension finance is still under the direct control of the Treasury and the system is run by Whitehall as just another department of government. The Social Security Administration is more autonomous, but its board of trustees is still dominated by the Treasury Secretary. In both countries pension surpluses have been routinely drawn upon to cover the government's own current account deficits – a practice which conceals and compromises the pension reserves.

Given that Social Security is cost-effective and nearly universal in its coverage why not allot to it the whole job of meeting the target 15 per cent of US GDP that will be needed by 2035 or thereabouts? At present Social Security pays out old-age pensions worth 3.5 per cent of GDP. To quadruple this figure would be a leap too far. Raising future entitlements to cover nearly twice as many over-65s will itself raise Social Security old-age pensions to 5 per cent of GDP over the next three decades. Ensuring that the programme really does this heavy lifting from its dedicated revenues is quite demanding. Earnings by employed seniors might be 2 per cent or a little more, but hitting the overall target of 15 per cent of GDP will require a system of secondary pensions with more diverse revenue sources. Like the US, Britain should build a secondary pension regime which obliges employers to contribute in a new way and which strips out the excessive costs in private provision. Even in continental Europe and Japan, with their more collectivist traditions, the shape of the problem will be very similar. As we have seen, successive 'reforms' may still leave current spending quite high but they have slashed entitlements due in three or four decades' time. Because the proportion of those aged sixty-five or over is set to continue rising in these countries, such cuts are either illusory or ominous, and quite likely both. In effect the citizens of these states will be faced with a task not unlike that which confronts British and US citizens, namely to reinforce and improve the basic public pension and to supplement it with a public mandated second tier, with the aim of delivering something like 15–20 per cent of GDP in order to maintain pensioners' relative incomes at no less than 70 per cent of average income.

The shape of the overall challenge is scarcely addressed in US debates and still does not figure prominently enough in UK discussions. Instead there is hand-wringing about the affordability of the present modest levels of Social Security, combined with intermittent attention to the grave problems besetting occupational and personal schemes. From the late 1980s advocates of so-called 'generational accounting' appeared who increasingly questioned both the viability and the equity of the Social Security programme. In part their method was the one already evoked in the first chapter – segregating the generations and examining whether they gain or lose from the programme, if the present value of their total contributions is set against the total value of their eventual benefits. Social Security is frequently portrayed in US public discussions as being on the brink of bankruptcy. Thus after noting that the programme will bring in a surplus for the next ten years, Howell Jackson wrote in the *New York Times*: 'Were the federal government to account for its Social Security obligations under the rules of accrual accounting which govern public companies, its financial outlook would be far worse. By the end of last year [2002], the Social Security system owed retirees and current workers benefits valued at $14 trillion. The system's assets in contrast, were only $3.5 trillion. These assets include not only the trust funds' current reserves ($1.4 trillion), but also the present value of the taxes that current workers will pay over the remainder of their working lives.'[12]

Using a similar methodology, Laurence Kotlikoff and Scott Burns offer an even more alarming prospective total fiscal shortfall of $51 trillion if both Social Security and Medicare – the health care programme for seniors – are taken into account. This truly astronomic figure looms over the 'infinite' horizon. Kotlikoff and Burns believe that the obligation on the Social Security trustees to estimate the programme's fiscal health over a 75-year period is quite insufficient. They cite a study estimating that while the 75-year horizon indicated a gap of $3.5 trillion, the deficit increased to $10.5 trillion over seventy-five years 'and beyond' simply for Social Security. The fiscal gap relating to Medicare is considerably bigger, largely because it has much more modest dedicated funding from payroll taxes, and was boosted to just over $40 trillion by the passage of a new prescriptions entitlement Act in November 2003. These authors argue that the size of prospective deficits begins to explode as soon as the base line for the mandatory 75-year projection moves from 2002 to, say, 2015. [13]

While forecasts do need to be made, the approach of the partisans of 'generational accounting' tries to do too much. The combination of distant horizons with arbitrary assumptions renders the projections overly alarmist. Quite small changes in the assumed annual growth rate of employment or productivity would lead to hugely different results over seventy-five or 150 years. Moreover, there is no good reason to assess Social Security's particular assets and liabilities as if it was a fund or business, nor to calculate the 'present value' of future contributions, using some inevitably rigid and unrealistic discount rate. Funds need to assess liabilities and assets in this way because they do not have mandatory future sources of revenue, as does Social Security. Contributors to the system have furnished benefits to their 'predecessors at large', and their own pensions will be paid by contributions from their 'successors at large'. This is laid down in the law. If a fiscal gap appears over the 75-year horizon, such as the possible $3.5 trillion shortfall in Social Security receipts, then the correct remedial measure is to phase in more revenue, either by raising contributions or through recourse to some other tax source. In 2005 the contribution rate of 12.4 per cent of income was only levied up to a given annual threshold – just under $90,000. The raising of this threshold would generate substantially more revenue.

A Scheme for Intergenerational Justice

The supporters of 'generational accounting' write as if there is something intrinsically unfair in taxing younger workers for the benefit of older retirees. While there is a need to avoid an unfair apportionment of burdens caused by varying cohort size – an issue to be confronted below – there is a broad schema of generational exchanges which also has to be borne in mind. Those who have received public education or educational subsidies will thereby have benefited from the taxes paid by their 'predecessors at large' in another way. With age cohorts of varying sizes it is a challenge to work out a fair balance between what is given and what is received, but this will not be achieved by nullifying generational interdependence.

Philosophically the publicly sponsored pay-as-you-go systems have been claimed to embody a contract between the generations. Each generation makes a contribution and each receives a benefit. Where there is economic growth this can stretch to pensions which rise with national prosperity, as long as there is a broad balance between age cohorts. A problem arises when generational cohorts are of very unequal size, because of 'ageing' and/or 'baby booms' followed by declining fertility. Rapid growth of output and productivity can absorb the strain but if growth slows, generational imbalance will make for awkward choices. Either (1) the members of the smaller cohort have to pay more than did the members of its larger predecessor in order to pay the latter's pensions; or (2) the pension received by the members of the larger cohort is scaled back so that contribution rates don't have to rise; or (3) contributions rates are raised, and pensions are cut, until a fit is found based on shared sacrifice.

These are not easy choices to make and yet they are difficult to avoid. There are many in the United States and Europe today who believe that their past contributions entitle them to the pensions that they were promised. As noted above, there has been great opposition to those politicians who wish to downsize public pensions and encourage people to make their own arrangements instead. But though wholesale reform is often rejected, entitlements are nevertheless often gradually and sneakily whittled down, with the real reductions not coming into force for a few decades. Some opponents of pension privatization claim that there is really no problem. But in most parts of the developed and developing world the demographic shock of ageing is large enough to be a major issue, requiring new sources of revenue.

In the United States the debate tends to focus on the future of Social Security which, although important and successful in the ways mentioned above, amounts to about 40 per cent of retirees' income today. Because of the severe problems afflicting private and occupational coverage – examined in the previous chapters – this proportion could rise in the future. The retired will need full Social Security benefit even more than before but they will also be keen to restore, or acquire, a decent second pension. The US Social Security faces a shortfall in 2041, according to the

2005 report of the programme's trustees, or by 2052, according to a report of the Congressional Budget Office in the previous year. The trustees estimated that solvency could be restored across the 75-year horizon, either by cutting benefits by 12.8 per cent or by raising contributions from 12.4 per cent of pay to 14.32 per cent of pay. These increases would have to be introduced immediately, effective in 2006. If action is delayed until the trust fund is empty then, according to the trustees, the payroll tax would have to be increased to 16.66 per cent of salary in 2041 and to 18.01 per cent of salary in 2079.[14]

Kotlikoff and Burns, as we have seen, would see such adjustments as too little, too late, because, in their view, the really big shortfalls are not yet on the 75-year horizon but will be by 2020. Given the uncertainty of the trustees' projections, the wait-and-see approach could be advisable. If US workers in 2079 really have to pay 18 per cent of salary towards Social Security this would not be such a dire prospect if the pension was a decent one. Swedish workers already pay 18.5 per cent of salary towards a publicly administered pension system. However this brings them a second as well as a basic pension.

With variable cohorts, pension provision inevitably raises issues of intergenerational justice, which are conceptualized in different ways by those committed to 'generational solidarity' and to the partisans of 'generational accounting'. The generational solidarity approach, in its most radical form, insists that the qualitative bond between parents and children makes any precise calculation of who gains and who loses unseemly and inappropriate. Supporters of loading all pension needs onto the pay-as-you-go systems incline to this approach, and regard talk of a crisis of the 'ageing society' as needless alarmism. They are understandably deeply sceptical of the claims of 'generational accounting'. As we have seen, the latter argues that each generation should pay its own way, relying on no help from parents or children. Risk-pooling within a generation is okay but not between generations. They hold that if modern states only came clean with implicit debts – the present value of their future pension liabilities, minus the present value of future payroll taxes – they would find that they are all staring bankruptcy in the face. They regard the attempt to impose this burden on today's children and those not even born as the height of injustice; to do so will halve the incomes of rising generations and cause untold social strife.

The 'generational accountants' approach to the justice issue is as open to question as their methodology. Generational accountants and privatizers, overlapping but not identical categories, like to argue that today's worker, paying his or her payroll tax (social security contribution), is making a bad investment since he or she is not likely to get a good rate of return. But if workers considered their payroll tax as a way of paying the pensions of their parents and those Peter Laslett calls their 'predecessors at large', then there would be no reason to expect a rate of return.[15]

The reasoning of the partisans of generational solidarity is very much to be preferred over that of the supporters of generational economics. But it is flawed nonetheless. Each generation has a right and duty to revise the social arrangements it finds in place. While they have obligations to their parents' generation these are not limitless. Talk of a literal generational compact would be wrong, since the newborn find many choices already made on their behalf. In Chapter 2, I referred to the debate on John Rawls's philosophy of justice and cited Brian Barry's observation concerning inter-generational justice. In a remark that bears repeating he writes: 'the key here is a willingness to claim and be claimed upon in virtue of a given principle. Justice must be fair from both sides . . . The point here is that we should think not of a choice made by a particular generation at a single point in time but of a collaboration over many generations in a common scheme of justice.'[16]

I think that such conclusions invite us to come up with arrangements for the equal sharing of the burdens of an ageing society – and, given the probability that these might be considerable, to find appropriate fiscal innovations to meet them. I have urged support for the formula that the overall scheme of pension provision should be adjusted so that the ratio of pensioner incomes to average incomes is held broadly constant, as formulated by John Myles.[17] Myles was developing this argument in relation to European pensions systems, which have historically supplied a comprehensive overall pension replacing two-thirds or more of pre-retirement income. Applying this approach to pension provision in the UK and US would consequently require a focus on overall post-retirement income. Where there is every likelihood that personal and occupational pensions would be inadequate and vulnerable, it would be important to sustain a decent level of public provision. Social Security in the US, which furnishes a little less than half of retirement income, should be protected as the stable core of income maintenance in old age. The Social Security programme is and should remain a DB scheme in which the benefit is not only inflation-protected but also geared to rising earnings. It should also be paid to all and not simply targeted at the poor, as this will help to retain public support and ensure decent benefit levels. While occupational and personal pensions are moving to the DC model which can fluctuate downwards, the Social Security element of retirement incomes should be as reliable and predictable as possible. Thus the best way to meet the target level for overall retirement income maintenance would be to protect Social Security benefits at their present level.

President George W. Bush has thus far been frustrated in his attempt partially to privatize Social Security. Many US voters rightly fear that diverting 16 per cent or so of the programme's revenues into personal accounts will fatally undermine its overall finances. However, wealthy backers will continue to press for 'compromise' plans to 'save Social Security', and these are likely to involve benefit reduction and 'implicit privatization'. In March 2006 the CBO website urged the need for a 10 per cent benefit cut and in June Hank Poulson, the former Goldman Sachs chief nominated as Treasury Secretary, also warned of the need for economies. But cuts, even if gradually achieved by means of weaker indexation, could drag millions below the poverty line who are only just above it now. There is also another danger. Some ambitious 'reformers' really look forward to converting Social Security into a programme targeted only at the poor, with the rest of the population left to the tender mercies of the market. This would deprive Americans of a residual element of shared security in a society that is already too exposed to uncertainty and social fragmentation.

At the present time in Europe and North America the overall income of the average pensioner is 70–75 per cent of average income. These averages do not, of course, tell us about inequality between pensioners, or in society at large. But they do indicate a generational ratio, with the older deemed to have lesser outgoings than those who still have the responsibility of growing families. I have been arguing that to maintain something like this overall ratio could be seen as a scheme of intergenerational justice. To do so would require a raising of future contribution rates but also, perhaps, a somewhat greater effort to pre-fund tomorrow's pensions by raising savings rates and obliging employers to contribute more effectively – the employers' contribution has plummeted with the switch from Defined Benefit to Defined Contribution schemes.

Inequality has risen sharply in most of the leading capitalist states over the last three decades, especially in the UK and US.[18] It is quite possible to address the issue of generational equity and yet also tackle the issue of a more equal distribution within pensioner incomes and average incomes.

Traditionally all public pension schemes have involved an element of redistribution from rich to poor, even if many still allowed those who had contributed more to receive a somewhat higher entitlement. Commercial pre-funded schemes obviously make no attempt at such redistribution though they do incorporate some risk-pooling. It should not be assumed, as it sometimes is by proponents of the 'generational solidarity' approach, that all pre-funding is inimical to redistribution, and that it cannot make a contribution to a sharing of the burden occasioned by demographic transformations. For example, restoration of the employers' contribution could help to build a pension reserve and a large generation like the famous baby-boomers still has some time to build up reserves so that all the costs of their future pensions will not have to be met from payroll taxes alone. However, we should bear in mind another of Brian Barry's observations here, namely that the whole process of 'saving' rests on certain assumptions – in particular a 'process of accumulation of capital'. I will be returning to the implications of this argument in a later section.

So we should not underestimate the very real problem of financing future pensions or count on prevailing tax regimes to accomplish the task. Because of the ageing phenomenon – lower birth rates as well longer life expectancy – the maintenance and improvement of future levels of pension provision will certainly require sources of finance other than pay as you go. This is all the more the case because the real problem is not that of delivering on the distinctly modest promises of Social Security in the US, or of a very modestly 'entanced' state pension in the UK, but rather that of ensuring decent pensions for all.

Unemployment Saps European Solidarity

The problem of fewer workers, more dependants, is here to stay. We know there is no easy fix . The ratio of workers to pensioners will be improved by immigration and by an increase in the age at which people stop working. But, as noted in Chapter 1, the help from these trends will be limited. Immigrants remit earnings home or bring elderly relatives, have fewer children and themselves live longer. Because of this the numbers of immigrants who have to be found to maintain the ratio of workers to retirees balloons to improbable magnitudes.[19] The likely extension of working life past sixty-five will be counterbalanced by longer periods spent out of the labour force at earlier ages.

Supplying income in the 'third age' is going to make growing demands but this is true of other social programmes as well. A realistic assessment of social provision in all its forms – including education and health – must count on rising not falling costs. Even governments gripped by neo-liberal dogma have had difficulty shrinking state budgets. Despite tax-payer revolts, and waves of austerity, state expenditures – if local and central budgets are both taken into account – still claims 30–45 per cent of GDP in most advanced countries.[20] In manufacturing industry, costs are continually reduced by productivity gains. But health and education cannot count on this type of productivity growth. They are people-centred and labour intensive. Reducing staff reduces service and achievement. This sets strict limits on possible gains in labour productivity and contributes mightily to the fiscal crisis of social provision. Private suppliers are also constrained by cost factors; they may try to pay inferior wages but they commonly add new layers of expense.

Meeting rising social costs from current budgets will not be easy. While voters can be brought to accept higher taxes, the resulting fiscal regime can be unstable if general taxes have to bear all the strain. Historically many of the costs of social provision have been met from identifiable and separate social insurance contributions or, as the jargon has it, hypothe-cated payroll taxes (NIC in the UK, FICA in the US). The dilemma here is that either the payroll taxes remain moderate (and insufficient) – as is still the case in the UK and US – or they are raised until they add a 'tax wedge' of 30 or 40 per cent on top of labour costs, as has happened in France or Germany. The continental European approach has dampened demand and raised labour costs. Both impacts lead to unemployment, but they are hard to separate analytically from other factors, notably the deflationary policies associated with the Maastricht agreement and lat-terly, the European Central Bank.

A recent quantitative study which sought to apportion responsibility for the rise in European unemployment concludes that 'the rise in labour taxes since 1970 has accounted for almost half of the rise in long-term unemployment'.[21] The increase in joblessness supposedly affects about a tenth of the labour force, but this understates its real extent which may well be half as great again or more. The over-50s, the under-25s, women and ethnic minority workers suffer exclusion from work on a consider-able scale. Notwithstanding the large prison and student population in the US, which reduces the proportion of those gainfully employed, US employment rates for the total population aged 18–65 over the last

AGE SHOCK

decade were still about fifteen points higher than the employment rates registered in France and Germany.[22]

While the stringent monetarist policies of the Central Banks dampened demand, so did hefty payroll taxes. The blame for high joblessness lay not with the level of pensions paid out, still less promised, but with the attempt to finance them from regressive payroll taxes alone. On the one hand Europe's baby-boomers carried a 40 per cent 'tax wedge'; on the other its not yet so numerous pensioners retained quite conservative spending habits. The combined effect was to aggravate the central bankers' deflationary efforts. The continental European model has its own very considerable strengths. Annual holidays are two weeks longer, and weekly hours of work are several hours shorter, than in the United States. Health care insurance is universal and access to university-level education cheap. Europe's handsome cities and towns still convey a sense of cared-for public space. Several formerly blighted industrial zones have been rehabilitated. In some countries publicly mandated pensions will replace over 60 per cent of income on retirement for another decade or so. While European macro-economic management has been poor, and fiscal policy timid and inappropriate, the underlying economy has many strengths.[23] Manufacturing productivity is higher than in the US and export performance is impressive, with no equivalent to the massive US trade deficits. There is no shortage of strong European enterprises. Looked at in the round, Germany and France are highly productive societies, they enjoy strong social infrastructure and most people have a good quality of life in often stunningly attractive surroundings. Such strengths have been celebrated, and the contrast with the United States and Britain drawn, in a recent work by Will Hutton.[24]

But the Achilles' heel of these core European states has been the failure to generate high levels of employment. As was seen in Chapter 3, continental Europe, on the one hand, and the United States and Britain, on the other, have different patterns of unemployment. In the United States and Britain it is 'good jobs' in manufacturing that have been destroyed, and overall employment levels have been boosted by an expansion of low wage employment in the service sector. In Germany and France good jobs have been retained, but jobs in the service sector have been harder to find and unemployment rose. In Germany, a payroll subsidy was to mitigate this trend (see preface, p. xxxiv).

Those excluded from the world of work and its influences become a prey to political demagogues – in France in 2002 one half of the unemployed voted for Le Pen, the far-right candidate. Three years later another section of the army of the unemployed – those of immigrant descent – rioted, burning many thousands of cars to demonstrate their frustration. The unemployed receive quite generous unemployment benefits in France but, it seems, welfare dependence does not promote social solidarity among its recipients. The eventual successes of 'reform' – which are now beginning to focus on near-term expenses rather than just future decades – stemmed from the disorientation and even demoralization generated by a decent pension system hitched to an inadequate, and to some extent inappropriate, financing mechanism.

The extent of European unemployment showed that the problem could not be, as the reformers sometimes claimed, that there were too few workers and too many pensioners. If the central bankers had pursued a different macro-economic policy some of the misery could have been avoided. Also helpful would have been a willingness to diversify the sources of pension finance in order not to overstrain the pay-as-you-go system of payroll taxes.

Swedish Wage-Earner Funds

These problems have been tackled in a more innovative way in Sweden and in some other smaller European countries. A hallmark of Sweden's mid-century 'Rehn–Meidner model' was devices to ensure that high employment was maintained. Rudolf Meidner and Gösta Rehn were the architects of the Swedish welfare state. Meidner was Chief Economist of the LO, Sweden's main trade union federation. A distinguishing feature of his approach was that social funding was harmonised with both a wage-bargaining round and the protection of high employment levels. Whereas Anglo-American companies have been encouraged to take 'contribution holidays' during upswings of the trade cycle, Swedish corporations were, and are, encouraged to stow operating profits in special tax-exempt reserves. And as early as 1959, after a hard-fought political battle, the Swedish Social Democratic government set up a pre-funded secondary public pension system.[25]

Anticipating the new social expenditures that would be entailed by an ageing and learning society Meidner came to believe in the need for strategic social funds – 'wage-earner funds' – to be financed by a share levy. This levy did not work like traditional corporate taxation which subtracts from cash-flow, and, potentially, investment. Instead Meidner's levy falls on wealthy shareholders, the value of whose holdings is diluted, not on the resources of the corporation as a productive concern. According to the original plan every company with more than fifty employees was obliged to issue new shares every year equivalent to 20 per cent of its profits. The newly issued shares – which could not be sold – were to be given to a network of wage-earner funds, representing trade unions and local authorities. The latter would hold the shares and reinvest the income they yielded from dividends, in order to finance future social expenditure. As the wage-earner funds grew, they would be able to play an increasing part in directing policy in the corporations that they owned.[26]

Meidner's visionary scheme was strongly supported by trade unions and the members of the Social Democratic party, but strongly opposed by the privately owned media, and by the '20 families' who dominate the country's large corporations. Opponents of the scheme claimed that it would aggrandize the leaders of the trade unions who would dominate the wage-earner funds. It was also alleged that the scheme unfairly favoured employees in the private sector, since they were to be the first to receive shares from the levy. After a scare campaign the Social Democratic government eventually diluted the proposed share levy but set up social funds financed by a more modest profits-related tax. However, by the 1990s these funds came to own 7 per cent of the Swedish stock market; to prevent them getting any larger, they were wound up by the incoming Conservatives in 1992 and the proceeds used to finance a string of scientific research institutes. So Meidner's plan has yet to be properly tried, though even in its dilute form it helped to propel Sweden to the forefront of the knowledge based economy.

Meidner's scheme had an ambitious set of objectives. While accumulating funds for future social purposes was certainly important, he also hoped that the wage-earner-funds would, in conjunction with the wage-bargaining round characteristic of the Swedish model, ease macro-economic imbalances, raise savings, and eventually allow substantial community and workplace input into business strategy. A recent assessment concludes that the policy as implemented, while modest in scale, achieved its main objectives and would have been even more effective if closer to the shape of the original proposals: 'Examination of the performance of the wage-earner funds system demonstrated that it achieved many, but not all, of the multiple objectives established for the funds to pursue. In macro-economic terms, their introduction and expansion was associated with increased collective savings, capital formation, economic growth, moderated labour costs, higher industrial employment and an improved inflation-unemployment trade-off. However their influence proved insufficient to counter destabilization caused by financial de-regulation, together with the resultant asset price bubble and outward flows of capital that ultimately undermined voluntary wage moderation.' [27]

Sweden experienced a sharp economic crisis in 1991–2 that shook confidence in the country's welfare arrangements and led to a change of government. Meidner had retired a decade earlier and bore no responsibility for the crisis. Nevertheless the incoming Conservatives and demoralized Social Democrats opted to dismantle and scale back secondary-pension provision. The 1959 legislation establishing the second pension had been preceded by protracted national debate, but it was now repealed by a deal between the larger parties almost without real discussion. While elements of the Rehn–Meidner model remained – including the wage-bargaining round, company reserve funds and pre-funded second pensions – there was a sweeping pension reform which installed what came to be called a 'notional defined contribution' system. Of course most pay-as-you-go systems establish a link between contributions and entitlements, but the size of the latter are determined by the salary earned in the last period of employment, making these Defined Benefit systems. The Swedish reform of 1995 introduced a new logic according to which the benefits are calibrated both by contributions to the system and by the overall rise in all pensionable income. The ratios are set so that benefit entitlements will always balance income to the system. Moreover the public pension authorities (PPM) also organize a pre-funded supplementary pension financed by 2.5 per cent of wages. The latter offers employees a menu of investment vehicles, all of which have to conform to stringent charge ratios, with annual fees around 0.3 per cent of funds under management. Most employees decline to chose a fund and so their contributions are allocated by the PPM to its own default fund.[28] Proponents of the reform see the new arrangements as combining affordability with reasonable future pension levels, in a country where ageing pressures are well below those of the core European states. Sweden's elder care arrangements remain generous but old-age pensions are set to rise from 10.6 per cent of GDP in 2004 to only 11.2 per cent of GDP by 2050, despite the fact that the ratio of those 65 and over to those aged 15–64 will rise from 26 per 100 in 2040 to 41 per 100 in 2050. The 'notionally defined contribution' pensions will thus see pension expenditure rise far more slowly than the rise in the elderly population and, on current arrangements, will leave Sweden paying its pensioners 11.2 per cent of GDP when Denmark, with a similar dependency ratio, will be paying 12.8 per cent of GDP.[29] In the next chapter I will explain why I believe that Meidner's bolder approach remains promising, though certainly lessons should be drawn from the Swedish experience. But prior to this it will be helpful further to explore the logic of pay-as-you-go pension funding.

The Logic of Pay-As-You-Go

Yesterday's three (or more) worlds of welfare capitalism are converging on an 'Anglo-Saxon' model, albeit that this model is in deep trouble in its homelands. Many countries are experimenting with commercial provision but historically nearly all of these regimes made some use of the pay-as-you-go system of financing, if not for the whole pension then at least for a substantial part of it. 'Anglo-Saxon' states such as the US and the UK have historically had much less generous public pensions than Germany or France, but nevertheless they all make use of not only pay-as-you-go but also of social security contributions made by every employee. In the United States the payroll tax or Federal Insurance Contribution – FICA – amounts to 12.4 per cent of every employee's earnings up to a threshold of $90,000 a year in 2005, rising to $94,200 in 2006. While there is a Social Security Trust Fund, the programme has always used current contributions to pay pensions. In the early days there was really no alternative since pensions were granted to retiring workers who had a very modest contribution history. Most public pension systems in the OECD states acquired their existing shape in the 1940s and 1950s at a time when there was great public pressure for decent pensions but inherited fund accumulation was meagre or non-existent because of the impact of war and postwar inflation.

For the most part these schemes were already up and running on a pay-as-you-go basis when, in an article published in 1959, Paul Samuelson furnished a theoretical account of why it would work. He saw it as a necessary measure of state-sponsored collectivism – even going so far as to invoke the shade of Friedrich Engels. In Samuelson's view, the state could run a pay-as-you-go system because it could do something denied to a commercial finance house – it could balance its books by counting on a contribution from those not yet born to pay the pensions of today's workers, who were paying the pensions of today's retirees. Samuelson was writing at a time when Western economies and birth rates were both booming, and these circumstances both helped to ensure that pay-as-you-go finance could produce a huge social gain for little or no fiscal pain. The almost simultaneous slow down in economic growth, and decline in the birth rate in the 1970s and after, created a tougher context. The pay-as-you-go method was administratively simple, publicly supported and highly efficient so it could still play an important part. But it needed to be properly calibrated, and if possible supplemented, to achieve balanced and fair results.

Two schematic mathematical models of the workings of a pay-as-you-go system will illustrate the problems involved.

The first, elaborated by Paul Johnson of the London School of Economics, is set out in Table 6.1. This gives a schematic representation of a pension system and shows successive cohorts of different sizes. Each cohort is represented by a letter – A, B, C, D, E, F, G and H. The size, contribution and receipts of each cohort appear in a column underneath the letter (in stylized numbers that could be millions of individuals for cohort size and otherwise billions of currency). Contributions and receipts are given both as a total and in per capita figures. Each cohort lives for two periods, contributing in the first and receiving in the second. The receipts of each cohort are equal to the contributions of its successor, and the amount of contributions directly reflects cohort size. The table shows how changing age-cohort size determines contribution adequacy. As Johnson writes: 'This hypothetical example demonstrates that an ageing population which first reduces the ratio of workers to pensioners, and then leads to an absolute decline in the number of workers, can progressively reduce, and ultimately render negative, the real rate of return produced by a pay-as-you-go pension.'[30] The table also demonstrates a declining pension yield even with rising cohort sizes, but a steeply declining pension yield once the size of cohorts contracts. The first column shows a generation which receives benefits but makes no contribution. The last two columns reflect the assumption that the system breaks down because the contributing generation withdraws from it.

Table 6.1: *Pay-As-You-Go:*
Varying Cohort Problem (With Collapse)

Cohort	A	B	C	D	E	F	G	H
Cohort size	2	3	4	5	6	5	4	3
Contributions per cap.	0	10	10	10	10	10	10	0
Total contributions	0	30	40	50	60	50	40	0
Total benefits	30	40	50	60	50	40	0	0
Benefits per cap.	15	13.3	12.5	12	8.3	8	0	0
Net individual gain (loss)	15	3.3	2.5	2	(1.7)	(2.0)	(10)	0

The table shows the declining yield in pension benefits per capita in a pay-as-you-go system if per capita contributions are held constant and the size of successive cohorts first grows and then contracts, followed by collapse as generation H exits the system leaving generation G with zero benefits. In reading the table bear in mind that each generation's benefits come from the subsequent, younger, cohort. Thus generation A makes no contributions but receives 30 from generation B; because it's a small cohort it receives 14 per capita. B contributes 30 but receives 40; because it's a larger cohort the gain is 3.3 per capita. C contributes 40 overall but receives 50, for a per capita gain of 2.5. Once contraction begins, with generation F, it receives back less than it puts in. The last two columns look at the collapse of the system, induced by the failure of generation H to contribute anything to generation G because of a perception that the programme had become a losing proposition.

Johnson points out that the possibility he sketches was known theoretically forty years ago – indeed if the assumptions are registered, it is compatible with Samuelson's equations. The crisis which overtakes the system cannot really be attributed to the last two columns, because these already assume collapse in generation G's total benefits column. The collapse is triggered by the negative returns to generations E and F, perhaps especially the latter. Yet there might be circumstances where a generation was prepared to accept receiving less than it contributed so long as the discrepancy was not too great. The schema does not tell us about any transfers from earlier to later generations which might offset net losses on the pension account. For example, earlier generations might be covering the costs of education and upbringing for the younger generation. Also the collapse in column G is caused by the exit of generation H, but the latter would have to be the result of either some external calamity (war) or, if not, of a political decision. However the larger cohort G will have more political clout than the smaller one, H, so the terminal political decision may not be made.

It is interesting to replay Johnson's schema without the assumption of collapse since this more nearly approximates the world in which we live, where pay-as-you-go systems have proved quite hardy but in which they deliver a less than adequate pension. Table 6.2 looks at benefits per capita if the population decline stabilizes and generations continue to contribute and receive as they did before with no systemic collapse.

Table 6.2: *Pay-As-You-Go:*
Varying Cohort Problem (Without Collapse)

Cohort	A	B	C	D	E	F	G	H	I
Cohort size	2	3	4	5	6	5	4	3	3
Contributions per cap.	0	10	10	10	10	10	10	10	10
Total contributions	0	30	40	50	60	50	40	30	30
Total benefits	30	40	50	60	50	40	30	30	30
Benefits per cap.	15	13.3	12.5	12	8.3	8	7.5	10	10
Net individual gain(loss)	15	3.3	2.5	2	(1.7)	(2.0)	(2.5)	0	0

Source: Adapted from Paul Johnson, 'Paying for Our Futures', British Academy Symposium, June 2005.

Once population growth and decline levels out the system reaches a sort of steady state in which there is no yield on contributions but benefits per capita recover to a level considerably above that obtaining in generations E, F and G. The absence of 'yield' could be a perfectly acceptable feature of the system if it is regarded as a mechanism for collective risk-pooling, whereby 'successors at large' repay 'predecessors at large' who have covered the costs of their upbringing and schooling. In this case the successive generations make and receive payments without 'yield'. Because generations overlap in time they can cover needed costs in the present, giving the present a layered texture in which younger parents are paying for young children and older children are paying for older parents.

However, even taking these considerations into account the table still identifies a major problem, namely that the absolute benefit per capita drops from 15 in the first column, to 7.5 in column G, before rising to 10 in column I. What this illustrates is that pensions drop heavily as a consequence of cohort imbalance. Let us put aside the exceptional deal received by the first generation and take a benefit of 10 as the target. Then there are three generations which receive less than they have contributed, and one that receives pensions that are only 75 per cent of the target level, which is eventually reached in the 'steady state' illustrated by the last columns. There is unfairness here and there is also a prospect of old-age poverty.

Johnson's own thought-provoking – and no doubt tentative – conclusion from his model was that fiscal measures should be introduced to reward those who had children and penalize those who didn't. Here one is disaggregating the generational approach to pinpoint individual and family responsibility for maintaining population levels. Since having children is a great investment of time and effort – and since it greatly benefits future retirees – perhaps it should be encouraged by rewards to those who have children (tax breaks, child allowances, free child care, free further education for mothers, parental leave and so forth). The global decline in fertility is linked to the higher standard of living that is often associated with small families. The onset of the consumer society has sometimes been spurred by the decision to buy a house, car, TV or dog, before having a first or second child. Johnson suggests redressing the balance a bit by levying a tax on those with few or no children, and offering a better pension to those who have done most to produce and rear a successor generation. Mothers – whether single or not – might, in such a view, be seen as heroines of the ageing society, and be guaranteed good conditions for rearing their children, with all necessary help from fellow citizens of both sexes.

Johnson's argument endorses the already very strong case for improving the pension rights of women. Existing public- and private-pension systems tend to link pension rights to contributions made from employment earnings, with little or no recognition given to the huge amounts of unpaid labour for which women are responsible in the home. International studies agree that, across cultures, women perform far more domestic labour than men.[31] Women are also over-represented in the teaching and nursing professions where, for meagre wages, they play a huge role in bringing up the successor generation. Paying good pensions and better wages to such educational and care workers would acknowledge their vital importance in ensuring society's future.[32] Reverting to a generational rather than gender perspective, Johnson's argument would also have to take account of the manifold ways in which those who pay taxes for education, or who help to raise the productivity of future workers, are making a contribution in a wider scheme of intergenerational support. Employees without children who pay taxes are directly helping to cover at least some of the costs of bringing up a new generation.

Nancy Folbre has urged that US Social Security should take account of child-rearing in its benefits structure – the more so since it fails to credit many women with extra benefits when they contribute to the programme. She writes: 'Since the 1960s we've seen a small increase in the number of people who have no children at all, and a big increase in the percentage of families maintained by women alone. Few of these mothers are eligible for any spousal benefits through Social Security. When they go to work for pay, their Social Security taxes are just as high as everybody else's. After their paid work is over they go home to take care of the kids, usually with very little financial or direct assistance from men. This activity of caring for kids is not considered work, even though it produces the next generation of tax-payers to keep Social Security solvent (and the next generation of workers who will actually take on the physical and emotional tasks of caring for the elderly).'[33]

Johnson's model abstracts from overall economic performance and the rising productivity that we have come to assume that the future brings. Rising output and productivity will stem from education and training, investments in infrastructure, technological and scientific advance, superior forms of coordination and so forth. Looking at the positive side of the ledger, the 'predecessor' generation will have laid the basis for these productivity gains through its own taxes, saving and innovation. At least partially offsetting this would be the depletion of natural resources. But we can hope to so arrange human affairs that the former outweighs the latter. This would then allow us to assume an economic advance that steadily diminishes poverty and raises prosperity. To illustrate how this might affect pension provision at a national level, I would like to turn to a schema which uses rising output to come to very different conclusions from those embodied in Johnson's stark 'collapse' model. But before leaving Johnson's model it must be admitted that the real world has witnessed both the collapse or erosion of pay-as-you-go systems, and their ability to withstand ferocious assault. The United States Social

Security system has again and again proved that it is, in the famous phrase, the 'third rail' of the political system – those who try to tamper with it get a sharp shock. On the other hand where there is overall economic breakdown or malaise, and a determined push to commodify pension finance, then pay-as-you-go systems can collapse. This happened in Chile in the early 1980s, though admittedly it took hyper-inflation, ballooning unemployment and a military coup to do it. In Europe in recent years the pay-as-you-go systems have been fairly drastically modified because of a much milder, but still tangible, deterioration in public life.

The French economist Bernard Friot draws up the schema represented in Table 6.3 to show that a steady and strong expansion in cohort size, combined with improved pensions, need not pose any insuperable problem for a modern economy. The main reason his figures work – and they are stylized numbers quite close to the real proportions of the French economy – is that he assumes that the economy doubles every forty years, an annual growth rate of 1.6 per cent, a figure that seems quite conservative.[34]

Table 6.3: *Projections of GDP and Pension Spending in France*

	1960	2000	2040
GDP (in euros of 2003)	750 bn	1,500 bn	3,000 bn
Pension spending	40 bn (5%)	180 bn (12%)	600 bn (20%)
Balance (in euros of 2003)	710 bn	1,320 bn	2,400 bn

The indicated increases in pension spending crudely reflect the rising proportion of the retired in the population. Because of the assumed overall expansion the balance of GDP left for all other claimants and purposes, including investment, still rises steadily by around 1 per cent a year. Friot's schema supposes an increase in the number of the retired from 40 for each 100 workers in 2000 to 80 for each 100 workers in 2040. Social security contributions rise from 8 per cent of income in 1960 to 25 per cent of income in 2000, and at least 40 per cent of income in 2040. Other taxes relating to health care, education and other government expenditure, including unemployment pay, would have to be levied on top of this sum, so this 40 per cent social security payroll tax for retirement pensions already begins to look less comfortable. Friot points out that wages and salaries only comprise 60 per cent of French GDP. Current

French income distribution is burdened by heavy transfer payments because around 10 per cent of the official labour force is unemployed.

Aware that the prevailing configuration of French GDP is problematic, Friot explores scenarios which would see the share of wages rise from 60 per cent to 70 per cent or even 85 per cent, but in the latter case – a visionary scenario – the country's investment needs would largely have to be met by employees, taken as a whole, from their 85 per cent share of GDP. In effect Friot is saying that the workers take over the system and the economy, making all necessary provision for investment. It is almost as if the pay-as-you-go system really could become the engine of socialism feared by Milton Friedman and other neo-conservatives, though it is not clear how this might be embodied institutionally. In the conclusion I will return to the key financing question. For now it is sufficient to register that a growing economy can indeed afford to pay decent pensions to a rising number of retirees, but this will not obviate some hard choices concerning how best this might be done and what principles can be invoked to effect a just apportionment of that burden between generations.

Modern capitalist economies are capable of expanding at between 1 and 2.5 per cent per year over the long term. Where there is still population growth, per capita GDP growth would obviously be lower. There is also the problem that the conventional way of assessing GDP fails to put a negative number on depletion of most natural resources, and puts a positive number on such better-avoided costs as building jails and paying prison guards. These considerations mean that the available resources for paying pensions and making other transfer payments are, perhaps, more limited than the annual growth figure by itself suggests. Nevertheless a well-run economy should be able to achieve genuine per capita economic growth. How should the extra resources be distributed?

I have generally adopted the argument of John Myles that a fair way of projecting future pension needs is to spread the burden of changes in relative cohort size between generations by keeping constant the ratio of average income to pensioner income. I have also argued that this should apply to overall income levels in retirement and not to basic pensions. In most advanced countries pensioner incomes are roughly 70–80 per cent of median income, after tax and transfers are taken into account. A crude assessment of needs will usually show that people who are over sixty or sixty-five years old, and who are retired generally have fewer expenses than those in their thirties and forties. They are less likely to have dependent children and they do not have job-related expenses such as travel. They are more likely to own their house outright. Putting a figure on the reduced living expenses of the older person is somewhat arbitrary, but one way of doing this is simply to register the already-existing ratio of retirement incomes to average income.

However, in the great majority of developed countries there is universal health coverage or health insurance, so this income figure does not include health costs. Pensioners are not required to pay out of their current income for medical care. In the United States the annual health-care costs of a person over sixty-five, as was noted in the first chapter, are something like four times greater than for someone under sixty-five, with much of the extra cost accruing in the last six months of life. While Medicare does cover many medical expenses it also requires complex and significant co-payments. European systems of health insurance have proved better at containing medical costs and preventing them from impoverishing the elderly.

I now return to issues I raised at the outset. Financing the costs of the new life course demands ever larger funds and a quite new model. The financial services industry has not proved equal to the task. I have dwelt on the poor returns received by most who are covered by pension schemes and plans. But the plight of the rest of the working population – those who have little or no coverage – is even worse. The 1990s saw an expansion of low-wage and casual employment which carried with it no pension or medical benefits, and which allowed no scope for long-term saving.[35] As might be expected, those without coverage – about a third of those reaching the age of retirement – include most of the poor, and many minority and female employees. However, some quite low-paid workers do have coverage, especially if they work in the public sector, while not a few middle-class employees will find themselves tossed into retirement with a derisory private pension. Spells of unemployment can easily hollow out a 401(k). Others, like the workers at Enron and Worldcom, held too much stock in one company – their employer – doubling their vulnerability.

For a variety of reasons, a third of those reaching retiring age will be solely, or almost solely, reliant on Social Security retirement income. Those who have had considerable spells of part-time work, unemployment, casual labour and low-paid labour will find that their entitlement is meagre. Living on Social Security alone would be a recipe for borderline poverty, as it is for many older women and minorities today. And full

Social Security entitlement still requires a contribution record which many lack. For these there is means-tested relief.

The more canny advocates of 'pension reform' (i.e. privatization) used to admit that the situation is bad. They said that the coverage problem could not be solved by voluntary means – even helped by such acts of 'implicit privatization' as raising the retirement age. They instead insisted that governments should step in and make it compulsory for all to buy commercial pension products. Many observers are worried that savings claim only about 5 per cent of GDP in Britain – and less in the US – compared with more than double this figure in Germany and France. Probably compulsion is required, but not the sort which would have everyone paying taxes to the commercial fund managers. The British Trade Union Congress has urged that the time has indeed come for compulsion and that it is the employers who should be compelled to restore their contributions to employees' pension funds. In a similar vein Howard Dean, then seeking the Democratic presidential nomination, pointed to the shrunken receipts of corporate taxation and urged that its contribution be raised.[36]

But this is not the approach of most 'pension reform' merchants who instead take their cue from a famous World Bank report of 1994, *Averting the Old Age Crisis*. This argued that all citizens should be obliged to pay over contributions to the fund managers to supply their main retirement income, with a basic state pension remaining only as a safety net. In the US the Cato Institute and other advocates of privatizing Social Security have urged that the programme faces bankruptcy and should be replaced by allowing individuals to set up their own share accounts with a proportion of their FICA contributions. If the young or the better off were able partially to exit the system in this way, it would ruin its finances without offering a better return to most of those who had been tempted.[37] If the Social Security programme does eventually face a shortfall this will be because, unlike most private pensions, it is inflation indexed. According to recent projections the deficit will not reduce payouts until around 2038–42.[38] What the programme needs is more resources, to furnish better pensions than are currently promised, not a shrinking contribution base.

When Bush's Commission on Social Security reported in December 2001 it was unable to agree on a route to privatization. Its three proposed methods for introducing individual accounts either incurred a shortfall or failed to maintain the level of benefits. In order to tackle transition costs – that is, to continue to pay the pensions of today's seniors, and those about to retire, while diverting contributions to the programme – the Commission found that it would be necessary to raise a huge loan, worth between $1 and 2 trillion. Some conservatives did not like this. Nor did they like the proposal that, because of the cost problem, the contributor would be restricted to a handful of five or six officially selected funds. These conclusions dented the case for privatization.[39] The latter had been further weakened, even before the stock market troubles, by arguments which took apart the case for privatization developed by the World Bank.

In 1999 Joseph Stiglitz, the then Chief Economist of the World Bank, co-authored a paper on the 'Ten Myths About Social Security System', which developed a powerful critique of the Bank's 1994 report.[40] Stiglitz and his co-author Perter Orszag urged that the attempts to discredit public programmes lacked evidence and theoretical rigour. While public agencies had proved very poor pension providers in some developing countries, the stock market in those countries had also proved to be unsafe receptacles for savings. In fact public trust funds have delivered good results in countries like Singapore and Sweden, contributing both to social provision and to economic growth. In the US and UK public sector pension funds have proved reliable pension providers, with superior cost-control. Other theoretical work by Douglas and Gale showed that a 'long-lived planner', using a mixture of assets, would supply better returns across several generations than a market model, which would be undermined by opportunities for generational arbitrage. [41] A paper by Thomas Michl and Duncan Foley has further explored the far-reaching changes which could be brought about by 'superfunding' of the Social Security system.[42] Finally, a change in the economic climate, and the rehabilitation of John Maynard Keynes, reopens the case for investigating the link between the financing of social security programmes and the overall conjuncture, a topic which Keynes debated with his colleague James Meade.[43]

The frustration of President Bush's attempt partially to privatize Social Security has great significance. US Social Security continues to enjoy high levels of support, and politicians will hesitate to challenge it openly. While both President and Treasury Secretary continue to press for partial privatization, the programme also faces the danger of a vaunted friend of the programme who claims that its benefits must be trimmed to make it affordable. The belief that the programme could face a fiscal problem, given existing contribution and benefit rates, is not confined to supporters of privatization. It includes, for example, Paul Krugman, one of Bush's most vociferous critics.[44] Given the difficulty of making such projections, it would be prudent to have additional sources of finance. For its part, the well-funded privatization lobby will strive to resurrect their cause at an opportune moment.

Notes

1 I have more on these momentous events in chapters 4 and 5 of *Banking on Death*.
2 Antoine Math, 'The Impact of Pension Reforms on Older People's Income', in Gerard Hughes and Jim Stewart, eds, *Reforming Pensions in Europe: Evolution of Pension Financing and Sources of Retirement Income*, Cheltenham 2004, pp. 105–38, p. 122.
3 Economic Policy Committee and the European Commission, Directorate General for Economic and Financial Affairs, *The Impact of Ageing on Government Expenditure: Projections for the EU25 Member States on Pensions, Health Care, Long-Term Care, Education and Unemployment Transfers (2004–2050)*, Brussels, February 2006, pp. 11, 33.
4 Francis G. Castles, *The Future of the Welfare State: Crisis Myths and Crisis Realities*, Oxford 2004, p. 126.
5 Pensions Commission, *A New Pension Settlement for the Twenty-First Century*, the Second Report of the Pensions Commission, London 2005, p. 293.
6 Nicholas Timmins, 'Treasury Challenges Cost of Revamped Retirement Proposals', *Financial Times*, 5 April 2006.
7 Pensions Commission, *A New Pension Settlement for the Twenty-First Century*, the Second Report of the Pensions Commission, London 2005, pp. 8–10.
8 See John Mirowsky et al, 'Links Between Social Status and Health Status', and Stephanie A. Robert et al., 'Socioeconomic Inequalities in Health', in Chloe E. Bird, Peter Conrad and Allen E. Fremont, eds, *Handbook of Medical Sociology*, 5th ed., Upper Sable River NJ, 2000, pp. 47–6 and 79–97.
9 Anne Case and Angus Deaton, 'Broken Down by Work and Sex', in David A. Wise, edn, *Analyses in the Economics of Ageing*, Chicago 2005, pp. 185–212.
10 The Reagan and Clinton attempts were briefly signaled in Chapter 2, above, but for a fuller account see *Banking on Death*, Chapter 6.
11 For a study which contrasts regional re-distribution in the US with its absence in Europe, see James K. Galbraith, Pedro Conceicao and Pedro Ferreira, 'Inequality and Unemployment in Europe', *New Left Review*, September–October 1999. For the impact on poverty, see 'Social Security Lifts 13 million Above Poverty Line: A State-by-State Analysis', Center on Budget and Policy Priorities, Washington DC, 24 February 2005.
12 Howell E. Jackson, 'It's Even Worse than You Think,' *New York Times*, 9 October 2003.
13 Laurence J. Kotlikoff and Scott Burns, *The Coming Generational Storm: What*

You Need to Know about America's Economic Future, 2nd edn, New York 2005, pp. 65–72.

14 'Social Security's Future: FAQs', Social Security Online, 12 October 2005, p. 4.

15 Peter Laslett, *A New Map of Life*, p. 249.

16 Brian Barry, *A Treatise on Social Justice,* vol. 1, *Theories of Justice*, London 1989, pp. 200–1.

17 John Myles, 'A New Social Contract for the Elderly', in Gosta Esping-Andersen et al., *Why We Need a New Welfare State*, Oxford 2002, pp. 130–72.

18 Data on this was supplied in Chapter 4 but see also John Hills, *Inequality and the State*, pp. 25, 29, 31.

19 Points elaborated in the first chapter, above, but see the UN Population Division, *Replacement Migration: Is It a Solution to Declining and Ageing Populations?*, New York 2000 and Neil Gilbert, *Transformation of the Welfare States: The Silent Surrender of the Public Responsibility*, Oxford 2002, pp. 33–4, 39.

20 OECD, *Revenue Statistics, 1965–2001*, Paris 2002, quoted by Martin Wolf, *Why Globalization Works*, p. 255.

21 Christopher Planas, Werner Roeger and Alessandro Rossi, 'How Much Has Labour Taxation Contributed to European Structural Unemployment?', Directorate-General for Economic and Financial Affairs, European Commission, Economic Paper no. 183, Brussels, May 2003, p. 12.

22 See the figures cited in 'Germany's Growth Performance in the 1990s', Directorate-General for Economic and Social Affairs, European Commission, Economic Paper no. 170, May 2002.

23 See Andrea Boltho, 'What's Wrong With Europe?', *New Left Review*, no. 23, July–August 2003, pp. 5–26.

24 Will Hutton, *The World We're In*, London 2002. (Published in the US in 2003 under the title *A Declaration of Interdependence*). In mid-2006 US unemployment was 4.6 per cent but, as in the UK and Europe, this offical measure omits those on disability stipends, who numbered 6.5 million, up from 3 million in 1990. Thirteen per cent of men aged 30–55 had no job, up from 5 per cent in the 1960s, with industrial lay-offs explaining much of these increases. See Louis Uchitelle and David Leonhardt, 'Men Not Working and Not Wanting Just Any Job', *New York Times*, 31 July 2006.

25 Jonas Pontusson, *The Limits of Social Democracy*, Ithaca NY, 1992; and Joakim Palme, 'Pension Reform in Sweden', in Gordon Clark and Noel Whitefield, eds, *Pension Security in the 21st Century*, Oxford 2003, pp. 144–67.

26 The original plan is set out in Rudolf Meidner, *Employee Investment Funds*, London 1978. For an account of the struggles over its implementation see Jonas Pontusson, 'Sweden: After the Golden Age', in Perry Anderson and Patrick Camiller, eds, *Mapping the West European Left*, London 1994, pp. 23–54.

27 Philip Whyman, 'Post Keynesianism, Socialisation of Investment and Swedish Wage Earner Funds', *Cambridge Journal of Economics*, vol. 30, no. 1, January 2006, pp. 49–68, p. 64.

28 Joakim Palme, 'Pension Reform in Sweden', in Clark and Whitehouse, *Pension Security in the 21st Century*.

29 European Commission, *The Impact of Ageing on Public Expenditure*, pp. 11, 52.
30 Paul Johnson, 'Paying for Our Futures', British Academy Symposium, June 2005.
31 Unifem, *The Progress of the World's Women*, New York 2000.
32 Care would need to be taken that such measures would not 'lock' women into a social role that some might not welcome or that men should share. We will later look at how decent pensions might be available to all and will urge that those who care for the ill and aged also deserve entitlement.
33 Nancy Folbre, *The Invisible Heart: Economics and Family Values*, New York 2002, p. 103.
34 For an overview of Friot's approach see Bernard Friot, *La puissance du salariat*, Paris 1998. The figures used in the text are taken from a seminar presentation at the University of Westminster, June 2005.
35 See Barbara Ehrenreich, *Nickel and Dimed*, New York 2001; Robert Pollin, *Contours of Descent*, New York 2003, pp. 45–7, 75. The 2001–2 recession raised the total number living below the poverty line by 1.7 million to reach a total of 34.6 million, see Lynette Clemetson, 'More Americans in Poverty in 2002', *New York Times*, 27 September 2003. From the standpoint of retirement provision even 'episodic' poverty eats into savings and reduces future income.
36 'Dean Seeks Deeper Corporate Tax Bite', *Wall Street Journal*, 17 October 2003.
37 For a searching critique of privatization see Dean Baker and Mark Weisbrot, *Social Security: the Phony Crisis*, Chicago 2000.
38 This is the range of estimates made by the Trustees, but it is impossible to predict the relevant trends at this distance in time. If a labour shortage ensues as the baby-boomers retire this is likely to force up wages and salaries, which would boost revenue to Social Security.
39 I outline the tug-of-war over Social Security in the US between 1980 and 2002 in Chapter 6 of *Banking on Death*.
40 The paper was delivered at a conference, and posted on the Bank's website, in 1999. It is published as Peter Orszag and Joseph Stiglitz, 'Rethinking Pension Reform: Ten Myths About Social Security Systems' in Robert Holzmann and Joseph Stiglitz, eds, *New Ideas About Old Age Security*, Washington DC, 2002. For evidence of the impact of the paper see the critique of privatisation in Nicholas Barr, *The Welfare State as Piggy Bank: Information, Risk, and Uncertainty*, Oxford 2000, pp. 87–157. See also Stiglitz, *The Roaring Nineties*, pp. 188–201.
41 A theoretical demonstration of the need for a 'long-lived' planner in pension provision was offered by Franklin Douglas and William Gale, 'Financial Markets, Intermediaries, and Intertemporal Smoothing', *Journal of Political Economy*, no. 3, June 1997.
42 Thomas R. Michl and Duncan Foley, 'Social Security in a Classical Growth Model', CEPA Working Paper Series II, New School University, Economic Policy Analysis, Working Paper no. 11, September 2001.
43 See the discussion of Keynes's 1940 pamphlet on 'How to Pay for the War' in Robert Skidelsky, *John Maynard Keynes: Fighting for Britain*, London 2002.
44 Paul Krugman, 'Social Security', *New York Times*, August 2003 and 'America's Senior Moment', *New York Review of Books*, 15 March 2005.

7

How to Finance Decent Pensions
– and Tame the Corporations

W hat is to be done about the prospect of increasingly inadequate and insecure provision for the ageing society in most advanced countries? The pension regimes of Europe, North America and Japan are converging on a failing model, which will combine a modest public pension covering nearly everyone and a range of private schemes which are either unreliable or costly, or both, and whose coverage is very patchy. Not only do reasonable projections of the retirement incomes generated by this 'divided welfare state' model suggest that it will fall far short of what is needed to protect relative pensioner incomes but medical costs and care costs of the aged will also grow, and add to the strain on public budgets.

In the first chapter I argued that the US will need to channel around 15 per cent of GDP to retirement incomes by 2035 if it is to maintain the relative incomes of its senior citizens, and subsequent chapters, especially Chapters 3 and 6, have underlined that US retirement incomes are not on course to reach anything like this target. Social Security is meant to supply 6.1 per cent of GDP for all its programmes by 2035, and around 5 per cent for old age pensions only. However, the trustees warned in their 2005 report that by that year there will be a shortfall in the revenues needed to finance Old Age benefits equivalent to 1.51 per cent of GDP. While this may be too pessimistic, it would be only prudent to prepare extra reserves in case it did come to pass. (The gap could be closed without loss of benefits by raising the threshold – $90,000 a year in 2005 – below which the FICA is paid, and/or raising the 12.4 per cent rate by a point or two, or by some new tax.[1]) Private sector pensions, whether DB or DC, are likely to yield much less than Social Security. With schemes closing, and heavy charges, private sector pensions will find it difficult to generate even 3 per cent of GDP, significantly above the level reached when both DB and DC schemes were in apparently good shape in the 1990s. Public sector funds might supply an extra 1 per cent of GDP and earnings of those over 65 as much as 2 per cent. So by 2035 there will be a shortfall of around 4 per cent of GDP.

In the UK, with its weaker state pension, the Pensions Commission warned of the probability of an even larger shortfall by 2050 as we saw in the first chapter. It went on to recommend an 'enhanced state pension' but this was to be paid for by raising the state pension age to 68 by 2050. Because benefit gain was counterbalanced by benefit loss overall state spending in 2050 under the recommendations was barely above the level that it would be under the then-current regime, (though at points in between it would be somewhat higher). The Pensions Commission mainly counted on reducing the GDP gap, and securing a better income replacement rate for retirees, by introducing a publicly-managed, low-charge, pre-funded programme, the National Pension Savings Scheme (NPSS), to be based on auto-enrollment of employees and compulsory matching contributions from the employer (on which more below). The Commission projected that the NPSS could build up a fund worth 20 per cent of GDP, which itself would comprise roughly a tenth of the value of all UK equities, corporate bonds and government bonds. The introduction of the NPSS would, it believed, offset some of the decline in income from DB schemes, adding just 0.7 per cent of GDP to pensioner incomes.[2] In consequence of this modest contribution and the weakness of the 'enhanced state pension' the Pensions Commission failed to fill the gap that it had itself identified.

The downsizing of public pension entitlements in many other OECD countries, including Italy, France, Germany and Japan, means that by a mid-century they, too, will face a shortfall in the range 3–6 per cent of GDP. These are all wealthy societies, of course, but this would not make the re-emergence of large-scale pensioner poverty any more acceptable. On top of retirement income are the already-mentioned medical and care costs which are already over 5 per cent of GDP in the United States.

The prospect of shortfalls will trouble not only those directly threatened but also those approaching retirement and their working age children. Those who have made a lifetime of contributions to pension and medical systems may not react to a descent to relative poverty and neglect with uncomplaining meekness. A realistic mixture of policies for raising and securing pension reserves, and for meeting other ageing costs, could be popular, even if it involved calling on the most comfortably off to make some sacrifice. Even in the age of globalization these are pressures which national governments will face and to some extent meeting them belongs to the realm of those things that 'go without saying'. They should be discharged without great fuss to leave us all to face the real problems of humanity in the twenty-first century.

An international poll conducted by Harris Interactive for the AARP found that the most favoured solutions to the problem of a possible pension shortfall were as follows: 68 per cent favoured 'raising taxes among higher paid workers', 37 per cent 'raising taxes for all workers'; 33 per cent raising the retirement age and 42 per cent increasing retirement benefits at a slower rate. The tax-the-rich approach was backed by 69 per cent of respondents in the US and 75 per cent in the UK.[3] Though the question was not asked directly, this pattern of replies suggests that quite a high number of respondents might have favoured the more effective taxation of the corporations and the wealthy, defined by their high net worth.

Searching for the Best Taxes

Curiously enough the public's willingness to consider proposals for the redistribution of income or wealth is not matched by any enthusiasm amongst economists for devising new methods for accomplishing this. Or at least this is the bias of the last three decades. In *Just Taxes*, a history of tax policy in the UK, Martin Daunton discusses the great variety of fiscal instruments proposed and developed in early and mid-twentieth century Britain which aimed at redistribution.[4] James Meade was an enthusiast for the capital levy and eventually won over Keynes to the idea that it could be a useful policy instrument. Other devices included the 'excess profits tax', 'estates duties', the 'capital gains tax' and taxes on 'unearned income'. Nicholas Kaldor, Thomas Balogh, Joan Robinson, Maurice Dobb and Sidney and Beatrice Webb, each had their own approach to these and other attempts to tax the rich in the interests of the community as a whole.

Whether in Britain or the United States, few now concern themselves with this type of taxation.[5] Instead the movement for tax reform usually means enthusiasm for cutting progressive taxes, or even for eliminating them, in favour of a flat tax or a consumption tax.[6] Schuyler Colfax, one of the most fertile legislative minds ever to be applied to US public finances, is an almost unknown figure, even among specialists, though he was the author of the first US tax on income in 1862. In the same year Colfax, a Republican, also proposed an imaginative scheme for taxing wealth in the form of stocks and shares. As a representative from Indiana he believed that elementary justice required that the new form of wealth should be expected to make its fiscal contribution: 'I cannot go home and tell my constituents', he declared, 'that I voted for a bill that would allow a man, a millionaire, who put his entire property into stock, to be exempt from taxation.'[7] Later the followers of Henry George expected great things from a tax on increases in commercial land value, arguing that such increases reflected windfall gains which reflected public infrastructure investment, and general economic advance, rather any effort on the part of the owner of the land. Several US states and cities have legislation permitting such taxes but these clauses are now all but forgotten. The Supreme Court had eventually ruled that the income tax was unconstitutional, so a large-scale campaign was needed, attracting Progressive and Democratic support, to pass an amendment explicitly sanctioning such a tax. The amendment passed in 1913, so this time the measure was not simply a wartime expedient.[8] Without income and corporation tax the United States could scarcely have become a modern power. But these days such campaigns for tax reform are more likely to be waged to abolish or reduce taxes than to find new ones. The jury of the Nobel Prize for Economics, which has shown esteem for arcane contributions to financial engineering and quantitative finance – and will sometimes issue multiple citations for such work – has rarely honoured anyone with an innovative approach to progressive taxation – the prize awarded to James Tobin in 1978 being one of the few exceptions.[9]

A solution to the pension crisis will require institutional as well as fiscal innovation. What is needed to prevent the return of pauperized old age is a strong, universal basic pension, financed largely by pay-as-you-go, supplemented by an equally universal, pre-funded secondary pension, financed by a tax on capital and engaging non-commercial fund management.

The basic pension could be very similar to the US Social Security pension, with a modest income-related element but with more generous qualifying conditions for those with broken contribution records, so that care-givers and the unemployed receive contribution credits. In the UK the Pensions Commission's proposed 'enhanced state pension' does not live up to its name and would be better if closer to the superior US Social Security pattern. The basic public pension would supply a 'defined benefit' pension, as does the US Social Security today. In both the US and the UK any surpluses that appear in the trust fund will be needed to finance future basic pensions. Over the medium or long run deficits could appear which should not be tackled by weakening the benefit but rather by raising the threshold below which the payroll tax is paid. In the US the Social Security trustees forecast a shortfall in the late 2030s or earlier 2040s. I will be outlining below a way of insuring against this possibility.

The second pension would deliver to everyone a useful supplement but would reward those who had made extra contributions of a financial (or non-financial) description with a somewhat higher pension. There would be credits for care work, or for an educational or cultural contribution. Devising fair ways of apportioning such entitlements offers some difficulties but not nearly so many as that of discovering a viable funding source. So, in the first instance, it is this latter aspect of matters that I focus on.

I have urged that conventional tax revenue should be drawn on sparingly, or not at all, because it is badly needed for education, health, child care and social infrastructure. Indeed the budgets for such purposes often include the pension costs of public sector pension schemes so it would be wrong to expect general tax revenues to take any more of the strain for pension provision – if anything such liabilities should be removed from departmental and local budgets where they eat into what is available for services. The yield of green taxes should be used to mitigate climage change. Payroll taxes will be sufficiently stretched ensuring good basic pensions and will not be able to contribute to second pensions as well. What other revenues might be drawn upon for pre-funding second pensions for all? There are a range of possibilities here, each of which could help to build a pension reserve, some of them particularly well tailored to the long-run nature of the problem. In my view the share levy proposed by Rudolf Meidner, and discussed in the last chapter, could play a crucial role but winning broad support for such an approach will certainly not be easy. Are there any other alternative sources of finance? Are there forms of partial pre-funding which could lighten the load bequeathed to future taxpayers? I will briefly consider these since, faced with a large task, every bit helps. And levying share-holders will seem fairer if the whole weight does not fall on their shoulders.

1. *Employee contributions and the 'matching' approach*

Employees themselves could and should make contributions to saving for their own retirement, according to their ability to do so. It is well established that the best way to build the legitimacy of universal entitlement is to require everyone to contribute. The contribution generates a widespread sense of ownership of the programme, as well as a source of finance. In contrast to payroll taxes the contribution rate should be progressive. The large numbers of US and UK employees who earn little more than the minimum wage should be given contribution credits. Care givers and the unemployed should also receive second pension credits. The current denial of pension rights to care givers is a scandal that should be ended as soon as possible. Flexibility in payment could be provided for by allowing every contributor to skip three years in every fifteen. Employee contributions of 3 to 5 per cent of income will raise serious sums, which can be boosted if it is possible to add extra matching pension rights to those who contribute more to the scheme. Contributors might receive an extra benefit worth $500 for every $1,000 they put in up to $3,000. If the resources can be found for such a scheme then the results are likely to be both more effective and more equitable than offering tax relief, since the latter, as we have seen, offers a much bigger incentive to the high paid than it does to the low paid. However the 'matching' approach requires some pump-priming so it does not solve the initial problem of raising resources. There is also the consideration that if employees are to contribute more then why not employers?

2. *Proceeds of public assets or sale of licences*

Governments with plans to license use of the airwaves, could vest them in pension funds benefiting all citizens. The public ownership of other assets could also yield revenues which could be applied to pensions, and in some special cases, such as oil states, this could furnish major funding. But often the purpose of public ownership would be to supply a socially advantageous service which profit-oriented enterprises have failed to provide. For example the sad state of rail transport in the UK following privatization – notably the failure to invest in infrastructure – suggests the need to return to public ownership. But the equally sad state of Amtrak, the publicly owned US rail network, also suggests that running such services on commercial lines negates the purpose of social ownership. Rail transport is worth subsidizing because, if properly managed, it can alleviate road congestion, reduce the emission of greenhouse gases and allow free or reduced travel to be offered to needy sections of the population, including the elderly. So the case for public ownership in such cases is not one which envisages such assets becoming major sources of revenue.

3. Betterment Levies

Governments could adopt a modern version of the Henry George device and place a tax on any increase in commercial site values – including the land on which shopping malls and luxury apartments are built. The rise in the value of commercial land is often the consequence of public infra- structure investments in roads and other amenities. Alternatively it is a by- product of general economic advance, offering the affected proprietors a windfall gain. For such reasons it is appropriate for increasing site values to be taxed as a source of public revenue.

4. Wealth Tax

There is also a case for considering a 'wealth tax'. The experience of several European countries suggests that this type of levy is quite practical but that it can run into serious loophole problems. This is because the threshold for the tax has to be set quite high if it is not unfairly to penalize small businesses, farms, and owners of homes that have become expensive urban real estate. As with taxes levied on estates bequeathed to heirs, reasonable and politically necessary exemptions to the wealth tax can be exploited by the truly wealthy. And since individuals or households will be taxed on their 'net worth' it would also be necessary to ensure that the valuation rules did not encourage indebtedness. At all events the tax take from wealth taxes is generally less than 1 per cent of GDP.

5 A Share Levy

I have left till last what is likely to be the best and most appropriate source of finance for pension systems, namely requiring all corporations employ- ing more than twenty people or with a turnover of over $10 million to issue new shares to a network of funds, with the rate of the levy to be calculated as a proportion of corporate profit or shareholder value. At a stroke this would restore the employers' contribution, which has fallen so low following the switch from DB to DC occupational schemes by many employers. During this same period, as we saw, corporations also become very skilled at tax avoidance so, if share levies were difficult to avoid, there would be a case for them on this ground alone. Another positive feature of the share levy is that it is impersonal, targeting corporations not individuals. Individuals do not have to declare how many shares they own and pay a tax on them, but instead corporations are required simply to issue new shares, something they do quite routinely, with the incidence of the levy calculated by reference to annual performance.

How a Share Levy Would Work

Corporations should not be thought of as rugged individuals living on their own. They are intimately dependent on their host society for law and order, for good communications, for access to markets, and for the availability of educated and committed employees. In the age of the disposable corporation they owe their very existence to a framework of public provisions and protections. The corporations and their owners enjoy considerable privileges and immunities. They have the privilege of personhood but only limited liability for the actions of the corporate entity they own. It is therefore perfectly just and necessary that they have a duty to the wider society and to the care of their workforce, and that this take the form of setting aside a portion of their annual profit. However, as we saw in Chapter 4, the corporate obligation is not best expressed in terms of a link between a specific company and a given employee. A system of social insurance should be diversified and should not shackle the employee to a particular employer. Nor, if it can be avoided, should companies be allowed contribution holidays when times are good and forced to contribute more when times are bad, as current DB arrangements require. When deflation threatens there can be another difficulty. In a deflationary climate forced cash levies, whether on individuals or corporations, undercut demand and threaten recession.

The levy is a way of meeting the increasing demands of social expenditure which does not distort the labour market and which can be better adjusted to the macro-economic environment than traditional tax-and-spend. The provision of pensions for aging populations will be amongst the heaviest of charges. If it is possible to furnish some of this provision without competing with current education and health budgets this would be highly desirable. As it happens these demanding conditions can be met.

In the last chapter we saw that it was in Sweden, where social expenditure first rose to claim more than a half of GDP, that Rudolf Meidner, one of the architects of the country's welfare state, drew up a variety of measures to ensure that it could afford its generous social arrangements. From 1959 the Swedish model already embraced the need for a prefunded second state pension so that all pensions would not have to be met from current taxation. In Meidner's original proposal the share levy was set rather high.– all companies employing more than fifty workers had to issue new shares each year, equivalent to the value of 20 per cent of their profits, and hand over these shares to a regional network of 'wage-earner funds'. The fund network could not sell the shares but were required to hold them to generate future income. These funds were to be run by boards of management representing workplaces and local communities.[10] Though the proposals were popular to begin with, the implacable opposition of Sweden's family-controlled large corporations, coupled with the half-hearted support of the Social Democrats, meant that its more radical aspects were never implemented.

Today we might set the share levy at 10 per cent of profits on any public company with more than twenty employees, or a turnover in excess of, say, $10 million a year. Private or closed companies could be required to issue bonds to a similar value, paying one per cent above bank rate and maturing in twenty-five years. These new shares and bonds would be divided between a central reserve fund and a regional network of pension funds. As Meidner envisaged, the shares (or bonds) would not be sold but would be held to generate future income. Indeed for an initial accumulation phase lasting, say, twenty-seven years, the dividend and interest payments would be re-invested in government bonds and real estate in order to diversify the assets held by the network and in order to further build up the resources available to fill the future funding gap. Once a target date was reached – say 2032 or 2037 – then the network would apply dividend and interest flows to paying second pensions. In what follows I will, for illustrative purposes, look at the effects of such a scheme in the US context. If Miedner's share levy could be made to solve US pension deficits than there is a good chance, given the extent of convergence noted above, that it would also help in other countries. (I will later draw on similar UK-based, and EU-based, calculations).

A share issue does not subtract from corporate cash-flow so it should not jeopardize investment programmes nor threaten employment. Increasing the number of shares in a company does not require the board to issue larger dividends, it simply means that the total dividend is shared more widely. A new share issue calculated in the way Meidner proposed – as a proportion of profits – acts as a sort of tax, like that on capital gains, on any profits-related growth in company value. It is, therefore, an asset tax and not an income-related tax. It slightly changes the distribution of property and its impact on the distribution of income is in consequence of this. The dilution effect on shares – perhaps 0.8 per cent a year – would be less than that of much willful behaviour by boards of directors. Employee stock options in the US, as noted above, ran at 19.5 per cent of profits in 2000, while M&A activity routinely involves using shares to make expensive acquisitions. Both these practices result in share dilution, often on a larger scale than that proposed here – and often in a less worthy cause.

Economists debate whether corporate taxation or payroll taxes are really passed on to the consumer in higher prices. It seems likely that under prevailing circumstances these taxes are indeed borne by the consumer.[11] With the share levy there is no doubt that it falls on a corporation's owners – and thus the rich, who own most shares. Indeed the richest 1 per cent of US households receive one half of all dividends and capital gains.[12] Of course it is also true that half the population own some shares, directly or indirectly. Even though the small shareholder would reap a considerable net gain from the levy great care would have to be taken to ensure that its workings were widely understood and that compensation was available to deserving and needy shareholders such as charities (on this more below).

Then there is the macro-economic context to consider. As noted above, there have been calls for compulsory employer contributions, but we should be careful that resulting budgets cuts do not threaten jobs. A compulsory share levy would supply a stream of assets which will generate income when it will be needed to pay pensions – in the future not the present. Using current taxes to meet future liabilities would be a mismatch. Corporations today often find it easier to give employees shares than to make a cash contribution to their pension holdings, but this company-specific form of share donation should not be encouraged because it violates the first rule of safer investing, namely diversification. The Meidner-style arrangements are diversified, not just between companies but also across time. In the initial accumulation phase cash income to the funds would be used to further broaden the types of assets held by the fund. It should be noted that dividends are much less volatile than share price. The goal of the funds would be to promote 'inter-temporal income shifting', enabling society to achieve a better balance of assets and to justly apportion the claims of present, past and future.

The Yield of a Share Levy Over 27 Years

At the heart of the new regime would be provision of a second pension to every citizen. The share levy would raise $141.7 billion to begin with – based on 'profits before tax' of $1.417 trillion in 2005 according to the US Flow of Funds data for that year[13]– rising to nearly twice this amount after twenty years as the economy grows and companies are induced to make a franker declaration of profits. A crackdown on tax loopholes and tax havens could be accompanied by a 5 or 10 point reduction in the existing rate of corporation tax, to yield roughly the same amount as today's higher nominal rate. The share levy would benefit from more accurate profit recognition. It would cause less distortions than existing corporate taxes. The shares raised by the new issues and the re-investment of their earnings would soon build up assets in the central reserve and in the regional network. An initial tranche of assets might be employed to strengthen the long term position of Social Security and to improve its future pay-out rates, especially for those who lack full entitlement because of broken contribution records or, in the case of older women, spousal irresponsibility. The growth of casual labor, part-time work and low-paid employment has weakened the entitlement of forty or fifty million Americans. The central reserve might commit, say, $20 billion annually, to strengthen the Social Security trust fund. It could use a similar tranche of receipts to strengthen the PBGC reserves, enabling it to improve its own pay-out rates and even negotiate to take over and run the individual corporate schemes. These share issues would vary in line with receipts and be channeled to these recipients on the strict under-standing that they were not to be sold for a lengthy period but were to be used to cover long term capital deficits.

The residue of about $100 billion annually would go to the regional network and would eventually enable it to supply a second pension to all citizens. If this was thought desirable a portion of the annual receipts would be available to offer matching funds for savers throughout the country up to a threshold amount, with the extra savings boosting the eventual value of the second pension. For an initial period – up to 2033 or 2037 – all earnings would be ploughed back into the trust and reserve funds. For a further period payout of earnings could be restricted to, say, 90 per cent of earnings each year. The state trust funds would be able to draw on the expertise of local universities in managing these assets and investing earnings.

I started out by estimating that maintenance of old age income will require 15 per cent of US GDP by 2033, with at least a further 5 per cent for medical and care costs. At present Social Security is meant to supply 5 per cent of GDP by that date, though its trustees forecast that it will by then have nearly exhausted its trust fund and be unable to pay full pensions by about 2040. In 2002 private pensions accounted for about 2 per cent of GDP, but close to a further 2 per cent – over $200 billion – was absorbed by the high cost of financial intermediation (fund management charges, brokerage charges, mutual fund profits and the like). The doubling of the numbers of retirees could raise this proportion a little but – given both the extent of private sector failure and the doubling of GDP over this period – not by much. Private pensions will not be able to supply is more than 2.5 per cent of GDP, and will do very well to attain that level. Public sector schemes should supply 1 per cent of GDP. The earnings of workers beyond the age of 65 might add a further 2 per cent of GDP. So there would be a 4 percentage gap by 2032 between what was available and what was needed simply to maintain pensioner incomes. How much of this gap could the new pension regime plug?

I have suggested that the levy should be set at 10 per cent of profits and that the pension fund network, the PBGC and the Social Security trust fund, barred from selling the shares they received, would instead hold them to use their future earnings to pay future pensions. I have also suggested that there should be a twenty-seven year 'accumulation' phase during which dividends would be re-invested in the funds. When US profits before tax were $1,417 billion in 2005, GDP was $12.5 trillion.[14] The levy would raise $141.7 billion and if we assume that profits rise by an average of 2.5 per cent a year and that the fund grows at 5 per cent a year then the fund would reach $10.9 trillion by 2033, (just a little ahead of the time when, according to its trustees, the Social Security trust fund will be exhausted). Matching contributions could attract a further $3 trillion or more.[15]

The $10.9 trillion fund should yield over $500 billion a year in earnings by 2033. Part of these assets could plug holes in the Social Security Trust Fund and PBGC but the lion's share woulds go to pay a second public pension to every retiree, with modest bonuses for those who had made a matching contribution. A yield of $500 billion by 2033 would amount to roughly 2 per cent of the then-GDP. At this level the share levy would be meeting at least half of the funding gap estimated earlier at 4 per cent of GDP level. This would be a very useful contribution but still leaves a small gap and other unmet ageing costs. If the new pension fund regime cracked down on excess costs in the financial services industry then perhaps DB and DC schemes could pay pensions worth 3.5 per cent of GDP instead of 2.5 per cent. This would bring the incomes of those sixty-five and over close to the target level. If age discrimination was successfully combated, and flexible working arrangements furnished to older workers, then post-retirement earnings might rise above 2 per cent of GDP. At the present time such earnings already comprise 21 per cent of senior incomes, with the incomes of older professionals making a large contribution. With policies to promote 'active ageing' reaching out to wider sections of the population, the contribution from this quarter could rise to 2.5 or 3 per cent of GDP in future. Adding up these various sources of retirement income we reach a total of around 14–15 per cent, with new sources of finance and rigorous reform of the existing investment industry making a crucial contribution. If the initial target was for some reason exceeded – or deemed to be overly generous in the first place – the extra resources would still be needed to meet other costs of the aging society.

The medical and care costs of the elderly already comprise over 5 per cent of US GDP, funded partly by the Federal government and partly by insurance and personal contributions. While there is certainly scope for the better control of US medical and care costs – too larger a theme to be tackled here – these are bound to grow as the aged population does. So the measures I have proposed are the bare minimum and still leave major problems to be addressed.

Theoretical and Practical Objections

The pre-funding part of these proposals have to surmount a theoretical objection. It is sometimes said that the pensions of the future will have to be met from the output of the future so that pre-funding is illusory and the most straightforward procedure is to finance pensions only through taxes paid by the workers of the future. For example John Eatwell, the Cambridge economist, argues as follows: 'Living standards are secured in retirement by acquiring monetary claims than can be used to purchase part of the contemporary flow of goods and services produced by the current workforce. The pensions problem is to ensure that retired people have a sufficient number of monetary claims to buy the goods and services they need and to secure the agreement (explicit or implicit) of the workforce to "give up" a share of the goods and services they have produced. The problem of this inter-generational transfer becomes significantly more difficult when the population in ageing, i.e. when the proportion of the population that has retired is rising due to falling birth rates and increased longevity. If the ratio of the retired to the working population is rising then the income that the working population must give up must also rise. The goods and services for the pensioners are "released" by the working population in two forms – saving or taxes. They are transferred to the pensioners either via the state, or via the monetary claims that the pensioners have built up. The direct transfer via the state (the PAYG pension) is clear. Less obvious is the fact that if the pensioners monetary claims exceed the amount the working population is willing to save, then either inflation will erode the value of pensions to equal savings, or the government will be forced to raise taxes to force "savings" on the working population.'[16]

Eatwell's argument was not directed against a Meidner-style share levy proposal but rather was aimed at those who exaggerate the scope for pre-funding. He concluded with a telling observation: 'The only advantage that can accrue to the government of a switch to private pensions is that it can disavow responsibility for the failure of privately accumulated funds to provide for pension needs.'[17] While he had good criticisms to make of funded pensions, his reasoning has gaps which would allow it to be used against attempts to use a Meidner-style levy. Eatwell fails to make clear what has happened in his scenario to property income and the returns to capital – namely dividends, capital gains, interest and rent. These constitute income claims quite different from tax or savings, which are hence not the only ways of getting future workers to yield up income. Under capitalism owners appropriate corporate profits; and this gives them dividends, capital gains and leverage over the corporation. Of course, if these arrangements have somehow disappeared, and only labour incomes are allowed, then pensions would certainly have to be paid exclusively from taxes on labour (perhaps echoing Bernard Friot's ideas mentioned in the last chapter).

But those who insist that the retirement income of the future will have to come from the production of the future do not usually envisage any such sweeping expropriation. In the absence of such a dissolution of prevailing property relations, workers are 'giving up' or 'releasing' a portion of the total output to owners and creditors and this could be applied to pensions. However, it would have to be by a deliberate

legislative act and course of policy. And it would be different from the
necessarily much more limited transfers that result from standard funding
by employees. Under most funding schemes workers will only acquire
such money claims through their own saving but – one of Eatwell's main
points – this past savings rate bears no necessary relation to the future
savings rate that might be necessary to absorb the cost of needed future
pension expenditures. Under the share levy extra saving by workers also
occurs but is simply a bonus. The levy itself is transferring a stream of
future claims on property income to the fund network, which is
allocating them to pension needs. Pay-as-you-go will still be pulling
its weight – indeed supplying a major stream of retirement income – but
it will have supplementary support.

One reason why income to capital can be so easily forgotten, or
bracketed out of the discussion, is that a chunk of it will be channeled to
investment, either directly by investment decisions, or indirectly by
capitalists' savings. Historically employees have often had difficulty
accumulating significant savings and capitalists have re-invested much
of their gross income. As Andrew Glyn has argued: 'Investment com-
plicates the picture since higher welfare spending could be at the expense
of capital accumulation rather than current consumption . . . It is a
fundamental problem for left-wing governments that "making the bosses
pay" by higher corporate taxation or a profits squeeze risks killing the
goose that lays the golden egg of investment and growth.'[18]

This is often a problem with swinging 'tax and spend' proposals, but, as
stated, it does not apply to the share levy. As already indicated , the share
levy does not subtract from the funds a company has available for
investment. In the initial accumulation phase the network's savings rate
would be very high. Capitalists, on the other hand, have probably
become more consumption-oriented. Glyn points out that in most
advanced countries the top ten percent of households receive 30 per
cent of national income and that there is scope for belt-tightening there.[19]
This group also garners well over a half of all property income and would
find its consumption squeezed by the transfer of a part of that income to
pensioners.

Glyn is keenly aware that social expenditure will require more than a
third of GDP and that revenue on this scale will require broad-based taxes
which cannot be raised simply from the rich: 'Realistically most revenue
for redistribution will have to continue to come from tax on wage or
salary income though this may be done in a more or less progressive

manner.'[20] While it is true that 'most revenue' will have to be raised in this way progressive taxation of financial assets could nevertheless play a strategic and important role both in supplementary pension provision and in overall redistribution. The focus would here be on the top 5 per cent and the top 1 per cent, recalling that the latter receive a half of all dividend payments and capital gains, and that this layer in the Anglo-Saxon countries has long ago abandoned the frugal ways of its Puritan fore-bears.[21]

Nicholas Barr has also wrestled with the argument that pre-funding of pension is illusory in his book *The Welfare State as Piggy Bank* (2002). Barr rightly stresses that the key to the affordability of future pensions will be growth in output and hence improvements in productivity. While the new regime would aim to promote healthy levels of investment and a dynamic macro-economic balance I do not wish to assume away the funding problem by simply anticipating such gains. Instead I wish to isolate the financial resources yielded simply by the share levy and trust fund network. Barr concedes that some pre-funding of pension obliga-tions can be achieved if there is a transfer of property rights to a fund which enjoys the consequent claim on future income streams. [22] Shares or bonds acquired through a levy would certainly meet this condition. If such shares were held by a network of public trust funds then the effect would be to reduce the national debt, and hence the servicing burden bequeathed to future generations. After the initial accumulation phase the funds would use dividend income and sales of shares that had been held for a minimum period – perhaps ten years – to pay pensions. The market volatility problem would be somewhat diminished, as noted above, because dividends are less prone to swings in value than shares. The trustees of the second tier funds would use smoothing techniques and actuarial adjustments to pay the universal second pension, the exact value of which would depend on overall economic growth.

There remains the danger that owners would be so upset by the levy that they would invest overseas instead. But it would only be rational to do this if investments within the jurisdiction were no longer profitable. A levy set at a level far below that of corporation tax would not wipe out all capital gains or distributed profit. If irrational capitalists nevertheless stampeded, then more rational capitalists would take their place. His-torically capitalists have been willing to brave much more onerous conditions. Nevertheless the potential for a 'strike of capital' would certainly make it more difficult for smaller countries, lacking in scarce resources, to apply the share levy. But the United States, the European Union, China, India, and the Mercosur countries of South America, represent such considerable opportunities for profitable investment that capitalists would not be induced to abandon them simply because they have to share their gains with a local pension fund network.

Each year the levy or 'social dividend' would re-distribute a tiny slither of share capital from wealthy individuals to all those who had rights in the pension fund system. Future generations would benefit. Relieved of onerous payments to rentiers and rich capitalists, future generations will have more resources available to pay decent pensions. Those responsible for overall economic management would have to ensure that investment needs are met so the extra boost for retirement income would really be supplanting – gently and gradually – the over-consumption of the wealthy. There was a time in the mid-twentieth century when capitalists' consumption was quite tightly constrained and the tax rate was quite high. The share levy implies a return to something like that social balance.

Today more than half of all Americans and Britons have some stake in shareholding, albeit that for most of them this will be a small stake and the shares will be held via an intermediary such as a mutual or pension fund. Nevertheless, opponents of the proposed levy would charge that it would rob the small man and the widow. Indeed pension funds themselves, as owners of shares, would suffer from the annual dilution of share values that the levy would represent. In fact a half of pension wealth is held by the richest ten per cent of the population and has benefited from generous public subsidy in the shape of tax relief. Share ownership as a whole is even more concentrated in the hands of the rich – the top 1 per cent – and it is anomalous that this form of wealth is subject to no tax or levy when every home-owner has to pay a tax or charge. The richest 1 per cent of US households own a third of US total assets (including housing), with the next richest 9 per cent also owning a little over a further third, so that the top 10 per cent own over two thirds of all assets, and the poorer 50 per cent own only 2.5 per cent of all assets.[23] The ownership of key financial assets – bonds, stocks, pooled investment funds and retirement funds – is even more unequal. [24] The levy would begin to redress this massive inequality.

Nevertheless, the objection to the principle of taxing shares would have to be considered very seriously. The case for the reform should stress not only that it would benefit the great majority, but also that share-holders themselves should welcome the construction of a network of responsible transactors, partly for reasons of general social justice, and partly because the trust funds would use their leverage to assert share-holder rights over and against irresponsible chief executives and their financial help-meets and hangers-on.

It would be quite possible to ensure that all pension funds received more than they lost from the levy. Reserving a portion of levy receipts to boost the reserves of the PBGC – or in the UK the Pension Protection Fund – would improve the insurance afforded to the remaining DB schemes. The aim would be to move away from the present flawed single-employer model, but only if employees could be persuaded of the benefits of this. Employees in blue chip companies might think that their best interests lie in staying with their employer as the ultimate insurer of their pension. But this does not take account of the fact that we live in the epoch of the disposable corporation and that, over the time required to pay out a pension, companies can be transformed from industrial champions to basket cases. Those joining the publicly sponsored scheme would gain better insurance, portability of their pension rights from one job to the next, and inflation indexing. While today's insurance system fosters moral hazard (employers who skimp still get forgiven contribu-tions) the new regime would be based on compulsory profit-linked contributions. For smaller personal investors there should also be a gain in that the pension fund network would offer lower cost savings vehicles and would finance independent and freely available research.

The share levy can be seen as a gentler and more subtle variant of the 'capital levy', a device adopted by some governments after the First and Second World Wars. Such a tax simply declares that a portion of all financial assets must be paid to the government. In conditions of war-induced breakdown governments sometimes resorted to a 'tax in kind' and such a tax, applied to financial assets, would be a capital levy. However the chaotic conditions that made such a levy necessary also hampered its execution. Hyper-inflation and currency breakdown could easily destroy the asset base unless the levy was used as part of a strategy for curbing inflation. Joseph Schumpeter, the great economist, experimented with such a levy when he was Austria's Minister of Finance. But the brevity of his occupancy of this post in 1919, the dire condition of the country's economy at this time, and the weakness of the government coalition meant that it was never put into effect. The Czechoslovak Republic made effective use of a capital levy in the 1920s, but the main contributors to it were ethnic Germans. The most successful and radical example of the implementation of a capital levy occurred, interestingly enough, under the aegis of the United States government. In 1946 the Japanese fiscal authorities, with the full encouragement and support of the occupying power, introduced a capital levy, with a sliding scale of charges rising from 10 per cent on fortunes over 100,000 yen and reaching 90 per cent on fortunes over 15 million yen.[25] A clause designed to discourage attempts to undervalue assets, stipulated that the public authorities could purchase any asset at the value assigned to it by owners in their return to the fiscal authorities. The large sums raised by the levy helped to cover urgently needed outgoings and to stabilize postwar Japanese public finances. The share levy remains a milder tax than the capital levy, and focuses exclusively on the ownership of assets which are currently not subject to taxation. It follows the asset and would tax those who hold equity in tax havens. It would gently dilute the equity holdings of hedge funds to the extent that they held equities for any purpose. It is an approach to corporate taxation that itself inhabits the financialized world and seeks to qualify the attempt by boards to monopolize the share issuance process.

Applying the share levy to the entire range of companies and concerns, including medium-sized companies, partnerships and private equity arrangements would pose technical problems, as does all taxation. However, notional partnership rights, and a portion of the 'carried interest' of a private equity deal, would serve as counterparts to the share levy. In applying the levy itself the fiscal authority should avoid using just one threshold or definition of what is to be taxed as that would tend to foster distortions and facilitate avoidance. That is why the size above which the levy applies might be specified using turnover as well as number of employees. In March 2004 the US workforce totaled 125 million employees, of whom 105 million were in the private sector. Three quarters of the private sector workforce – 77 million workers – were employed by concerns with twenty or more workers, and 89 million workers worked in those with more ten or more workers. Employees at large concerns are better paid, on average, than those at small concerns, and profits per employee are also probably higher – the 12 million employees of companies with between ten and nineteen employees earned $94 billion in the first quarter while the 11.4 million workers who work for the 5,400 establishments with more than a thousand employees earned $170 billion.[26]

The UK Pensions Commission has recommended that there should be auto-enrolment in a National Pension Savings Scheme (NPSS). Employ-ees would be able to opt out but if they did not then they would have to contribute 5 per cent of salary, and their employers would be required to contribute 3 per cent of salary, to the scheme, which would credit these contributions and then manage the resulting funds.[27] Anticipating that these arrangements would be burdensome for small employers the Commission suggested special arrangements, and a special support fund, to facilitate this important extension of coverage. The proposal that the NPSS be a publicly organized, non-commercial body was welcomed by the Consumer Association and trade unions but was attacked by the National Association of Pension Funds (NAPF) and the Association of British Insurers (ABI). Some members of the main employers organiza-tion, the Confederation of British Industry (CBI), after initial misgivings gave the proposals their guarded approval but some of its members, joined by the Institute of Directors, representing smaller companies, were worried about the burden of being compelled to make a cash contribu-tion worth 3 per cent of wages.[28]

The proposals of the Commission might be a little uncomfortable for some sectors of the financial services industry but most of the latter prefer to concentrate on the better paid and the wealthy. And while the NPSS would itself be publicly run it would, rather like the Swedish PPM, channel all contributions to these suppliers of financial products who would keep costs below 0.3 per cent of fund value each year. A few very large providers might find this useful business. While the arrangements might suit providers with wide brand recognition, and in a position to reap scale economies, many ABI members would find no gain.

Britain's centre-right coalition government, formed in 2010, accepted the Commission's scheme, with the NPSS now to be known as the National Employee Savings Trust (NEST). The NPSS/NEST fund might have some features that could be adapted to solve the technical problems – such as coverage of small employers – required to make the share levy and fund network a practical proposition. However, the 'auto-enrolment with opt out' approach to contributions is the wrong solution, especially at a time of recession and generally depressed incomes, since it will weaken demand and prove onerous to the low paid. A better approach would be to offer a tapered contribution credit to those on below-average wages. While the original UK Commission proposal remains a highly regulated regime of commodification, the Meidner-type approach leans, instead, towards de-commodification, by weakening the link between entitlement and cash-contributions. But, curiously, the share levy would be less burdensome to those seeking to run a business. When it comes to contributing to employee pension funds, US corporate management has always preferred to issue shares rather than cash. Following the collapse of Enron a large amount of business lobbying was successfully devoted to defending this traditional practice.

The Scope for Re-regulation

In earlier chapters I have drawn on the work of a remarkable group of professionals and critical insiders in the field of regulation and fund management, notably John Bogle, the founder of Vanguard, Eliot Spitzer, the New York attorney general, Arthur Levitt, former chairman of the SEC, Joseph Stiglitz, former chief economist at the World Bank, and Nomi Prins, a former managing director at Goldman Sachs.[29] This diverse group is united in calling for more rigorous and effective public regulation of corporations and financial markets. Existing regulatory structures should be given more powers, and new rules of disclosure should be applied. Interestingly most of these experts would like to strengthen the power of shareholders in relation to chief executives and boards of directors; and to enhance the ability of plan members to monitor and discipline those who manage their savings. The share levy and the social fund network would complement and reinforce such efforts and would ensure that every citizen and employee would benefit.

In September 2003 Spitzer urged fund managers to use their power to check abuse and promote better corporate governance, and the mainly public sector activist funds sought to follow his advice. John Bogle believes that the finance houses have perverted the clear intent of the legislation which established their fund management concerns: 'The starting point for considering how to fix mutual fund America is the reiteration of the lofty words to the preamble to what is essentially the mutual fund industry's constitution, the Investment Company Act of 1940: "the national public interest and the interest of investors" require that mutual funds be "organized, operated, and managed . . . in the best interests of share holders, rather than in the interests of advisers, underwriters or others". Note that the law of the land says nothing about balancing the interests of managers and fund owners. If you visualize a scale, the law would have all of the weight put on the shareholder side, and none of the weight on the side of the fund management company.' [30] Bogle urges that mutual funds should be required to conform to mutual principles, with members given the opportunity to appoint directors who will monitor the fund managers ands change them if necessary.

The authors I have cited, and the public debate occasioned by the scandals, has led to a string of proposals for the more effective regulation of corporate and financial affairs which it is not possible for me to review here. However some ideas are worth noting briefly. Corporate audit is still deeply unsatisfactory, plagued by conflicts of interest and with only four companies able to audit large international companies. The time has come to set up a public audit service, leaving accountancy services to the private provider. The reform of mutual funds and the introduction of the new social fund regime could be combined with a new and more rigorous regime for all tax-favoured retirement funds. The aim would be to strip out the fat layer of excess costs by setting ceilings on fees and marketing spend. Funds which failed to comply would attract no further tax relief . And full cost-disclosure would be a legal requirement.

The United States already has a regional regulatory structure – that of the Federal Reserve system – which could help to invigilate the workings of the network of trust funds and the reform of other savings and investment institutions. Currently the regional Federal Reserve system is meant to possess this sort of competence but over-represents business interests and under-represents communities. However if the system was reformed it could assemble the necessary expertise as well as represent community interests. Currently representatives from local consumer, labour and civic groups comprise only about a tenth of the membership of the 9-person regional boards, while there is now representation for companies with financial ambitions, such as Wal-Mart and General Electric.[31] The regional Federal Reserve offices have often attracted competent staff but a reform of these structures might confine board representation to elected officials and qualified experts, in roughly equal proportions, while providing for business interests to be legitimately expressed via consultative panels.

A network of public trust funds could encourage the spread of higher quality pension coverage by establishing basic operational criteria. These should oblige pension schemes to report to, and consult, their members at regular intervals. Such consultation would concern investment priorities not pay-out rules, which should be laid down to ensure fairness between current and future retirees. Schemes could also be encouraged to adopt mildly redistributive pay-out rules, which would allow somewhat higher rewards for those with greater lifetime contributions, but with a progressive narrowing of income differentials. Pension tax breaks could be confined to funds which refuse to lend out stock for shorting operations and commit to hold a high proportion of their shares for five years or more.

Likewise the pension funds could foster Socially Responsible Investment (SRI). They will automatically receive a diversified portfolio of equities and will be banned from selling them. But their voting power at AGMs would still give them significant and growing leverage. They could not micro-manage the companies whose stock they held. But if they concentrated on a few large and important issues – and did so one at a time and with some coordination – then they could have an impact on such issues as executive compensation, labour rights and sustainable production and sourcing.

If the pension fund network had a growing say in corporate policy, some fear that the mass of beneficiaries would become no less wedded to the cult of 'shareholder value' and the bottom line than Wall Street. Of course this would be a danger – indeed share ownership is widespread enough to make it already a danger. Under the proposed arrangements there would be argument about how pension trust fund votes should be used and there would certainly be concern that, in due course, decent pensions would be paid. But a strong case could be made that building a healthy economy for the long run is not best achieved by inflicting poor conditions on the workforce, poisoning the environment or wasting scarce resources. The funds would be invested right across the major indeces and their holdings in any one company would be tiny. If asked to vote on, say, whether Wal-Mart should allow its workforce to join a union, or Exxon be encouraged to drill for oil in the Arctic, or Gap source its garments from exploiters of child labour, the funds could not read off the answer on a simple economic calculus. Their members would have to decide what sort of world they wanted to live in, one which denied workers' rights or one which did not, one which ravaged the environment or one which guaranteed sustainability. Perhaps there would eventually be some impact on the pension they received twenty or thirty years later but it would not be easy to say what it was. (Wal-Mart workers who want a union will find it difficult to persuade their stubborn employer so they would do well to consider, as part of their strategy, an SRI campaign aimed at funds which invest in the company.)

The fact that every citizen was a proxy shareholder via the funds held to supply them with retirement income would open the way to new constructions of shareholder interests. Today's corporations often neglect the social cost of their malpractices and negligence because it does not show up in their accounts. But a 'universal investor', such as a pension fund for the whole community, would not be able to escape such 'externalities'. The representation of communities, and their involvement in such debates and decisions, would not guarantee the right outcome but they would establish a structure within which progressive outcomes could be argued for, as is already happening in several large public sector unions. Moreover communities, trade unions and consumers' groups would not need to abandon any of their other efforts to change, correct or influence corporate behaviour. The trust fund network would simply be an extra channel or arena for pursuing the interests of their members and of society as a whole.

Companies are frightened of the reputational impact of campaigns against them if they violate what are seen as decent and commonly-accepted standards. But the adjustments they make are often purely cosmetic. Even if they respond in good faith the mechanisms of market competition may mean that others will pick up, and profit from, the bad practice which had been targeted.

Would the trust fund network have any stake in such corporate bad behaviour as extravagant compensation of chief executives or elaborate transactions undertaken for the sole purpose of avoiding tax? Shareholders often show their unhappiness with corporate greed but not with CFOs who promise to ensure that the corporation pays less tax next year by using a tax haven, or devising a sham investment in tax-favoured social infrastructure. While citizen-shareholders will certainly be concerned about the pension they are due to receive, they could well be persuaded that corporations should be doing their bit, and not leave individual tax payers to shoulder all the burdens. Plan members who stood to benefit in future from the share levy would also be aware that this would be diminished by corporate tax avoidance.

The leading states are already tightening up on tax havens because of their usefulness to money launderers, illegal arms traders and terrorist networks. The proposed new pension fund network would have good reason to press for even more effective controls. The potential gains are very large.

The primer on *Taxes and Business Strategy* by Myron Scholes and Mark

Wolfson insists that the taxing authority is already a de facto 'investment partner' in every enterprise, but, as we saw above, went on to show how 'tax planning' could exploit that partner's lack of information[32]. At a Senate hearing in October 2003 a consultant estimated that tax havens had been used to evade $14–18 billion of taxes in 2000 alone. It was explained how US corporations had disguised profits as infrastructure leases in a scheme known as 'lease in, lease out' or Lilo.[33] Over a five-year period the total of lost taxes was $85 billion. A strengthening of IRS powers along the lines of the New York state Martin Act, used by Spitzer, would help tackle this problem. At present there are legal rulings that the tax advice which accountants gives to companies is protected – as confidential client information – from scrutiny by the Internal Revenue Service.[34] The IRS also has limited staff and a limited vantage point. Not surprisingly the contribution of corporate taxation to Federal revenue has fallen from 30–40 per cent in the 1960s to less than 20 per cent in recent years.

If the new network of funds had its own expert analysts the tax authorities' partnership with business could become more equal and effective. If shareholders had greater expertise, legal powers and legitimacy they could assist the chronically short-staffed taxing authority to track corporate revenues and secure social objectives. The network of social funds would have legitimacy because all citizens would have a stake in them, and they would be able to hire the necessary expertise. Today the brimming profits which corporations brag about to quarterly conferences with analysts and shareholders, mysteriously turn to losses by the time they report to the IRS. The pension network would be in a good position to find out what was really going on.

Both the US and the EU authorities have the power to take on the tax havens but have lacked the will. The revenue staff are perfectly willing to pursue tax evasion but are not helped to do so by the treasury officials and finance ministers. It is interesting that South Korea, a medium-sized state, has decided to take on the corporate tax evaders by denying double taxation privileges to a list of territories and states which act as tax havens: 'From July 1 [2006], investment income derived in Korea, including interest, dividends and capital gains earned by foreign investors located in designated tax havens will be subject to domestic Korean withholding tax rates – usually 27.5 per cent – regardless of double taxation treaties. Ireland, Belgium and the Netherlands are being considered for the list of tax havens, along with controversial offshore centres such as Labuan in

Malaysia. Lawyers say tax authorities will be able to review all transactions conducted through the listed "havens" during the previous five years . . . European multinationals and banks such as Standard Chartered, Deutsche Bank, ING and BNP Paribas could be hit by the inclusion of European Union countries, but the changes may also affect US banks including Citibank and JP Morgan.'[35] The share levy system would also be able to focus on revenues generated within a jurisdiction, and to insist on enough information to be able to spot such devices as transfer pricing and thin capitalization.

The social funds could be about producing wealth as well as distributing it. In a world where stock exchanges are already of greatly increased importance, the social funds could help to protect productive enterprises from 'financialization'. They could promote socially responsible business objectives and assert a degree of popular control over the accumulation process. Because the network of pension funds would have significant power in corporate affairs, it would need to develop its own cadre of financial specialists and, as we have seen, would have reason to assist the tax authorities to monitor and enforce fiscal regulations. The effect of the levy would be to bring about a very gradual 'nationalizing' effect on ownership, in the sense that the trust fund network would build up shareholdings in all corporations which were generating revenue and making profits within the jurisdiction.

The inflow of dividends and matching contributions would supply the network with liquid assets which it would use to diversify its investments. A limited portion of these revenues – say no more than a tenth – could be invested in regional enterprises and in special public bonds issued by state or municipal authorities to meet urgent infrastructure needs. These bonds would be able to count on a mixture of rents and guarantees to deliver real returns of around 4 or 5 per cent annually. In this way a portion of the cash income accruing to the social funds could be used to meet, say, the need for cheaper housing in metropolitan districts, an area where trade union-sponsored funds have already made a valuable contribution.[36] In the UK the government has offered banks generous guarantees in return for supplying the finance needed to build hospitals and schools. It would be better if such terms were given to a not-for-profit trust fund network dedicated to meeting ageing costs.

What if a profitable corporation wished to become still more profitable by closing its plant in one locale and opening it in an overseas region where labour was cheap? The attractions of such a course of action can easily be exaggerated by those who take no account of the open and hidden costs of distance, with its accompanying inflexibility and lost time. It is not usually registered that wage costs are often only a small proportion of overall cost, and that any company whose output embodies dozens, or scores, or hundreds of components, will usually combine items from different regions with greatly varying management, wages rates, skills, natural resources and transport facilities. Germany, the United States and Japan are still the world's major exporters despite the relatively high wages received by their workers. The market share of Ford and GM in the United States is being squeezed by Toyota and Nissan, with vehicles made in Japan or North America. Being close to the largest market has many advantages. Those who invoke the economics of 'comparative advantage' often neglect the heavy pollution costs of long-distance transportation. If these costs were properly taken into account in fuel prices, as they should be, this would encourage local sourcing and stimulate regional trading networks.

But even after taking such factors into account a corporation might find some relocation of production facilities to be profitable. The fund covering the region affected by the closure might still oppose such a move, especially if they believed local potential was being underestimated. If they appealed to fellow shareholders to oppose outsourcing, they might not succeed but it would be worth a try. If the move succeeded in boosting performance, all shareholders might benefit, but the notional small increase in their future pension would not compensate workers who had been thrown out of a job. However this sequence would not be rooted in, or facilitated by the existence of the fund network. In a globalized economy, regional, national and local authorities would need to step in to ensure new jobs in the affected area. It would be the job of such authorities to ensure, if possible, that those they represent are able to benefit from the workings of comparative advantage, workings which often require public intervention. While the social fund network does not remove such dilemmas, it would give local communities extra resources and mechanisms with which to address them.

In much that I have written I have assumed that US and UK economic structures are rather similar. Yet UK shareholders have more rights than do their US counterparts. They can more easily put motions to AGMs and replace directors. In the wake of the scandals there was pressure for more shareholder rights in the US, as we saw in Chapter 5, but the concessions made so far to this are fairly modest. Yet even in the US the future probably lies with empowering shareholders as a check on CEOs and boards of directors. The meek behaviour of crony boards faced with arrogant and greedy CEOs has strengthened the demand for directors to be more answerable to shareholders. In the UK the somewhat greater powers of shareholders have probably helped to restrain CEO self-indulgence a little, at least outside the financial sector itself.[37]

But greater shareholder power in the UK is also associated with more negative features. The large institutions have displayed very little commitment to the companies in which they invest and have been ever-willing to accept the blandishments of corporate raiders and foreign bids. The result has been the transfer into the hands of foreign corporations of great swathes of the British economy. After a recent spate of such deals Will Hutton pointed out: 'Some 20 years ago, the Royal Bank of Scotland fought off a foreign take-over and argued that it would be good for Scotland and Edinburgh to be the home of an independent bank, complete with Scottish head-quarters, rather than become part of another company's, and country's, dream.'[38] Unfortunately RBS soon compromised this gain by embarking on a hugely expensive, leveraged, takeover of a large Dutch bank, rendering itself highly vulnerable to the 2007–9 shock.

The share levy, as noted above, would begin to return some ownership and leverage to local communities. Applied internationally it would also furnish a mechanism whereby, in all countries and regions, communities could acquire a growing stake in the multinational corporations active within their borders. The smarter multinationals already realize that their overseas divisions need to be 'nationalized,' with boards of directors and senior executives drawn from the countries in which they operate. As the share levy became an international norm it would spread local ownership as the natural complement of this process.

Implementing the Fund Network

The aim of the measures I have outlined is both to anticipate the predictably heavy costs of the forthcoming retirement of the baby-boomers and to foster the emergence of informed and socially accountable economic agents who can reinforce the external regulation of banks and businesses by regulation from within and below by shareholding bodies which represent all citizens. In the wake of the scandals, the new management at Worldcom introduced a measure which, however limited, hints at future possibilities: 'The firm's website will host electronic "town hall" meetings for shareholders to make proposals to management. Ideas that win the support of, say, 20% of shareholders, must be put to a vote at the next annual meeting.'[39]

At the present time 'shareholder democracy' is not really democratic because share ownership, even in pension funds, is so unequally distributed. The proposed share levy and the egalitarian norms that would apply to the new pension funds, would begin to give every citizen a shareholding stake, and would do so in a collective form that would make for both low costs and greater clout with corporations. Moves to render corporations more responsive to their owners already have considerable legitimacy and this would grow if the whole community had an ownership stake. This outcome might also be reached by routes other than those sketched here – for example through investment of the fruits of a wealth tax, or as a result of raising taxes on high incomes, putting the proceeds in the stock and bond market, and allowing a logic of 'superfunding', as described by Thomas Michl and Duncan Foley.[40]

The current 'Anglo-Saxon' pattern of financial and corporate power, with all its problems, will not last forever. It will come under increasing pressure for a radical transformation of its modus operandi. The possibilities that I have invoked are extrapolations and mutations of trends which can already be observed. I do not think that they are unilaterally or unequivocally progressive and desirable. For example, SRI can be quite illusory, and shareholding, even if indirect and egalitarian, could engender its own blinkers and false perspective. But I do believe that, together with other democratic transformations and movements, the measures I have outlined could open up pathways to a progressive future and furnish the context for addressing the special costs of an ageing society.

I have advocated a share levy similar to that proposed by Rudolf Meidner, yet his proposals were first watered down by the leaders of Sweden's Social Democratic party and then the funds transferred to research institutes by the Conservatives in 1992. One could say that Meidner's proposals were never properly tested or, alternatively, that they failed to garner the support which all ideas need if they are to succeed. As we saw the Meidner plan was strongly opposed by the family-owned business conglomerates. They rightly saw it as a threat to their control of so much of the Swedish economy. The scheme had a number of design features which were exploited by opponents. It appeared to favor private sector workers over public sector workers and no specific purpose was proposed for these 'wage-earner funds', as they were called. The scheme gave a big role, some claimed an overweening role, to the trade unions. The Social Democratic government was induced to dilute many of the provisions of the scheme, reducing its incidence, eliminating wage-earner representation, and allowing for cash contributions as well as new issues. Notwithstanding the fact that it was never implemented the plan suffered from the (temporary) backlash against the Social Democrats in the early 1990s. If care was taken to construct the scheme in ways that were intelligible to the great majority, and to ensure an accountable fund, the outcome could well be different. The pressing nature of today's pension finance issues could give a sharper focus to the scheme. The fear of trade union power, which opponents of the plan were able to mobilize in Sweden in the 1980s, is now less common than a fear of high-handed employers. Sweden's '20 families' had a lot to lose from implementation of the scheme, whereas today family control of corporations is becoming rarer. [41]

Surely globalization rules out more stringent taxing of corporations? It has rightly been argued that globalization has often furnished an alibi to governments that were anyway keen to adapt to the corporate agenda. I have already urged that it would be easier for large states or regions – the US, the EU, Japan, China, India – to introduce the share levy than for smaller states which have less leverage over large corporations.[42] However it should be noted that many states are now able to levy corporation tax at rates of 20 per cent or more, and to raise serious sums in this way. In principle the share levy should be no more difficult to calculate or levy than corporation tax. Indeed, as noted above, issuing new shares is easier than finding cash.

In principle the social fund approach differs from schemes for employee self-ownership. It avoids the concentration of risk and danger of 'enterprise egoism' that some employee self-ownership schemes can foster. The social funds would encourage good employment practices but would also define and develop a general social interest apart from the particular interests of those who work for a given enterprise.[43] Employees already have a large stake in the enterprise for which they work; the fund network would give them a stake and a say in a wider economy. However, in Banking on Death I envisaged that a proportion – say no more than 10 per cent – of the shares raised by a levy on large companies could go into an enterprise-specific pool. This would give workers a further stake in the success of the companies they were working for while not making this their major source of savings.

The world's most successful example of worker self-ownership is the Basque Mondragon group. It grew from 8 cooperatives in 1960 employing 395 worker members, to 92 cooperatives in 1980 employing over 18,000 worker members. By 2004 the group was Spain's seventh largest corporate entity, with combined assets of 18.6 billion euros and 70,000 worker members. The group produces electrical goods, auto components, machine tools, furniture, is involved in major construction projects, and operates a retail chain. It maintains important research and training programmes. Not only is the group diversified in its activities but its overall growth was facilitated by its own bank, the Caja Laboral Popular, and an Enterprise Board, which guided each new start-up. By 1995 the Caja had 1,380 employees and was a major force in the Basque region. During a formative period finance made a crucial contribution to the group's expansion and coherence and it still furnishes some discipline to each member of the group. In the late 1980s overall leadership of the entire group was vested in a 'Cooperative Congress', representing every constituent cooperative, and an elected Standing Congress Committee.[44] The regional funds might establish, with appropriate autonomy and audit, enterprise boards and finance arms that took some inspiration from the modus operandi of the Mondragon Group.

I have stressed the dangerously 'pro-cyclical' features of current DB pension fund arrangements, encouraging asset booms and aggravating downturns. Since pension expenditures, and the revenues needed to pay for them loom so large in national accounts their precise incidence can be varied in ways that tame the business cycle and counterbalance inflationary or deflationary dangers. When inflation threatens to get out of hand then employers and staff can be encouraged or obliged to increase their cash contributions; when deflation looms then the emphasis can fall on asset levies, so demand will not be diminished. John Maynard Keynes – probably influenced by his Cambridge colleague the 'liberal socialist' James Meade – advocated the raising of contributions for a national social security trust fund in 1940 when the outbreak of war threatened to bring about excessive inflation. In a pamphlet entitled *How to Pay for the War* he advocated a system of 'deferred pay' as a substitute for increasing income tax. In his scheme five per cent of pay would be paid into special accounts controlled by independent social institutions; money from these accounts could be drawn down at a later period to cover health or retirement needs. In Keynes's scheme a postwar capital levy would ensure that there were enough resources to meet all needs when the draw-downs began.[45] Very much in the spirit of Meade and Keynes, Jane D'Arista has proposed a new 'macro-prudential framework. to encompass all pension and mutual funds, furnishing their beneficiaries with insurance, rather than supplying that insurance to the financial institutions.[46]

The Meidner approach included a number of arrangements designed to counterbalance the business cycle, including pre-funding secondary pensions, a national round of wage negotiations and a scheme whereby Swedish companies could stow away tax-free profits in an 'investment fund' during boom periods, and draw them down when times were more difficult. These aspects of the Rehn–Meidner model help to explain why, over the long term, Sweden has been able to combine high levels of welfare and pension provision with low levels of unemployment.

The Shape of the New Pension Regime

In most countries today there is still a basic state pension. In the pension regime I am sketching the basic state pension would be raised until it was 40–50 per cent of median income. This priority should be mainly achieved by means of increased thresholds for the payroll tax, using mainly pay-as-you-go but with some pre-funding. The enhanced basic pension should be paid in full to all citizens (at present many are not entitled to it because of limited contribution records or failure to comply with a means test). The universal secondary pension system would aim to supply 30 per cent of median income, or of their own previous income, up to three times average income, whichever was the higher. The matching contribution method would enable people to raise their entitlement. There would be some variation in retirement income, reflecting different contribution records. As in today's occupational schemes contributions would be calculated as a proportion of income for those in employment. Those who were unemployed, or caring for dependents, would benefit from contributions paid on their behalf from the pension reserve.

A ceiling would prevent the rich from building up extravagant levels of entitlement. The principles used here would resemble those already used to calculate a sliding scale of retirement income according to contributions in the US Social Security system and in the UK SERPS (State Earnings-Related Pension Scheme). In 2004 British financial regulations set an upper limit of £1.5 million on the size of an individual's tax-favoured pension pot. The adoption of the matching contributions principle would also curb excessive relief going to the rich and would ensure that the pension fund system would give the best rewards to those on a broad range of average incomes than to the rich.

It would be possible to use assets raised by the share levy in a number of different ways. They could be wholly devoted to existing public pension provision as an extra layer of provision – say a top-up to existing entitlement under Social Security in the US or the UK's existing State Second Pension and SERPS. In this case all the resources raised by the levy would be handed over to the existing trust funds. However, it could well be better to avoid over-centralization by setting up the previously-suggested network, with a central body channeling the proceeds of the levy to trust funds in every state, province or region, according to their demographic characteristics. This would create a more decentralized pattern of fund management. And since some regions or states are themselves rather large (for example, California, New York) the regional bodies could, if they wish, organize networks of their own so long as each citizen received the same entitlements and opportunities.

Using the levy to reinforce Social Security, and to add an extra layer to it, would build on its present strengths. The value of Social Security entitlements to a thirty-year-old employee on average earnings has been calculated at over $300,000; this is the sum that such a worker would have to pay to an insurance company to acquire such protection. Measures that would restore confidence in the system and increase its generosity would be welcome to its particpants. Furthermore, using the existing systems of public administration would have cost benefits. Since entitlements in existing schemes are already individualized, several features of the regime I have suggested would be easily incorporated. When an individual moved from one state or region to another, then they would carry their entitlement with them. And the various trust funds could be made democratically accountable, with actuarial safeguards for generational equity. This regionally-distributed model would still mean that there would not be one big public trust fund, with the over-accumulation of power this might imply.

In *Banking on Death* I suggested that individuals might have rights in three different funds – based on region, occupation, leisure pursuit, and school or college.[47] All members of a fund – whether beneficiaries or contributors – were to have an equal voice and vote on its policy. However, the audit process would ensure that funds kept to actuarially fair pay-out rates, so that the goal of paying future pensions was not jeopardized by excessive payments in the present. The expertise of universities could be drawn upon to strengthen fund management. The audit process would seek to ensure that pension money was invested in deserving projects and not exposed to undue risk. Basing pension funds on alumni associations, resident groups, occupational groups, sporting clubs and other affinity groups, would help to promote participation and reduce costs. The audit of funds in the network could be undertaken in the US by the revamped regional Federal Reserve banks.

However, it might be that this is needlessly complicated and that all shares raised by the levy would be best channelled to a pension reserve trust fund in each state or province or region. Whatever organizational form was chosen the pension funds should be run by elected officials, staffed by skilled professionals and bound by actuarially fair rules of disbursement. They would be expected to undertake their own research into corporations whose stock they owned and would have an interest in combating tax avoidance since the flow of donated shares would profit. The research conducted by these public trust funds would be made available to all shareholders, since, even after the Sarbanes–Oxley reform of 2002, the mass of shareholders are still at a disadvantage compared to banks. While shareholders would lose by a small dilution of the value of their shares each year they would gain by the appearance of a new and increasingly powerful agency capable of defending shareholder interests (where the latter don't conflict with social responsibility – for example, the struggle to rein in executive compensation).

Pension funds are, of course, a form of capitalist property, albeit a collective one, and would remain so even when reformed and 'socially regulated'. Consequently it would be necessary to monitor their working to check that market forces did not generate new inequalities or sources of social division.

The essential features of the proposed system are the diversity of sources of finance, including the share levy, and the steps taken to foster non-commercial custodianship, social responsibility and democratic accountability. These principles could be worked out in a number of different ways reflecting different institutional legacies and popular understandings. I have also suggested that in the US case, existing public institutions such as the Social Security Administration, the state level trust funds, the regional network of Federal Reserve Banks, and the Pension Benefit Guaranty Corporation, could all be drawn upon to help administer or regulate the new regime. While some of these institutions give representation to elected officials there would certainly be scope for more accountability.

Transitional Measures Towards Responsible Accumulation

In Chapter 5 we saw that the public sector funds have sometimes supported campaigns to improve corporate governance and to promote social responsibility. Responding to pressure from social movements and trade unions, CALPERS, the Californian Public Employee Retirement System, announced in early 2002 that it would review all its investments with the aim of promoting fair employment practices. CALPERS controls $130 billion of investments. It announced that it might withdraw from investments in companies which are implicated in dangerous working conditions and the denial of trade union rights. However, funds which practice SRI now more typically use a strategy of engagement than one of boycott and withdrawal. This approach particularly appeals to trade union-influenced funds. These have themselves secured representation on trustee boards and have discovered the new information and leverage that this can give them even in today's pension regime.[48]

'Engagement' involves direct approaches to management, backed up by the use of 'activism' at AGMs to publicize and penalize bad practice. Funds which benefited from the share levy would naturally own shares in a great variety of concerns and would sometimes be barred from selling those shares. For them this type of engagement – 'voice' rather than 'exit' – makes the best sense, as it begins to do even for today's index-tracking funds. Michael Calabrese has pointed out that the strategy of engagement allows social funds to avoid the predicament of 'having no ownership rights at the companies they most want to change'.[49]

The pension trust funds would, thus, be expected to play an active part as shareholders in promoting good corporate governance and the avoidance of socially or ecologically harmful practices. The policy-holders' stake in any one corporation will be very small and their financial return will not mature for quite a long time. I believe that in these circumstances it will be possible to persuade majorities that social injustice and ecological irresponsibility are not the best way to build healthy enterprises nor to contribute to long term fund value. After all, the generality of citizens may well have to pay for the cost of this irresponsibility and injustice long before they can claim any tiny and notional super-profit it might generate. The social funds could thus seek both to promote responsible accumulation and to offer the generality of citizens a chance to participate in shaping the future of their communities. The boards of the Anglo-Saxon corporation would, in consequence, also need to be made far more accountable to shareholders.[50]

I have suggested that regional funds could be allowed, indeed encouraged, to channel a limited portion of their surplus revenue – say no more than 20 per cent – to meeting local investment needs. Quebec's 'quiet revolution' and the Hydro-Québec project demonstrated the contribution which local pension fund investment could make to regional development.[51] As with Mondragon, the effectiveness of the Quebec solidarity funds no doubt testifies to a pre-existing sense of community, but it also seems to have expressed and reinforced it. Similarly Peter Self has proposed that 'super-annuation funds' should be made available for 'longer-term investments which would yield environmental benefits (such as more durable products or energy savings), or which would make a socially informed use of the many new and disturbing inventions (such as genetic engineering) which would otherwise be left to commercial exploitation'.[52]

Measures encouraging corporate social responsibility should be seen as a complement rather than an alternative to government legislation aimed at corporate abuses, the more so since the new regime would itself require legal backing. There will be bad practices which should simply be outlawed, and other usages which it may be more appropriate to limit. The internal reinforcement of good practice at which the new pension trust funds should aim would have the further advantage that it could help to discourage bad practices in all areas where the enterprise was active as an investor or purchaser, including those outside its home jurisdiction.

My proposal that pension funds should be encouraged to follow 'socially responsible' policies was singled out for criticism in some reviews of *Banking on Death* – notably those in the *Economist*, in the *TLS* (by John Chown), and in the *Guardian* (by Howard Davies, the then-Director of the UK's Financial Services Authority).[53] It was urged that pension contributors would only accept traditional profit-maximizing approaches to investment. But this objection underestimates how discredited such strategies still are in the wake of the late nineties share bubble. And it fails to register the new respectability of SRI.[54] Both the NYSE and the FTSE now both organize SRI indeces. These are early days and the procedures and criteria used in drawing up such lists are still rudimentary. In the future they will be refined and elaborated not abandoned. Indeed some observers believe that the day of the 'universal investor', whose investments are so diversified that they do not properly have 'externalities', has already dawned.[55] The true interests of beneficiaries do not automatically entail benign and progressive policies, but they do offer scope for constructing arguments and campaigns which will methodically target the irresponsible practices that shift cost and risk to the wider community. Such is the complexity of the market system that gains in one area may well lead to off-setting losses in another. But, over time, the incremental logic would be to stimulate social invigilation and to furnish those campaigning against corporate abuses with significant allies within the corporate structure itself.

Any reform of pension funds aimed at making them engines of social self-management should take heed of the experiences of each country and in particular of the different historic form of social conquests. It would be absurd to introduce Anglo-Saxon-style individualized pension plans to a country where they were unknown only to reform towards a more collective model. Paradoxically the global spread of stock markets makes share levies possible and necessary in a widening circle of countries. It also increases the need for robust regulatory institutions, capable of evaluating annual accounts, and, in the case of public utilities, prices and programs of investment. It is usually not difficult to see the ways in which the share levy and the funded approach can be used to strengthen existing systems of pension provision.

Within a decade or two the social funds would become an important force in the corporate world but it would take them half a century before they were approaching a dominant position. Even then this would not be a suppression of capitalism, nor of all the social evils that is has encouraged or permitted – inequality, heedless consumerism, unemployment, hucksterism and noxious social divisions based on status. In the end it is just a single measure whose overall impact would depend on the balance of social forces and the outcome of fundamental battles over the future evolution of society.

The proposed pension fund regime would gradually bring about a restructuring of economic relations in the direction of a sort of 'stakeholder capitalism', with communities and employees having a collective stake in corporate property.[56] There would be much greater equality between citizens, since every citizen would have a significant stake in the property regime. Membership in a fund would carry with it the right to regular information and consultation on the fund's policies. The share levy would, over time, transfer the ownership and control of decisive assets into the hands of working people and the citizens generally. The device would check market-related tendencies towards inequality within its jurisdiction. It would give citizens and workers real leverage over the economic process as a whole, not simply the workings of a given enterprise, as in some schemes of worker self-management. There would be no encouragement to enterprise egoism, and no unhealthy concentration of risk, as in some ESOPs schemes. Employees and citizens would themselves have to address the tensions and trade-offs between current and future interests. They would do so within a framework that did not, as in today's 'financialization' and 'generational economics', reduce future needs to present values, or assume that every arrangement and relationship should be abandoned once a financially superior alternative is sighted. The fact that decisive assets are held by non-commercial funds will allow them to weigh non-commercial considerations and will, at least partially, 'de-commodify' the social entity exercising ownership. Social movements and workforces would have greater scope to influence investment decisions.

The new pension fund regime would not suppress market relations and would still make use of market signals. It would thereby hope to simplify price formation and avoid the difficulties and complexities of non-market price formation and coordination, as in many variants of planned economy or participatory economics. The combination of markets and of a species of share-ownership would still yield decisions, and determine comparative prices, more economically than procedures that require everyone to inform themselves about, and participate in, every decision. The latter is not only cumbersome but can also find it difficult to allocate voting power (since, for example, the workers at a larger enterprise should not always outvote the workers at a smaller one).[57]

The proposed pension fund regime is, in some ways, close to the schemes of 'market socialism' and 'socialization of the market' theorized, respectively, by John Roemer and Diane Elson, and their ideas might be drawn upon to give it greater coherence.[58] Unlike such models, the proposed regime of 'responsible accumulation' aims to address the specific failures and vulnerabilities of 'grey capitalism'. While it addresses some sources of inequality, unemployment, exploitation and alienation it will not remove them all. For example, though it might offer some openings to 'fair trade', it might make little direct impact on international inequality – except to the extent that more egalitarian countries tend to be less mean in their trade and aid policies. Employees in the advanced countries might be persuaded that they should use their new leverage with multi-national corporations to encourage better labor standards. Doing so would help to discourage a business strategy based on driving down labor costs and replace it with one orientated to developing the potentially huge domestic market in such emerging economies as China and India – better labour standards and living conditions are needed to help maintain the momentum of growth in these countries. This is the direction that Japan, South Korea, Taiwan and Singapore have already followed and it furnishes better results than multiplying sweatshops.

The new regime might also prove to be unstable, or transitional to some other, hopefully more equitable and advanced socio-economic regime. At a certain point the remaining structures of capitalism might well need to be replaced or transcended to the extent that they generated new types of inequality, insecurity and alienation. My own guess would be that such a regime would not simply suppress all the institutions of 'financialized' capitalism but would find progressive and democratic uses for some of them in an increasingly non-capitalist context.

While my proposals may seem fairly limited from a radical anti-capitalist perspective, they are likely to be far-reaching enough to provoke stiff resistance. The proposed measures give the majority tangible gains and build on already-functioning institutions. But many already own shares or have membership in a pension scheme and they would need convincing. Share-ownership is heavily concentrated among the rich but people who owned shares worth anything from a few thousand dollars to $150,000 could be made to feel that the measure was harming their interests, even though the implicit tax was a very modest one and even though they would benefit from the new, universal layer of coverage. Existing shareholding wealth would be diluted by less than 1 per cent a year, on average – perhaps just 0.691 per cent in 2004. It could be that some shareholders would appreciate the new institutional pressure for good governance. Chief executives might not welcome the new investors, but the share levy would pose less problems than do corporation taxes, since the levy makes no cash demands on the company – it simply directs the dividends to a different group of shareholders. The measures would not, of course, be welcome to many CEOs or most of the very rich but the important task would be to persuade the great majority of citizens and employees that they were practical, reasonable and responsible.[59]

Members of existing schemes would also need to be re-assured and persuaded of the merits and justice of the share levy. Those in schemes that are not in deficit might be inclined to oppose their employer being levied for a universal system. As noted above, it could be arranged that every genuine pension fund received more than it lost from the share levy. But beyond the arithmetic of cost/benefit as many as possible would need to be won over to the idea that the pensions-and-ageing-society crisis is a major one and needs to be addressed by radical measures. Curiously enough many conservative or neo-liberal commentators do recognize that crisis, though they invariably focus on one aspect – and that the lesser one – of the crisis, namely the affordability of Social Security. As I have argued, the problem should rather be seen more broadly as the overall costs of the ageing society.

In the introduction I cited Paul Krugman's critique of those who 'perceive the issue of an aging society not as it is – a medium-sized issue that can be dealt with through ordinary changes in taxing and spending – but as an immense problem that requires changing everything.'[60] I insisted that the problem was pretty large, but conceded that the US could fail to address it, and try to muddle through, but only at the cost of growing misery and unhappiness.

A more optimistic scenario could be mapped if the Federal government broke with 'business as usual' and moved energetically to sponsor a new pension regime with new resources. If real economic growth was achieved over the next half century the Social Security problem should be rather modest. As the 9/11 panic wears off immigration rates could rise, which would help a bit. If public money was available to back a high-quality network of public nurseries, and if generous support and leave was available for parents of young children, then the birth rate might rise a bit. Public funding and encouragement for an active ageing programme would raise the proportion of sixty and seventy year olds in work. But a 'golden package' like this, with the virtuous circle that it would engender, is unlikely to be assembled by an administration that is unwilling to make corporations do their bit, and unprepared to tackle greed on Wall Street and in the boardrooms.

The share levy and other measures I have discussed robustly address the yawning crisis of pension provision. They could raise large sums at a time when the extra costs of an ageing society, knowledge-based economy, and unstable environment, are likely to be very large. They could also help to subsidize free time and freely-chosen work. There are few alternative proposals which can claim the same. Moreover, the network of social funds would have some ability to invigilate and curb corporate abuse, though only in conjunction with a wider framework of regulation and thanks to pressure from the generality of citizens and social actors. I have striven to show that the interlinked proposals are all based on tendencies or practices already present in today's 'grey capitalism' while avoding the latter's vices. They represent a practical next step rather than a fully worked-out model of an alternative economy.

Notes

1 See the discussion in Peter Diamond, 'Reforming Public Pensions in the US and the UK', *Economic Journal*, vol. 116, February 2006, pp. F94–118, especially F115.

2 Pensions Commission, *A New Pensions Settlement for the Twenty-First Century: the Second Report of the Pensions Commission*, London 2005, pp. 8–18, 129–34, 284–302.

3 Harris Interactive, 'International Retirement Security Survey', AARP Global Aging Program, 21 October 2005. The AARP is the American Association of Retired Persons.

4 Martin Daunton, *Just Taxes: the Politics of Taxation in Britain*, 1914–1979, Cambridge 2002.

5 For a collection focusing on obstacles rather than opportunities see Joel B. Slemrod, ed., *Does Atlas Shrug? The Economic Consequences of Taxing the Rich*, New York 2000; and for a revealing study of the successful campaign to repeal inheritance taxes see by Michael J. Graetz and Ian Shapiro, *Death by a Thousand Cuts: the Fight Over Taxing Inherited Wealth*, Princeton NJ, 2005.

6 See, for example, George R. Zodrow and Peter Mieszkowski, eds, *United States Tax Reform in the Twenty First Century*, Cambridge 2002. It is possible to design a consumption tax that has some progressive features because such taxes usually kick in above a threshold such as $15,000 a year. But by its nature a consumption tax does not aim to tax savings, including reinvested profits, at all, a measure likely to favour the wealthy. To guard against misunderstanding I should make it clear that if one studies closely the US

National Tax Review, or the publications of the UK's Institute of Fiscal Studies, one will come across occasional articles or working papers canvassing more effective taxation of corporations or wealthy individuals and I will cite a few examples below.

7   W. Elliot Brownlow, *Federal Taxation in America*, Cambridge 1996, p. 26.

8   See Steven R. Weisman, *The Great Tax Wars*, New York 2003.

9   The prize was for several aspects of his work. The 'Tobin tax' was designed to curb speculative movements of capital. Note that in the UK there has long been 'stamp duty' on the purchase of shares as well as property. It raises useful revenue and acts as a very mild restraint on speculation. Its presence has not stopped London from thriving as a major financial centre.

10 Rudolf Meidner, *Employee Investment Funds: An Approach to Collective Capital Formation*, London 1978.

11 Joseph A. Pechman, *Federal Tax Policy*, New York 1983, pp. 135–40.

12 Edward N. Wolf, 'Who Are the Rich? A Demographic Profile of High-Income and High-Wealth Americans', in Joel B. Slemrod, ed., *Does Atlas Shrug? The Economic Consequences of Taxing the Rich*, New York 2000, pp. 74–96, p. 90. According to this study the top 1 per cent also, at this time, garnered 22 per cent of proprietory income (i.e. income from ownership of private businesses), 25 per cent of all interest payments and 31 per cent of royalty, rental and trust income. These figures relate to 1992 and wealth concentration has subsequently grown, as we saw in Chapter 4. Another contribution to the collection makes the argument that there is much scope for more progressive taxation. Robert Frank, 'Progressive Taxation and the Incentive Problem', pp. 890–507.

13 United States of America, *Flow of Funds*, 9 March 2006, pp. 13, 14.

14 Ibid.

15 If the return was 4.5 per cent then the eventual total would be $10.2 trillion by 2033. I have chosen 5 per cent bearing in mind that Martin Feldstein, the most intellectually formidable advocate of privatizing Social Security, usually assumes much higher rates of return (either 7 per cent or 9 per cent). For refinements to the levy scheme, see Robin Blackburn, 'The Great Pension Gap', *Challenge: The Magazine of Economic Affairs*, published by M. E.Sharpe, July–August 2003, pp. 91–112 and for the UK in 'How to Rescue a Failing Pension System: The British Case', *New Political Economy*, December 2004 and 'How to Plug the Gap', Catalyst-Forum website, June 2005.

16 John Eatwell, 'The Anatomy of the Pensions "Crisis" and Three Fallacies on Pensions.', Judge Institute Working Paper, Cambridge University, posted 5 February 2003, pp. 13–14.

17 Ibid.

18 Andrew Glyn, *Capitalism Unleashed: Finance, Globalization, Welfare*, Oxford 2006, pp. 160–1.

19 Ibid., p. 161.

20 Ibid., p. 176.

21 The surfeit and waste produced by the 'self-consuming' of the well-off, and sometimes mimicked by those not so well off, is evoked by Richard Sennett,

The New Culture of Capitalism, pp. 138–57.

22 Nicholas Barr, *The Welfare State as Piggy Bank*, Oxford 2002, pp. 96–101. He also points out that any measure that pays down debt handed to successor generations makes it easier to pay future pensions.

23 David Wessell, 'US Rich Are Still Getting Richer', *Wall Street Journal*, 2 March 2006.

24 I have already cited Wolff's calculation that the top 1 per cent of households received a half of all dividends and capital gains in 1992 (Wolff, 'Who Are the Rich', in Slemrod, *Does Atlas Shrug?*, p. 90.) Household panel data contained in 'Recent Changes in U.S. Family Finances', *The Federal Reserve Bulletin*, February 2006, found that the poorest 25 per cent of households had median financial assets of just $1,400, the next 25 per cent had median financial assets of $11,200, the next 25 per cent median financial assets of $56,500, and the next richest 15 per cent median financial assets of $214,800. The richest 10 per cent had median financial assets of $753,500. The latter's median holding of retirement funds was $212,400, of pooled investment funds $148,100, of stocks $129,900 and of bonds $95,900. The poorest 75 per cent of households had a nil median holding of bonds and very modest holdings of other investment vehicles (p. A13). Note that, quite apart from disclosure problems generated by the tax shyness of the rich, panel data and 'median' figures are not good at pinpointing the holdings of the very wealthy.

25 Barry Eichengreen, 'The Capital Levy in Theory and Practice', in Rudiger Dornbusch and Mario Draghi, eds, *Public Debt Management*, Cambridge 1990, pp. 191–220.

26 US Bureau of Labor Statistics, *Quarterly Census of Employment and Wages*, February 2005.

27 Pensions Commission, *A New Pension Settlement for the Twenty-First Century: The Second report of the Pensions Commission*, London 2005, pp. 7–8, 353–404. See also Pensions Commission, *Implementing an Integrated Package of Pension Reforms: The Final Report of the Pensions Commission*, London 2006, pp. 16–39.

28 He is also the author of *Just Capital*, London 2002, a study of contemporary capitalism that urges a mild version of the 'stakeholder' philosophy.

29 John Bogle, *The Battle for the Soul of Capitalism*, pp. 191–240; Levitt, *Take on the Street*, Nomi Prins, *Other People's Money*, pp. 265–97; Joseph Stiglitz, *The Roaring Nineties*, pp. 281–319.

30 Bogle, *The Battle for the Soul of Capitalism*, pp. 191–2.

31 Wal-Mart is seeking to develop a finance arm using the ILC (Industrial Loan Corporation) structure.

32 Scholes and Wolfson, *Taxes and Business Strategy*, pp. 3–4.

33 Joshua Chaffin, 'Mystery Witness Lifts the Lid on US Tax Dodgers', *Financial Times*, 22 October 2003; David Cay Johnston, 'Crackdown on Tax Cheats Not Working, Panel Says', *New York Times*, 20 October 2003.

34 Cassel Bryan-Low and Glen Simpson, 'KPMG Has Win in Tax-Shelter Case', *Wall Street Journal*, 17 October 2003.

35 Anna Fifield, 'S Korean Tax Haven Blow to Hit Investors', *Financial Times*, 6
    March 2006.
36 See Gordon Clark, *Pension Fund Capitalism*, London 2000, pp. 210–34, and
    Archon Fong, Tessa Hebb and Joel Rogers, eds, *Working Capital: the Power of
    Labor's Pensions*, Ithaca NY, 2001.
37 'Shareholder Democracy: Battling for Corporate America', *Economist*, 11
    March 2006.
38 Will Hutton, 'UK For Sale: One Careless Owner', *Observer*, 12 February,
    2006.
39 'WorldCom's Revenge', *Economist*, 30 August 2003.
40 Thomas R. Michl and Duncan Foley, 'Social Security in a Classical Growth
    Model', CEPA Working Paper Series II, Economic Policy Analysis, Work-
    ing Paper No. 11, September 2001.
41 Jonas Pontusson on 'Sweden: the People's Home in Danger', in Perry Anderson
    and Patrick Camiller, eds, *Mapping the Left in Western Europe*, London 1994.
42 I have outlined how the share levy could be introduced by the EU in
    'Capital and Social Europe', *New Left Review*, no. 34, July–August 2005, pp.
    87–114.
43 Following Žižek, who adopted the term from Karatani, I would suggest that the
    inter-relationshiop of the social fund and the enterprise could held to establish a
    'parallax view'. See Slavoj Žižek, 'The Parallax View', *New Left Review*, 29, July–
    August 2004, and K. Karatani, *Transcritique: Kant and Marx*, Cambridge 2003.
44 See Robert Oakeshott, *Jobs and Fairness: the Logic and Experience of Employee
    Ownership*, Norwich 2000, pp. 448–93 and the website of the Mondragon
    Cooperative Corporation.
45 John Maynard Keynes, 'How to Pay for the War', *Collected Writings*, Vol. IX,
    London 1972.
46 Jane D'Arista, 'Including Pension Funds in the Macro-Prudential Frame-
    work', paper presented at the conference on 'Pension Fund Capitalism and
    the Crisis of Old Age Security', CEPA, New School for Social Research,
    September 2004.
47 Blackburn, *Banking on Death*, pp. 465–539.
48 See Archon Fong, Tessa Hebb and Joel Rogers, eds, *Working Capital: the
    Power of Labor's Pensions*, Ithaca NY, 2001.
49 Michael Calabrese, 'Building on Success: Labor-Friendly Investment Ve-
    hicles and the Power of Private Equity', in Fong, *Working Capital*, pp. 93–
    127, p. 120.
50 Some of the problems here are addressed by William Greider, 'The New
    Colossus', *Nation*, 15 February 2005.
51 Kevin Park, 'Late Nationalism: the Case of Quebec', *New Left Review*, no.
    11, September–October 2001, pp. 35–54.
52 Peter Self, *Rolling Back the Market: Economic Dogma and Political Choice*,
    Basingstoke 2000.
53 'Matters of Life And Death', *Economist*, 30 August 2002; John Chown, 'Live
    Long, Work Long', *TLS*, 23 August 2003; Howard Davies, 'Cracking the
    Nest Egg', *Guardian*, 24 August 2003.

54 For a guide to SRI by an established practitioner see Amy Domini, *Socially-Responsible Investment*, Chicago 2001.
55 See James Hawley and Andrew Williams, 'The Emergence of Universal Owners', *Challenge*, vol. 43, no. 4, July–August 2000, pp. 43–61. Also the writings of the 'share activist', Robert Monks, *The New Global Investors*, Oxford 2001.
56 For a rather similar approach see Gar Alperowitz, *America Beyond Capitalism*, New York 2004.
57 I explore some of these problems in 'Fin de Siècle', *New Left Review*, no. 185, January–February 1991; also published in Robin Blackburn, ed., *After the Fall: the Failure of Communism and the Future of Socialism*, London 1992.
58 See John Roemer, *The Future of Socialism*, New York 1994 and Diane Elson, 'Socializing the Market', *New Left Review*, ser. 1, no. 172, November–December 1988.
59 No doubt attempts would be made in the United States to obtain a ruling from the Supreme Court declaring the share levy unconstitutional; on the other hand, as noted in Chapter 3, Chapter 11 courts have actually required companies to issue shares to the PBGC.
60 Paul Krugman, 'America's Senior Moment', *New York Review of Books*, 15 March 2005.

Epilogue:
Living in the Presence of Our Future Selves

In the Introduction and first chapter I wrote about the broader challenge of the ageing society and the need to acknowledge its likely costs. Instead of investing in the prospect of a productive 'third age' in which the over-65s would be able to make a new contribution to the wider society, the partisans of pension reform were instead relying on financial coercion' and arousing false hopes in the capacity of the commercial sector. I urged that the 'divided' pension regime character- istic of the United States and Britain was not a good model for other countries and that pension 'reform' in Europe now meant that they, too, were heading for a serious shortfall in provision of retirement income in coming decades. In subsequent chapters I have focused on the pitfalls of commercial pension funding and provision, and of the financialized world of which pensions are increasingly a part. Chapters 3, 4 and 5 set out just how inefficient, costly and insecure the commercial manage- ment of pension funds has been in the United States and Britain. They also showed that the richest tenth of the population had garnered the lion's share – fully one half – of the tax relief offered as an incentive to pension saving.

In Chapter 6 I argued that public-pension systems using pay-as-you-go finance had an indispensable role to play in meeting future retirement needs because they were very cost-effective. But it would not be wise to rely on these systems alone for all retirement income support. Instead, in the last chapter, I sketched ways to plug a gap in pension provision, using a share levy on all corporations to set up a regional network of social founds. The funding network would furnish second pensions to every- one. They would also give a voice to all – from young adults to the truly aged. Everyone would have a vote on the membership of the trust-fund boards and issues of general investment policy could be put to a general vote. To link the paying of second pensions to the setting up of social funds which give a voice to all citizens may seem an odd proceeding. Yet there is a definite logic here. The trust-fund boards would not decide on the basic criteria for distributing pensions, since this would be a respon- sibility of national policy. But they would be able to monitor the working of the major economic enterprises, ensuring that they were good employers and good citizens. By stages the new regime would not only de-commodify pension provision but also stabilize and de-commodify a part of the apparatus of production and exchange.

The combination of ageing costs, a voracious consumer capitalism, the probability of ecological shocks, and the devices of financial engineering, is highly unstable. The future outlook is bleak, with mounting inequality, new dangers of poverty, continual cuts in social outlays, short-termism, amnesia and a pervasive discounting of the future. Every individual and every institution is encouraged to use financial techniques to carry out a continuous assessment of whether or not they are maximizing their returns. As the accountants' phrase has it they must, at regular intervals, 'mark to market' all their assets and liabilities. Taking their cue from current prices and performance they must be prepared to jettison under-performing assets or operations in favour of more promising arrangements. Contracts with employees, suppliers and customers must be open to continual renegotiation. In such a view the institution or enterprise has no past. And so far as possible its future should be bound up in immediately visible opportunities. In the field of pension provision the result is the 'generational arbitrage' which follows if each cohort is isolated from its predecessors and insists that risk-pooling should always be within — and never between — generations.

This is why the young are saddled with loans to pay for their own education, the elderly are forced to subsist upon the fruits of their own savings and those in-between are plunged into insecurity. This vision is the reductive ideology of a financial system blind to solidarity between generations and dedicated to the delusion that present prices truly reflect what we owe the past or what we might hope for from the future. It is also self-destructive. Identity and equity are lost in a completely fungible world where everyone exits as soon as an unwelcome cost shows up. While we do not need corporations with souls, it does help if corporate leaders see their enterprises as more than a random bundle of assets and possibilities. Financialization further concedes sovereign rights to the hedge funds and derivative markets, making rigorous regulation or accounting almost impossible. Even profit soon becomes notional and unprovable in such a world.[1]

Progressive liberal and left-wing thought resists these trends but sometimes even some of its most eminent proponents remain attached to what might be called the 'myth of the homogeneous present'. We are urged to entrust all social provision to the annual budget, to ignore capitalist control of the surplus, and to discard the artificial convention of pre-funding future obligations and liabilities. This can harden into a myth of a homogeneous and unending present.

But what is valued in public-pension systems is their universal character, their promise to honour past contributions and the generational interdependence that they embody. Payroll taxes have an indispensable part to play in such public systems but in practice few PAYGO regimes have entirely dispensed with operational reserves and pre-funding. The ups and downs of the trade cycle and the disparate size of age cohorts of the population mean that a degree of pre-funding is needed to smooth the returns to succeeding groups of the population. The most celebrated, or bemoaned, example of the latter is the anticipated passage of the famous baby-boomers into retirement around the years 2010–30. But the rise in longevity and the drop in the birth rate in all countries means that payroll taxes would have to rise continually if they were to supply the same level of benefit to a rising proportion of the population over sixty-five. I have earlier suggested that it will be inconvenient, regressive or counter-productive to put all the weight of pension provision on payroll taxes, though they are bound to remain the mainstay of public provision. I have urged that they should be supplemented by some pre-funded provision and that such pre-funding is not illusory, as is maintained by the proponents of the homogenous future-present.

My contention is that capitalism is a social system where a chunk of future output is mortgaged to the owners of capital and that this produces a complex layering of claims on future output. Some of those claims will be from capitalists and some from workers, and both social groups will spend/consume some of their entitlement and save/invest other portions. The system of pre-funding I have proposed could be seen as a way in which the network of social trust funds gradually accumulates claims to the future social surplus at the expense of capitalists and rentiers. For a considerable period the network might save/invest all or most receipts from their asset holdings. But as specific needs for extra funding present themselves the network could be permitted to devote income to meeting entitlements, whether to retirement income support, medical care or educational provision. In making pension disbursements the network should be subject to actuarial principles that aim to treat each successive generation fairly, moderating and limiting any variance in the overall relationship between average wages and average pensions. Another constraint on disbursements would be the need not to 'crowd out' necessary investment in social infrastructure and sustainable means of production.

Until very recently the institutions of capitalism represented a particular way of reconciling present and future. Riven by class and neglectful of the planet's fragility, they nevertheless crudely ensured the development of the apparatus of production. I have urged that the techniques of hyper-capitalist financialization represent a flattening or reduction of the perspectives of capitalist accumulation. The model of 'responsible accumulation' represented by the social fund networks would aim to restore a sense of what is owed to the future and to the past. In appropriating the congealed claims on the future represented by private ownership of the means of production it would not seek in a spendthrift manner to devote them all to present needs. Instead it would be sensitive to a democracy of the generations, which would bequeath possibilities to our children and grandchildren that were at least as good as, and hopefully better than, those we currently enjoy ourselves.

I have concentrated on the way in which the specific problem of ageing in the new life course might be addressed rather than a host of other problems. The financing method I have explored has the considerable advantage of taking some of the strain off current tax and future revenues, leaving them potentially more available for other programs. While the share levy is a good match for pension obligations it could not do much to help pressing current needs. The fact that the shares are held for a considerable time is essential to the overall working of the scheme.

Recently Bruce Ackerman has proposed that substantial capital sums – perhaps $80,000 – should be bestowed on every individual once they reach 18 or 21 years of age and thereafter leaving them great latitude in how it should be used. He proposes that this should be paid for by a 2 per cent tax on wealth above a threshold, say $230,000.[2] This would be an egalitarian measure and would lift most of the burden of debt from the young. As I pointed out in the first chapter, Roberto Mangabeira Unger favours a similar scheme but would restrict the purposes on which the grant could be spent, confining it to education, house purchase, starting a business or some other substantial and relatively permanent investment.[3] Whatever the details there is a strong case for endowing each individual with an educational allowance, in addition to existing provision. A wealth tax would furnish one way of paying for such a programme. Alternatively a betterment levy, or tax on increases in the value of commercial land, could supply some of the needed funds. At present the owners of such property enjoy a windfall whenever an increase in general productivity, or in public improvements, makes their holdings more valuable. It would be more appropriate to ensure that such bonuses accrue to the educational system which will have helped to nourish them.

It is easy to slip into the vocabulary of exchange when addressing relations between the generations, either affirming or denying a generational contract. But we should be careful not to conceive of this relationship either, on the one hand, as a simple economic transaction or, on the other, a pure gift relationship. We owe something essential to our parents but it is not explained by the language of contract, which implies either too little or too much. Too little since it relates to our very identity – there can be no equality between these contracting parties. Too much since, after all, we must each live our own lives – the contract theory could, if we were not careful, lead to limitless obligation, patriarchy or matriarchy. I suggest that we don't want our parents to become our dependents, since that would diminish us as well as them. If it is a purely physical frailty, that is quite enough of a problem without compounding it by economic dependence. On the other hand there is merit in Unger's proposal, also cited in the first chapter, that everyone should undertake some caring role, whether in relation to the elderly or young children.[4]

I have vigorously repudiated what Veblen called the invasion of everyday life by 'business principles', and many of the developments I have cited vividly illustrate what he termed the 'natural decay of business enterprise', its failure to constitute a civilisation.[5] But in his otherwise fine polemic he was at least half-wrong to bemoan the fact that money was substituting for relations between family members. The pension claimed as a right by the citizen allows independence and dignity to the parent and to their children alike. Veblen was half-right because this is nothing to do with a business deal, but half-wrong because the money-form allows for a looser bond than that between individual giver and receiver.[6]

Faced with the catastrophes of climate change, and the need to temper their ravages, it will be necessary to impose heavy carbon taxes and to rein in consumption, sometimes in quite imperious ways. This will only be acceptable to the public if the rich are also obliged to tighten their belts. The sharp polarization of wealth in recent times is beginning to prompt arguments for progressive taxation.[7] While there is certainly scope for raising tax rates on high incomes, the rich have ways of avoiding conventional incomes taxes. Meidner's share levy is a direct and simple tool for promoting economic equality and for fostering a degree of social control over corporate power (without, of course, removing the case for better regulation too). If some of the larger developed or developing states succeed in curbing corporate power in this way they will also help to establish new global norms which can benefit smaller and less well-placed states. The share levy itself is a device which, as noted in the last chapter, could be used gradually to oblige multi-national corporations in all parts of the world to confer ownership on local communities and to forster local training and talent. While legislation enacted by national states would be required to set up such processes, they would themselves eventually operate at regional and global level. Social funds at a regional level could be established in ways that redress the exclusion of large sections of the population from basic economic decision-making.[8]

It is now a long time since governments have dared to tackle the corporations and ask whether their owners might be obliged to contribute more to the wider society, without which their own profits would be impossible. I believe that Meidner's attempt to safeguard the 'Swedish home' is the most far-sighted attempt to think through the types of 'economic democracy' that are needed to guarantee generous social outlays and to restore a degree of social control to an accummulation process now gripped by a heedless and destructive consumerism which is incapable of surmounting the stress, debt and inequality which it has itself created.

Without a more generalized awareness of the challenges facing humanity radical solutions will not command the overwhelming support they need. The already-alarming evidence of global warming and the havoc it will cause may well help to bring about in the twenty-first century that 'great compression', triggered by war, which was witnessed in the middle decades of the twentieth. But the need to confront the costs of the ageing and learning societies will also supply necessary elements of this new awareness. If our civilization does confront the spectre of destruction then social funds would have a double role in both re-distributing wealth and furnishing an extra vehicle or channel of social representation and control.

Some critics of *Banking on Death* complained that the expropriation it proposed – however gradual – would arouse the bitter enmity of all shareholders and that this would doom the proposal.[9] This is certainly a serious consideration and it received some attention in the last chapter. The objection acknowledges that steady and consistent implementation of the share levy would be effective – otherwise there would be no reason to fear it. The conclusion must surely be that care should be taken to extend support for, and understanding of, the needed measure – and not at all that less effective measures are desirable because the very wealthy would be happy with them.

Because the novel element in my package is the social fund it might seem that I have illusions that they would be able by themselves to transform the large corporations. I do urge that the social funds should selectively seek to steer the corporations in which they have a stake towards greater social responsibility. But I readily concede that this is only one – and not necessarily the most effective – of the ways in which to re-shape the functioning of corporations. Legislation, regulation and invigilation by social movements and trade unions also have a crucial part to play. And the corporate form itself may well need to be transformed through such interventions.

In *The Importance of Disappointment* (1998) Ian Craib, the social and psychoanalytical writer, observed: 'In our everyday lives, we are simply not aware of the structures of ownership and control of industry and finance capital, of the ways in which decisions are made, of underlying tendencies in the markets which push people into these decisions; we cannot see any underlying pattern. If however we give up the idea of such a social structure lying out there somewhere, it is like letting go of a proffered lifebelt in a strong flowing river, leaving us only to be carried along by the current. The same is true in our personal lives; we need to hold onto some idea of ourselves as maintaining some consistency beneath the multitude of things we do, that happen to us, that we experience, or our world will feel as if it is collapsing.'[10] In words that have lost none of their timeliness he also wrote: 'We are aware of the immensity of the risks of being in such a huge system, in effect a system of global interconnections; if the system is global then the disasters – ecological, military and economic – can be global too.' Craib concluded that the challenge was to re-embed social institutions, and find a connection and balance between our fragmented social identities, the cycle of nature and the life cycle.

The approach I have sketched aims to identify strivings in this direction. As yet there are only random points of contact between youth protests, anti-globalisation movements, trade unions, pensioner movements, indigenous peoples' movements, advocates of SRI, and defenders of welfare and social provision. Yet as Ian Craib observed we are all being borne down the torrent together and can work on the lifebelt – even lifeboat – idea together.

Notes

1 Many relevant examples are cited in Randy Martin, *Financialization of Daily Life*, Philadelphia PA, 2002. See also Arlie Russell Hochschild, *The Commercialization of Intimate Life*, Berkeley 2003. Reasons to believe that financialization promotes an intertemporal dimension of dispossession are explored in Robin Blackburn, 'Finance and the Fourth Dimension,' *New Left Review*, no. 39, May–June 2006, pp. 39–72.

2 See Ackerman's contributions to Eric Olin Wright, ed., *Redesigning Distribution: Basic Income and Stakeholder Grants as Cornerstones for an Egalitarian Capitalism*, London 2005, pp. 43–67, 209–16.

3 Roberto Mangabeira Unger, *What Should the Left Propose?*, pp. 80–1, 159–60.

4 Ibid., pp. 94–5

5 Veblen, *The Theory of Business Enterprise*, pp. 177–90.

6 And we should see such a device as the modern equivalent of institutions which have preserved the strength of the elders of the tribe in other societies. Thus amongst the !Kung of South West Africa the widow is allotted a portion of the game killed with the aid of her husband's spear.

7 Recently two powerfully argued books have appeared developing the case for greater economic equality. See Richard Layard, *Happiness*, London 2005 and Andrew Glyn, *Capitalism Unleashed*, Oxford 2006. Researchers at the UK's Tyndall Centre, UMIST, have urged that every individual should have an annual carbon ration, with the possibility to sell and buy unused portions. While there are modestly redistributive versions of this proposal so far as individuals are concerned this is not the case for corporations. A combination of a tax on corporate fossil fuel consumption and the share levy could be an effective complement to carbon rationing. (see Tyndall Centre on Climate Change, 'Domestic Tradable Quotes', Technical Report, no. 39, December 2005). Carbon rationing is semi-egalitarian because, at least in its progressive versions, it obliges the rich who wish to exceed their quota to pay those poorer citizens who have a ration to spare. But it leaves the rich with a more visibly greedy lifestyle, and has difficulty rationing corporations, and it is these circumstances which recommend the share levy as a complementary measure.

8 And to this extent would respond to some of the criteria for global justice urged by Nancy Fraser in 'Reframing Justice in a Globalised World', *New Left Review*, no. 36, November–December 2005.

9 This includes both Göran Therborn's very generous consideration of *Banking on Death* in *New Left Review*, no. 22, July–August 2003, pp. 133–42, and Doug Henwood's in my view excessively stringent objections in his paper, 'Pension Fund Socialism: The Illusion That Just Won't Die', presented at the Conference on Pension Fund Capitalism at the New School for Social Research, September 2004.

10 Ian Craib, *The Importance of Disappointment*, London 1998, p.94.

Afterword:
Social Protection after Globalization:
Proposal for a Global Pension

The universal, publicly financed old-age pension has been a popular and effective means for reducing poverty and extending social citizenship in all developed states. In the age of globalization it is right that this tried and tested device for protecting the livelihood of the elderly should be installed at a global level, by means of a pension paid at a modest rate to all older persons on the planet, to be financed by a very modest tax on global financial transactions and corporate wealth.[1]

In the first instance the global old-age pension could be set at $1 a day, bearing in mind that even this small sum would help to lift hundreds of millions of the aged out of poverty in every part of the globe. Poverty is still strongly associated with old age, and especially with gender and old age.

State pension schemes greatly help to limit old-age poverty in the developed world, but have not abolished it. In the developing countries pension arrangements reach only a fifth of the population, and are often very modest anyway. The *UN World Economic and Social Survey 2007: Development in an Ageing World* explains:

> 80 per cent of the world's population do not have sufficient protection in old age to enable them to face health, disability and income risks . . . In developing countries alone, about 342 million older persons currently lack adequate income security. That number would rise to 1.2 billion by 2050, if the coverage of current mechanisms designed to provide old age income security is not expanded. The demographic transition poses an enormous challenge . . . For the unprotected the notion of retirement does not exist; they must continue to rely on their work, which is a greater challenge for those in advanced age (80 years or over). To survive, older persons also count on the support of the family and the community, which, if also resource-constrained, may not be able to offer solid social insurance. In this regard, older persons who are single, widowed or childless (particularly women) face an even higher risk of destitution.[2]

Poverty and inequality are so great in today's world that quite limited remedial measures can have a large impact. There are 2.5 billion people living on less than $2 a day, with a probable majority of the elderly falling within this category. The poorest tenth of the world population receives only 0.7 per cent of global income; meanwhile, the richest 10 per cent commands 54 per cent of global income. In this 'champagne glass' world, the well-off sip at the glass's brimming bowl while the impoverished or struggling remainder supply the slender stem. In such conditions, $1 a day is less than a rounding error to the wealthy, yet would be a lifeline to the global aged poor.[3]

The link between pension entitlements and formal employment is bad for women and bad for all those outside formal employment. Because women live a few years longer than men, the majority of the elderly are women, and because women's unpaid labour in the home does not count as a contribution to all private, and most public, pension systems, over three-quarters of the elderly poor are female. Moreover the older woman's work of caring for other family members is not just a question of the past but continues in the present as she cares for her spouse, her grandchildren and the sick.[4] In countries afflicted by HIV/AIDS older women are essential to family survival as they take on their children's parenting role. Over 60 per cent of orphans in South Africa and Zimbabwe, and 50 per cent of orphans in Botswana, Malawi and Tanzania, live with their grandparents.[5] If a reliable way could be found to channel $30 a month, or $90 a quarter, to the aged in the developing countries this would not only massively reduce poverty but would put resources in the hands of those who could make good use of them.

Today women comprise 55 per cent of those aged 60 and over worldwide, 65 per cent of those aged 60 plus in North America and 70 per cent of those aged 60 plus in Europe. Worldwide, women comprised 63.5 per cent of those aged 80 and above in 2005, a figure that is expected to drop slightly to 61.4 per cent by 2050.

The frail and vulnerable 'old old' are the most rapidly growing age cohort in all parts of the world. There were 88 million persons aged 80 and above worldwide in 2005, a figure that is projected to rise to 402 million by 2050 according to the UN Population Division mid-range projections. Already in 2040 there will be 98 million persons aged 80 plus in China, 47 million in India and 13 million in Brazil.

The forecast absolute numbers of the old have the credibility that they concern people already born. They could only prove false if there is some large-scale rise in the death rate, due to epidemics or other catastrophes, which would be very much against a well-established trend. But the relative size of the older population could be prevented from rising so quickly if there were a dramatic rise in the birth rate. In most advanced countries the birth rate has dropped well below the replacement rate, which is an average of roughly 2.1 children per woman. In Europe the birth rate has dropped to between 1.2 and 1.8 children per woman, with 30 per cent of women having no children and many limiting themselves to one. This overall trend is well established throughout the developed world and is now evident in the developing world as well. Because the decline became steep three or four decades ago, its consequences will be with us for a long time. While both increased longevity and a lowered birth rate contribute to the ageing of populations, if the latter drops more heavily than the former rises, the population shrinks.

The Japanese birth rate has dropped to an average of only 1.3 children for each woman in her childbearing years. For the first time Japan's population actually dropped in 2005, by a few thousand, and between 2005 and 2030 it is set to fall from 127 million to 100 million.[6] By mid-century, fifty states will have populations lower than they were in 2000 and the total world population could well be declining by the last decades of the century. If shrinking populations are combined with other measures to ease the pressure of population on resources, and to reduce emissions of greenhouse gases, it could well be very positive. Nevertheless, the likely costs of an ageing society will still have to be met and these will be high.

Formal retirement income schemes cover fewer than 15 per cent of the world's households. Even states like India and Chile, with growing economies and considerable administrative capacity, fail to deliver basic pensions. Chile's pension system has been held up as a model yet leaves 40 per cent of the population entirely uncovered, and furnishes weak coverage to another 40 per cent. India's old-age pension is means tested and amounts to only $2 *a month* for those able to claim it.[7] While India's poor urban-dwellers are not poor enough to claim, its poor rural population finds it too costly to do so. (A 'pension walla' may collect the pittance but will charge a heavy commission.)

As populations age further, this places great strain on the elder care arrangements in family and kinship networks.[8] At the present time in the developing world, 75 per cent of older people still live together with their children and grandchildren; this contrasts with the developed countries where 73 per cent of the elderly live on their own. However, in all regions the number of the elderly living either on their own or only with their spouse is rising.[9] Older people living on their own are at most risk of poverty, especially where there is little or no pension provision. But where the larger family unit is poor, rising numbers of the dependent elderly aggravate poverty. Of course live-in elder persons can help with childcare and other tasks, but if they are entirely without income this can be a factor nudging a family below the poverty line. Even a very modest pension would help to alleviate this uncomfortable tension. The global pension should suit both residential patterns and strengthen the ability of families to confront their problems, whether encompassing co-residence or not.

At present most of the official reports relating to 'old age' in the more developed OECD countries put those aged 65 years and above in this category, while the global statistics presented by the UN Population Division define the old as those aged 60 and over. Because life expectancy is lower in the less developed regions, it might well be appropriate to pay the proposed global pension to those aged 60 and over, while raising the qualifying age to 65 and over in the OECD states. (Alternatively, one might use each country's pension age as the qualifying age – or calibrate that age to local life expectancy in some way – but these more complex approaches will not be attempted here.)

At the suggested qualifying ages – 65 for the OECD, 60 elsewhere – there are some 560 million men and women who are in the older category today. The cost of introducing a global pension of $1 a day in the next few years would be around $205 billion a year – one-fifth of the projected cost to the US of the Iraq War, or one-half of the annual US military budget prior to the Iraq invasion. The cost will double by around 2030, however, and treble by mid-century: ageing is going to climb steeply in coming decades because of rising longevity and a falling birth rate. These trends are strongest in the rich countries and most rapidly developing states, but they are not confined to these regions. Just as urbanization occurs with or without economic development, so does ageing of the population. While the former process is leading to 'a planet of slums',[10] the latter is making for a global blight of destitution in old age.

By 2050 the UN Population Division expects there to be 2 billion persons aged 60 or over worldwide, with 1.6 billion of these in the less developed countries. An ageing demographic is most marked in Europe and Asia but it is advancing elsewhere too. Africa had only 48 million persons aged 60 and over, comprising 5.2 per cent of the total population, in 2005; but by 2050 the size of this older group in Africa is set to quadruple to reach 207 million, comprising 10.3 per cent of total population. By 2050 Africa is expected to have more older persons than Latin America and the Caribbean (with 187 million aged 60 and over), and nearly as many as Europe (with 229 million of that age). By 2050 Asia, a category that includes India and China, is expected to have no less than 1,249 million older persons, comprising 24 per cent of the population.[11] The large Asian states will achieve a degree of prosperity long before this but they will still need to find ways of meeting the costs of an ageing society and ensuring that the elderly do not get left behind. The global pension could help to identify a shared worldwide problem, and manageable and cooperative ways of meeting it.

It is often claimed that the ageing of the population can be offset by immigration. The projections I have quoted assume the continuation of current trends in migration. While migration flows can mitigate the ageing effect on a country-by-country basis, they cannot, of course, reduce the ageing of the global population. Indeed, in so far as the migratory flow is from more 'youthful' populations to regions where the birth rate is much lower, and life expectancy longer, it is likely that migrants will adopt the demographic patterns of their hosts, a process that will itself increase ageing effects in the global population.

There are very few countries in the world which have arrangements adequate to the rising future need for the care and support of the elderly. In the developing world and poor countries the aged are often sunk in absolute or extreme poverty, while in the richer countries they suffer relative poverty. As aged populations double or treble both these problems will grow. In a recent critical examination of official projections, I give reasons to believe that both the US and EU are on course to a shortfall in resources dedicated to these purposes of around 4 per cent of GDP by 2035.[12] In continental Europe per capita public pensions are to be heavily slashed – roughly cut in half. In the US and UK occupational pension schemes have lost much value or are under threat, and individual schemes have poor coverage and are inefficient. Commercial suppliers of private pensions spend heavily on marketing, customization and salaries, and many exploit the tempting information gaps between knowledgeable provider and bemused customer. Even though favoured by lavish tax concessions, the financial services industry has failed to furnish adequate pension coverage to those on low and medium incomes. If private financing of pensions fails so many in the rich countries, because of cost ratios and information asymmetry, it will be even less appropriate in developing countries.[13]

The global pension I propose would be a universal social insurance scheme, not an aid programme. It would channel financial resources directly to the elderly in communities – whether rich or poor, urban or rural. The costs of administration would, so far as possible, be spent in those communities. It would be a non-means-tested as well as a non-contributory 'social pension', as has been recommended by the NGO, Help the Aged International. Requiring pension recipients to undergo a means test is demeaning and discourages the poor from saving. It can easily stigmatize the elderly, especially older women. The tax system could claw back some of the money paid to the better off while the really wealthy may pass up the $1 a day.[14]

Anthropologists have identified an interesting characteristic of village support networks in parts of West Africa: the young men of the village are encouraged to constitute work teams to help all villagers to carry out urgent tasks at difficult moments of the planting and harvesting cycle. The anthropologist is able to work out that this help is far more important to some – such as older widows – than to others, but this differential need is not rendered visible in a way that would highlight neediness or compromise dignity. The more successful welfare states, as we know, have also practised universalism in the interests of broadening support and maintaining respect for the recipient, who is not singled out as an object of charity.[15]

A cheque for $90 a quarter would not banish old-age poverty in the advanced countries, but it would reduce it a little. It would be welcomed by many of the elderly, making a modest but useful contribution to their straitened budgets. In richer countries there are still stubborn pockets of poverty among the aged – especially among older women. In the US as many as 45.5 per cent of older women living alone have incomes that are less than 50 per cent of median income. In Sweden, one of the world's most advanced welfare states, the figure is 16.5 per cent, whereas in the rest of the EU states the figure for this index of old-age poverty ranges between the Swedish and the US level.[16] As programmed entitlement cuts are made to European pensions, poverty rates will soar. In the United States, President Bush's plan to weaken Social Security was defeated, but already there is talk of 'saving' the programme by means of future benefit reduction. A campaign for the global pension would draw attention to old-age poverty and encourage all governments, according to their means, to do more to combat it.

Worrying as the economic outlook is for the elderly in most of the

OECD countries, the situation is, of course, worse in much of the former Soviet Union, and worse still in many parts of Asia, Africa and Latin America, where the aged in the countryside and the slums often have no coverage at all – circumstances which could themselves supply their own grim corrective to the assumption that recent improvements in life expectancy will be maintained.

Reaching Out to the Excluded

But, you may ask – why single out the aged? Why not tackle poverty at any age? Over the last several decades mounting concern at the horrendous dimensions of global poverty has prompted a variety of schemes to reduce it. But despite the proliferation of such measures there are no international programmes specifically dedicated to tackling poverty among the old. The widely cited Millennium Development Goals (MDGs) do not include a single aspiration directly related to support of the elderly. The only goal that would be relevant – though the aged are not specifically mentioned – is the commitment to make sure that nobody is living on less than $1 a day.

International action on poverty is dominated by a development agenda such that specific measures are recommended on the grounds that not only do they achieve a worthy objective – say, the education of women – but they also stimulate economic growth. The plight of the elderly often does not lend itself to such arguments, since few of them are likely to be protagonists of development – and since this plight may not be alleviated even by successful economic growth.

So far there have only been two world assemblies devoted to the problems of the elderly, the first of which was held in Vienna in 1982. This assembly registered some important issues, but its main focus was on ageing in the more developed countries. Two decades were to elapse before the convening of the second world assembly on the problems of the old, held in Madrid in 2002. It identified a checklist of priorities for national policy with regard to older people while urging, in a locution that sought to harness the growth agenda to its own concerns, that the old should become 'full participants' in the development process.[17] The new UN report, *Development in an Ageing World*, recognizes the need for a dramatic widening in pension provision – and signals that $1 a day would be a good beginning – but stops short of proposing any global programme to tackle the problem, which is thus left to national governments and existing aid efforts.

In urging the case for a global old-age pension, I do not mean to slight the claims of bare humanity or the efforts of those who campaign for the need to alleviate the poverty of other groups, such as young mothers or AIDS sufferers. In the unequal and strife-torn world in which we live there are several, or many, ways in which poverty may be overcome. Peace would be the best help for the very poorest in strife-torn lands. Successful economic development, such as has taken place in China over recent decades, lifts many out of poverty and furnishes a more hopeful context in which to advance anti-poverty strategies. But China also shows that even – or especially – the most rapid growth may not banish absolute poverty, in the countryside or in new urban centres.

Some believe that the best anti-poverty programme would be a global Basic Income Grant (BIG). This could not be set at much less than $1 a day and would thus be ten times as costly as the global pension. In a later section I show the affordability of the pension, but a qualitatively greater effort would be required to set up a global BIG. No doubt the champions of BIG would still see that effort as eminently justifiable. Perhaps they could also see the global pension as a useful stepping-stone to BIG.[18]

I believe that a global pension would command support in ways that would extend the general case against poverty. In the richer countries there is widespread uneasiness at the danger of growing relative poverty amongst the old at home and an unhappy awareness of the worse plight of the very deprived in the poor countries. In the developing and under-developed countries there is the more specific alarm or guilt that is occasioned by the poverty, actual or impending, of parents, grandparents, uncles and aunts. And reasonably, if less altruistically, young couples also aspire to live in a different dwelling from their parents (and parents-in-law), something which is still rare in the developing world. Such sentiments have helped to generate support for old-age pensions in the developed states, and are likely to do so again in the developing world.[19] Overall a global old-age pension, if it could be realistically financed and delivered, would enjoy substantial legitimacy and would in no way detract from other efforts to combat relative or absolute poverty. That legitimacy can only grow in an ageing planet. Today the majority of the old are poor: tomorrow the majority of the poor may well be old.

Unfortunately, the very size of the ageing problem inhibits its solution. One dollar a day does not sound much, but it would represent a very considerable burden to the budgets of many developing states. The old-age pension at 65 or 70 was introduced in the developed countries at a time when the numbers of those reaching such an age were still quite low – 5 per cent of the population rather than the 25 per cent or more now in prospect. There is also the problem that governments today in all countries are expected to supply universal health care and education, and to sponsor ambitious development programmes.

The UN report *Development in an Ageing World* points out that national pension schemes are so modest because there are so many claims on the revenues of poor governments. It identifies sixty developing countries, many of them approaching medium levels of development, where the cost of financing a pension of $1 a day would only represent 1 per cent of GDP. However, it grants that this money would still be very difficult to find because of the pressing needs of other important programmes. The report observes: '. . . in low income counties there may be competing demands on scarce government resources. For example in Cameroon, Guatemala, India, Nepal and Pakistan, the cost of a universal basic pension scheme [of $1 a day] represents as much as 10 per cent of total tax revenue. In Bangladesh, Burundi, Côte d'Ivoire, and Myanmar, it is equivalent to the public health budget'.[20] And then it adds: 'How to finance a basic pension scheme may therefore need to be determined in close coordination with the resource allocation process (as well as the use of development assistance) for other social programmes'.[21]

Pension programmes were adopted in the richer countries at times when market failure had demonstrated the misfit between commercial mechanisms and social protection. Some business leaders saw retirement schemes as a way to raise productivity, while some political leaders hoped that their introduction would head off social unrest. The experience of the Second World War both increased political pressures and demonstrated the ability of modern tax systems to generate massive revenues and hence to underwrite large-scale social provision. There is plenty of social unrest in today's world – radical advance in Latin America, oil strikes in Nigeria, tens of thousands of demonstrations and strikes each year in China are amongst the many signs that there is an unmet popular appetite for social justice and protection. *Development in an Ageing World* argues that resources would be better used if aged farmers were able to retire with a pension and hand on their land and tools to the younger generation.[22] This echoes an argument that was made in New Zealand and Denmark, countries that pioneered pension provision in the nineteenth century.

But even where there is political pressure and a claimed development rationale, scarce resources make it very difficult for governments to pledge money to pensions on the scale that ageing demands. Just as the national welfare state found revenues based on industrial incomes and profits in the past, so today revenue should be sought from taxing the circuits of globalization.

How to Pay for the Global Pension

I have explained that only $205 billion a year would be needed, to begin with, for the proposed global pension. But it would be necessary to reckon with the need for a more than doubling of revenues within a generation and the building of a substantial fund now, while ageing effects are still comparatively modest, to help finance extra pension payouts in the middle decades of the century. Moreover, there should be a commitment to raise the global pension in line with the growth of overall average incomes so that the old share in future prosperity.

Raising the necessary finance for a global pension – together with something extra for administrative costs – will certainly require a serious effort. The fiscal devices adopted should ideally relate to the workings of the global economy taken as a whole so there would be a wide and dynamic tax base.

Three types of impost are peculiarly well suited to such a task: a mild tax on international currency transactions, a tax on the fuel used on international flights, and a mild tax on corporate wealth. The calculations which follow are simply rough-and-ready exercises designed to establish that the global pension and grant can be easily financed by the proposed taxes.

The famous Tobin Tax applies to the sale or purchase of currencies and has been urged as a measure to curb currency speculation.[23] But it could be applied mainly as a revenue-raising measure. Set as low as 0.1 per cent – or a one-thousandth part of each transaction – the tax would not be worth evading but would still raise large sums globally. Common estimates of the amounts that could be raised each year from a Tobin Tax on currency transactions ranged from $100 billion to $300 billion in the late 1990s. It seems reasonable, therefore, to postulate a yield of at least $150 billion annually from such a tax in, say, 2012 or thereabouts.

At present the fuel used on international flights is almost untaxed and costs the airlines about $50 billion a year. A doubling of the price of fuel might help to cut consumption by a fifth or a quarter while still raising $30 billion. Much of the yield from green taxes should be used to invest in other measures designed to mitigate global warming. But tying at least some of the revenue – say, half of it – to a universally recognized good cause would be defensible. While $15 billion a year would be a help, other sources of revenue would still be needed.

The third source of revenue I propose is a mild levy on share values or on share transactions. There could be a requirement on all companies employing more than fifty employees, or with a turnover of more than $10 million, to pay a tax of 2 per cent on their annual profits, to be paid either in cash or, in the case of public companies, by issuing new shares of that value to the fiscal authority (private companies could issue bonds, and partnerships, including private equity partnerships, could issue nominal partnership rights).

The effect of requiring the issuance (for free) of new corporate securities is to dilute the value of existing holdings. Because there is such huge inequality in the ownership of shares and bonds – the richest 1 per cent own half of all shares – the tax is very progressive. All genuine pension funds would be compensated for the impact of share dilution on their holdings.[24]

Two important features of these arrangements should be noted. Firstly, they would apply to profits made anywhere in the world. Secondly, companies would be able to discharge their obligation simply by issuing a new security rather than by subtracting from their cash flow. Large US and UK corporate pension fund sponsors have complained about the burden of making cash payments to the Pension Benefit Guaranty Corporation and the Pension Protection Fund, the insurers of their 'defined benefit' pension schemes. In some cases companies have been in such difficulties that payments were impossible. This has led to US 'Chapter 11' bankruptcy-protection courts to require the issuance of new shares as an alternative way of making a contribution to their insurer. In the UK the Pensions Regulator has made similar provisions requiring cash-strapped companies to issue shares to the Pension Protection Fund.[25] Employees will stand to qualify for the new pension but would certainly welcome a type of contribution that does not weaken their employer in any way.

The profits tax/share levy would be at a modest rate – a tax of 2 per cent of profits should raise about $140 billion annually. Assessing the share levy at 2 per cent of profits is simply a convenient way of measuring a company's operations; it might need to be supplemented by other metrics (gross profit, capitalization) to avoid distortions and evasion. The fact that the levy works by means of share dilution means that even those holding their funds in tax havens would not escape.

In case of any problem with the share levy – an admittedly radical device – there exists a readily available substitute, namely stamp duty. This tax has a long history in Britain and elsewhere, and has been highly successful. It has been levied at a modest rate in the UK on the buying and selling of shares for over two centuries. Its success shows that a very modest charge on a large volume of transactions can yield large sums at a low cost, with high levels of compliance and without harmful side effects. It is currently levied at a rate of 0.5 per cent of each share transaction (other than those by market makers) and raises about £3 billion ($6 billion) annually. While derivative contracts pay no stamp duty, any sale of underlying shareholder assets does attract the tax. The Confederation of British Industry, a business lobby, argues that the stamp duty is weakening London's position as one of the world's leading financial centres. But the thriving state of London finance belies the argument. The UK Treasury is anyway greatly attached to an impost that is so difficult to avoid and so easy to collect – this is done, at very low cost, as part of CREST, the central share-settlement system. China's financial authorities have a similar device which they use in a 'Tobin Tax' way to dampen speculation – but it also raises large sums.[26] Several European states, including Switzerland and France, have similar, very mild imposts, applying to bonds as well as shares.

In case of any shortfall in the yield of the taxes already suggested, or of implementation difficulties, a global stamp duty or FTT (Financial Transaction Tax) would fill the gap. According to the World Federation of Exchanges global share transactions ran at $70 trillion in 2006, which would yield 'stamp duty' revenue, at UK rates, of $350 billion. (Interestingly, James Tobin himself advocated what he called a 'transfer tax' on share dealings, with an eye to raising revenue as well as dampening speculation.[27])

It will be recalled that a half-share of the Tobin Tax on currency transactions already raises $150 billion towards the global pension, and that the fuel tax on international flights should raise a further $15 billion annually. Thus, to begin with, an extra $40 billion a year would be needed from the share levy (or share transaction tax), to meet the immediate annual cost of $205 billion. This would allow the remainder of the sum raised by the share levy – $100 billion each year – to accumulate in the Global Pension Fund (GPF) network as a strategic reserve pledged to meet the anticipated rise in the numbers and proportion of the aged. The various taxes would be collected by national fiscal authorities with assistance from appropriate international bodies such as the IMF and IATA. Revenues would be paid to the global office of the GPF for consolidation with the world fund.[28] Consolidation of assets by an international agency would ensure a highly diversified portfolio, but the agency would itself be required to distribute the assets it receives to the global network at regular intervals. This regional network of around a thousand local offices of the Global Pension Fund would be responsible for paying the pension and would receive resources in line with their region's demographic characteristics. In the interests of building up its reserves, the GPF network would use its cash revenue to pay out current pensions but hold all the new shares and other securities to generate larger revenues in the future, when they will be needed. During the initial 'accumulation' phase it might be wise to reinvest dividend income in public bonds.

Because the GPF network would not buy or sell shares it would have less scope for making mistakes. The knowledge that the Global Pension Fund network would not sell the shares it held would also be a factor of stability and would prevent it from weakening the companies in which it had stakes. By around 2034 total assets in the GPF network could amount to $7.7 trillion.[29] If cash payouts began at this time, and the annual yield on capital was around 3 per cent, this would be $257 billion for that year. Each regional office would hold around $7.7 billion in assets and receive $257 million in revenue. This element of pre-funding, added to other revenue sources, would help the global pension payouts to keep pace with the rising numbers of the aged. Note that while dividend income can fluctuate it is less volatile than share price, and there are ways of smoothing such receipts.

The global pension would be a universal scheme benefiting everyone who reaches old age. The receipts of the currency-exchange tax and the levy on corporate wealth would obviously be larger in rich parts of the world than in poor ones. However, currency transactions and corporate profit trails often lead to havens and developing states where taxes are low or non-existent. The currency tax and share levy would be light but they would apply everywhere. The overall workings of the global pension – if financed in the way suggested – would redistribute from rich to poor. On the other hand, the participation of every territory – no matter how small or poor – would be essential to the effective workings of these levies.

Citizens of richer countries should be pleased at the comprehensive scope of the new arrangements, which would require potential or actual tax havens to report currency movements and profits at companies they allow to register in their territory.[30] The global pension would give those in richer countries rights to a modest pension supplement, and as a flat-rate benefit would help the less well placed more than the comfortably off everywhere. It would do most to reduce poverty where it is worst – in the countryside and neglected urban areas of the underdeveloped and developing world. Last but not least, it would promote more transparent and responsible corporate behaviour and nourish a worldwide organization dedicated to social welfare.

The Fund Network: Tasks and Opportunities

The regional network of funds would be bound by actuarially fair rules of distribution and would be required to hire professionally qualified personnel. The network would also furnish democratic representation to local communities. The holding of stakes in a great variety of companies would in principle give the regional network a say in how these shares would be voted. The impact of the network on the management of any given company would be very small, but each regional fund would be able to influence issues of general principle, such as respect for labour rights or compliance with environmental standards. On some issues the entire network might agree to set standards; on others, the thousand or so regional offices worldwide could frame their own approaches. The network would thus give a say to local communities who are often ignored by large corporations.[31]

However, the primary duty of the regional and national network would be to organize the cheap and effective disbursement of the global pension to all who qualified for it. In many countries the task could be subcontracted to the national pension authorities. Where these still had weak coverage, assistance might be sought from – and costs shared with – post offices, local microcredit unions and public sector employees' schemes. The latter exist in many countries where national administration is ineffective or even non-existent. Namibia has developed effective means for delivering the old-age pension, employing mobile ATM machines activated by fingerprint ID.

The old-age pension would not dictate social policy priorities for national budgets. Some governments already make quite good provision for older citizens (for example, South Africa) or for continuing education (for example, Cuba). As the pension and grant came on-stream, governments would have the option to rebalance their budgets towards other programmes if they wish. The effect of the global programmes would rather be to guarantee a basic minimum for the old and for young people, leaving it to national governments to decide how to build on, or complement, such provision.

The regional reserve funds of the GPF could also be given some scope to invest their surplus income in ways which best answer to local needs and perceptions. Elected officials and their professional advisers would need a framework where there was a balance between socially useful investment and security for the future. The best practice of public sector pension funds would be one benchmark here. They have shown that a strictly defined portion of income can be invested in, say, affordable social housing, with results that benefit the community in the present while also supplying good security for the future.[32]

In the past, national and local governments owned real estate and public enterprises, and financed their activities with taxes on income and residential property. Local and national debt furnished a key source of finance. In the globalized and ageing world, governments in a position to do so appear to believe that there is advantage in building up reserves and 'sovereign funds' (such as the publicly controlled 'future funds' run by Australia, China, Norway and Singapore). The GPF would permit a global diffusion of such provident funds. (Fair trade schemes also partake of such a pre-funding logic when the proceeds from the premium price paid by customers are used to build locally controlled social funds.)

There is no doubt that arranging for the local administration of the global pension would be a demanding task and that there should be regular audits and inspections to make sure that the cash reaches its intended recipients. Distributing money in smallish sums should prove easier than delivering complex aid packages involving construction, storage and salaries for a large staff. If the fund network were required to use local personnel and pre-existing non-commercial facilities (as mentioned above), then the cost-sharing this involves would itself boost local financial administrative capacity. The fund network could also organize appropriate training programmes for administrators. Universal public pension schemes, whether pay as you go or pre-funded, have proved much cheaper to run than private schemes. Administration costs should amount to no more than 1 per cent of the fund each year, and quite possibly less.

Given the rising number of the aged in the poor as well as rich world, the adoption of a single standard – a pension of $1 a day – would be the assertion of an important egalitarian principle. While traditional cultures nourish respect for the aged, recent debates on social justice in the era of globalization stress the need to assure the livelihood of the poorest, a category within which the old loom large.[33]

The global pension should be established for its own sake, as a measure of social justice. But it is worth adding that the relative conservatism of the tastes of older people usually means that their expenditures tend to foster local suppliers. The Andropov government in Russia in the late 1990s discovered that the resumption of pension payments to older citizens had a stimulant effect on the whole national economy. Other political leaders who saw the strategic importance of universal pensions include Lopez Obrador, the former mayor of Mexico City, who established a municipal old-age pension, and Nelson Mandela who insisted that all older citizens should be entitled to the public pension, making South Africa one of the few developing states with universal pension provision – in honour of the latter achievement, the global pension might appropriately be named for Mandela.

For the proposed measures to be effective, they would have to be supported by the world's main economic powers and regional groupings. Some may think the entire approach doomed by this consideration. But while securing such support would not be easy, each of these powers and groupings does admit some duty to promote measures of social security. The scheme aims to benefit every part of the world in one way or another and would offer a small but tangible measure aimed at counteracting the problems generated by wild globalization. A campaign for a global public pension would enable many important issues to be ventilated and very likely would lead to detailed improvements in the measures proposed. In the age of national welfare states the most broadly popular measures were those promoting security for the aged and opportunity for the young. As we seek to extend social policy in the age of globalization we should introduce these values and measures at a worldwide level.

The practicality of the global pension is enhanced by its very modest dimensions. Many other schemes for global redistribution involve much greater resources. However, extreme disparities and the division of the world – and each of its regions – into many economic zones actually permits rather modest measures, such as those I propose, to have quite disproportionate anti-poverty effects – and all without even being an anti-poverty programme. It's worth adding that the dollars being paid into and out of the proposed funds would be real dollars, not reconstructed PPP dollars.[34] They would be dollars stitching the world together and generally gaining in purchasing power as they do so. It would also be important that every older person would be entitled to the pension, and that the source of the funds would be the globalized 'space of flows'.[35]

An important feature of the global pension is that it would seek to channel cash directly to the aged. This chimes in with the conclusion to a recent World Bank Poverty Research paper on global inequality by Branko Milanović:

> When Russia faced its worst crisis, aid, instead of being given to the corrupt Yeltsin regime, should have been disbursed directly in cash to the most needy citizens. An international organization . . . could have simply used the existing structure of the Russian state pension rolls, and distributed cash grants to some twenty million Russian pensioners. That would be money much better spent than giving the same amount of money to the government. And citizens would have fondly remembered receiving cash aid from the international community rather than blaming that same international community for transferring funds to corrupt leaders. Today the same or similar approach could be adopted in many countries . . . The approach is simple and powerful. It involves three steps: raise money from the globally rich, do not deal with the governments of either rich or poor nations, and transfer funds in cash to the poor. While supporters of an exclusively private-sector driven globalisation may resent the idea of vesting a tax-raising authority for the first time in history into a global agency they cannot fail to notice that the very process they support undercuts, in an ironic twist, their own position. They will ultimately realize that their self-interest lies in supporting some form of global action to deal with both poverty . . . and inequality.[36]

While I commend the spirit of this, the sweeping dismissal of any role at all for the state could compromise the egalitarian objective. It could even open the door to the financial services industry – an industry which, quite apart from corruption issues, has exorbitant costs and no pretence of democratic structures. Furthermore, even a corrupt and authoritarian state can be better than no state at all. The aim of the reserve fund network would be to coax states to accept and respect a programme that would be beneficial to their citizens. The network of pension reserve funds would help to strengthen civil society while requiring legislative support from the state, and thus appear not counterposed to it. While paying out money to individuals, the regional offices of the reserve fund would aim to develop as a locally accountable collective structure. These points registered, Milanović's argument is welcome and adds to the case for a global pension.

The global pension would contribute significantly to the 'security in old age' envisaged in Article 25 of the *Universal Declaration of Human Rights* and to the 'existence worthy of human dignity' referred to in Article 23 of that declaration. UN agencies and conventions have helped to focus global attention on the problems of children, of women, of the sick and disabled. The Second International Assembly on Ageing in Madrid in 2002 issued good advice to member governments, which is endorsed and elaborated by the 2007 *World Social and Economic Report*. But, as yet, the plight of the aged and the prospect of a surge in their numbers are still not addressed by a specific international agency or by a programme with global scope. The global pension would represent a tangible step in the right direction.

Appendix: Twinning the Old-Age Pension with a Youth Grant?

The pension proposal stands on its own but also serves as a new point of departure, both for better provision for the aged and, perhaps, for similar help for other problematic life stages. While the insecurity of the ageing and the old has been neglected, so has the misery of another vulnerable age cohort – the young. Half of those aged 14 to 20 are neither employed nor at college. Worries for old age and despair at the situation of the young have surfaced both at the ballot box and in the street. They cannot be further ignored and now attract the attention of international organizations and a wider public.[37]

Many in these two age groups have little prospect of finding decent work at reasonable wages. In the knowledge-based society the young would be better off anyway if they had the resources to pursue education or training. Reducing the economic pressure on the young and the old will also reduce the pressure of labour market competition on those aged 20-65, promoting better wages and living conditions. In doing so it would help to strengthen labour solidarity, displace sweatshops and address the fundamental imbalances which bedevil the world economy. Older people themselves might feel happier to receive a pension if finance were also available to the young, especially resources that would allow them a better start in life. If we set aside a privileged minority in both categories there is reason to see young adults and the elderly as the excluded generations. Age, gender, race, class and illegal status work in different ways, but whether separately or conjointly, these factors often very much intensify vulnerability and exploitability. In the case of the young, the structural exclusion of the majority is also linked to the super-exploitation of a sizeable minority, in a familiar pattern where difficulty in finding a job leads those affected to accept substandard employment.[38]

So I suggest that the proposed global pension be matched by equivalent financial help to young people. The cost of supplying every younger person with $1,500 for educational and training purposes on reaching the age of 15 or 17 would be very similar to that of paying the global pension of $1 a day. I suggest here, therefore, that the rates on the taxes already proposed be increased to allow an extra $150 billion annually be raised to be dedicated to young adults – the young could be offered a lump-sum grant of $1,500 to use for education or training when they reach the age of 15 or 17. Small as this sum would be in richer societies, it would not be a negligible one. Matching the global old-age pension with help for young people would begin to assert a new balance between life stages in a scheme of generational equity. (The value of the youth grant would need to keep pace with economic growth but the size of the youth cohort is set to decline, limiting the future cost.)

A youth grant would symbolize a concordance of the generations. While it could transform the possibilities of the young person in poor countries, it would still be welcome to most of the young in wealthier lands. Young people are now greatly burdened by the rising cost of acquiring skills and education. They also generally welcome an extra modicum of independence from their parents. Even in some of Europe's most advanced welfare states, such as Sweden, young people living on their own figure disproportionately in the poverty statistics because they opt to live on their own.

The network of reserve funds established to administer the global pension could also be asked to oversee distribution of the youth grant. While some of this expenditure would help to finance educational or training projects the young persons should be encouraged to act as the active and responsible bearers of the entitlement, and allowance should be made for their own maintenance expenditures. The age of eligibility for the youth grant might vary a little between countries, with that age being a little lower in developing countries (such as 14 or 15). It might not be advisable to pay all the proposed youth grant in cash to the young persons whom it is to benefit, but it would be good if as much as possible took forms that would be very tangible to the recipient. The prospects of young people are damaged by high dropout rates from school, unavailability of training and apprenticeship, unemployment, high incarceration rates, and inappropriate or damaging work.

In Bangladesh school-dropout rates for young girls were greatly reduced when they were paid a modest sum for completing an extra year – the money compensated for lost earnings. In Kenya the provision of free school uniforms has greatly reduced dropout rates among both boys and girls – it has also reduced young girls' unwanted pregnancies.[39] It is a sad fact that the proportion of 15-year-olds who have dropped out of school is in the 35–45 per cent range in even such quite developed states such as Turkey, Mexico and Brazil.[40] The global youth grant could also help to fund 'second chance' programmes for the 'lost generation' of former child soldiers, 'gang mites' and teen prison inmates. This grant could underpin wage subsidies for post-secondary school employment with clear educational and apprenticeship value.

The 1960–62 Cuban 'campaign against illiteracy' was strikingly successful in reducing the country's illiteracy rate from 34 per cent to 4 per cent in the space of a few years. It mobilized already literate urban youth to teach country-dwellers how to read and write (as well as giving the former firsthand experience of rural deprivation). Higher literacy contributed to the subsequent successes of Cuban educational and medical programmes. A global youth grant could be used to help finance such a programme and to draw young people in as educators as well as recipients of education. While not recalling this experience, the World Bank report on *Development and the Next Generation* notes low literacy rates in many poor countries and observes an anomaly that makes relevant the Cuban literacy programme: 'Within poor countries, youth unemployment is concentrated among those who are educated and from high-income families.'[41]

The proposed youth grant could be introduced once the global old-age pension was already a proven success. Alternatively, the new global approach might have a better chance to fly if it had two wings from the outset . . .

Notes

1   First published as 'A Global Pension Plan', *New Left Review*, ser. 2, no. 47, September–October 2007, pp. 71–92. I would like to thank Jay Ginn, Diane Elson, Susanne Paul and Manuel Riesco for comments and suggestions.
2   UN Department of Economic and Social Affairs, *World Economic and Social Survey 2007: Development in an Ageing World*, New York, June 2007, p. 89. Hereafter: *Development in an Ageing World*.
3   UN Human Development Report 2006, 'Beyond Scarcity: Power, Poverty and the Global Water Crisis'.
4   The disproportionate domestic burden on women is a theme of the successive reports of UNIFEM. See, for example, *The Progress of the World's Women*, New York 2000.
5   *Development in an Ageing World*, p. 95.
6   'Greying Japan: The Downturn', *Economist*, 5 January 2006. These trends are well discussed in Göran Therborn, *Between Sex and Power: Family in the World, 1900–2000*, London 2004, pp. 229–59.
7   The yawning gaps in pension provision are well documented in Larry Willmore, 'Universal Pensions for Developing Countries', *World Development*, vol. 35, no. 1, 2007, pp. 24–51. For India see Rajeev Ahuja, 'Old-Age Income Security for the Poor', *Economic and Political Weekly* (epw.in), 13 September 2003.
8   A strain described in Jeremy Seabrook, *A World Growing Old*, London 2003.
9   *Development in an Ageing World*, pp. 93–95. These co-residence patterns mean that there are fewer 'elderly households' in the developing world and help to explain why the data of old-age poverty in the developing world is less clear-cut than for the developed world. The large, multigenerational family often gives tangible reality to the phrase 'generational solidarity'. But rising numbers of older people in poor households will aggravate their problems, while availability of a pension would ease them.
10 Mike Davis, *Planet of Slums*, London 2006.
11 These figures are taken from *World Population Prospects: The 2006 Revision*, available on the website of the UN Population Division.
12 See pp. 61–74 of the present volume. In this book I draw on recent forecasts made by the UK Pensions Commission, by the Economic Policy Committee of the European Commission, by the US Congressional Budget Office and by contributors to *OECD Economic Studies* to identify the size of this shortfall. While those over 65 are set to double in absolute number within a

AGE SHOCK

generation, and to become between a fifth and a quarter of the total population, their share of income will – under current public and private arrangements – be stuck at around a tenth of GDP. Simply to maintain pensioners' relative incomes at their present level would require an extra 4 per cent of GDP. There is still significant pensioner poverty today but matters will become much worse by 2030 and 2040, as already-enacted reductions in entitlement come into effect. If the UK government succeeds in its plans for a National Pension Savings Scheme it will reduce the projected shortfall of over 4 per cent of GDP by only 0.7 per cent of GDP by 2050 (*Age Shock*, p. 266).

13 *Development in an Ageing World* notes some of the weaknesses of private provision but does not register the structural problem of heavy charges, stemming from exorbitant salaries, profit-gouging and marketing costs. In a section of Chapter 4 entitled 'High Finance and Distressed Debt', I also urged that credit derivatives based on subprime mortgages and private equity deals would not be good for pension funds.

14 The case for non-means-tested pensions is powerfully advanced in Willmore, 'Universal Pensions for Developing Countries'.

15 John Van D. Lewis, 'Domestic Labor Intensity and the Incorporation of Malian Peasant Farmers into Localized Descent Groups', *American Ethnologist*, vol. 8, no. 1, February 1981, pp. 53–73; and Richard Sennett, *Respect in a World of Inequality*, London 2003.

16 Timothy Smeeding and Suzanna Sandstrom, 'Poverty and Income Maintenance in Old Age', *Feminist Economics*, vol. 11, no. 3, November 2005, pp. 163–86, p. 167.

17 The website for Global Action on Aging (globalaging.org) contains links to most of the literature produced by international organizations on this subject. Since 2002 there have been some signs of growing attention to the situation of the elderly. The hitherto marginal position of the old in international anti-poverty discourse admits of an exception which really does prove the rule. In 1994 the World Bank issued a famous report entitled *Averting the Old Age Crisis*; its subtitle was *Policies to Protect the Old and Promote Growth*. This report advanced a critique of public pensions schemes and urged their replacement by new provisions which would force every citizen to enrol with a commercial pension provider. It claimed that this would foster growth by deepening capital markets. I discuss the counterproductive effects of this advice, and its repudiation by a later World Bank chief economist, in Robin Blackburn, *Banking on Death or Investing in Life: The History and Future of Pensions*, London 2002, pp. 225–78, 402–8. For the shaping of international development priorities see Paul Cammack, 'Attacking the Poor', *New Left Review*, ser. 2, no. 13, January–February 2002, pp. 125–34.

18 The pension would not only be easier to finance, it would also proceed from an argument that is easier to make – appealing to the widely accepted view that the elderly are deserving of support. No such consensus yet exists concerning support for able-bodied adults. Likewise, while the claims of infants are certainly very strong, offering young mothers financial incentives

to have children does not promote their best interests. However, in an appendix I do address the predicament of another often-excluded cohort, those aged 14–20.

19 In stressing the moral legitimacy of arguments for a global pension, I don't mean to imply that narrower arguments will not also be made. In the early twentieth century the advocates of public pensions in the 'old rich' countries sometimes urged that allowing the over-70s to retire from the workforce would boost productivity. Today, chiming in with the development para-digm, the argument is also sometimes heard that a pension will allow the older farmer to retire, handing the land over to sons or daughters who will work it more productively.

20 *Development in an Ageing World*, p. xvi. Why does the report make this 'experiment' of a pension of $1 a day? I do not believe that my advocacy of the measure at the hearings in February in any way prompted it. The explanation is rather that extreme poverty has long been defined as $1 a day. Moreover, the report conceives the pension as paid by each state, not as a global programme.

21 Ibid.

22 Ibid., p. 57.

23 For the Tobin tax see James Tobin, *The New Economics One Decade Older*, The Elliot Janeway Lectures in Honor of Joseph Schumpeter, Princeton 1974, p. 88; Jeffrey A. Frankel, 'How Well Do Foreign Exchange Markets Function: Might a Tobin Tax Help?', NBER Working Paper No. 5422, Cambridge MA 1996; Keiki Patomaki, *The Tobin Tax: How to Make It Real*, *Helsinki: Finnish Institute for International Affairs, 1999; Joseph Stiglitz, Globa-lization and its Discontents*, New York 2004.

24 The use of a general share levy to establish reserve social funds is associated with the work of Rudolf Miedner, chief economist of the Swedish trade union federation, the LO, and architect of the Swedish welfare state. I supply a fuller account of its workings in Chapter 6 of *Age Shock*.

25 I give examples of this court-mandated share issuance in *Age Shock*, pp. 134–5, 142. The judges were no doubt in part prompted to take this measure because of records of corporate irresponsibility which I document in Chapters 2 and 3 of this book.

26 See Geoff Dyer and Jamil Anderlini, 'Beijing Could Reap $40bn Share Tax Bonanza', *Financial Times*, 4 June 2007.

27 James Tobin, *Full Employment and Growth: Further Keynesian Essays on Policy*, Cheltenham 1996, p. 254. Note that by this time share dealings were taking place in many countries, small and large, which did not have stock exchanges – Tobin made his original proposal in 1974.

28 The GPF might maintain offices in such important financial centres as Zurich, Cyprus, Mauritius, Singapore and so forth, chosen with a view to strengthening compliance.

29 I am assuming that profits rise at 2.5 per cent a year and that returns of 5 per cent a year are ploughed back into the fund for an 'accumulation period' of 27 years. The reserve fund proposed here based on a 2 per cent profits levy is

of the same size as the US Federal reserve fund proposed in *Age Shock*, based on a 10 per cent levy on US corporate profits alone.

30 The scope for tightening up regulation of tax havens was explored by an IMF official in Vito Tanzi, *Policies, Institutions and the Dark Side of Economics*, Cheltenham 2000. Most tax havens are offshore operations dependent on the UK, Netherlands, France and the United States, but all are dependent on exchanges with the OECD countries and could easily be brought into compliance with international reporting standards if the will was there. Quite apart from concern at money laundering, the treasuries of the stronger states have their own reasons for wishing to curb such tax-avoidance practices as 'transfer pricing' and 'thin capitalization'. The IMF and the OECD have already made progress in standardizing reporting standards relating to currency transactions and company profits. In order to flourish as a tax haven, an OFC (Offshore Financial Centre) must now have minimum legal and accounting compliance staff; investors themselves shun attempts by some would-be 'havens' such as Liberia or Nauru in favour of locales that can inspire confidence, such as Bermuda, the Cayman Islands, the Channel Islands, the British Virgin Islands, Mauritius and Cyprus (all of which are current or former UK dependencies). See 'Places in the Sun', *Economist*, 22 February 2007. The real problem in applying a global currency transaction tax and profits tax would come from states like Switzerland and Singapore; but this resistance could be overcome if the EU, the US, Japan and China were agreed, and if the public authorities in these financial centres were given some role in implementation of the scheme.

31 I elaborate a similar proposal for a share levy to feed a regional network of pension reserve funds in *Age Shock*, pp. 272–7. If such a scheme were already in operation in a given jurisdiction then the global levy and pension could be just a layer of it. In *Age Shock*, I suggest a levy equivalent to 10 per cent of profits; the global levy could either be added to, or carved out of, this revenue. I am indebted to Rudolf Meidner, architect of the Swedish welfare state and chief economist to Sweden's main trade union confederation, for the basic idea of the share levy and fund network.

32 Gordon Clark, *Pension Fund Capitalism*, Oxford 2000, pp. 21–34; see also Archon Fung, Tessa Hebb and Joel Rogers, eds., *Working Capital: The Power of Labor's Pensions*, Ithaca NY 2000. The experience of the Mondragon is also relevant. I discuss such questions further in Robin Blackburn, 'Economic Democracy: Meaningful, Desirable, Feasible?', *Daedalus*, vol. 136, no. 2, Summer 2007, pp. 36–45.

33 See Thomas Pogge, *World Poverty and Human Rights: Cosmopolitan Responsibilities and Reforms*, Cambridge 2002; and Nancy Fraser, 'Reframing Justice in a Globalized World', *New Left Review*, ser. 2, no. 36, November–December 2005, pp. 69–88.

34 The approach here strives to register the reality of wildly divergent economic spaces in order to break it down, rather than simply to revel in diversity.

35 Manuel Castells, *The Rise of the Network Society*, Oxford 1997.

36 Branko Milanović, 'Global Income Inequality: What It Is and Why It

Matters', World Bank, Policy Research Working Paper No. WPS 3865, March 2006, pp. 29–30.

37 The World Bank has weighed in with a report that complements *Development in an Ageing World*, namely its *Annual Development Report 2007: Development and the Next Generation*, Washington 2007. (Henceforth: *Development and the Next Generation*). For the dimensions of youth exclusion from decent work and continuing education, see especially pp. 99–100.

38 It is interesting to note that when Thomas Paine elaborated a costed, universal old-age pension proposal he also argued for young people to receive a lump sum of €15 at the age of 21, both to be paid for by a 10 per cent inheritance tax: see Thomas Paine, 'Agrarian Justice (1795)', in *The Thomas Paine Reader*, Michael Foot and Isaac Kramnick, eds, Harmondsworth 1987, pp. 471–90. The special claims of youth are urged by Bruce Ackerman and Anne Alstott, 'Why Stakeholding?' and 'Macro-Freedom', in Bruce Ackerman, Anne Alstott and Philippe Van Parijs, ed, *Redesigning Distribution*, London 2006, pp. 43–68, 209–16.

39 These examples are cited in *Development and the Next Generation*, p. 18. The report also notes that over 8 million girls and boys are believed to be subjected to very damaging work and a further 20 million to stultifying industrial employment (p. 115). The value placed on school uniforms by young people in a Kenyan refugee camp is brought out by Dave Eggers in *What Is the What: The Autobiography of Valentino Achak Deng*, New York 2007.

40 *Development and the Next Generation*, p. 70

41 Ibid., p. 99.

Index